Tariffs, Trade and European Integration, 1947–1957

THE FRANKLIN AND ELEANOR ROOSEVELT INSTITUTE SERIES ON DIPLOMATIC AND ECONOMIC HISTORY

General Editors: Arthur M. Schlesinger, Jr., William vanden Heuvel, and Douglas Brinkley

Tariffs, Trade
and European Integration,
1947–1957

From Study Group to Common Market

Wendy Asbeek Brusse

St. Martin's Press
New York

ISBN 0-312-16518-8

Library of Congress Cataloging-in-Publication Data
Asbeek Brusse, Wendy, 1965-
   Tariffs, trade and European integration, 1947-1957 : from study   group
to Common Market / Wendy Asbeek Brusse.
      p. cm.
   Originally presented as the author's thesis (Ph.D.—European
University Institute, Florence 1991).
   Includes bibliographical references and index.
   ISBN 0-312-16518-8
   1. Tariff—Europe—History. 2. Europe—Commercial policy—History.
3. Europe—Economic integration—History—20th century. 4.
European Economic Community—History.   I. Title.
   HF2036.B78 1997
   382' .7'094 dc21   96-39531
                                                           CIP

Design by Acme Art, Inc.
First edition: July, 1997

10 9 8 7 6 5 4 3 2 1

Contents

Acknowledgments

This book originated from a Ph.D. dissertation submitted at the European University Institute in Florence in 1991. I am greatly indebted to the Institute's intellectual and financial support for this project, and in particular to all those associated with its research project 'Challenge and Response in the History of the European Communities' who provided advice, encouragement and friendship throughout the research. I also wish to thank Jacques Pelkmans, whose detailed comments on my dissertation helped to improve the argumentation of this book. Any errors of fact, interpretation or judgment remain, of course, entirely mine.

The following institutions have provided archival material for this thesis: the Algemeen Rijksarchief in The Hague; the Bundesarchiv in Koblenz; the Public Record Office in Kew; the National Archives in Washington, D.C.; the Archives Nationales in Paris; the Auswärtiges Amt in Bonn; the Ministerie van Economische Zaken; the Ministerie van Financiën, the Ministerie van Buitenlandse Zaken and the Ministerie van Algemene Zaken, all of which reside in The Hague; the Ministère des Affaires Étrangères (Ministerie van Buitenlandse Zaken) in Brussels; the Archives of the European Communities in Florence; the Fondation Jean Monnet in Lausanne and the Roosevelt Study Center in Middelburg. I thank all the archivists and officials who have helped me and have provided advice on the source material.

Finally, I wish to thank my former colleagues at the University of Leiden's Economic and Social History Department and my present colleagues at the University of Groningen's Department of International Organization and International Relations for their unfailing support for my teaching and research activities.

List of Abbreviations

ABCM	Association of British Chemical Manufacturers
AKU	Algemene Kunstzijde Unie
BDI	Bundesverband der Deutschen Industrie
BLEU	Belgium-Luxembourg Economic Union
CEEC	Committee on European Economic Cooperation
CET	Common External Tariff
DIHT	Deutscher Industrie- und Handelstag
ECA	Economic Cooperation Administration
ECE	Economic Commission for Europe
ECSC	European Coal and Steel Community
ECUSG	European Customs Union Study Group
EDC	European Defense Community
EEC	European Economic Community
EFTA	European Free Trade Association
EPC	European Political Community
EPU	European Payments Union
ERP	European Recovery Program
FRUS	Foreign Relations of the United States
GATT	General Agreement on Tariffs and Trade
GNP	Gross National Product
HA	High Authority
IBRD	International Bank for Reconstruction and Development
ICI	Imperial Chemicals Industry
IDAC	Import Duties Advisory Committee
IMF	International Monetary Fund
ITO	International Trade Organization
MFN	Most Favored Nation
MRP	Mouvement Républicain Populaire
NAF	Dutch-American Fuse Company (Nederlands-Amerikaanse Fittingen Fabriek)
NATO	North Atlantic Treaty Organization
NFU	National Farmers Union
OEEC	Organization for European Economic Cooperation
R&D	Research and Development

RTA	Reciprocal Trade Agreement
RTAA	Reciprocal Trade Agreement Act
SITC	Standard International Trade Classification
SPD	Sozialistische Partei Deutschland
UN	United Nations
UNRRA	United Nations Relief and Rehabilitation Administration
WEU	Western European Union

Archival References

AEC	Archives of the European Communities, Florence
AN	Archives Nationales, Paris
ARA	Algemeen Rijksarchief, The Hague
ARA, MAZ	Algemeen Rijksarchief, Ministerie van Algemene Zaken
ARA, MEZ	Algemeen Rijksarchief, Archieven van het Ministerie van Economische Zaken
ARA, MR	Algemeen Rijksarchief, Ministerraad
ARA, REA	Algemeen Rijksarchief, Raad voor Economische Aangelegenheden
BA	Bundesarchiv, Koblenz, Germany
BA, B 102	Bundesarchiv, Koblenz, Bundesministerium für Wirtschaft
BA, B 136	Bundesarchiv, Koblenz, Bundeskanzleramt
BA, B 146	Bundesarchiv, Koblenz, Bundesministerium für den Marshall Plan
CHP, RSC	Cordell Hull Papers, Roosevelt Study Center, Middelburg, The Netherlands
FJM	Fondation Jean Monnet, Lausanne, Switzerland
MAE	Ministère des Affaires Étrangères, Paris
MAE, AD, DE-CE	Ministère des Affaires Étrangères, Archives Diplomatiques, Direction des Affaires Économiques et Financières, Service de Cooperation Économique
MAE (Bel)	Ministère des Affaires Étrangères, (Ministerie van Buitenlandse Zaken), Brussels
MAZ	Ministerie van Algemene Zaken, The Hague
MBZ	Ministerie van Buitenlandse Zaken, The Hague
MBZ, DGEM	Ministerie van Buitenlandse Zaken, Directoraat Generaal voor Economische en Militaire Samenwerking
MEZ	Ministerie van Economische Zaken, The Hague
MEZ, BEB	Ministerie van Economische Zaken, Directoraat Generaal voor Buitenlandse Economische Betrekkingen

MEZ, DGHN	Ministerie van Economische Zaken, Directoraat Generaal voor Handel en Nijverheid
MFin	Ministerie van Financiën, The Hague
NA	National Archives, Washington, D.C.
PRO	Public Record Office, Kew, U.K.
PRO, BT	Public Record Office, Board of Trade Archives
PRO, CAB	Public Record Office, Cabinet Papers
PRO, FO	Public Record Office, Foreign Office Archives
PRO, PREM	Public Record Office, Prime Minister's Papers
PRO, T	Public Record Office, Treasury Archives

List of Tables

List of Illustrations

Introduction

There is something distinctly puzzling about the economic and political environment of the 1950s. Never before in history did there exist such a widespread belief in the virtues of free trade and competition, and never before was the free trade doctrine so generally accepted. The inter-war experience of economic nationalism that had led to progressive production, trade and welfare losses had entrenched Western European and American countries' commitments to an open international economic system. The Cold War climate, in which authoritarian Soviet socialism challenged liberal Western capitalism, further enhanced these beliefs. And yet, never before were Western European governments more prepared and better equipped to intervene in the domestic economy and to promote exports in order to obtain full employment and high levels of consumption and investment.

It is this paradoxical mixture of Keynesian economic nationalism and liberal economic internationalism, of neomercantilist policy and free trade ideology, that has long fascinated historians, political scientists and economists studying this period. For those interested in trade policy issues of the era, some further intriguing questions emerge from this puzzle. How open was the international economic system and how committed were governments really to reducing tariff and nontariff barriers to trade? Were protectionist countries in Europe mainly pursuing noneconomic, politically motivated trade policies, as some historians and economists have suggested? Were their policy choices the outcome of pressure groups' activity within the political economy? Did the United States, through its hegemonic position, secure a liberal international trading system, and did European governments gradually undermine this policy by opposing trade liberalization? What were the contributions to trade liberalization of international institutions such as the General Agreement on Tariffs and Trade (GATT) and the Organization for European Economic Cooperation (OEEC), and why did the latter give birth to two separate trading blocs in Europe?

There exist many works that have dealt with some of these commercial policy questions, but it is not often that these issues have been integrated into a study of the early origins of the European Common Market. This is somewhat surprising, given that trade policies are inextricably linked to the history of the European Common Market. After all, it was the customs union that underpinned the Treaty of Rome of 1957 and that prompted the six founding members to surrender authority over tariffs and quotas.[1]

With the opening up of archival material from the 1950s, various historical, archival- based works have appeared that focus on individual attempts since 1947 to create European trading frameworks as part of the wider process of strengthening economic and political ties between Western European nation-states. Some of these works indeed also discuss the regional trading frameworks such as Benelux, the Franco-Italian customs union, the European Coal and Steel Community (ECSC) and the European Economic Community (EEC).[2] Yet they either tend to deal with only one of these plans for regional integration, or they stop before a more thorough examination of the various national tariff policies that contributed to the creation of these plans, sometimes on the assumption that they represented issues of a mere technical, "low politics" nature.[3]

It would be wrong to attribute this lacuna to the relative newness of archival research on economic integration, to the limited perspectives of historians or to their horror—doubtless justified—of dry tariff schedules and tedious customs union proposals. Economists have tended to stress the relative insignificance of tariff barriers to the economic development and national economic policies of the 1950s. Usually, their arguments are twofold. First, tariffs were, and still are, considered a lesser evil than quotas and payment restrictions. Their impact on trade flow and trade policies is therefore seen as less crucial. Second, it was nontariff barriers to trade, not tariffs, that dominated postwar trade and payments, at least until 1954. Several economic and historical analyses of commercial developments before that period therefore highlight the OEEC's attempts to eliminate quota barriers and gloss over tariff proposals.[4] If tariffs are discussed, this is usually within the context of the first GATT rounds.[5]

Economists have been more concerned with the process of preferential tariff and quota elimination that began in 1958 with the start of the Common Market's transitional phase toward completion. This process was the impetus for extensive research into the trade and welfare effects of maintaining, reducing and eliminating tariffs.[6] At the same time, it renewed interest in levels of tariff protection in force on the eve of the EEC's creation, and it stimulated the debate on the measurement of tariff protection.[7] Such research accepts the EEC's formation and the resulting gradual disappearance of autonomous tariff policies as an economic fact and therefore does not focus on the *tariff origins* of the EEC.

More recently, scholars of international political economy have brought trade policy issues of the early postwar period back into the limelight. They examine the relative openness of the postwar trading system, the workings of the GATT regime and the link between trade and security, often in connection with the ongoing debate over the role of the United States in creating and maintaining the postwar economic order. Despite renewing the interest in tariff policy issues of the 1950s, their work has not yet resulted in similar contributions on the trade policies of European countries in this period.[8]

ARGUMENT AND PLAN OF THE BOOK

The argument of this book is that European tariff policies and plans for tariff reductions did matter in this period, even though the economic boom of the 1950s was so powerful that tariff rates themselves may not have had much impact on *overall* levels of trade expansion.[9] It traces the Common Market's tariff policy roots from an historical perspective and tries to explain why, after more than a decade of multilateral plans for trade cooperation, its six founding members were finally prepared to surrender the larger part of their autonomous trade policies and eliminate the tariff barriers between them. In doing so, it addresses systematically a number of relevant trade policy issues relating to the following questions: Was the creation of the EEC easier because tariff protection and tariff policies after 1945 had entirely lost the prominent position they held in the 1920s and 1930s? But if that were so, why is it that the customs union emerged as the cornerstone of European economic integration? Did customs unions develop as a first and intermediate step toward worldwide trade liberalization? Why then did the Six not eliminate their tariffs much earlier, and why not within GATT, on a worldwide basis? Why did so many policymakers embrace the classical free trade doctrine and yet for a long time refused to surrender their frontier protection? Why, if tariffs merely represented a purely technical, and therefore "low politics" element of European economic integration, did it take the EEC members more than ten years to determine all the tariff levels for their common external tariff? Why, if tariffs were economically irrelevant, or at least trivial, until the mid-1950s, did the period between 1947 and 1957 witness so many abortive plans for the multilateral reduction or elimination of European tariffs?

Before explaining the way in which these questions will be addressed, we should pause to clarify beforehand some of the concepts used to analyze the different trade and tariff agreements.[10] The term *integration* will be used here in two different contexts, namely that of "economic integration" and of "European integration." Economic integration is defined here as the outcome of a process by which economies are drawn more closely together as the result of increased mobility of goods, production factors or both. The term *European integration,* by contrast, will be used only in the restricted sense of the effective pooling by national governments within Europe of sovereignty into a supranational body. It thus excludes all those looser institutional forms of interdependence or intergovernmental cooperation that fall short of this.[11] Consequently, the concept of European economic integration is reserved for the outcome of a process of economic integration which involves the pooling of sovereignty.

The multilateral tariff plans examined in this study are those that involve attempts at increasing the mobility of goods by reducing or eliminating tariff barriers among two or more European economies. To avoid ambiguity, the concepts used to describe these different approaches will be summed up and explained here:[12]

- worldwide tariff reductions: Tariff cutting on a nondiscriminatory basis (implemented within GATT)
- preferential tariff reductions: Tariff cutting on a discriminatory basis (for example, within the system of Commonwealth Preferences or among a group of European countries)
- preferential tariff elimination: This may involve:
  - a free trade area: intra-group tariffs are eliminated
  - a customs union: Intra-group tariffs are eliminated and a common external tariff is formed toward nonmember countries

• sectoral tariff elimination: Removing tariffs within one specific industry or economic sector

The research method chosen to examine these European tariff plans starts with the premise that they cannot simply be divided into those that were concerned with the pooling of sovereignty (i.e., with European economic integration, such as the ECSC, the Beyen Plan or the EEC) and those that merely aimed at reducing or eliminating tariffs on an intergovernmental basis—often outside the framework of the Six. It is clear that all these plans were linked because they represented foreign commercial policy responses to a common set of national or international imperatives, albeit they were experienced in different ways in different countries. To focus solely on those involving the six eventual founding members of the EEC would be to distort the reality of the historical process. For this reason, a problem-oriented approach is offered which examines the multilateral tariff plans and tariff issues across the range of international trading frameworks of the period, such as the OEEC, GATT and the Council of Europe. From the start of this research, the OEEC's prominent role in tariff issues suggested that to highlight tariff matters and to ignore quota policies would be equally distorting.[13] As will be shown, the OEEC's Trade Liberalization Program had such a large impact upon European tariff policies that quotas have to be treated as an integral part of the tariff analysis.

Figure 1 shows the various multilateral tariff initiatives launched in the decade after 1947 and the international fora in which they were presented. The names at the top represent the frameworks or organizations in which the tariff plans were launched, and the arrows show if the plans were referred to another framework for discussion. The starting point for our research is the first postwar proposal for the creation of a European customs union launched at the so-called Conference on European Economic Cooperation. From there, we follow the multilateral European tariff plans that were presented within the OEEC, GATT, the Council of Europe and the framework of the Six. We will end the study with the negotiations for the Common Market between 1955 and 1957. For the sake of completion, figure 1 also shows the link between Britain's Plan G for an industrial free trade area and the eventual formation in 1958 of the European Free Trade Association, even though the EFTA negotiations fall outside the scope of this book.

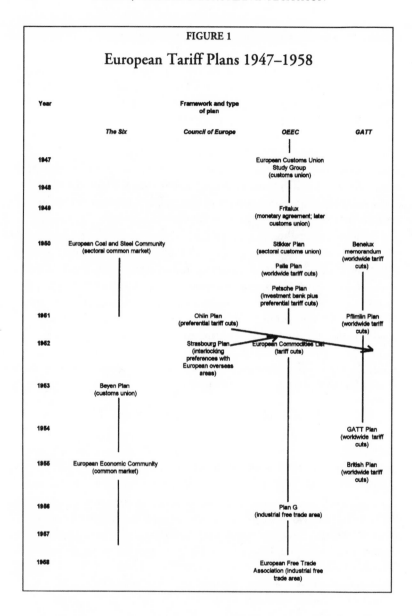

FIGURE 1

European Tariff Plans 1947–1958

As figure 1 indicates, the ECSC, the Beyen Plan and the EEC form only one explanatory route in the chain of multilateral tariff initiatives conceived by European states. Quite often, different plans were discussed simultaneously within different frameworks, suggesting that for at least some countries the tariff issue was important enough to push it at various instances and in many different international institutions. In 1952, for instance, the OEEC members discussed a plan for tariff reductions among them, while most of them met at the same time within GATT to examine yet another tariff plan. In addition, six of these states were also considering the pros and cons of the Beyen Plan for the creation of a customs union.

A multi-archive study on postwar tariff policies necessarily requires certain self-selected restrictions to the subject.[14] One choice concerns the extent to which the study is embedded into the broader historical and economic literature on European trade liberalization. Since the book's main focus is on the period from 1947 to 1957, it is in the first chapter that an introductory outlook is offered on the historical patterns of protection, on the main arguments for imposing tariffs and on the evolution of national tariff policies. Also, no attempt is made within this book to tackle adequately one of the most painstaking of all tariff issues: the measurement of tariff protection. This is why the appendix discusses some problems involved in making international comparisons of tariff schedules and also points at the limitations and possibilities of the methods available.[15] A third choice lies in the issue areas examined. By concentrating on the tariff plans and commercial policies of the late 1940s and 1950s, the book does not examine the military and political events that have influenced the shape, timing and nature of European economic integration. It should be stressed from the outset that two main incentives for the drive toward greater integration since 1947 were the need for Franco-German political reconciliation and for West Germany's military and political (as well as economic) integration into Europe in the wake of fears of Soviet communism. While these aspects of European integration will receive mention as part of the wider international political events of the period, they will not be analyzed here, since that has been done elsewhere in many contemporaneous and recent historical contributions. To give just two concrete examples: In chapter 2 most attention is concentrated on the tariff aspects of the European Coal and Steel Community negotiations, even though the reader is made aware that these negotiations involved many broader and more crucial issues of a political nature. The Beyen Plan for a European customs union among the Six is discussed without an in-depth treatment of the debate on the European Defense Community and the Political Community, of which it was a component. These self-imposed limitations in discussing the prehistory of the EEC are adopted only to serve the brevity and clarity of argumentation; they should not be interpreted as attempts to offer one-dimensional explanations. A further limitation is that the book deals predominantly with the tariff policies of national governments. It considers nation-states as actors in an international network of economic and political relations, without offering a deeper analysis of events at lower, domestic levels of decision making that influenced their policy choices. This choice had to be made because it would require yet another vast layer of empirical research to cover systematically such decision making and bargaining processes at sectoral, private or political party levels. The final chapter, however, offers three case studies that highlight aspects of the interaction between domestic decision making on tariff policy and tariff bargaining at the international level.

The European tariff plans set out in figure 1 provide some guidance to the thematic structure of this book, since chapters 3, 4 and 5 all deal with the three most important frameworks within which several of these plans were discussed: the OEEC, GATT and the Six, respectively. The book starts with a chapter that begins by placing the postwar trading era within the wider context of patterns of free trade and protection, and by summing up the mainstream arguments for imposing tariffs. It then discusses various general approaches toward explaining protectionism and, in the second part, offers an overview of national commercial policy developments up to 1945.

Chapter 2 examines how commercial developments in the 1930s influenced and shaped the postwar international trading system of GATT. It subsequently moves away from this worldwide economic framework to the problems of regional economic recovery within Europe and to the early plans for regional trade cooperation among the recipients of Marshall aid. While these early plans all failed to come about, they paved the way for the negotiations in 1950 leading to a sectoral European common market in the coal, iron and steel sectors.

Chapter 3 highlights the tariff issue that emerged within the context of the OEEC, shortly after this organization began its attack on quantitative restrictions to intra-European trade. This initiative brought tariff protection back into the limelight and provoked a long and heated campaign by the so-called Low Tariff Club against the disparity of tariff levels prevailing within Europe. Before turning to the plans resulting from the Club's crusade, an attempt is made to assess and compare tariff levels across countries and industries. These assessments are used throughout the book as a frame of reference for examining the European tariff debate.

In chapter 4 the main emphasis lies on proposals for reducing European tariffs within GATT, the framework originally designed to foster tariff negotiations. After the Torquay round of 1950, GATT suffered severe setbacks, partly because it tried to deal with tariffs in isolation from other forms of protection such as quantitative restrictions, subsidies and state trade. Even so, GATT played a role in setting the parameters for European states' freedom to maneuver in tariff matters. As we will see, it also turned into a vital battleground confronting European and American trade policies. This development, too, strengthened the search for a preferential trading block in Europe.

Chapter 5 directs us toward trading cooperation among the six ECSC members by examining the Dutch proposal for a supranational European customs union that was launched in 1952 during the talks for a European Political Community. Their Beyen Plan represented a further attempt, alongside earlier proposals made within the OEEC and GATT, to force down tariff barriers and to create a permanent set of trade rules that firmly and irreversibly linked their economy to a preferential zone of freer trade within Europe. The failure of the Political Community temporarily halted these efforts, but another proposal for European economic integration followed in 1955, this time presented by all three Benelux countries. The remainder of the chapter highlights the tariff aspects of these negotiations that eventually led to the formation of the Common Market.

The final chapter discusses domestic and international factors influencing national tariff policies of three European countries: Germany, the United Kingdom and the Netherlands. It traces how the governments of these countries used their tariff instruments, how they coped with opportunities and constraints resulting from international tariff bargaining and how—and to what extent—such influences impeded or stimulated tariff reductions in Europe.

ONE

The Patterns and Politics of Protection in Historical Perspective

Patterns of free trade and protectionism have long been of great interest to students of international trade issues. Central to their work are such questions as: Why do swings between free trade and protectionism occur in history, and what are their consequences for economic growth? Why do governments turn to tariff protection if the gains from free trade and the benefits from unilateral tariff cuts are so widely accepted? Why did nontariff barriers become so prevalent in the twentieth century? By turning to some of these analytical and historical issues, this chapter will provide a background to the subsequent chapters on postwar trade policies. It will examine the international pattern of protectionism since the nineteenth century and the tariff policies that emerged in the United Kingdom, continental Europe and the United States. It also explores some explanations for these historical swings between free trade and protectionism, which may shed more light on the central theme of this book: the origins and nature of Europe's tariff plans between 1947 and 1957.

THE ANALYTICAL FRAMEWORK

Conventional international trade theory explains that under perfectly competitive conditions (i.e., where the market prices for goods and services reflect the social marginal costs of their production and the social marginal benefits of their use) free trade provides the optimal trade policy. The unrestricted transfer of goods and services across national borders will improve world and national welfare since it allows countries to maximize the gains from their comparative cost advantages. This logic, which descended from Adam Smith and David Ricardo, has become one of the most widely admired and accepted doctrines of modern economics. Almost universally embraced by Western economists and politicians alike, it became part of the consensus underlying the postwar international trade order.[1]

However, despite its widespread acceptance, the free trade logic has also caused economists many a headache. One main reason is that protectionism seems to have been a recurring feature ever since an integrated world economy emerged in the mid-nineteenth century.[2] A period of relatively free trade, such as that between roughly 1850 and 1870 when Britain and several other trading nations adopted free trade policies, is usually succeeded by a period of protectionism. Moreover, genuinely liberal trade policies, based on unilaterally opening up one's home market, seem to have been the exception rather than the rule. Trade specialists are thus faced with a remarkable discrepancy between the overwhelming logic of free trade theory and the empirical evidence of recurring protectionism.[3]

Before examining some of the more common explanations for this discrepancy, we first should explore these long-term historical patterns of free trade and protectionism more closely. When do they occur and how widespread are they? Although there is no unanimous agreement on their exact timing, importance or economic impact, the general trends suggested in various economic historical surveys can, for the moment, be summarized as shown in table 1.1.[4]

Britain's gradual liberalization of taxes on industrial raw materials since the 1820s and its eventual abolition of the Corn Laws in 1849 set in motion a major swing toward free trade. Many continental countries subsequently reduced tariff barriers in the 1850s and 1860s, but during the Great Depression of the 1870s and the rise of nationalism, the general trend was toward protectionism. Although there were some brief interruptions, and even though Britain only introduced tariffs in 1916, protectionism prevailed well until the end of the Second World War. Between 1945 and the slowdown of world economic activity in the early 1970s there again occurred a widespread move towards trade liberalization. After the postwar boom ended and

TABLE 1.1

Patterns of Free Trade and Protectionism

Period	Trend toward free trade	Characteristics
1850-1870	increasing	Britain sets swing in motion
1870-1945	decreasing	Widespread tariff rises on Continent, but not in Britain until 1930s
1945-1970	increasing	Widespread trade liberalization among industrial countries
1970-1990	decreasing	'New' protectionism after the economic recession and the collapse of Bretton Woods

Source: See chap. 1, note 4.

the international monetary system collapsed in the early 1970s, the world economy again entered a phase of increased protection.[5]

While the historical literature seems fairly unanimous on the timing of these international patterns of free trade and protection, there is little agreement on their causes. Why they occur, and also why tariff protection in general is so prevalent, remains controversial. Below, we will consider some of the more common answers offered by economics, economic history and international political economy. A sophisticated discussion underlies these various explanations, but here we will merely give a simplified version of arguments for and against imposing tariffs.

ARGUMENTS FOR TARIFFS

Although economists have generally supported the classical theory of international trade, they have also identified early on exceptions to the rule that free trade is always the optimal policy. Thus, it has been suggested that one solid—and purely economic—reason for using a tariff is to exploit one's monopoly power as an importer. By imposing what is called an 'optimum tariff' on a product of which a country is a large importer, that country can maximize the gains in real income from improving its terms of trade in such a way that this will compensate for the welfare loss associated with imposing that tariff. It may enrich itself but only at the expense of world welfare, since there is a misallocation of economic resources.[6] Most economists agree that there are several practical difficulties involved in using this strategy. Not only do monopoly positions occur rarely, but also their exploitation through optimum tariffs requires detailed knowledge of elasticities and cross-elasticities of supply and demand for a wide range of products, knowledge that is usually not obtainable. A further consideration is that monopoly tariffs may render short-term benefits but that retaliation by other countries may well cause long-term damage.[7]

Since tariffs normally discourage imports by increasing the prices of imported goods relative to those of domestically produced goods, they also may be imposed to improve a country's balance of trade and to preserve or increase its foreign-exchange reserves. However, economic analysis indicates that in developed countries these aims can usually be obtained more effectively by other direct instruments of macroeconomic policy that, unlike tariffs, neither distort price structures nor result in a suboptimal allocation of production factors.[8]

A more customary motive for imposing tariffs is to maintain or increase employment in specific sectors. By discouraging imports of certain products, tariffs may encourage in the short run domestic economic activity and raise incomes. In the long run, this income rise may even offset the reduction in overall imports resulting from these restrictive tariffs.[9] However, it is more likely that other unprotected domestic industries will suffer, either directly from higher input costs or indirectly from wage inflation or upward pressure on the exchange rate.[10] Ultimately, therefore, the choice for sectoral tariff protection is a political one, which concerns the distribution of economic welfare among different groups within society.

Yet another historically important economic reason for levying tariffs is to collect revenue. After all, they can be administered and collected relatively easily and are paid at least partly by foreigners. Theoretically it is possible to set a revenue tariff that brings in maximum revenue. A government trying to do this has to take account of the difference between the short- and long-term revenues it will derive from the tariff. In the short run, a given tariff may bring in more revenue than in the long run, since it will stimulate import substitution.[11]

Perhaps the most dominant economic explanation for temporary tariff protection is rooted in the infant industry argument developed during the mercantilist era and further popularized by thinkers such as Alexander Hamilton and Friedrich List. This assumes that some newly starting firms and industries need maturing time behind a protective tariff wall to train labor, to explore new markets, to develop new technologies and to obtain economies of scale or to produce external economies. By raising the price of the imported good relative to the domestically produced good, the tariff offers protection from competition by older, more competitive industries abroad.[12] It implies a subsidy to the producer but also a higher price for the consumer, whose demand therefore may be limited. Thus, it is often argued that direct subsidies offer a more effective way of protecting infant industries than tariffs, since they do not tax the consumer directly.[13]

STRATEGIC TRADE POLICY AND THE POLITICAL ECONOMY OF PROTECTIONISM

While the law of comparative advantage suggests that unilateral free trade is the optimal trade policy because it maximizes economic welfare, it is based on assumptions only rarely true of the real world: that perfectly competitive markets exist in which returns to scale from production are constant. Influenced by the rise of neomercantilist policies, trade theorists since the early 1980s have loosened these strict assumptions and have begun focusing on trade policies under imperfect competition. They have developed the argument that a governmental strategy of unilateral protection may improve national welfare. Just as a unilaterally imposed optimal tariff may exploit monopoly power, the unilateral use of import duties or export subsidies in oligopolistic industries may lead to competitive advantages and rising profits that may increase national income.[14] Briefly the argument is that large economies of scale along with high research and development (R&D) costs entail high fixed costs and large risks for businesses. To yield a return on such major initial investments, firms require growing sales volumes, and if their collective market shares at home are too limited to reach the minimum scale needed for breaking even, access to foreign markets and control over the domestic market become vital. It is at this point that the national government may successfully step in by protecting the home market with a tariff and by stimulating production with an export subsidy.[15]

What are the main implications of this strategic trade theory for practical trade policy? To a large extent, they resemble observations made earlier for protection under monopoly or infant industry conditions. There may exist industries with a small number of firms, with limited market entry and increasing returns to scale in which intervention may improve national welfare. Under certain circumstances governments will therefore have an incentive to introduce protectionist measures and to support domestic firms' efforts to compete internationally. Yet they will find it extremely difficult to obtain all the information needed to determine an optimal strategy. In addition, even if such information is available and an optimal policy is devised, other governments will probably retaliate, thus damaging national and global welfare.[16] And such retaliation is all the more probable in R&D-incentive industries, since these are often subject to national policies motivated by considerations of economic, political and military prestige.[17] Paul Krugman, one of the pioneering strategic trade theorists, has aptly summarized this dilemma, stating that:

> The economic cautions about the difficulty of formulating useful interventions and the political concerns that interventionism may go astray combine into a new case for free trade. This is not the old argument that free trade is optimal because markets are efficient. Instead, it is a sadder but wiser argument for free trade as a rule of thumb in a world whose politics are as imperfect as its markets.[18]

Both orthodox and strategic trade theories affirm that the *distribution* of the welfare gains from trade may not be equal for all. Protectionism tends to benefit some groups in society at the expense of others. The implications of this seem obvious: Levels of protection are influenced by interest groups. The economic and political examinations of their activities have generally pursued three types of analysis, one focusing on factorial explanations of protectionism, another on firm and sectoral theories and a third on so-called public choice approaches. Together, these different approaches form part of a broad analysis known as the political economy of protectionism.[19] Let us discuss their contributions.

The first, factorial analysis, rests on the assumption that countries will specialize in and export those goods whose production uses the factor relatively abundantly available within their economies. Thus, a country that has plenty of capital (relative to another country) will specialize in the production and export of capital-intensive goods, whereas a relatively labor-abundant country will specialize in labor-intensive products. This leads to the conclusion that industries using their countries' abundant factor will gain from a move toward free trade, since the international specialization that follows will increase the demand for and thus the relative return to that factor. Similarly, industries using the relatively scarce factor will lose from such a move toward free trade and will gain from more protection. The political implication is that a free trade policy will be pursued once the political representatives of the abundant factor have obtained sufficient power.[20]

Closer examination of this factorial model raises some questions. One major problem is that the empirical evidence hints at a convergence of interests among the political representatives of labor and capital.[21] Trade unions and capital owners are not seldom lobbying for the same type of trade policies. Moreover, the factorial model assumes that production factors are entirely mobile across countries and industries, an assumption which at least in the short term runs into difficulties. Firm and sectoral trade policy models try to anticipate these problems. They assume, first, that production factors are either immobile or can move across firms and sectors only at considerable costs, and second, that capital and labor within a specific firm or sector will always adopt identical trade policy positions.[22]

Public choice approaches to studying protectionism have further expanded the analysis of special interest group activities within political systems. Generally speaking, they focus on the interaction between politicians supplying protection and organized interest groups demanding it. Governments or individual politicians tend to satisfy producer demands for protective legislation (such as higher tariffs or subsidies) in exchange for financial and electoral support. Consumers usually do not enter the picture, since they tend to form a large unorganized group of individuals whose per capita income losses from protection are usually much smaller than producers' per capita income gains.[23]

It is one thing to identify the interests behind tariff protection that operate at the factorial, the sectoral or the national (governmental) level, and quite another to explain patterns of tariff protection across countries and over time within the international economy.[24] In the latter case, the international political economy literature has pursued some further lines of inquiry, many of which rest on or combine elements of the more familiar economic explanations for protectionism discussed earlier. Since it would require at least another long description to examine these studies in detail, the next section will outline only the key elements and hypotheses of four such approaches. These center on, respectively, the role of ideas and ideologies, of business cycles, of international diffusion of production and of changes in the international distribution of power (see the summary in table 1.2). For analytical purposes they will be presented as separate theories, but it is worth bearing in mind that there exist many models and concepts that combine elements of these approaches into other chains of causation.

The first approach is what one may call the intellectual or "ideational" explanation. It assumes that ideas do not necessarily reflect underlying interests, but that they can exert independent influence on

TABLE 1.2

Approaches to Explaining Movements toward and Away from Systemic Openness

Ideational approach	Business cycle approach	Surplus capacity approach	Structural approach
Ideas and ideologies	Economic contraction or expansion	International diffusion of technology and industrial production	Changes in the international distribution of power
Belief systems of decision-makers	Expected utility of protection versus free trade	Sectoral performance below capacity	Ascent or decline of hegemony
Institutional change	Collective action of organized interests	Legislative action to protect sectors	(Institutional lags)
	Legislative outcome		Trade policy preferences
Trade policy	Trade policy	Trade policy	Trade policy

Source: Adapted from W. Thompson, L. Vescera, "Growth Waves, Systemic Openness, and Protectionism," *International Organization* 46 (1992): 501. The ideational approach is partially taken from Fischer, "Swings Between Protection and Free Trade," 29 (see chap. 1, note 1).

trade policy by shaping the belief systems of intellectual elites, the general public and decision makers. Britain's unilateral move toward free trade in the early nineteenth century is often quoted as a policy outcome that can be—in part—explained by ideas and belief systems. The assumption is that the classical economists Adam Smith and David Ricardo and their followers had a crucial influence on the belief system in Britain by introducing the notion that free trade always serves the general interest.[25] In a variation on this theme, many authors also stress that these classical economists provided the intellectual foundations for the free trade bias prevailing among subsequent generations of economists in the nineteenth and twentieth centuries.[26] This liberal ideology is also said to be institutionalized or "embedded" into the GATT worldwide trade regime.[27]

A second, business cycle explanation of trends in protectionism has also long enjoyed popularity among historians, political scientists and economists. In essence, it argues that downswings in business cycles enable protectionist interest groups to bear strong collective pressure for protectionism upon their governments, which in turn are more receptive to such pressure in times of economic recession. During business upswings, by contrast, organized interest groups and governments can more easily perceive the gains from free trade and they will therefore lend stronger support to a free trade orientation.[28] Indeed, many analysts explain the moves toward international openness of the 1860s and the 1950s in terms of strong economic upswings, whereas they see the "beggar-thy-neighbor" policies of the Interbellum and the "new protectionism" of the 1970s and 1980s as outcomes of downswings in the business cycle.[29]

The surplus capacity theory of protectionism is concerned with more fundamental, structural economic changes that may be more persistent than those resulting from the business cycle. It holds that the widespread diffusion of new technology and production methods results in increased international competition shifts in market positions and more capital-intensive production methods. These developments periodically cause a situation in which the productive capacities of major industries substantially exceed levels of demand at prices high enough to sustain employment and adequate returns on investment. The more extensive and persistent this surplus problem, the stronger these industries' demands for protection.[30]

One rather different but influential contribution made by international political economists concerns the "structural" approach to explaining free trade and protectionism.[31] Commonly known as the theory of hegemonic stability, this body of thought contains a wide variety of strands and interpretations, ranging from the neoliberal to the realist and neorealist. Here, we shall discuss one of its best known variants, the hegemonic stability analysis first suggested by the economist and economic historian Charles Kindleberger and subsequently modified by Stephen D. Krasner.[32]

Kindleberger's original work of 1973 established a link between Britain's economic decline, America's rise to international power and the outbreak of the Depression. He argued that the existence of a stable international economy depended on the presence of a single hegemonic power that operated as a stabilizer. Only the dominant power with the largest stake in the international system could be expected to take responsibility for and bear the costs of maintaining relative stability. If there was more than one power in charge, the temptation to "pass the buck" or to revert to mercantilist "free riding" would ultimately lead to the breakdown of the system.[33]

Following Kindleberger, Stephen Krasner argued that economic openness is more likely to develop in periods when a single hegemonic state (defined as a state that is "much larger and relatively more advanced than its trading partners") is still increasing its relative economic size and technological lead. In that phase, the hegemonic state prefers an open economic structure because this improves its aggregate national income, rate of economic growth and political power. In Krasner's view, "such a state has the interest and the resources to create a structure characterized by lower tariffs, rising trade proportions, and less regionalism."[34] Taking three indicators—tariff levels, ratios of trade to national income and concentrations of trade within regions of varying development levels—he distinguished five different phases of increasing and decreasing international economic openness since the early nineteenth century. For the hegemony theory to "fit," each phase of increasing openness would have to coincide with a rise in the hegemonic state's international economic power and each phase of decreasing openness with that state's declining economic power. Krasner's original hypothesis met his empirical data for three periods but failed to explain the periods 1900-1913 and 1918-1939. Therefore, he subsequently amended it by allowing for a "delayed reaction" in the international trading system. Changes in economic power, he argued, are not immediately translated into changes in the distribution of political power and in the social and institutional structures involved in trade policy-making. There is also a time lag between changes in economic hegemony and the policy changes that eventually alter the degree of international economic openness.

Two elements in Krasner's approach are of direct interest to our research on tariffs plans in the 1940s and 1950s. First, when examining tariff levels and tariff policies, it is extremely difficult to ignore national institutional structures and national decision-making processes. Even if one adopts the systemic level of analysis, as Krasner originally did, one is inevitably confronted with the question of the societal or institutional mechanism through which systemic changes (for example, declining economic hegemony) will influence domestic policies. If changes in tariff protection are used as indicators of systemic "waves," this question becomes all the more urgent, because unlike quantitative restrictions or exchange controls, tariffs are normally subject to parliamentary scrutiny. Second, like so many other authors before and after him, Krasner concluded that as far as the period 1945-1970 is concerned, "it is neatly explained by the argument that hegemony leads to an open trading structure . . . "[35] However, he also notes that his indicators produce an ambiguous record. While tariff levels were gradually reduced during the various GATT rounds, ratios of trade to gross domestic product were relatively large in the early 1950s because of rising commodity prices, yet they did not increase until the early 1960s. In addition, regional trade concentration only began decreasing after 1960.[36]

Timothy McKeown's 1983 study of Britain's trade policy in the nineteenth century and his later analysis of the long-run pattern of imports in the United States and Western Europe each reject hegemonic stability theory as an adequate explanation for international economic openness. His first work supports the "revisionist" interpretations of economic historians such as McClosky and Irwin, who have argued that Britain's tariff policy in the nineteenth century did not lead to a "Golden Era" of free trade. It concludes that on the few occasions that Britain pressed for tariff reductions it almost invariably failed, even during negotiations with small countries. Britain did not really use its hegemonic power to try and obtain tariff reductions as a *quid pro quo* for British diplomatic, economic or military support.[37]

McKeown's other, quantitative study is also interesting for our purposes. It presents industrial capitalist countries' proportions of trade to income in nominal and value terms over seven periods between 1880 and 1987 and uses these outcomes as indicators of trends in relative openness.[38] The value series confirm the familiar view that the 1930s and 1940s were decades of relative closure while the years 1880-1900, the 1920s and the period 1973-1987 were phases of relative openness. However—and this seems more remarkable—the value figures also suggest that during 1948-1958 the international trade system was only marginally less closed than during the years 1930-1938. On a volume basis, this period seems even more closed that the years 1930-1938.

The degrees of regionalization and bilateralism also suggest that the immediate postwar period was less open than commonly assumed. Between 1938 and 1954, regionalization of world trade increased within all trade regions while degrees of bilateral balancing measured for France, the United Kingdom, the United States and Germany were all higher in the postwar years than in the era 1928-1938.[39] McKeown therefore rejected even the rather cautious observations of some analysts that the postwar trading system was one of "freer" rather than free trade. In his view, "The contention that the post–World War II era has been more open than previous ones is strongly supported only when openness is measured by trade volumes rather than values, and when the years since 1972 are included."[40] Rather than explain relative economic openness in terms of hegemonic power, he suggests that economic growth rates in the years *preceding* changes in trade growth may offer more adequate explanations.

Although it is easy to go along with the critics of hegemonic stability explanations for systemic openness, it may well be that the alternative long-run analysis described above is still spurious. Even if one accepts the use of the hegemonic state's proportion of total trade as an indicator of his influence over the trading system, the reasoning remains imprecise and ambiguous. For instance, once the intervals for the interwar and postwar years are broken down further into subperiods, it emerges that the ratio was relatively low in the first four postwar years and subsequently rose quite rapidly. This underlines the fact that such empirical assessments are extremely sensitive to the definitions used and the periodization adopted.[41]

Clearly what unites all the political economy approaches is that they offer explanations for patterns of international economic openness and closure that are based on trade flows rather than trade policies. If we want to establish if and to what extent trade flows and commercial policies interacted, we should take a closer look at developments on the national level.

COMMERCIAL POLICIES SINCE
THE EARLY MODERN STATE SYSTEM

The rise of the modern state is inextricably linked to the growth of the international market economy.[42] The perpetual struggles since the fifteenth century between European monarchs, noblemen and merchants to control resources produced various power centers, ranging from absolutist states and highly dispersed empires to networks of merchant city-states. Each state emerged from an intricate web of conflicting and overlapping interests. By the seventeenth century each state conducted a policy often described now as mercantilism, aimed at obtaining a net surplus of money by encouraging foreign exports and discouraging foreign imports. It was this money surplus that enabled the state's survival in times of war. Internally, the state strengthened its position by dismantling domestic trade barriers and by broadening revenue sources through taxation.[43]

One common mercantilist trading practice involved creating trading monopolies through capture of the most profitable international trading routes. By taking direct control of trade flows in the Indian Ocean region, Portuguese, English and Dutch merchants maximized trade profits and minimized overseas money spending. By supervising, taxing and re-exporting imported goods, the state received profits and revenues from trade and managed to offset deficits with other vital trading areas such as the Baltic. As a result, throughout most of the seventeenth century, Holland and later England operated as the two dominant and rivaling states that shared control of the East Indian trade flows through companies exercising monopoly power. They built up large financial and military power centers that strengthened their external and internal power.[44]

Against this background of ever closer relationships between state building and national economic performance, a debate on "freedom of trade" developed throughout Europe, and in particular in England. Initially—that is, until the 1690s—this debate focused on the role of the monopoly trading companies, which excluded some groups of merchants and which were blamed for trade losses. By the end of the eighteenth century, a new middle class of English merchants and industrial capitalists facing ever tighter government controls over profits demanded more freedom from state intervention on all fronts. They embraced a liberal philosophy and the "classical" free trade ideology advanced in the writings of Adam Smith and David Ricardo.

Nonetheless, it would be too simple to propose an "ideational" explanation of Britain's unilateral move toward free trade. Britain initially used preferential entry to its domestic market as leverage for negotiating preferential market access abroad. In the early 1820s it began concluding reciprocity treaties with most-favored-nation clauses. Under such clauses, the tariff cuts that Britain granted on products imported from one country were extended to the same products derived from all other countries. This attempt at multilateral trade liberalization, however, had only limited success.[45] Not until 1860 did the most-favored-nation clause become a regular feature of international trade agreements.

Britain's impressive industrial lead created a need for new foreign markets and cheap raw material imports that eventually triggered its free trade orientation. The awareness that revenue arguments for tariffs began to lose weight facilitated this unilateral move. With the exception of duties on luxury items such as coffee, tea, tobacco and wine, many revenue duties had become either redundant or inefficient, at least when compared to other revenue sources such as income tax. In the 1820s, when the government achieved annual budget surpluses that lessened its financial problems, it made a cautious start with fiscal reforms.[46]

The British tariff debate reached its climax in the 1840s with the campaign to repeal the Corn Laws that protected British landlords from foreign corn imports. As interest group explanations suggest, manufacturers and a coalition of other politically vocal groups united in the Anti–Corn Law League succeeded in popularizing the case for free trade and noninterventionism. Minimizing international and domestic trade restrictions, their argument ran, would maximize national productivity and national economic welfare by increasing the division of labor. These proponents of free trade of course recognized that the welfare gains from unilateral tariff elimination would not benefit all groups on equal terms. The resulting income redistribution would benefit industrial laborers and manufacturers, who would see raw materials and food prices decline, while it would damage landlords that were previously protected. However, the League popularized the view that since the nation's overall welfare would increase, free trade was ultimately in "the general interest."[47] This perception eventually won the day because it was endorsed by increasingly powerful groups in society.

The unilateral repeal of the Corn Laws in 1846 accentuated Britain's rising productivity and expansion in world markets. In exchange for easier access to its domestic market, Britain could expand its manufacturing exports abroad. This, in turn, promoted trade liberalization elsewhere in Europe. In France, Napoleon III pursued a conscious policy of tariff reform aimed at cutting the costs of imported inputs and improving industrial competitiveness. By relying on his significant power and by offering tactical concessions to opposing industrialists, he could cut duties on bar iron, wool, machinery and various other products.[48] These commercial initiatives eventually culminated in the celebrated Cobden-Chevalier Treaty with Britain, which is commonly considered the onset of a golden era of free trade lasting until the 1880s.[49]

Had it not been for the spread of liberalism and nationalism, Britain's unilateral tariff cuts might not have had much international impact. Demands for political liberty and economic progress created a

climate in which calls for free enterprise and free trade fell on fertile soil.
As Sydney Pollard has so poignantly described:

> The demand for the independent nation state became closely associated
> with the demand for freedom of capital, even though that might mean
> impoverishment for the peasant and repression for the worker. Thus was
> created the fateful bond between the two most powerful drives in
> nineteenth-century Europe, nationalism and industrialization or 'eco-
> nomic progress.'[50]

In Europe, national liberation and unification initially seemed to coincide with trade liberalization and industrial growth. The unification of
Italy in 1861 but even more so the creation of the German Zollverein
under Prussian leadership illustrates this very well.

The Prussian tariff of 1818, which established zero rates for raw
materials, 10 percent rates for manufactures and revenue duties of up to
30 percent for colonial products, was among the least protective in Europe.
It reflected the interests of the Prussian Junkers, who were keen to expand
grain exports to Britain in exchange for imported manufactures.
Paradoxically, many states within the German confederation criticized this
tariff as being either too liberal or too protectionist and convoluted.
Despite these reservations several smaller and medium-sized states joined
the Prussian Union because they received generous shares of total revenues
and because their own agricultural and commercial interest groups were
very powerful. In 1831, these states formed the Prussian Customs Union.
Two years later, the existing Bavarian Customs Union and the Prussian
Union established the German Zollverein, an internal market uniting 18
former states and 23.5 million people. In the decades to come, the
economic and political power of this union would pull the remaining
German states into the Zollverein.[51]

The Anglo-French Treaty between the two largest international
traders served to inspire Prussian policymakers. They pursued a low-
tariff policy to satisfy their trading interests and to block Austrian
accession to the Zollverein.[52] Other, smaller states in Europe also
modified their tariff policies. The Netherlands introduced a tariff
reform that set a 5 percent ceiling on industrial imports, while Italy,
Spain, Portugal, Norway and Sweden dismantled their prohibitive and
excessively protective rates. These smaller and larger states together
formed a network of bilateral treaties that embodied the most-favored-
nation principle and that further lowered tariff levels.

TARIFFS AND PROTECTION IN
THE GOLDEN ERA OF FREE TRADE

Now what did this move to lower tariffs imply for overall levels of tariff protection since the nineteenth century? If we pause for a moment to look at the customs duties on manufactures prevailing in Europe and the United States before and at the height of the free trade era, some interesting observations can be made. What the figures confirm is that the United Kingdom was alone in adopting a policy of total free trade; various smaller countries such as Sweden, the Netherlands and Switzerland had reduced their duties already before the Cobden-Chevalier agreement, but they represented only a small proportion of Europe's market. By 1875, these countries and Germany had cut their rates on manufactures to averages below 10 percent. In the 1860s and 1870s, several other nations such as Russia, Austria-Hungary, France, Spain and Denmark also reduced tariffs or abolished various import prohibitions. It should be noted, though, that they retained average tariffs close to or above 15 percent. Furthermore, Belgium (after its separation from the Netherlands in 1830) and the United States both raised tariff protection.

A closer look at the United States suggests that this country had a long history of tariff protection and was indeed "the mother country of modern protectionism."[53] Its early industrial development and subsequent economic spurt were based on excessive investments, large natural resources and a vast and rapidly expanding domestic market opened up by major transport improvements and protected by high tariffs.[54] In 1791, well before List's standard work justifying infant industry protection appeared, America's first secretary of the treasury, Alexander Hamilton, had developed similar views. He argued that industrialization without tariff protection would be impossible, because under free trade young industries would be overpowered by their more efficient foreign counterparts before ever reaching the stage of full competitiveness. True to this philosophy, America's moderately protectionist duties of 1789 were raised during subsequent tariff reforms, leading to averages for manufactures of around 35 percent by 1816. As some research suggests, these duties favored dominant manufacturing interests in the Northeast and parts of the Midwest over large midwest agricultural exporters. Tariff levels reached an all time high in 1829, and throughout the nineteenth century they belonged to the highest in the industrialized world.

There is evidence that trade liberalization in the Golden Era of free trade was neither as widespread nor as long-lasting as is sometimes assumed. It probably remained limited to areas in Europe and it came to a halt after just one decade, when the Austrian-Hungarian Empire introduced two tariff increases in 1876 and 1878 and Italy followed suit. Britain did not raise its most-favored-nation duties but instead increased discrimination by expanding preferential treatment of Empire trading areas. Germany raised its official tariff levels in 1879, but its policy change was not as drastic as it seemed to outsiders. At the insistence of its manufacturing interests, the German government negotiated with major traders separate commercial agreements that incorporated lower tariff levels and that lasted twelve years. After that period, however, German agricultural rates soared again. Only Belgium, the Netherlands and Britain continued to pursue their previous free trade policies.

The end of freer trade and the gradual return to protectionism may well have been linked to the economic downturn since the 1870s.[55] Per capita growth in Europe had reached an annual average rate of 1.6 percent during 1850-1870, but it declined to an average rate of 0.6 percent in the two following decades, a level well below even that of the 1830s and 1840s. Growth rates of European export volumes slowed somewhat later, falling from an annual average of some 5 percent in the period 1840-1870 to 2.8 percent in the two decades following. This slowdown of economic growth and of trade expansion can be attributed almost entirely to cheap overseas grain that began flooding European markets after 1866 and that damaged total agricultural production in continental Europe. Because some 60 percent of the continent's population still worked in agriculture, the subsequent fall in incomes depressed overall levels of industrial demand and triggered a general economic slump.[56] Initially, many governments reacted by increasing agricultural import duties. Once the depression spread, however, they responded to calls for protection from industrialists, who were harmed by rising labor costs, falling demand and mounting international competition.[57]

THE END OF THE GOLDEN ERA

As we saw earlier, the spread of freer trade during the second half of the nineteenth century reflected a widespread belief that Britain's strong performance as an industrially successful nation vindicated the liberal doctrine. Even so, the credibility of this conviction declined after 1870, partly because the doctrine failed to address problems of economic backwardness, and partly because of mounting economic, political and military competition among industrialized countries. Awakening nationalism in connection with the rise of new nation-states such as Italy and Germany merely strengthened the protectionists' case, especially since higher tariffs also provided the higher revenues needed to meet the states' rising expenditures on armaments, education and social services.[58]

What were the economic consequences of this return to protectionism? Perhaps paradoxically, the rise in tariffs was accompanied by the recovery and expansion of Europe's production and exports. As Bairoch has shown, during the 20 years following the return to protectionism the annual growth rate of GNP (in volume terms) increased by more than 100 percent, whereas the volume of export rose by more than 35 percent compared with the previous two decades. Europe's foreign trade expansion did slow down in the first decade, but in the second phase it surged at rates faster than those during the ten years of free trade preceding 1870. Trade grew faster in European countries adopting protective tariffs than in Britain, which maintained a liberal trade policy.[59] Whether there existed a causal relationship between protectionism and income growth, however, remains a matter of debate.[60]

It seems likely that the increase in protectionism initially damaged British manufacturing exports and benefited industrializing countries such as Germany, the United States, Italy and France. British exports of iron, steel and woollen products lost ground in the United States, Germany and elsewhere in Europe. In the long run, though, the impact of tariff protection may have been fairly modest because Britain's competitors became ever more efficient and quickly outgrew the need for shelter from imports. Furthermore, Britain itself switched to new export lines and markets; it began specializing in finer quality cotton exports to sheltered colonial markets, in cheaper cotton exports to less developed countries and in semi-manufactured exports such as yarn and pig iron. Its exports thus continued to expand, even though their overall role in world trade gradually declined.[61]

Despite the rise of protectionism, world trade rose somewhat faster than world production between 1880 and 1913. Indeed, if we consider the entire period of 1800-1913, trade growth outpaced production growth. Per capita foreign trade growth averaged 33 percent per decade over this period, whereas world output grew at an average rate of 7.3 per decade. As a result, the volume of foreign trade per capita had increased more than 25-fold by 1913, compared to an increase in *per capita* world output of just 2.2-fold. The main factors underlying this unprecedented trade expansion were most countries' growing propensities for trade, linked to the emergence of a worldwide network of multilateral trade and payments based on economic specialization. Like other multilateral systems that had existed before 1870, such as the triangular flows between Britain, Western Europe and the Baltic, this network assigned a central role to the United Kingdom; yet unlike the older systems it entailed a much more complicated and interlinked set of trade and investments relations involving almost all parts of the world. As a result, by 1913 some 25 percent of total world trade had become multilateral in character.

Britain's key role emerged from its growing deficits with regard to continental Europe and the United States, and its smaller deficits with regard to Canada, South Africa and Egypt, which it could offset by favorable trade balances with India, Australia and the Far East. India in particular proved crucial to Britain; by absorbing large quantities of manufactures, this area managed to offset almost 40 percent of total British deficits. In addition, India played a pivotal role in the international system by maintaining heavy export surpluses with Britain's creditors: continental Europe, the rest of the British Empire, China, Hong Kong, and to a lesser degree also the United States and Japan. The United States' important position followed from its import surplus with the Tropics (in particular India and Brazil) and its rapidly increasing export surplus with the so-called Great Plains countries (i.e., Canada, Australia and Argentina). The latter, in turn, generated the favorable trade balances that continental Europe needed to pay for its growing imports from Britain.[62]

While by 1913 virtually all regions of the world had been drawn into the international economy and North America and Latin America had rapidly expanded their shares, Europe continued to dominate world trade. It still held almost 60 percent of world exports and more than 65 percent of world imports. The bulk of this share, some 40 percent, consisted of intra-European trade. In addition, more than 20 percent of world trade involved Europe's imports from non-European countries and another 15 percent Europe's exports to non-European countries. In other words, trade among non-European countries accounted for less than one quarter of total trade. The pattern of these trade flows had changed quite markedly between 1870 and 1913. Industrialization and population growth in combination with the exploitation of primary produce in new overseas regions had reduced Europe's dependence on intra-regional trade and had increased trade interdependence with the overseas areas.

PROTECTIONISM AFTER 1914

The First World War and the Great Depression were two events that further enhanced overseas industrial development behind protective barriers. The outbreak of war disrupted established trade channels both among European states and with their overseas suppliers. It forced them to regulate foreign trade, to ration and allocate scarce economic resources and to promote import substitution. Manufacturing industries developed particularly fast in Japan, India, Australia, Brazil and several other Latin America countries that managed to boost domestic production when European competition disappeared. Some of these industries collapsed with the return of normal peacetime trading conditions, but many others were kept alive through high rates of tariff protection. Competing overseas industries were thus created in iron and steel, machinery, chemicals, paper, textiles and pharmaceuticals, which pushed up growth rates in these newly industrializing countries.[63]

In Europe, too, protection and state intervention lingered on well after the war had ended. One reason was that the new states in Central and Eastern Europe that had emerged from the peace settlement immediately introduced an additional 12,000 miles of tariff frontiers, thereby cutting off some industrial areas from their rural hinterland and disrupting various existing transportation links.[64] Their governments began protecting infant industries, mines and agricultural produce behind import barriers, which often provoked retaliatory protection. Currency disorder, inflation, war damage and reparation obligations initially added to this disintegration because they impaired the restoration of a sound financial system, delayed production and trade recovery and enhanced the use of exchange controls, quantitative restrictions and tariffs.[65] Among the other states in Europe, protectionism also flourished. By 1925, France, Germany, Italy, the Netherlands, Switzerland and Belgium had all raised their tariffs whereas Britain had reintroduced them (see table 1.3). These often served to shelter infant industries or to improve countries' bargaining positions in commercial negotiations. Increasingly, tariffs and other commercial policy instruments also began to be used to avoid balance of payments problems and to preserve employment.[66]

TABLE 1.3

Average Tariff Rates on Manufactures, 1925, 1931 and 1950
(WEIGHTED AVERAGES; IN PERCENT AD VALOREM)

	1925	1931	1950
Austria-Hungary	16	24	18
Belgium	15	14	11
Denmark	10	n.a.	3
France	21	30	18
Germany	20	21	26
Italy	22	46	25
Netherlands	6	n.a.	11
Russia	R	R	R
Spain	41	63	n.a.
Sweden	16	21	9
Switzerland	14	19	n.a.
United Kingdom	5	n.a.	23
United States	37	48	14

n.a. = not available
R = numerous and important import restrictions on manufactures that limit any meaningful assessment of average tariffs prevail

Source: Bairoch, *Economics and World History*, 40 (see chap. 1, note 53).

The American Congress' decision in 1922 to adopt the Fordney-McCumber tariff caused widespread anxiety among commercial diplomats. The fact that the world's largest producer of manufactures and most important creditor nation raised its customs duties to unprecedented and nonnegotiable levels completely blocked any progress in trade liberalization.[67] After all, no country would be prepared to grant reciprocal tariff cuts to another if these also benefited free-riding Americans. Unconditional most-favored-nation treatment therefore lost ground and regional preferences and discriminatory agreements gained acceptance. In 1927, the League of Nations summed up the impact of such acts of economic warfare: "Europe remains to-day with its tariff higher and more complicated, less stable and more numerous than in 1913. Moreover, Europe has failed to restore its former system of commercial treaties, and the habit has developed of putting tariffs designed for purposes of negotiating into force before those negotiations take place. . . . the obstruction remains higher than before."[68] At the World Economic Conference in the same year, several governments tried to reverse this trend. They called for drastic tariff cuts and for abolishing quantitative trade impediments. They also pleaded for unconditional most-favored-nation treatment and for long-term treaties that promoted tariff stability. However, any remaining hopes for freer trade were crushed with the outbreak of the worldwide depression. As prices dropped, foreign direct investment collapsed and industrial output fell, governments tried to avoid mass unemployment by creating yet another layer of tariffs, quotas, export subsidies and exchange controls. The United States shocked the international community by introducing still higher tariffs under the Smoot-Hawley Act of 1930 (see table 1.3). This move immediately provoked retaliation as other countries tried to preserve export levels and protect domestic jobs.[69]

The financial crisis and the depreciation of the British pound sterling in September 1931 gave the final blow to the remainders of a normal trade and payments system. Further competitive devaluations, tariff rises and foreign exchange controls followed, and in their wake separate currency blocs emerged: the Gold bloc (comprising France, the Netherlands, Switzerland and Italy until 1934, and Belgium and Luxembourg until 1935), the Reichsmark bloc (with Germany and Italy after 1934, parts of Southern and Eastern Europe and Latin America), the Dollar bloc and the Sterling area. Each of these blocs tried to expand internal trade by diverting trade away from outsiders. And within these blocs, each country pursued its own economic policy that gave national recovery top priority.[70]

Britain abandoned what was left of its free trade policy and adopted the Import Duties Act. This fixed tariffs of some 10 percent on foodstuffs and semi-manufactures, and rates of between 20 and 33 percent on manufactures. In 1932 Britain also negotiated mutual preferential access with its Commonwealth partners under the Ottawa Agreements. Its retreat within the Sterling area resulted in a rise in the ratio of internal trade to total Sterling trade and in a growing share of Sterling bloc trade in world trade. The proportion of Sterling bloc exports to total sterling exports rose from 40 percent in 1928 to 47 percent ten years later. Sterling bloc imports increased only marginally, from 35 to 37 percent over the same period.

In other blocs, policies for trade expansion had mixed results. The Reichsmark bloc countries in Eastern and Southeastern Europe all applied strict trade and exchange controls. They experienced mounting trading difficulties with third countries and a steadily growing economic and political dependence on Germany.[71] Due to a strong surge in bilateral trade with Germany, internal trade rose spectacularly; expressed as a proportion of total bloc trade, it more than doubled between 1928 and 1938. Yet the share of Reichsmark imports in intra-European trade declined while that of Reichsmark exports rose by just 1.6 percent. Within the Gold bloc, by contrast, trading links remained much looser. Only French trade with Switzerland and Belgium and Belgian trade with the Netherlands held some importance. Furthermore, Belgium and France strengthened ties with their overseas territories. As early as 1928, the area known as Metropolitan France had created a customs union with the remaining areas of the French empire, which steadily reduced imports from the outer regions.[72]

Belgium, the Netherlands and Luxembourg initially sought cooperation with Scandinavian countries to promote mutual trade and economic disarmament. Twice in the interwar period did they sign agreements to stabilize tariffs and to remove quota restrictions. Yet both times a competitive scramble for export markets blocked effective cooperation. The Scandinavian states subsequently began tightening links with the United Kingdom. After leaving the gold standard in October 1931, they stabilized their currencies with depreciated Sterling parities and concluded bilateral trading agreements to secure their exports to the British market.[73]

During the Depression the objectives and instruments of foreign economic policy broadened. While the range and precise workings of these instruments varied, they can be divided generally into those aimed primarily at influencing the flow of individual goods and those that intended to control payments directly. The first category includes, apart from tariffs, quantitative trade restrictions and import prohibitions, whereas the second embraces exchange controls and several types of bilateral trading arrangements. We will briefly discuss each of these nontariff instruments and their objectives; they became an integral part of European commercial policies in the 1930s and in years after the Second World War.

There are two main reasons why countries increasingly rejected active tariff policies and resorted to quantitative restrictions. One reason is that tariffs are largely ineffective in times of sharply declining prices. Some countries found a remedy in regularly revising their rates to keep pace with price falls or in adopting sliding scale tariffs, the rates of which increased as prices dropped. Both methods, however, were difficult to operate and administer. Moreover, since in many countries tariff changes required parliamentary approval, their practical use as quick way to reduce import flows was limited. Another reason was that many tariff rates were bound by bilateral treaties. Raising these would almost invariably lead to retaliation and would augment the risk of a trade war.

Quantitative trade restrictions provided direct and effective measures for controlling imports. They usually took the form of licenses or quotas, which fixed imported quantities in advance. This meant that the authorities responsible for administering the permits would judge each potential import transaction individually. They were able to limit imports of a commodity to an exact, fixed amount (usually by taking the previous year's requirements), irrespective of supply and demand conditions or price levels prevailing in domestic and foreign markets. Whereas foreign importers might still "jump" a tariff wall by reducing their prices to sufficiently low levels, a quota or license could restrict import quantities of even the most competitive foreign producers. In addition, since import quantities could be determined in advance, these restrictions could be used quite effectively to secure the maximum possible trade advantage from bilateral negotiations or to protect the balance of payments. Import quotas and licenses therefore often coincided with a system of exchange controls.

Official exchange controls on private foreign currency transactions compelled exporters to surrender to the monetary authorities the currency they received from exports abroad and required importers to purchase from these authorities the foreign currency they needed. Governments determined the official rates at which foreign exchange was sold and bought. One objective of such controls was to avoid the outflow of foreign or domestic capital during financial crises, such as those occurring in late twenties and early thirties. They were also necessary if a country wanted to avoid a currency depreciation. In notorious debtor countries these temporary restrictions encouraged direct government intervention to control the demand and supply of foreign exchange, to administer protection on a product-by-product basis (by limiting the foreign exchange allocated for specific imports) or to increase revenue by setting higher exchange rates for selling than for buying.[74]

Foreign currency scarcity and exchange controls stimulated the conclusion of bilateral trading agreements to ensure that payments for traded goods balanced out in a given period. In this way, national governments could maintain trade at relatively high volumes without accumulating soft currencies and losing scarce currencies or gold. Sometimes these bilateral arrangements took the form of compensation agreements involving straightforward barter trade. More often they included a system of offsetting bilateral claims known as "clearing." If two countries negotiated a clearing arrangement, they agreed to settle all individual transactions between them in terms of their respective currencies.[75] To keep control over the type of trade conducted, governments usually reinforced these clearing arrangements by a system of licenses and permits.

While clearing enabled mutual transactions to expand, structural imbalances in bilateral trade could eventually cause transactions to stagnate, since the amount of currency in the clearing account was limited. In that case, the surplus country could either wait until the clearing account favoring the deficit country had been built up again, or it could advance credit to that account, thus allowing exports to resume. From the mid-1930s onward, Germany began using this mechanism in the bilateral clearing system to build up an import surplus and to "borrow" from states that depended on access to its large market. It purchased large quantities of raw materials and agricultural products from countries in Eastern and Southeastern Europe, paying high prices in terms of local currency. Once these states had built up large claims, the German authorities forced them to take massive quantities of unwanted products and to pay high prices for the scarce, wanted manufactures they did make available for export. In this way, Germany tied these trading partners to its market and increasingly exploited their economies.[76]

Bilateral payments agreements were another type of arrangement, involving economies with and without exchange controls. Unlike clearing agreements, they covered a wide range of transactions and included normal methods of foreign exchange payments. Apart from allowing countries previously hit by the Depression to regulate and expand trade, they also tackled the problem of financial and commercial assets that had been "frozen" in blocked currency accounts. By creating an export surplus with the creditor country and by paying an additional sum in convertible currency, the exchange-controlled country could gradually liquidate its debts with the creditor country.

The extraordinary circumstances of the Depression and the resulting trend toward autarky had a profound impact on the growth and pattern of world trade. The rate of growth in total world trade per decade dropped from an average of close to 40 percent in 1881-1913 to 14 percent in the years 1913-1937. Moreover, measured on a per capita basis, world trade grew less fast than world output in the interwar period, even though there existed marked variations between the 1920s and 1930s. In the years of the Depression, world production received a greater blow than world trade, but when the international economy began to climb out of the slump and industrial production recovered, it was trade recovery that lagged behind.

This weak trade performance was still more pronounced in Europe. The period between 1913 and 1937 saw a decline in Europe's share of world trade from 60 to 50 percent and a decline in intra-European trade of almost 20 percent. Whereas the volume of Europe's commodity production increased by some 15 percent from 1918 to 1928 and by another 15 percent in the period 1928-1938, the volume of intra-European trade remained unchanged in the first decade and declined by more than 10 percent in the second decade. At its lowest point, in 1932, Europe's industrial production dropped to 72 percent of its 1929 level and exports to 62 percent. By 1936, industrial production managed to surpass the 1929 level, but exports still lagged behind. They remained at least partially trapped in a network of bilateral trading agreements and import restrictions.[77]

The Second World War enhanced governmental control over the economy. Exchange controls and bilateral trade agreements became more common and stringent than ever before to ensure that financial reserves and economic resources maximized the war effort.[78] By 1942, the dominant axis power, Germany, had conquered Western, Central and Eastern Europe and had submitted these regions to its war economy, whereas its axis partner Japan had done the same in large parts of the Far East. From then on, economic transactions between the sovereign states opposing this axis consisted largely of immense supplies (covered under the Anglo-American Mutual Aid arrangement) being sent by the United States to Britain and to the other Commonwealth countries.[79] Until its termination in August 1945, this so-called Lend-Lease system involved goods and services totaling 43,615 million U.S. dollars. Almost 70 percent went to the United Kingdom, along with other parts of the British Empire, and another 25 percent to the Soviet Union. These supplies greatly reduced payments among the Allies and allowed the British government to concentrate on war production and military operations.[80]

The success of wartime cooperation and the Allied victory in August 1945 could not conceal the inherent instability of the postwar international economy. Some of these weaknesses were rooted in the Interbellum and merely emerged more glaringly as postwar planning began to take shape. Others resulted directly from the physical destruction, debts and international political tensions that the war had brought about. But whatever the precise nature of these problems, in all nations relief and reconstruction relied on a large system of domestic and frontier controls that had been tuned to perfection during the Depression of the 1930s and the war. Furthermore, whether nurtured by free trade or by protectionist ideologies and traditions, governments after 1945 felt that their role went far beyond the most urgent tasks of economic recovery and corrective economic action. How this influenced postwar commercial strategies will be discussed in the following chapter.

TWO

The Foundations of the Postwar Trading System and the First Regional Plans for European Trade Cooperation

The nineteenth century witnessed the maturing of what is still the most influential perspective on international trade: the free trade doctrine. The theory that universal free trade would bring maximum trade advantage was so forceful that it acquired widespread support in economic and political thinking. Because Britain, as the world's most powerful nation and mecca of economic theory, maintained a policy that stimulated trade liberalization elsewhere, the period between 1840 and 1880 gradually captured the imagination as the Golden Era of free trade and economic progress. In a similar vein, the 1930s Depression and the Second World War acquired mythic proportions as phases of universal protectionism, interventionism, economic discrimination and totalitarianism. The architects of the postwar international order drew many lessons from those two historic episodes that eventually found their way into the institutions of the new worldwide economic system known as Bretton Woods.

In Western Europe, however, this economic order initially had to give way to a separate scheme for economic aid and reconstruction known as the Marshall Plan. While the Marshall Plan's immediate aims were to speed up the Continent's economic recovery, strengthen its economic and political cohesion in the wake of mounting Cold War tensions and ease the transition toward worldwide multilateralism, its indirect impact was to move Western Europe on a course toward regional economic integration. As we will see in this chapter, soon after 1945 Western European countries launched several regional trading plans that developed a momentum of their own.

POSTWAR PLANNING FOR INTERNATIONAL TRADE

American beliefs and lessons were among the most influential forces shaping this postwar international order. The dominant power during and after the war, the United States did much of the groundwork for the monetary and trading rules embodied in the Atlantic Charter of 1941 and in the Mutual Aid Agreement concluded with Britain. Later on, American preoccupations also found their way into the Bretton Woods system and the multilateral trading system envisaged in the Havana Charter.

One of these preoccupations stemmed from the belief that monetary factors had caused the economic depression. The wave of international speculation in 1931 that had wrecked the banking systems of Germany and Austria, the subsequent exchange controls, and the devaluations of the pound sterling and its dependent currencies were seen as the reasons why the sharp recession of 1929 had turned into a lengthy and destructive economic depression. The innovations embodied in the Bretton Woods system were therefore specifically designed to prevent such monetary disasters. The system represented a return to the fixed exchange rates embodied in the gold exchange standard, but this time with the pound and the dollar as the key currencies maintaining free convertibility into each other and into gold. The International Monetary Fund (IMF) had to provide all the safeguards needed to avoid monetary disasters. It would furnish monetary reserves to defend currencies against speculative moves while also limiting countries' freedom to impose exchange controls or to devalue their currencies. In the immediate postwar years, though, these IMF provisions were suspended during a transitional period in which countries struggled to achieve economic recovery.[1]

In the area of trade, the interwar experience of trade collapse, regionalism, retaliatory tariff making, offensive trade controls, bilateralism and economic nationalism had fueled calls for worldwide multilateralism.[2] The logic of multilateralism had greatly influenced American Secretary of State Cordell Hull, who in the 1930s had tried to establish worldwide liberal trading arrangements. Hull had adopted the traditional arguments that specialization would promote economic welfare and overall prosperity, which he saw as two prerequisites for peace. Multilateralism in the sense of equal and universal access to foreign supplies and outlets would counterbalance the competitive scramble for markets and resources that usually caused modern imperialism and warfare.[3] Only an institutionalized commitment among major trading powers to apply the most-favored-nation clause (MFN clause) would sustain this principle.[4]

This conviction had certainly not found universal support. During the Lend-Lease discussions, for instance, the British negotiator John Maynard Keynes had taken a rather different stance. As one American delegate observed:

> Mr. Keynes, as an economist, has been preoccupied with the problem of unemployment which dominated the depression period. His economic theory pertains to conditions existing under economic depression. He has felt a need for economic controls in such circumstances. Since a national government has been the only authority which could exercise such controls, he approaches the problem from a nationalistic point of view and has tended to disregard the effect of such an approach on international relations. Perhaps because he feels that any scheme of cooperation would involve further contributions by the United States, and because of hesitancy in suggesting this, he tends to disregard the possibility of instituting through cooperative measures international economic controls which, in taking account worldwide betterment, might better serve ultimate British national interests.[5]

In subsequent paragraphs we will see that such fundamental disagreements on the priorities and instruments of national economic reconstruction also figured prominently in postwar planning meetings between the Americans and continental European governments.

During and after the war, American negotiators advanced their ideas for a worldwide trading institution in the Suggested Charter for an International Trade Organization (ITO). This provided the document of discussion for three postwar conferences in London (1946), Geneva (1947) and Havana (1948), at which detailed trade rules were agreed on. The final, radically modified text that eventually emerged from these discussions became known as the Havana Charter. The Charter included an extensive set of provisions and rules designed to regulate national policies on trade and related issues, with chapters on tariff and nontariff barriers, restrictive business practices, employment and economic development. It also authorized the ITO's establishment as a permanent institutional framework supervising these trade rules.

Although the signatories of the Havana Charter eventually all subscribed to the general nondiscrimination principle, it had taken a series of highly protracted negotiations between the United States and Britain before this compromise had emerged.[6] The Charter's early "London" draft had contained a general ban on quantitative restrictions, in line with American views that such barriers would inevitably lead to economic discrimination, inefficient production and major political tensions. It had also included an escape clause permitting member countries to impose restrictions for balance of payments reasons, provided these were equivalent to exchange restrictions authorized by the IMF. However, the main controversy had centered on whether these restrictions could be applied discriminatorily. This touched the very heart of national economic policy because discriminatory restrictions provided effective instruments for protecting selective domestic economic activities and for shifting trade into specific regional patterns.

While the Charter negotiations continued, the British gradually succeeded in revising the American draft rules in two main ways. First, countries would be allowed to take discriminatory measures to avert the pending danger of a decline in their foreign currency reserves. Also, they could relax such measures in a discriminatory way if this enabled them to obtain more imports than a nondiscriminatory relaxing of measures. Second, the length of the transition period during which discrimination was allowed would no longer be specified. Theoretically, it could last forever. The only control mechanisms incorporated were regular reviews of the discriminatory quotas still remaining after March 1952.[7]

The looser, general ban on quotas had been one major reason for American discontent with the Havana Charter; tariff preferences was another. To understand why this was so, we must go back to 1947, the year that Congress, under the Reciprocal Trade Agreement Act (RTA), provided the Executive branch of the government with the unprecedented power to cut American tariffs by up to 50 percent, in exchange for reciprocal concessions from its major trading partners.[8] Since this mandate would expire after three years, the American government had insisted that a series of international tariff negotiations (commonly known as a "round") take place in the same year, parallel to the Charter negotiations in Geneva. The results of these tariff bargainings were included within a General Agreement on Tariffs and Trade

(GATT), a separate, provisional code containing the Charter's rules on trade policy.

American delegates had been extremely keen to use their mandate for an all out attack on the British system of Commonwealth preferences. What had motivated them was not merely a deep-rooted dislike of discriminatory measures but also a sharp awareness that domestic political support for the trade program had been waning since the Republican victory in the Congressional elections of 1946. By using its tariff-cutting powers to eliminate Commonwealth tariff preferences, the Democratic Truman administration had hoped to gain the business community's backing for the RTA program and for the Charter. In turn, this should have secured Congressional support for the ITO.[9] However, the American declaration of war on Commonwealth preferences had aroused hostility among British Conservative backbenchers and had hardened the British government's opposition. During the Geneva round American negotiators had therefore secured only a handful of commitments (known in GATT's language as "consolidations" or "bindings") not to raise tariffs during the next three years and a few cuts in British preferences in the Commonwealth. This disappointing outcome had badly damaged Anglo-American commercial relations, whereas it had also diminished the ITO's chances with Congress.[10]

Eventually, the writing on the wall was Congress' insistence on renewing the RTA for only one year instead of the usual three years, as well as its introduction in 1949 of a peril point clause to the Act. This provision meant that a Congressional Tariff Commission would scrutinize in advance all tariff concessions that the government planned to offer at future GATT rounds. Even though the Democrats repealed this clause when they regained their majority in Congress one year later, they could not turn the tide. By then even the more free trade–minded spirits were increasingly critical of the Havana Charter. Some representatives claimed that the Charter's rejection in principle of quotas was unduly limiting American policies for full employment. Many others argued that its original, more radical ban on quotas had been totally undermined to accommodate vested interests.[11] The overriding sentiment was one of disappointment with the new worldwide institutions of the postwar order.

The American architects of Bretton Woods had believed that after a short transitional adjustment phase one politically and economically stable world order would quickly come about. The IMF, the ITO and their political counterpart, the United Nations (UN), would together form the institutional pillars of the new international community and, as Cordell Hull had put it at an earlier time, become the agents of "worldwide betterment." By 1947, these expectations were largely shattered. The UN was hopelessly divided and paralyzed by the growing enmity toward the Soviet Union, which had maintained its troops in the East and had actively encouraged the establishment of communist regimes. Hostilities escalated in the course of the year. In March, shortly after the British planned to withdraw troops from their intervention against the communists fighting in the Greek civil war, President Truman announced a strategy of "containment" that had profound implications. It proposed to resist the advance of communist influence by giving military and economic assistance to individual countries that were at risk of losing independence to undemocratic forces. America would also actively encourage the political and economic unity of Europe, for only a strong and united Europe seemed capable of containing communism without requiring a permanent American presence in Europe.[12] In the course of 1947, this regional approach undermined the political clout of the UN and institutionalized the division between East and West in Europe still further.

Like the UN, the Bretton Woods institutions were incapable of meeting postwar challenges. The IMF lacked both the reserve funds needed to eliminate currency controls and the authority to impose its rules effectively. The depth of its failure became obvious with the faltered attempt in 1947 to restore sterling-dollar convertibility. In the space of six weeks, an American loan to facilitate the restoration of sterling convertibility was depleted and IMF provisions had to be suspended. Meanwhile, the ITO's chances of Congressional approval dwindled further and the American government eventually abandoned attempts to get it ratified. Because of this fiasco, the provisional GATT became the only worldwide framework for multilateral trade negotiations. It contained almost all the commercial policy rules of the Charter, but it lacked the power to force its members (the so-called Contracting Parties) to participate in tariff-cutting rounds and to bring their existing legislation in line with the GATT rules. It also left out the Charter's sections on full employment, restrictive practices and commodity agreements.[13]

The premature collapse of Bretton Woods clearly reflected a growing discrepancy between wartime planning for a smoothly working economic order and the reality of postwar recovery in Europe. Such plans underestimated the impact of political and military instability on the international economy and also the need for corrective measures to restore structural economic imbalances. Moreover, they failed to appreciate adequately the extent to which the Depression and the war had changed the role of the state in economic policy. These events had turned national ministries into giant corporations, and ministers of finance, economic affairs and agriculture into all-round managers involved in large scale relief, distribution and resource mobilization. In the aftermath of the war, national governments emerged as the only agencies capable of meeting the immediate relief and recovery requirements. A new development was that these governments, supported by an overwhelming majority of their populations, all had assumed policy goals that no longer stopped at the task of recovery but rather aimed at actively promoting long-term economic and social welfare. State intervention, although adopted with varying degrees of intensity, gradually surfaced as the new orthodoxy that could count on broad popular support. Frontier controls on commerce, those traditional instruments of state intervention, thus became part of a wide range of economic policy tools employed for ever broader policy objectives.

EUROPE'S TRADING SITUATION

This new climate explains to a large extent why, paradoxically, postwar commercial policies embraced all those trading practices that had been perceived generally as instrumental to the outbreak of economic and military warfare in Europe. Just as in the 1930s, governments suspended tariffs and relied on quotas and exchange controls to allocate their scarce resources for reconstruction purposes. When they had exhausted their foreign currency reserves to meet the constant demand for hard currency imports, they often sought refuge in strictly bilateral trade agreements. Economic transactions became largely a bilateral affair, relying on the exchange of precisely defined quantities of strictly essential goods and on reciprocal credits that permitted some flexibility in the volume of trade. Such arrangements dominated the pattern of European trade, and it was only through such measures that intra-European trade could take place at all.[14]

The major problem was that the war had destroyed large parts of Europe's productive capacity, capital income from foreign property holdings and multilateral trade and payments flows within the area and between it and the rest of the world. Countries thus had to assume large debts for reconstruction purposes while trying to recover production and step up commodity exports. Germany's defeat and the Allied decision to curb its economic potential, however, severely hampered these efforts, since Germany had been the most pivotal player in Europe's production and trading system. In 1928, it had consumed more than 19 percent of Europe's exports and supplied almost 18 percent of its imports. Capital goods formed the bulk of Germany's exports. Even in 1938, Germany had still supplied more than 1,060 million U.S. dollars' worth of metals, machinery and chemicals, amounting to some 42 percent of intra-European trade in these products and 30 percent of Western Europe's total exports to other areas. Ten years later the figure had dropped to a mere 122 million U.S. dollars. It was not until 1951 that Germany's total exports to the OEEC countries would surpass their prewar level.

The German economy's delayed recovery increased Europe's dependence on the dollar area as a source for imports of foodstuffs and capital goods, because only the United States could meet the Continent's needs for a wide range of manufactures. The disruption of triangular trade with the third world economies accentuated this dependence. Traditionally, Europe had run a large trading surplus with these primary producing countries which, in turn, had run a surplus with North America. After the war, however, Europe could no longer earn dollars from this triangular trade, either because war destruction prevented these countries from resuming exports to the dollar area or because import substitution policies had meanwhile diminished their demand for European products. True, there were partially successful attempts by France and Britain to strengthen mutual trading links with their former colonies and dependent territories and to deflect trade toward their currency areas, but as comprehensive and permanent solutions to the dollar problem such policies were inadequate.

What further widened the dollar gap was the breakdown of Western Europe's trade with Eastern Europe. Before the war, this area had been a major supplier of grain imports.[15] The main European importers had traditionally derived some 15 percent of their grain imports from Eastern Europe (including the USSR). By comparison, 22 percent came from the dollar area and 39 percent from Latin America. War devastation and deflection of trade toward the Soviet Union meant that after 1945 Eastern Europe supplied less than 7 percent of Europe's total grain imports.[16]

Cereals made up the largest single item in Europe's total dollar expenditure. In the period 1948-1950, the United States supplied 56 percent of its needs, and this percentage increased to 66 percent in the period 1951-1952. In each of these phases, cereal requirements accounted for 40 percent of the entire trade deficit with the dollar area. Petroleum products were another major item for dollar expenditure. In 1938, more than 40 percent of Europe's total imports came from the United States, Venezuela and Mexico. After the war, both the absolute value and the share of Europe's imports from these countries dropped, but petroleum still represented one of the main drains on Europe's dollar resources.

Generally speaking, European governments had two policy options available to tackle their dollar problem: to increase direct exports to the United States or to diminish their dependence on American imports. The first alternative proved to be extremely hard for most European countries, given the supply constraints on their production, the product mix of their exports and the incipient protectionism of the American Congress. The second option offered better prospects for dealing with the short-term problems of war destruction and hard currency shortages. Furthermore, this option supported the domestic industrialization programs that national governments advanced to underpin their structural policies for economic growth, full employment and social welfare.

In the short run, though, their reconstruction measures merely increased trade and payments difficulties. The high and sustained levels of capital imports and investments needed for industrialization initially augmented both the dollar gap and the imbalances between European creditors and debtors. Having emerged from the war with comparatively strong economies, creditor countries such as Switzerland and Belgium had initially fostered intra-European trade expansion by adopting liberal import policies and by granting large export credits. As balance of payments problems persisted elsewhere in Europe, however, these countries were no longer prepared to grant new credits. They began insisting on the payment of old credits and the balancing of bilateral trade flows. It meant that trade was first pushed into other, still less efficient channels and in the long run failed to expand any further.

THE MARSHALL PLAN

It was against the background of acute European trade and payments constraints and of growing antagonism between the Soviet Union and the United States that the American Secretary of State George Marshall announced a European Recovery Program (ERP) for massive dollar aid.[17]

Its immediate objective was to prevent a collapse of trade and payments flows. It intended to reduce the danger of inflation, increase productivity and social stability and forestall the threat of a communist overthrow in France and Italy. Ultimately, though, the objective was nothing less than the Continent's transformation into an integrated economic and military stronghold against Soviet communism. An economically strong and united ally would be a strong military partner and could eventually carry its share of the common defense burden. Furthermore, only a viable and integrated Europe could make the transition toward a worldwide economic system. The ERP thus embodied the Truman administration's new containment strategy, linking American economic and security interests to the goal of uniting Europe.

Immediately following the war, the Americans had contributed some four billion U.S. dollars in aid to Western Europe on an piecemeal basis through the United Nations Relief and Rehabilitation Administration (UNRRA) and other programs. In 1947, however, they were determined to commit aid for a comprehensive, coordinated four-year program drafted by the European governments themselves. In this way, they believed, American dollar aid and guidance would not be squandered on competing national schemes that served merely to reinforce the autarkic tendencies already present. Rather, it would be used to advance closer economic and political unity in Europe. On the American side, the Economic Cooperation Administration (ECA) would administer the scheme whereas a permanent organization in Europe would hold responsibility for its collective implementation.

The French Foreign Minister George Bidault and his British colleague Ernest Bevin, were among the first to respond to Marshall's offer. They invited all European governments to a conference to be held in Paris in July 1947. After a brief and angry confrontation at a premeeting in Paris with Russian Foreign Minister Vyacheslav Molotov, the Soviet Union and in its wake Czechoslovakia, Hungary and Poland, declined the invitation. Those other countries that did accept included all Western European democratic countries and occupied West Germany, Greece, Turkey and Portugal. Together, these 16 nations formed the Committee on European Economic Cooperation (CEEC) that would subsequently, in April 1948, set up the Organization for European Economic Cooperation (OEEC), the permanent organization charged with coordinating Marshall aid.[18]

It is beyond the scope of this book to deal with the extensive deliberations that took place between Western European and American delegates at the Paris conference, but it is worth stressing that in this setting the first fundamental disputes and misconceptions emerged on the aims, degrees and forms of European economic cooperation. Many American promoters of Marshall aid saw the customs union concept as remarkably useful to their economic and political plans for Europe. Common knowledge assumed that market size was one vital determinant of economic growth and productivity. It suggested that small nations lacked the resources and the domestic demand to exploit the advantages of modern technology. Their industries would eventually lag behind in competitiveness, since they would be dominated by small circles of producers intent on limiting production through restrictive practices. Removing trade impediments between markets and uniting them into one large customs union would allow producers and consumers to reap the full benefits of large scale production and specialization. Moreover, with rising numbers of producers it would become more difficult to enforce restrictive trade practices so that competitiveness and efficiency would increase still further. All this would induce a gradual convergence of productivity and income levels between areas previously separated. Social tensions would eventually fade away, thereby simultaneously undermining the appeal of communism.[19]

The example of the unified U.S. market lent an extra dimension to American support for European economic integration in the 1950s. What better to win over the skeptics at home than to present God's Own Country as its model?[20] After all, many Congressmen believed that their own highly productive and dynamic economy conclusively demonstrated the advantages of a unified market. If American funding could assist in transforming Europe's jumble of national economies into an attractive market for U.S. exports and foreign direct investment, why not support the project? The Economic Cooperation Act of 1948 undeniably played on such sentiments by producing all the buzzwords likely to please Congress. One of its opening paragraphs began with the statement:

> Mindful of the advantages which the United States has enjoyed through the existence of a large domestic market with no internal trade barriers and believing that similar advantages can accrue to the countries of Europe, it is the declared policy of the people of the United States to encourage these countries through a joint organization to exert sustained efforts as set forth in the report of the Committee for European Economic Cooperation signed at Paris September 22, 1947, which will speedily achieve the

economic cooperation in Europe which is essential for lasting peace and prosperity.[21]

Of course, the odd mixture of economic theory and political ideology that some customs union champions adopted did not pass unchallenged. Well before Chicago School economist Jacob Viner published his famous analysis of the trade-creating and diverting effects of customs unions, there were those who maintained that such unions made suboptimal alternatives to unilateral tariff cuts. At best, they would result in trade growth among members if the impact of removing their mutual trade barriers outbalanced the reduction in their trade with outsiders.[22] At worst—and not unlikely—the union's common external tariffs (CETs) would be so high as to damage outsiders, one or more member states, or even overall world trade.

Standard tariff theory did not offer much guidance either, since it argued that under fixed terms of trade there were no good economic reasons for maintaining tariff barriers at the frontier of the union. Indeed, by the mid-1960s economic theorists formally demonstrated that discriminatory tariff reductions are always inferior to nondiscriminatory ones. From an economic perspective, therefore, pursuing regional economic integration in the form of customs unions or preferential tariff reductions made very little sense.[23]

In postwar Europe, the American example of a liberal economic and political union also met its share of disbelief and apprehension. It proved hard to show that large markets generated higher levels of productivity and income than smaller ones, especially since some small economies such as Switzerland and Sweden had very high rates for both indicators. Nor did there seem to be direct evidence of a link between the number of firms and levels of productivity within particular branches of industry.[24] Some of the most efficient American firms operated in highly concentrated branches of industry. Finally, the suggestion of achieving a more equal income distribution, greater social harmony and balanced growth through market integration failed to convince those in Europe that were entirely committed to the creation of a welfare state. Indicative is this verdict of British Foreign Office officials:

> American talk of a Customs Union in the context of the Marshall offer is evidently largely based on the hope that it would prevent some of the maldistribution of economic development which seems to be foreshadowed in some of the individual national plans. They probably tend,

however, to overlook the extent of the painful readjustments which a Customs Union would mean in the existing economic policy both industrial and agricultural. It would mean (as would ex hypothesi be its intention) the decline of industry here in favour of its competitor elsewhere with all the attendant dislocation. . . . . This seems politically unthinkable in a European world in which all Governments are increasingly feeling their way to methods of planning aimed at mitigating the effect on their citizens of the more extreme rigours of the free inter-play of economic forces.[25]

Within liberal economic circles, too, some doubts surfaced on the feasibility of a genuinely free and competitive internal European commodity market. Who would guarantee that European states really completely eliminated all their obstacles to intraregional trade? Would not they collude to mitigate the unpleasant side effects of increased competition? Many interwar customs union programs had in fact enhanced existing restrictive practices and boosted new ones among national and international firms. Who could prevent these firms from introducing such practices after 1945?

Such skeptical views, it should be stressed, did not become part of conventional thinking. Generally, the European public began to view customs unions as a good thing because they involved tariff reductions and were often associated with political integration,[26] even though the historical evidence for such an association was rather feeble. Free trade–minded policymakers, moreover, were usually also positively inclined toward customs unions since they tended to focus rather more on the benefits from trade creation than on the possible damage from trade diversion, especially since there was still very little economic research to guide them. It was thus quite common to sing praise of customs unions, no matter what exactly they would look like. The logic was that "A customs union creates a wider trading area, removes obstacles to competition, makes possible a more economic allocation of resources, and thus operates to increase production and raise planes of living."[27]

From the American point of view, sponsoring a European customs union still entailed some practical dilemmas. First, the U.S. government had to reconcile the regional discrimination that such a union would entail with the nondiscriminatory, worldwide approach to trade liberalization embodied in the General Agreement on Tariffs and Trade.[28] Second, it had to reconcile its endorsement of such essentially discriminatory regional agreements with its longstanding condemnation—after all less complete—of the discrimination of Commonwealth preferences. In an effort to impose consistency into their government's position, American experts devised a detailed set of rules and conditions that any form of regional economic integration would have to meet to secure GATT's approval. Yet, as we shall see below, even with these rules, clashes over the consistency of such arrangements with GATT's worldwide trading principles were simply unavoidable.

GATT'S RULES FOR REGIONAL ECONOMIC INTEGRATION

The Havana Charter (and later also GATT) embraced the unconditional MFN clause as the main principle governing international trade. Its practical implication was that the Contracting Parties had to grant each other MFN treatment. On the other hand, any preferential trade agreements already in existence at the time of signing the Geneva Agreement in 1947 were still accepted. These included—to name just a few—the British system of Commonwealth preference and the preferential tariff agreements of France and Belgium with their respective overseas territories and dependencies. The members of such preferential areas had agreed to give one another a more favorable tariff treatment than they would third countries, yet without entirely eliminating their mutual tariffs.[29] To avoid a widespread use of such preferential tariff rates, the GATT rules froze the so-called preferential margins (i.e., the difference between the MFN rate and the preferential rate) either at their existing 1947 levels or at levels agreed to during negotiations. One direct implication of this "no-new-preference" rule was that any reduction in MFN rates would automatically result in a reduction of preferential margins. American negotiators to GATT thought that with this principle they could gradually destroy British Commonwealth preferences during successive tariff rounds.

Originally, the ITO Charter had also included a short section recognizing customs unions as historically evolved and approved exceptions to the MFN principle. By 1947, as negotiators drafted the provisional GATT pending the Charter's ratification, they expanded this section to highlight free trade areas and customs unions as important legitimate forms of regional integration. After all, they reasoned, both types of arrangements go much further than a preferential tariff area because they entirely eliminate internal tariffs and other trade barriers. Within GATT these should therefore be set apart from other, more limited preferential tariff arrangements (i.e., Commonwealth Preferences) that the Americans so fervently condemned. Furthermore, they assumed that once countries had succeeded in establishing a free trade area, their next step would be to form a customs union. Not only would this avoid many administrative complexities involved in defining the origins of goods moving within the area, it would also improve their bargaining position with regard to third countries.[30] It was at French insistence that the negotiators accepted yet another concession. To avoid economic shocks following the sudden removal of internal trade barriers, they tolerated interim agreements leading to a free trade area or customs union. These allowed states to reduce protectionism gradually over a longer period, provided they followed "a plan and a schedule" to prevent them from halting the process somewhere along the way.[31]

The General Agreement on Tariffs and Trade recognized free trade areas and customs unions provided their members would eliminate trade impediments "to substantially all the trade between them." Obviously, members of a customs union also had to apply a uniform system of trade barriers to nonmembers. This system should be "on the whole no more restrictive than [its] general incidence before the creation of the customs union."[32] As GATT expert Kenneth W. Dam has shown, both phrases provided sources of infinite debate. Not only is "substantially all the trade" a very vague indication for the extent to which members had to remove trade barriers, it is also unclear whether it refers to the total elimination of all but a few barriers or to the almost total elimination of all internal barriers.[33] It makes a large difference whether member states reduce all their tariffs by, say, 80 percent or whether they abolish all trade barriers covering 80 percent of their trade. In the latter case, they exclude no less than 20 percent from the workings of the customs union.

The GATT rules on a union's CET regime toward nonmembers were equally vague. It could hardly be otherwise. With national tariff schedules usually containing more than two thousand individual items, there existed no generally accepted method for measuring the tariff incidence of a single country, let alone comparing those of several. Therefore, whenever member states negotiated a customs union, they had ample opportunity to manipulate the "average" CET. If, moreover, their proposed regional arrangement did not fall within the existing stipulations for free trade areas and customs unions, member states still had one last recourse: the so-called "waiver." GATT could waive the rules if a two-third majority of its members voted in favor. In the event, this waiver procedure became the rule rather than the exception because hardly any regional agreement succeeded in meeting the GATT criteria, however loosely formulated. As we shall see, the European Coal and Steel Community and the European Economic Community both owe their recognition to such waivers and, by implication, to American support for special regional economic schemes.[34]

EARLY EUROPEAN DISCUSSIONS FOR REGIONAL ECONOMIC INTEGRATION

While American analysis represented a major strand in regional economic integration discussions, it would be wrong to suggest that the early proposals for European integration were all American-inspired. Other incentives came from Europe itself, where usually somewhat different perspectives emerged on the Continent's problems and needs. The various groups of European federalists that derived inspiration from prewar programs for a pan-European Union and from ideas developed within wartime resistance movements saw the essential problem in the anachronistic nature of the European nation-state.[35] In their opinion, the Depression had demonstrated the impossibility of isolating domestic economies from international influences, certainly without simultaneously causing grave social and political harm to their citizens. It seemed doubtful whether Europe's fragmented national markets could meet the new demands of mass production already posed by the United States and latent in the Soviet Union. Only the speedy creation of a federal union based on common political institutions and an integrated single market could provide the answer to such challenges.

Ironically, while European federalists and American decision-makers helped popularize this belief in the need for a unified European market, it was national governments that, each with their own agenda, gave these discussions real meaning. They initiated the first postwar negotiations and they were responsible for molding early customs union models into regional agreements equipped to serve their own specific needs and aspirations. As early as 1943, for instance, the governments-in-exile of Belgium and Luxembourg (whose economic union, the BLEU, dated back to 1921) had signed a monetary agreement with the Netherlands, establishing cooperation in exchange rate management and mutual credit supplies. One year later, the three governments signed an agreement for a customs union between their economies that was eventually established in 1948 and that became known as Benelux. The founding fathers of Benelux had been the Belgian Minister of Finance

Camille Gutt and his Dutch colleague Johannes van den Broek. Both considered the customs union a useful instrument for promoting economies of scale and a vital line of defense against a trade decline during economic recessions. Their wartime expectations were based on the assumption that the complementarity of industrial Belgium and agricultural Holland would offer good prospects for expanding production and trade. They also assumed that the customs union would enable entrepreneurs within their own region to maintain or expand mutual trade, while trade elsewhere would collapse because governments reverted to isolationism. For small, trade dependent economies such as the Netherlands and Belgium this seemed the only way to safeguard export interests in times of mounting protectionism.[36]

In 1938, the Netherlands had relied on Germany for more than 21 percent of its imports. Belgium's export package promised the fulfillment of some of its needs, particularly in the area of basic metals, construction materials, chemicals and certain semimanufactures. This arrangement offered Belgium the opportunity to expand its industrial base and the Netherlands the opportunity to reduce its dependency on dollar imports. The latter, however, came at the cost of increasing Dutch reliance on Belgium; it already depended entirely on the Belgian government's continuing readiness to extend commercial credits.

For the Netherlands there remained the problem of what to do with the economic capacity devoted to exports it had traditionally sent to Germany. Belgium did not need Dutch shipping services and could only absorb an agricultural surplus at the expense of limiting its own output. Both countries therefore initially had to accept an imbalance between the treatment of industrial and agricultural products, a problem only partially resolved in 1947. In that year, a protocol was signed whereby the Netherlands became a preferential foreign supplier of Belgian agricultural imports. Yet while their mutual preferences immediately resulted in expanding intra-Benelux trade, the structural economic imbalances between the BLEU and the Netherlands gradually became more problematic; in 1947, the Dutch balance of payments deficit with Belgium was by far the largest in Western Europe. Further trade liberalization between the three partners would only worsen this situation.

Despite these complications, the three states introduced a CET in January 1948 and subsequently agreed to abolish their mutual quotas and domestic trade controls and to establish full convertibility between their currencies by January 1950. Tactical economic considerations were behind this decision, as the Dutch prime minister explained to the cabinet. In his view, Benelux had initially served quite nicely as "a facade" and "an advertising object."[37] He had been willing to abandon the entire project, but all of a sudden escape no longer seemed possible. After all, as he had put it, "agreements have been made and dates named."[38] In the end, the Belgians accepted a so-called pre-union phase and they also agreed to waive Dutch hard currency payments. The Dutch deficit problems would eventually be solved within the European framework known as the European Payments Union (EPU).

While these three governments-in-exile discussed proposals for economic integration, the French had also undertaken several attempts to enter their arrangement. In 1944, they took the initiative to sign a mutual economic consultation agreement with Belgium, the Netherlands and Luxembourg. Known as the Conseil Tripartite, this agreement supposedly aimed at coordinating policies toward Germany and also in the fields of raw materials, social security, employment, taxation, quotas and tariffs.[39] However, for France it involved much broader, interlocking economic and security objectives. The French government wanted to expand production and exports into the vacuum left by Germany, preferably within a structure that offered permanent economic security and freedom from cut-throat competition with that country. A customs union or perhaps some other more limited preferential settlement with the Benelux states might have met this aim.

By consuming more than 13 percent of total French exports in 1938, neighboring Belgium and Luxembourg were France's largest single export market. They also made up its second largest source of imports, although the gap with France's main supplier, Germany, was considerable. By comparison, the Netherlands had less to offer in terms of exports and imports, even though a customs union would allow French industry to expand its share of the Dutch market at the expense of German producers. Whereas Belgian and Dutch tariff levels were fairly low and similar in structure, the regional arrangement that France envisaged would necessarily have much higher tariff walls. To protect French farmers against Dutch agricultural exports, it would also have to exclude the agricultural sector from the free movement of goods. This meant, though, that the Dutch would need access to the German market for their agricultural exports and traditional shipping services. And since that in turn depended on the Netherlands' ability to purchase German imports, the French scenario would inevitably run into difficulties.

Expectedly, the Dutch reaction to the French proposals was one of suspicion. Despite weakening commercial ties since 1934, Germany still occupied a key role in Dutch foreign economic relations as a main agricultural export market, major supplier of manufactures and raw materials and economic hinterland for Dutch seaports. As late as 1938, almost 15 percent of total exports had gone to its eastern neighbor Germany, of which more than 41 percent was of an agricultural (and perishable) nature. Germany had also been by far the largest exporter into the Dutch market, supplying some 50 percent of imported fertilizers, 47 percent of total machinery imports and 42 percent of imported steel goods. All these products were essential to reconstruction requirements. Dutch policy therefore steered toward supporting Germany's economic revival and restoring bilateral relations with that country. It rejected participation in a customs union dominated by France and surrounded by high tariff walls directed against Germany.[40]

The Belgians, too, observed France's modernization plans for heavy industry with growing anxiety. If French long-run targets for steel production were attained, Belgium would lose its share in the French market.[41] It also seemed doubtful whether other Belgian industries would receive freer access to French domestic markets in return. Likewise, the Belgians would presumably lose traditional export opportunities and transit trade earnings in Germany. For this reason, the Belgian government tried to shelve the customs union issue by maintaining that any regional agreement should first be examined at the GATT conference in Geneva. When the French renewed their advances in 1947, Belgian politicians remained cautious.

THE EUROPEAN CUSTOMS UNION STUDY GROUP

Despite this reluctance in Belgium and the Netherlands, French delegates grasped the opportunity offered by America's integration drive to relaunch their project at the CEEC in Paris. Backed by Italy's foreign minister, the committed federalist Carlo Sforza, France declared it would embark on a customs union with Italy. It also invited all 14 other states present to join negotiations for one large Western European customs union. This formal declaration should have compelled the United Kingdom and the Benelux governments to react positively. However, any rejoicing proved premature. To circumvent an outright refusal, Benelux and British representatives to the conference persuaded the other delegates to install a European Customs Union Study Group (ECUSG) in

Brussels.[42] There, the union could be discussed in greater detail without any formal commitments.

The question worth posing here is whether France's invitation to all ERP countries signaled a change in its foreign policy toward Germany. The answer is intricate. The first signs of change were already visible in June 1947, when Bidault had to abandon his proposal for Germany's permanent weakening and grudgingly accepted plans to create a Federal Republic of Germany.[43] At a subsequent meeting with Benelux delegates in Paris, head of the Quay d'Orsay's economic section Hervé Alphand hinted that a customs union might eventually include Western Germany.[44] The American government, he knew, still hoped that France and Britain would take the lead in talks for an OEEC-wide customs union. These talks could parallel the customs union negotiations between Italy and France and the other customs union discussions between Greece and Turkey and among the Scandinavian states—all of which suddenly mushroomed at the CEEC and that eventually failed. However, neither the Quay d'Orsay nor any of the other French ministries were as yet ready to take on economic competition in a pan-European customs union.

Britain's role in this customs union issue added to the general climate of skepticism. Despite its crucial position, the United Kingdom kept a low profile. True, in the summer of 1946 the foreign secretary, Ernest Bevin, already had held talks on a Franco-British customs union.[45] Whereas these economic discussions had stranded, both countries had meanwhile made progress in the field of defense cooperation. In March 1947, they had concluded the Treaty of Dunkerque, a pact for military assistance in the event of a German attack. In the course of the year, Bevin seems to have become convinced that only a larger Western European economic and political union that obtained an American military assurance would provide a real guarantee for Europe's safety in the wake of a Soviet attack. The dilemma was that the political and economic aspects of Bevin's proposal did not receive enough support within the British cabinet. Despite all his efforts, ministers eventually reached a negative verdict in 1948.[46]

A British interdepartmental study of 1947 argued that the long-term economic gains from joining a customs union would probably outbalance the loss of Commonwealth preference that inevitably followed, but it would mean an intolerable loss of freedom in policy-making. This assessment was firmly rooted in the conviction that once Britain had joined, "union control" would penetrate all levels of national policy formulation. It was felt that even if Britain tried to steer a middle course by promoting maximum gains from economic integration without infringing domestic policy commitments, it would eventually meet the union's interference in monetary and political affairs. Therefore, the study's final recommendation was to seek forms of economic cooperation less binding than a customs union since "It may be doubted whether democratic Governments would be willing, in spite of the economic advantages which the Union might bring with it, to give any international body the ultimate power to suggest or enforce the devaluation of their currencies and to exercise some of the other controls outlined."[47]

This judgement appeared crucial for the cabinet's formal decision in September 1948. Britain should continue participating in the European Study Group but it should also stress that closer economic cooperation in smaller, individual OEEC projects was more realistic. After all, "nothing would be gained by attempting to establish a western European customs union." Bevin, too, confirmed that "anything in the nature of a formal customs union or a federation of western European states was out of the question."[48] Pressed by increasing fears of a Soviet attack on Europe, he had meanwhile switched attention to closer defense cooperation, which the Americans had made a prerequisite for their military engagement in Europe. The outcome of his efforts was the Brussels Treaty Organization for a Western Union among Britain, France and the Benelux countries. In 1949, the North Atlantic Treaty Organization (NATO) would further enhance and expand this military agreement.

Although Britain now no longer felt a need to initiate closer cooperation in Europe, it neither wanted nor needed to express a public "no" to customs union talks within the Study Group. In March 1948, the Group produced a first progress report, which neatly summed up the many technical and economic problems involved in the project: creating a common customs administration and a system for levying revenue duties, calculating tariff averages to fix the CET, selecting the method and timing of internal tariff cuts and adopting a tariff nomenclature. It glossed over deep-rooted policy differences between countries with high average tariff levels and those with low ones. On the one hand it supported claims that a customs union would inevitably stimulate maximum use of productive capacity and rising productivity and standards of living. On the other hand it also warned against sectoral problems involved in tariff cuts and called for exempting various industries. It called for removing tariffs gradually, either individually or across-the-board, over successive stages. In either case it recommended a long transitional period, allowing for the temporary use of quotas and subsidies to avoid severe economic disruption.[49]

By the end of 1948, as most governments had lost patience entirely with the customs union discussions, a second, equally ambiguous report appeared. It said that there existed "fewer difficulties in the way of the formation of a Customs Union than might have been expected."[50] A closer look at the same report, however, gave no reason for optimism. Even for the less problematic sectors it often recommended maintaining protective barriers. For instance, it assumed that frontier controls on organic dyestuffs, machine-made lace, electrical equipment and coal tar and pitch could be replaced by unionwide cartel arrangements. Fears of "keen or abnormal competition" resulted in the advice to "mitigate the most damaging effects of competition" in the pharmaceutical industry, to "regulate the trade" in paper products and to maintain import restrictions for machine tools. The Sub-Committee on Iron and Steel, with a touch of nostalgia, recollected the happy days of the International Steel Cartel of the 1920s that fixed prices and stabilized markets.[51] Some French delegates from the business community quite bluntly advocated European cartels both as shock absorbing devices and as protection against excessive American and German competition. They clearly saw the Brussels Group as a convenient forum for colluding without prying Americans.[52]

THE FRITALUX INITIATIVE

Meanwhile, in April 1949, French Minister of Finance Maurice Petsche launched a plan for an economic agreement with Benelux and Italy that first appeared as the Petsche Plan and later developed into the so-called Fritalux project. Initially, German participation was far from his mind. In its original version the plan aimed at the eventual removal of quantitative controls on goods, capital and labor, but only in those economic sectors unlikely to suffer. It would begin by introducing a system of flexible exchange rates between the members that would help to correct the imbalances in their mutual trade and payments. Tariff barriers would be left untouched in this operation.[53]

There were two pressing practical reasons explaining the shape and timing of these new French proposals. In January 1949, the Belgian government had decided to suspend all exports to France until April because of the enormous size of the French trade deficit. Just two months later, the French economic council rejected the treaty for a full customs union between France and Italy. The Franco-Italian project—only shortly before presented to the American Congress as "of historical importance for Europe as a whole"—came to a very painful halt.[54] Petsche's proposal envisaged restoring commercial relations between France and Belgium and satisfying American calls for quick achievements in the field of European integration.[55]

When Dutch government officials discovered the details of the plan, they immediately objected to flexible exchange rates and to eliminating capital controls on the grounds that these measures, if taken in isolation, would merely strengthen existing monetary imbalances between the four economies. They suggested starting instead with abolishing mutual impediments to trade in goods and services by forming a customs union that included Germany from the outset.[56] Combined with the salutary effects expected from the September devaluations on the Franco-Belgian payments problem, it was this Dutch proposal that again cooled French interest in their own plan. So things would have remained had not the head of the ECA, Paul Hoffman, made a memorable speech before the OEEC's Council meeting in October 1949 in which he mentioned the word *integration* no fewer than 16 times. Hoffman stressed that Congressional approval for further Marshall aid depended on significant and coordinated progress toward European integration. Instead of demanding one pan-European customs union, the Americans would now also welcome smaller regional groupings, provided that these did not block further progress to greater European integration and did not involve introducing new barriers or raising existing ones. They even offered 150 million U.S. dollars in support of such regional integration schemes.

"The phrase struck, but the ambiguity remains," is how one State Department official later described the impact of the expression "European integration."[57] The Americans had failed to turn the OEEC into an early model for a Western federal government largely because the British government had insisted on creating a strictly intergovernmental organization, equipped with a ministerial council that decided by unanimity.[58] They were now prepared to redress their ambitions for a pan-European political and economic union, since too much pressure merely accentuated the divergences among the European themselves and with the Americans. The United Kingdom still resisted closer economic and political ties with the Continent. The Benelux states and

France favored smaller regional groupings in more limited economic areas, but they disagreed on the nature of Germany's involvement in such arrangements. The ECA's launching of the term *integration,* therefore, expressed the search for a new and conveniently vague compromise between widely different aims and expectations on both sides of the Atlantic, even though it inevitably also caused new conceptual confusion.[59]

With the ECA's blessing of restricted regional groupings, the French found their scheme for economic cooperation with Italy and Benelux, now appropriately called "Fritalux," back on the political agenda. To cope with Benelux demands they initially offered to consider German membership at some later stage, as they had done for previous schemes. In January 1950, though, they suddenly agreed to include Germany if the United Kingdom raised no objections. Yet it soon dawned that their offer was not so generous. France knew of Britain's reluctance to such a construction and also realized that the ECA began to have second thoughts on Fritalux because it did not include any measures for genuine monetary policy coordination and might not even alleviate Europe's payments problems. ECA officials therefore eventually withdrew their original 150 million U.S. dollars premium for the scheme and began pushing for a new, multilateral payments system to replace the Payments Agreements of 1948 and 1949. In addition, they supported an all-out, OEEC-wide attack on quantitative restrictions to trade. In the course of 1950, these efforts would bear fruit. The negotiations that began after the currency realignments of September 1949 eventually led to creation of the European Payments Union, which aimed at gradually establishing full convertibility within Europe. The EPU pooled European surpluses and deficits while providing debtor countries with automatic credits. Parallel to this, the OEEC introduced a Trade Liberalization Program to relax quota restrictions on intra-European trade. Fritalux was now shelved for good.

The OEEC's activities in the field of European trade liberalization also implied the timely abortion of the wider European customs union. After having released its final report by the end of 1948, the ECUSG continued working on low-key tariff matters such as collecting customs data and refining product nomenclatures and statistics. In the course of 1950, the Group received permanent status. From then on it continued life as a purely technical organization called the Customs Cooperation Council, concentrating on drafting a uniform European tariff nomenclature (the so-called Brussels nomenclature). Ironically, the British insisted on the Group's change of name; they wanted to avoid it ever again being hijacked by European customs union enthusiasts.[60]

As we have seen, the Quay d'Orsay had already concluded that its initial version of a wider European customs union excluding Germany proved neither realistic nor prudent. The Benelux countries still rejected anything but the complete participation of Germany on equal terms; the British were entirely against it; and, more importantly, the longer France postponed a settlement over Germany, the smaller were its chances of safely encapsulating that country's economic and military potential within a European framework.[61] Toward the end of 1949, Allied controls over Germany's production capacity were already being relaxed and the powers of the new supervisory authorities were ill-defined and as yet untested. With or without the added complication of surrendering frontier controls against Germany that a customs union would imply, German industry's reemergence was already a certainty. In addition, in Britain and the United States voices were raised in favor of some form of German military contribution to the defense of Europe.[62] The new foreign minister, Robert Schuman (who had succeeded Bidault in July 1948), and Jean Monnet, head of the French planning authority, the *Commissariat au Plan,* were well aware of this political reality. Therefore, they switched tack and began looking for a more limited but solid European "community of interest" that could cope with all these problems and that could involve Germany from the start.[63]

THE SCHUMAN PLAN

Asked in 1948 whether free trade in the European iron and steel sector was feasible, steel experts of the Brussels' Study Group had hinted that "the European iron and steel market was very stable before the war, due to the existence of the International Steel Agreement, of which nearly all the Study Group Countries were members."[64] Less than two years later, Robert Schuman proposed the immediate formation of a common market between the coal, iron and steel industries of France, Germany and all other European countries willing to join. Tariffs, quotas and other impediments to goods in these sectors would be removed immediately, while barriers to labor and capital would disappear over time. The industry would be placed under the control of an independent supranational body, later called the High Authority (HA), responsible for "the most rational distribution of production at the highest possible level of productivity."[65] The architect of the plan was Jean Monnet, not only an authoritative administrator but also an enthusiastic supporter of European unity. His proposal set the stage for the 1952 creation of the European Coal and Steel Community (ECSC) by France, Germany, Italy and the Benelux countries. It represented the first successful attempt at eliminating intra-European tariffs and quotas within one economic sector. Had the steel barons been silenced by the forces of free trade or had they returned in some "integrationist" disguise? What had changed that could explain Schuman's radical proposal addressed at the newly established Federal Republic of Germany?[66]

One important change concerned the situation of the European steel market. In 1947, all European states had considered the steel industry the key to industrial recovery and they had all planned drastic increases in steel output. Two main assumptions underlay their planning. First, domestic demand for steel was high and would remain high as per capita consumption increased. Second, the restrictions imposed by the Allies would limit German output. Thus, the other European manufacturers could take over former German export markets and regulate their production.[67] Nowhere was the latter assumption more crucial to government planning than in France. According to the forecasts of Monnet's second modernization plan of 1947, French output of crude steel should have doubled by 1950. One year later, it should have overtaken Germany and have penetrated new export markets. Yet this time, too, reality did not live up to expectations or hopes. In 1950, it was Germany that was able to surpass French domestic steel production because the American representative to the Allied Control Commission did not enforce production limits originally agreed upon by the Allies (see table 2.1).[68] Moreover, it was Germany that appeared unharmed by the slackening demand for steel that had occurred in France and in the rest of Europe in 1949.

Germany's industrial and military revival also endangered the steady supply of its coal and coke to France. In 1949, France depended for almost 70 percent of its total coal and coke consumption on imports from the Ruhr. Since June 1948, the Allies had put an International Ruhr Authority made up of American, British, Benelux and French representatives in charge of distributing the area's resources, but the French government questioned this body's ability to maintain German coal supplies at their present level. At some stage, the Germans might single-handedly reduce their own coal output and begin importing American coal. Equally, they might attempt to obtain

TABLE 2.1

Crude Steel Production within the Schuman Plan Countries, 1950

Country	Production in 1000 tons	Production as percentage of total production by the Six
FRG	12120	38.2
France (+ Saar)	10548	33.2
Belgium	3792	11.9
Luxembourg	2448	7.7
Italy	2364	7.5
Netherlands	480	1.5

Source: UN, Research and Planning Division of the Economic Commission for Europe, *Economic Survey of Europe in 1951* (Geneva: United Nations Publications, 1952), 181; the figure for the Netherlands is taken from Milward, *The Reconstruction of Western Europe*, 367 (see chap. 2, note 14).

TABLE 2.2

Coal Production within the Schuman Plan Countries, 1950

Country	Production in 1000 tons	Production as percentage of total production by the Six
FRG	11232	51.5
France (+ Saar)	6600	30.3
Belgium	2736	12.5
Luxembourg	0	0
Italy	negligible	negligible
Netherlands	1224	5.6

Source: United Nations Economic Commission for Europe, *Economic Survey of Europe in 1951* (Geneva, 1952), 180 (see chap. 2, note 75).

production limits on French steel in return for secure coal supplies. Germany would thus regulate and dominate the European markets at the expense of France's industrial expansion.[69] In 1950, this scenario was no longer unthinkable. Already the three foreign ministers of Britain, the United States and France planned to meet in London on May 11 and 12 to discuss the future of Germany and the Ruhr Statute, and the French feared this conference would decide to relax production controls in Germany yet again.[70] The Schuman Plan, announced to the world on May 9, 1950, had to ward off these dangers by placing the German and French coal and steel industry under the same supranational organization. It should assure equal access to raw materials and establish permanent control over Germany's economic and military potential.

REACTIONS TO THE SCHUMAN PLAN

The West German government under Chancellor Konrad Adenauer immediately recognized that the French design could mean a breakthrough in Franco-German relations and in European cooperation. The years 1949 and 1950 had already witnessed quite a few suggestions to organize heavy industries on a European scale, the best known of which was probably the European Movement's Westminster scheme of April 1949 for coordinating production in European basic industries. German officials also had taken up the idea of replacing the unilateral control mechanism of the Ruhr Authority with an international organization that could pool German and French coal and steel.[71] It was no accident that the coal and steel industries figured so prominently in all those proposals; these sectors occupied a vital role in reconstruction planning and could boast a long history of international cooperation among governments and private interest groups. What most distinguished the Schuman Plan from all those earlier schemes for regional integration was that it was French and that it treated Germany as an equal partner. For the first time since the end of the war, France broke radically with its traditional policy by offering Germany the prospect of close and lasting cooperation within Europe on the basis of full equality. Germany accepted the offer with both hands.

In Britain, by contrast, reactions to the Schuman Plan tended to be rather cool. As we saw earlier, in 1948 the government had decided to stand aloof from continental European arrangements, a position extended to other eventualities and formally endorsed in January 1949. It had made this position clear in response to Hoffman's speech and during the bitter debates with the federalists in the Council of Europe, the framework for European political cooperation created in the same year. When the French initiative was launched, therefore, the British policy line was plain from the start, allowing the cabinet to respond in a coordinated manner without having to consider the details of the Schuman Plan.

The British government under Attlee saw Schuman's proposal as a valuable step toward Germany's reconciliation with France and the West, but it had serious qualms about its likely impact on Western Europe, the Atlantic Community and the British position within them.[72] It feared that the French bid for leadership, even though strongly supported by the Americans, might lead to a deep split in Europe between the countries accepting a community governed by the supranational authority and the states, including Britain, that were unwilling to surrender national sovereignty. This rift, in turn, could weaken the larger Atlantic Community, which the British saw as the only alliance strong enough to contain Germany and to deter the Soviet Union. Under the circumstances, however, they felt in no position to counter this threat because Monnet soon made it evident that they should either accept the supranational character of the proposal immediately or stay outside the negotiations.[73] Only failure of the Schuman Plan negotiations could therefore allow Britain to recapture the initiative.

Before looking at the course of the negotiations, it is worth examining what was at stake for the four countries that did accept Schuman's invitation. To start with Belgium and Luxembourg, the answer that the figures suggest would be: everything. Together these two countries were the third largest steel producers, after Germany and France (see table 2.1). Belgium alone was the third largest coal producer among the Six (see table 2.2), whereas coal and steel contributed more than 16 percent to its total GNP.[74] In addition, about 764,000 people, or 28 percent, of the total working population found employment in the coal and steel industries.[75] Both sectors depended heavily on trade with neighboring economies. Belgium imported some 80 percent of its iron ore from France. Although the coal mines could meet domestic demands in normal times, domestic steel producers also needed imports of German coal at times of high demand. Moreover, almost half of Belgium's steel exports went to France, Germany and the Netherlands. Luxembourg's dependency on the steel industry was even more striking: it provided 88 percent of exports and absorbed about 25 percent of the total active population.[76] Only 3 percent of total steel output stayed on the domestic market, and all coal came from abroad. Eighty percent of these coal supplies came from France, the Saar and Germany. In addition, it imported 40 percent of its apparent iron ore consumption from France. Therefore, Belgium and Luxembourg had no other option but to join Germany and France at the negotiating table.[77]

In the Belgian case, to accept a common market was not to welcome it. Belgian coal mines were the most costly in Europe due to geological factors, ineffective organization and high wages. Through subsidies, cartel arrangements with steel companies and price fixing they continued production at full capacity to meet the need for coal during the reconstruction boom. Even so, had demand slackened, and they became exposed to competition within a common market, Belgian mines inevitably would have faced drastic output reductions and job losses.

Therefore, the Belgian government entered the negotiations by demanding the equalization of labor costs among the Six.

The Dutch government had quite different demands. Wages in its nationalized mines were among the lowest in Western Europe. They seemed crucial for maintaining competitiveness in export industries dependent on coal and steel inputs (such as coal-based chemical industries and electrical equipment industries). The government feared that by accepting Belgian demands for wage equalization it would enter a "high-cost club" that could wreck the national system of wage bargaining. Wage demands would spread quickly to other sectors, thus undermining competitiveness elsewhere in the economy. Moreover, if the supranational HA received just half the powers envisaged in Monnet's original proposal, the plans for expanding the IJmuiden steel mill might have to be postponed or even abandoned.[78] Despite these dangers and despite its insignificant role as a supplier or consumer of coal and steel, the Netherlands could not afford to reject the proposals. The country imported almost 85 percent of its total steel needs from the BLEU, France and Germany alone, and 50 percent of its entire domestic coal consumption.

There were additional economic motives of a more general nature for joining the common market for coal and steel. Ever since the first discussions on Germany's future in the Conseil Tripartite, the Dutch had felt that a strong and outward looking German economy would be the key to their own recovery. This, as we have seen, had determined their policy at the CEEC, in the ECUSG and during the Fritalux negotiations. In 1949, the French refusal to meet German competition on an equal footing formed the obstacle to Fritalux. This time France was paving the way for Germany's economic integration into Europe. The Dutch had to follow that road.

Italian reactions to the Schuman Plan were mixed. Most Italian steel was manufactured at high prices as a result of low productivity and lack of domestic resources. Almost one third of total apparent steel consumption had to come from abroad, at high transport costs. Moreover, Italy's steel industry's modest fifth position on the list of steel producing future member states and its isolated existence behind high tariffs did not foreshadow a rosy future in the common market. Like the Dutch, the Italians had embarked on a major expansion of steel capacity, partly financed by ERP loans and counterpart funds.[79] If the community were to limit the expansion of steel output, the Italian plans would be under heavy scrutiny. Admittedly, in spite of the industry's alleged "hot house" existence and vulnerability to competition, some of its branches could gain from the common market. Steel refining could benefit from a reduction in the price of imported scrap and coal, always assuming that equality of access to raw materials was assured. This could allow producers to specialize further in the manufacture of finished products and special steels. Nonetheless, the government and most industrialists agreed that the industry needed safeguards against future French, German and Belgian competition once trade barriers came down and glut occurred.

NEGOTIATING THE COAL AND STEEL COMMUNITY

One of the Schuman Plan's basic principles was the immediate and unconditional removal of tariffs and quotas on trade in coal and steel between the members. This broke radically with existing thinking on economic cooperation and with the old cartel image of coal and steel. It also helped to convince the Americans of the revolutionary nature of the undertaking. To see whether the Schuman Plan really deserves this claim to fame, we will first explore the role of tariffs and quotas in the coal and steel market and subsequently examine the marketing arrangements eventually agreed upon.

The first thing worth noting is that tariffs represented only one of many distortions to competition in the European market for coal and steel. Their effect was also less important than that of other widely used measures, such as differential freight rates, doublepricing, production and quota agreements and exchange controls.[80] Except for Italy, which had imposed a tariff of 15 percent on coke, all members of the future community imported coal duty free as a result of shortages in Europe. The main coal producers, the United Kingdom and Germany, used a system of double pricing for domestic consumption and exports. Thus, domestic coal prices were kept at a lower level to support economic recovery. Belgium used coal subsidies for the same reasons. France also subsidized coking coal imports from Germany to keep prices in line with the selling price of coke for its domestic consumers.[81] In the Netherlands, interference in coal prices went further still, since the government-owned mines charged the same price throughout the country, regardless of differences in transport costs.[82]

Differential freight rating was another frequently used method of favoring some producers over others. Rough estimates for railway transport suggest that discriminatory rates increased transport charges

TABLE 2.3

Tariffs in Percent Ad Valorem on Iron and Steel in the Schuman Plan Countries, 1950

Product	Benelux	France	Federal Republic of Germany	Italy
pig iron	1	25	5	10
ferromanganese	0	12	7	135
ingots	1	9	.13	0
plates and sheets	3	11	15	20
shapes and sections	5	15	22	0
rails	4	18	23	20
cast-iron tubes	8	20	16	25
hydroelectric conduits	7	25	8	45

Source: W. Woytinsky and E. Woytinsky, *World Commerce and Governments: Trends and Outlook* (New York: Twentieth Century Fund, 1955), 282.

by up to 10 percent.[83] There were several methods of discrimination. Sometimes railway freight rates for the same product varied between the country of origin or destination. On other occasions, special concessions favored some producers or consumers within a country, or railway freight rates were "broken" at the frontier. In Germany, the railways had different charges for different firms, different regions and even different domestic routes. Similarly, French railways charged 60 percent more for carrying coal and coke on the partially international route from the Ruhr to the steel center in the Lorraine than for the entirely domestic route Lorraine to the north of France, even though the distance was virtually the same. Discriminatory freight rates could therefore have the same effects as production subsidies or as import or export duties.

In the iron and steel sector tariffs did play a role (see table 2.3) but they seldom offered adequate security against dumping practices or discriminatory freight rates. For this reason, most steel producers preferred to rely on other, more effective measures of protection. Italian producers formed the exception to this rule. Since they could set their own tariff levels in the producer committees advising parliament, they preferred tariff protection. Other measures such as quotas or subsidies would have implied government involvement in the steel industry and that was exactly what these industrialists wanted to avoid.[84] In Belgium and Luxembourg, coal and steel producers were less choosy in matters of protection. They relied on government measures and government-sanctioned cartel agreements to obtain adequate shelter, but they still enjoyed a freedom from state intervention that was almost unique in the postwar European steel sector.

One central issue in the ECSC negotiations was whether to eliminate all distortions to competition and trade (other than tariffs and quotas) overnight or only gradually, after a period of transitional arrangements. Since the first alternative would entail the risk of disrupting traditional trade patterns and of causing massive unemployment, it was never seriously considered. The Monnet memorandum of May mentioned price fixing and production quotas as options during a transitional period. It stressed that these measures could be temporary only and that tariffs and quotas on trade would be abolished from the start. After the transition, price-fixing and other inequalities in competitive conditions would be abolished and there would be free competition within the common market.[85] Two funds would be available during the interim phase from which loans could be supplied to prepare industries for the new situation. These would both be financed largely from levies on coal and steel production. The first one, the equalization fund, would help to avoid sudden, large scale unemployment by temporarily financing exploitation losses of existing firms. Subsequently, the second—adaptation—fund would come into operation either to lend such firms further support for modernization schemes or, if they could not possibly meet competition, to offer alternative employment to the workers affected.[86]

If transitional measures were essential, how long should they last and who should be responsible for their implementation? The French draft of the Schuman Plan simply stated: five years, under supervision of the HA. This answer, though, was widely contested. Some industries, such as the high-cost coal mines in Belgium and several protected steel industries in Italy, were likely to need extensive funding to adapt to the common market if they were to survive at all. But if they had to be financed through production levies they could damage the competitiveness of other viable end users. Much would therefore depend on the criteria for determining the nature and amount of the funds, as well as their financing.[87]

The issue of the funds divided countries into two main groups. On the one hand there were Germany and the Netherlands, who preferred limiting the scope of the funds and minimizing the levies, which no doubt they themselves had to pay for. Belgium, France and Italy on the other hand pushed for large community funding for such extra tasks as retraining the unemployed and indemnifying firms in the coal and steel sector. Italy even demanded an open-ended commitment for unemployment compensation, but that claim faltered at an early stage in the talks. As for the question of the adaptation fund, negotiators eventually agreed to limit its use. Industries would receive loans rather than grants, the costs of which had to be shared equally between the HA and the national governments.[88] Contrary to original intentions, however, the fund would be permanent, allowing firms to receive support even beyond the transitional period.

The solution found for the equalization fund was far more complex. The governments agreed that this should be financed from a temporary, gradually regressive levy on coal to cover exploitation losses. The fund would operate as a price equalization mechanism by charging a levy on coal sold by producers whose average costs were below the weighted average prices prevailing in the future Community.[89] In this way, the low-cost German and Dutch mines would not only contribute to the restructuring of high-cost coal mines in Belgium but they would also indirectly subsidize Belgian steel producers by reducing the price of coking coal. The Belgian government, however, demanded still more. It would pay 50 percent of the costs of the equalization measures provided two conditions were met. First, during the restructuring phase Belgian output would be reduced by no more than 3 percent annually. Second, subsidizing would be allowed to continue up to three years after the end of the transitional period. These demands were not dropped until the last stage of the negotiations, when the Six governments eventually accepted a maximum production levy of 1.5 percent.[90]

In theory, the system of transitional and permanent adaptation measures allowed for the immediate creation of an internal market free from quotas and tariffs. The other alternative, a more gradual, phased removal of such barriers, had been rejected at an early stage because it would undoubtedly tempt governments to postpone these trade liberalization measures to the last moment. By contrast, a "plunge" into the common market was expected to secure member states' immediate and full commitment to the project.[91] In practice, though, the removal of tariffs and quotas to internal trade in coal and steel did not happen overnight, despite the presence of transitional arrangements designed to smooth the process. The reason was that the governments only accepted immediate liberalization measures after they had introduced two important, temporary exemptions.

The first exemption concerned Italian tariffs on steel and coke. Early on, negotiators had conceded that Italy could continue imposing duties on imports of steel and coke during the transitional period. The Italian government could use its high bargaining tariff levels for steel (rather than its much lower applied tariffs) as the starting point from which gradually to abolish steel tariffs after the transition period had ended.[92] These bargaining rates varied from 10 percent for pig iron to 23 percent for most finished steel products. It received a similar concession for coke production, for which it could temporarily maintain the original 15 percent tariff on coke imports.

The second exception to the immediate removal of internal trade barriers benefited Belgian coal. As mentioned before, Belgian delegates had formulated a long list of last-minute demands to safeguard their coal mines from immediate closure. This tactic was successful, for they received permission to "retain or set up, under the control of the High Authority, mechanisms making possible the separation of the Belgian market from the common market."[93] In practice this meant that Belgium could impose trade restraints to protect the coal industry against competition from member states. Even so, the government would never use this clause in the treaty. It realized that the most inefficient mines had to be closed at some stage. What better than to shift responsibility for this politically painful but economically inevitable process to the supranational HA?[94]

Whereas the provisions on internal trade left little either to chance or to the powers of the HA, those on the Community's external trade were deliberately vague. The French suggested charging the HA with controlling excessive imports and with determining maximum and minimum tariff levels toward nonmember countries. Within this margin, governments would be free to impose their own duties. However, the Benelux governments refused to accept this solution, which they feared would ultimately boil down to an upward adjustment of low tariffs. Directed by the Dutch, who were horrified at the thought of price increases for British iron ore and scrap imports, they demanded a unitary tariff that had to be as low as possible.[95] France and Italy seemed prepared to accept the Benelux tariff levels, at least as the bottom of any new tariff band and only in exchange for freedom to impose quantitative restrictions on "excessive" imports, but Germany rejected such compromises. It had no intention of abandoning the bargaining tariffs it had so carefully drafted in preparation for the forthcoming GATT conference in Torquay.

It is striking to see that, once freed from the straightjacket of a common Benelux tariff policy, Belgium and Luxembourg, too, slipped back into what may be described as old tariff policy habits. Characteristically, they did not support the Dutch crusade against tariff increases. This is not to say that they would have accepted happily the drastic increases proposed by Italy, but merely that they considered a slight increase in some Benelux tariffs useful for protectionist and bargaining purposes. Thus, when the negotiations on the CET reached their final stage, Belgium and Luxembourg confessed their preference for raising the Benelux tariff. They agreed to leave the issue to the unanimous decision of the Council of Ministers if no other solution was found. It meant the Dutch government had to accept a compromise. It eventually accepted minimum and maximum tariffs that were based on the Benelux levels. These maximum levels would come into force if the tariff negotiations for iron and steel with the United Kingdom (during the GATT round in Torquay) failed.[96] In addition, Benelux received a tariff quota to satisfy their needs for steel imports during the transition period. Fixing the precise CET was left to a unanimous decision by the Council of Ministers once the ECSC Treaty was signed.

In April 1951, the governments of the Six signed the Paris Treaty for the ECSC. It established neither the complete customs union, with free movement of goods in *all* economic sectors that the Americans had originally wanted, nor the supranational common market under full control of the HA envisaged in the original French proposal. Perhaps the best description is that of a sectoral common market, because it did establish the free movement of goods, labor and investments within the coal, iron and steel sectors. Even that did not entirely fit the GATT rules, because the transitional arrangements were never carefully fixed beforehand in a plan and a schedule. Yet the ECSC's importance to Franco-German economic and political relations overruled such—as some would say, legalistic—considerations. It joined both nations in a community of interests and it created the framework for Germany's new economic, political and ultimately military role within Europe.

Only an optimist would have assumed in 1947 that the ECUSG would become the driving force behind European economic integration. Earlier, the French initiatives for closer economic cooperation with Benelux had suggested that these remained futile unless the three Allied powers settled Germany's future. Before the war, Germany had played a crucial role within Europe's trading pattern. Its autarkic trade policies had heavily upset the precarious continental economic balance and had eroded welfare among its small, dependent neighbors. Few European governments after the war doubted that this country, whether permanently paralyzed or revitalized, would again greatly influence their own performance. Therefore few were willing to prejudice their role in future economic and political events by joining a pan-European customs union.

The British distanced themselves from initiatives for a European customs union because these seemed to clash with national policy objectives. For more than seven years, the study finished in 1948 would remain the only serious attempt made by a British government to assess the implications of joining. Throughout that period, successive British cabinets happily employed a caricature of European integration whenever any new efforts threatened to upset the status quo. They greeted such plans with a mixture of suspicion and contempt, seeing them as products of unrealistic thinking among continentals and Americans. Only officials at lower levels in the departmental hierarchy occasionally escaped this type of bureaucratic policy formulation. But they usually lacked the political clout to induce changes.

The belief that a European customs union would severely undermine national policy sovereignty was as much part of the early federalist illusion as it was part of the British government's caricature of European economic integration. The British expected that such a union would automatically imply the transfer of many national decision-making powers to some higher, supranational level. The practical experiences of the Study Group tell a different story. Continental European governments appeared very keen and well equipped to avoid the disruptive effects of trade liberalization. They, too, carefully considered the impact of the customs union on their political sovereignty, on the distribution of economic resources within their boundaries and on their national programs for economic recovery and welfare growth. If ever a European customs union were to come about, it would be a painstaking balancing act that offered prospects of net benefits to all member states.

The Benelux customs union, although much praised by the Americans, was the perfect example of such a balancing act. While the Benelux partners made an impressive and inspiring start by eliminating their internal tariffs and by introducing the CET almost overnight, they allowed quantitative restrictions and cartel agreements to survive for a long time. A set of preferential market-sharing arrangements gave the Dutch agricultural producers conditional access to the BLEU market. In exchange, industrial products from the BLEU could freely enter the Netherlands as long as the Belgian government provided the credits. The Dutch government also held a commitment to limit its industrialization efforts to those sectors that did not compete directly with Belgian industrial production.[97] Throughout the 1950s, economic cooperation within Benelux would prove to be a trying venture. Other than incidentally, political cooperation hardly emerged. However, the immediate economic gains from Benelux cooperation should not be underestimated. From 1948 to 1958 the relative share of imports from the Netherlands into the BLEU doubled, whereas the BLEU's export share in the Netherlands increased 40 percent. The Netherlands' preferential rights in the BLEU market had a large influence on its trade and helped to swing its deficit around.[98] In addition, Benelux provided the three governments with the largest market for industrial products in OEEC Europe, an asset that inevitably strengthened their negotiating position during the talks for a wider European customs union.

The ECSC's role in European integration was obviously entirely different from that of the ECUSG and Benelux. Its main incentive was political and its impact on European political stability was momentous. The Schuman Plan marked the first step toward the supranational organization of Europe. It also made a vital contribution to the prevention of any future war between France and Germany. This explains why the Americans were prepared to push it through GATT under the waiver arrangements of article 25, despite some qualms among outsiders such as Norway, Sweden and Denmark.[99] Apart from political objectives, however, the project had economic aims which originated in French policymaking. It aimed at safeguarding French access to the rich coal resources of the Ruhr after the dissolution of the International Ruhr Authority. At the same time, it allowed Germany's production potential to recover beyond the artificial limits fixed by the Allies without posing the danger of German economic domination, because the supranational authority in charge would consist of independent experts rather than governmental delegates. Moreover, by aiming at pooling one sector of the economy only, the French steel industry could profit while the other, weaker sectors of the economy remained protected.

The proposal for a sectoral common market (as opposed to the international planning institution for the steel industry suggested earlier by European federalists and socialists) also clearly showed that Monnet had anticipated hostile reactions to overt dirigisme. A planning authority would be fiercely resisted by German and French industrialists and might even be rejected by the American administration. A sectoral common market, by contrast, could count on broad support within the United States and among political parties and public opinion in Europe. Moreover, Monnet and many other Euro-enthusiasts hoped it might one day provide the platform for further economic and political integration.

THREE

The OEEC's Tariff Debate

To many postwar governments, the abortive talks of 1948 on the Western European customs union seemed to prove the political impossibility of simultaneously eliminating tariffs and quotas in times of economic instability. It was quantitative restrictions and not tariffs that they saw as the greater evil to Europe's trade expansion. Quotas embodied the crisis management and beggar-thy-neighbor policies of the thirties, as well as the symptoms of Europe's postwar trade and payments problems.[1] The reasons for this distinction were twofold. First, quotas removed the flow of trade from the working of the price mechanism under normal market conditions; if a stipulated quantity of imports was reached, not even the most efficient producer could increase its exports into the country imposing that quota. Tariffs, by contrast, could actually stimulate cost efficiency within both the exporting and importing countries, since cheaply produced exports goods could still jump the tariff wall. Second, as the 1930s had demonstrated, quotas were extremely suitable for hidden discrimination because their management and apportioning was usually left to the discretion of governmental bureaucracies. Tariffs, on the other hand, were often considered legitimate, democratically guarded trade policy instruments for countries imposing them and sometimes problematic but nonetheless clearly visible and constant barriers for countries facing them. And besides, reducing intra-European tariffs had little practical significance as long as quotas remained the main mechanisms for regulating European trade.[2]

The assumptions above also underlay the OEEC's decision in 1949 to concentrate on relaxing quotas in intra-European trade by launching the Trade Liberalization Program. As Paul Hoffman, U.S. special representative in Europe, stressed in his famous October address to the OEEC Council, Europe would now aim for "the freest possible movement of goods and persons in Europe involving the removal of quantitative restrictions, free movement of funds, and *the use of tariffs as a cushion and not as a quantitative restriction.*"[3] Hoffman's statement highlights the assumption that European governments would have the right to rely on some tariff protection once quotas were being relaxed, but that these rates would be moderate and certainly not heavily protectionist. It also reflects the awareness that while the OEEC had not yet officially abandoned its objective to promote a single European market free from quotas *and tariffs,* its members had in fact agreed to leave tariff matters to the competencies of the worldwide GATT. This ad hoc structure would have to provide the framework in which tariff cuts could be negotiated on a regular, worldwide basis and tariff disputes would be discussed and settled.

This artificial and ambiguous separation of postwar trade policy competencies between the OEEC and GATT may have been understandable in the light of America's persistent—albeit increasingly troublesome—efforts to pursue simultaneously European regionalism and worldwide multilateralism, but it certainly muddled trade policy bargaining among European states and between these and the United States. Such a separation may also be understandable in view of the distinct reputation of quotas. However, since quotas and tariffs (despite their differences) both had become so clearly part of the same "toolbox" of national policy instruments, it became increasingly unrealistic and perverse to deny their fundamental linkage in trade policy matters. And yet this is exactly what many postwar European governments did.

In Europe several major OEEC members quickly responded to domestic pressure for offsetting the loss of quota protection resulting from the Trade Liberalization Scheme. They either reintroduced previously suspended, prewar tariff schedules or they launched entirely new rates, often with generous "bargaining" margins aimed at negotiations in GATT rounds. Such actions provoked a series of tariff disputes with the governments of the trade dependant, low-tariff countries of the Netherlands, Belgium, Luxembourg, Denmark and Sweden, which insisted on linking the issues of tariff reductions and quota and bringing both under the OEEC's realm. By 1951, faced with the slackening pace of tariff cuts within GATT and with a growing influx of competing industrial imports, they increasingly criticized the OEEC's virtual neglect of tariff issues and eventually in 1954 threatened to halt its scheme for eliminating quotas. Ultimately, as we will see, it was such dissatisfaction on matters of trade policy that provided powerful incentives to launch new European schemes for preferential tariff cuts.

THE OEEC'S TRADE LIBERALIZATION PROGRAM

In 1948, the OEEC had emerged as the framework for channeling Marshall aid and, at least officially, for achieving "close and lasting cooperation between the participating countries."[4] Its Council, a supreme authority made up of representatives of all the member states, remained in permanent session but its level of representation varied according to the weight of matters under consideration. It received practical assistance from an Executive Committee of seven annually appointed national delegation leaders. This Committee, in turn, was assisted by a permanent staff under the direction of the secretary-general. Voting in the Council normally followed the unanimity rule. Once a decision was taken, it was binding to all members, but implementation was left to each individual state. As a result, the OEEC had neither the powers nor the resources to force compliance by direct action.[5] This is why the pace of the Organization's Trade Liberalization Program was often set by its slowest member.

The Trade Liberalization Program was ready in June 1949. In November, OEEC members agreed to remove before the end of the year quantitative restrictions on at least 50 percent of their imports from the OEEC area in 1948 (see table 3.1).[6] Indeed, they all met this target without too many problems, since they began by removing quota restrictions in those sectors where these were no longer necessary or effective, such as various raw materials and goods for which postwar shortages on the domestic market had disappeared.

The deadline for the next step of 60 percent was fixed at October 1950 and formally laid down in a Code for Liberalization.[7] This Code urged the OEEC members to remove quotas "as fully as their economic position would permit," in exchange for equivalent efforts by their trading partners. It also committed states to avoid discrimination both with regard to liberalized imports and imports still under quota restrictions. This rule was qualified by the recognition that balance of payments deficits and serious economic disturbances counted as legitimate reasons for suspending liberalization measures. Countries claiming to face such problems would, however, have to reintroduce

TABLE 3.1

The OEEC's Trade Liberalization Program, 1949–1955

Council decision of:	Target:	Target date:
July 1949	Immediate steps toward progressive elimination of quotas. Trade liberalization as complete as possible.	1951
November 1949	50 percent of imports from OEEC area	15 December 1949
January 1950	60 percent of imports from OEEC area	As soon as EPU established
September 1950	60 percent	4 October 1950
With adoption of Code:	75 percent overall and 60 in each of the three product categories	1 February 1951
January 1955	90 percent overall and 75 in each of the three product categories	1 October 1955

Source: F. Boyer and J. Sallé, "The Liberalization of Intra-European Trade in the Framework of the OEEC," in *International Monetary Fund Staff Papers* 4 (1955), 179-216.

liberalization measures within 18 months. In the meantime, the Organization had the right to study their case and recommend domestic measures to facilitate quota abolition.[8]

In June 1950, most countries were within close reach of the 60 percent requirement, thus bringing the OEEC average to 56 percent (see table 3.2.). This promising result prompted the Council to set a new target for February 1951. By that date, members should have liberalized no less than 75 percent of their total OEEC imports in 1948 and at least 60 percent for each of three product groups: food and feeding stuffs, raw materials and manufactured goods. A glance at the percentages reached by June 1951 suggests that this new target had begun to put some pressure on domestic producers. While Portugal, Switzerland, the United Kingdom and Italy surpassed the overall target of 75 percent, Austria, Denmark, Germany, Greece, Iceland and Norway fell far short of this requirement. Various countries also failed to meet the target of 60 percent liberalization *within* the three products groups. This revealed that many states had only reached the overall target by removing quotas on "essential" imports such as raw materials, grain products and specific capital goods needed for their economic recovery. When such restrictions were lifted, achieving higher targets necessarily involved damaging vested domestic producer interests or interfering with austerity programs. It was at this point that the trade liberalization process slowed down. Indeed, when the second target date appeared, progress stagnated and the

TABLE 3.2

Percentage Liberalization of Intra-European Trade, June 30, 1950–1959

	1950	1951	1952	1953	1954	1955	1956	1957	1958	1959
Austria	53	-	-	36	76	82	90	90	90	90
BLEU	56	75	75	87	87	88	91	96	96	96
Netherlands	55	66	75	92	93	93	91	96	96	96
Denmark	53	50	68	76	76	76	86	86	86	86
France	58	75	-	-	51	75	82	-	-	91
Germany	47	-	77	90	90	90	92	93	94	92
Greece	..	..	..	..	..	95	95	95	95	76
Iceland	-	41	41	-	29	29	29	29	29	29
Ireland	64	75	75	75	77	77	90	90	90	90
Italy	54	76	100	100	100	99	99	99	98	98
Norway	39	51	75	75	76	75	78	81	81	81
Portugal	53	83	100	93	93	93	94	94	94	94
Sweden	53	75	75	91	91	91	93	93	93	93
Switzerland	81	85	88	92	92	92	92	91	91	91
Turkey	42	63	63	-	-	-	-	-	-	-
United Kingdom	57	90	46	58	80	84	94	94	94	95
OEEC average	56	65	66	71	81	84	89	83	83	90

- = liberalization officially suspended
.. = liberalization not officially reported

Source: Organization for European Economic Cooperation. *Twelfth Annual Economic Review* (Paris: Organization for European Economic Cooperation. 1961). 185.

OEEC's Trade Liberalization Program experienced severe setbacks because Germany, the United Kingdom and France all reversed their liberalization trend (see table 3.2). Already by the end of 1950, the German government faced a growing balance of payments deficit caused by a strong surge in domestic demand and aggravated by a lag in income from its exports.[9] Three months later, it was forced to suspend liberalization measures. Although domestic measures swiftly reversed the deficit, this "de-liberalization," as it was called, severely damaged trade performances of the other members, who lost access to their major export market overnight. In November 1951, the United Kingdom suddenly also reduced its liberalization percentage from 90 to 61 and subsequently even to 46 percent. Only in 1953 did the British government gradually increase its share of officially liberalized imports. France was the third major European economy to de-liberalize. By mid-1952, it reintroduced a licensing system for all its imports, and it was not until the end of 1953 that the French government increased its liberalization percentage to a mere 8 percent.

While the reversibility of these quota liberalization measures caused major disruption and uncertainty in trade, it was certainly not the only deficiency in the Trade Liberalization Program. Negligence of tariff barriers was another. Since tariff policies were not considered an OEEC affair, all tariff issues should normally be handled by GATT. This provisional forum, however, had not developed into the firm, authoritative and vibrant organization for multilateral tariff cuts that some officials in Europe and many in the U.S. had hoped for.[10] Governments of the Benelux states, Denmark and Sweden, in particular, had expected that regular GATT rounds would gradually reduce and eventually abolish protective tariffs. During the first rounds in Geneva (1947) and Annecy (1949), they therefore had cut and consolidated many of their own rates, which were already comparatively low anyway. In exchange, they hoped to receive reciprocal access for their exports once a European payments system had also relaxed exchange controls and import restrictions. Other European nations had been more cautious during these GATT rounds and they had been preparing for the time when tariffs would again serve as tools for protection and trade bargaining. Despite the Trade Liberalization Program's easy start and initially modest impact on effective levels of protection, such countries swiftly responded by activating their tariff schedules. This can be illustrated by following their first steps toward restoring tariffs.

RE-ERECTING TARIFF BARRIERS

As early as 1947, France introduced some previously suspended tariffs after pressure from domestic industries. It also drafted a completely new tariff schedule of mainly ad valorem rates.[11] For several products such as chemicals, paper and some types of machinery, these new import duties were so high that imports came to a halt, and French firms needing these products as inputs were greatly handicapped. It meant that such rates had to be suspended only months after their reintroduction.[12] In 1948, when this new schedule was presented to the second GATT round in Annecy, it had provoked an uproar among the Contracting Parties, who argued that France had violated the GATT rule forbidding an upward revision of tariff schedules. The French negotiators formally insisted that the new schedule's overall levels equaled those in force in the period

1936-1938.[13] Informally, however, they admitted to having raised "sensitive" tariffs in order to limit the damage that the Trade Liberalization Program would inflict upon various domestic sectors.

Italy, too, had entered the GATT round in Annecy with a new tariff schedule. Its levels had been drafted by the most influential representatives of agriculture and industry, who based their recommendations on the expected competitive strength of each domestic sector as well as on bargaining considerations: Not only should tariff levels provide adequate shelter from foreign competition, they should include an additional margin for international tariff negotiations. In devising the structure of their new tariff schedule, they had followed a principle that governments traditionally applied to protect industry: the higher the share of value added that went into a product, the higher also its customs duty. The actual Italian rates, however, usually surpassed those of other Western European countries. Italian calculations estimated average levels for steel products, vehicles and equipment at some 30 percent ad valorem. Agricultural rates were usually 25 percent. Such tariff figures epitomized—to quote the Italian liberal politician and federalist Luigi Einaudi—"protectionism that brought back the high noon of vulgar Mercantilism."[14]

The Annecy round did not end the tariff debate in Italy. The newly drafted schedule not only raised fierce opposition abroad but also at home, where liberals and socialists feared drastic rises in prices. At their insistence, the government had to work out a temporary "compromise" schedule, the levels of which were below the so-called legal rates.[15] However, to Italy's European trading partners this was only a small consolation. They still faced high barriers and they also feared that industrial lobbyists would at any time insist on reimposing the higher, legal ones.[16] It is therefore all the more unexpected that the opposite actually happened in 1951, when Italy cut most tariffs by another 10 percent because its payments surplus was growing so rapidly. To avoid a loss of bargaining power and to satisfy domestic producers, though, all these reductions were officially only temporary.[17]

The West Germans were the third to draft a completely new tariff. They neither had been allowed to attend the first GATT round in Geneva nor to attend the ITO negotiations in Havana. Moreover, they had been forced to accept the Havana Charter and to grant unilateral MFN treatment to all Contracting Parties on the basis of their prewar tariff rates, which were still very low.[18] In 1948, the Allied High Commission had finally agreed to independent West German participation at the forthcoming tariff round in Torquay. The Germans were even allowed to draft their own revised tariff schedule, although the Allied High Commission retained responsibility for its final version.[19]

At the third GATT round in Torquay in the autumn of 1950, German tariff negotiators presented a schedule designed to offer adequate protection in the absence of quantitative restrictions. They, too, had added generous bargaining margins, which had by now become all too common, despite Allied warnings against such negotiating tactics. A German tariff commission had modeled this new schedule on the high tariff levels prevailing in 1937 and had subsequently carefully modified downward all those tariff lines that had clearly exceeded existing European averages. Tariff experts had made more than 130 tariff comparisons to ensure that the average tariff per chapter of the so-called Brussels nomenclature was within close range of average tariffs in France, Italy, Benelux, the United Kingdom and the United States. The tariff comparisons made at the time by the German experts designing their country's new schedule illustrate this method (see table 3.3).[20] These tariffs did meet GATT's rather vague obligation that also applied to free trade areas and customs unions: "on the whole" they did not exceed previous rates.[21] Consequently, the Contracting Parties might be able to object to individual German tariffs that were relatively high, but they could never oppose and reject entire chapters of the new schedule on the grounds that these violated GATT rules.

The Americans in the High Commission demanded cuts in several high tariffs on agricultural products, textiles, iron and steel products, aluminum, paper products, cars, dyestuffs and some other goods. However, for all except a few cases the German government managed to resist their pressure.[22] Germany could thus enter GATT with a bargaining schedule designed to strengthen its negotiating position. What the French government had done in 1948, the Germans repeated two years later. Understandably, this caused a shock to all those European exporters who were heavily dependent on the German market.

What this brief overview of major European countries' trade policies shows is that by 1950, tariffs had made a return as instruments for protection and trade bargaining in France, Italy, West Germany and Britain. In line with their commitments under the Trade Liberalization Program, these countries, except France, began relaxing their quantitative import restrictions, but they also reactivated previously suspended tariff rates or, in the case of Germany, introduced entirely new schedules. To discover the implications of this commercial

TABLE 3.3

Some Tariff Comparisons Calculated by the German Tariff Commission, 1950

German Tariff Chapter no.	Description	Benelux	France	Italy	West Germany*	Average
32	tanning and dying extracts	4.4	17.8	23.3	16.0	15.4
40	rubber and rubber products	9.0	13.0	17.0	17.3	14.1
48	paper and pulp	16.5	23.5	27.0	19.5	21.6
58	carpets	19.3	22.7	31.0	27.0	25.0
70	glass and glassware	12.0	21.0	36.3	19.7	22.3
73	iron and steel	4.0	14.0	21.3	15.3	13.7
76	aluminium	5.7	24.0	37.7	14.0	20.4
87	lorries	17.3	25.7	39.0	24.0	26.5
91	optical instruments	13.0	25.5	31.0	11.0	20.1

* new West German tariff

Source: P. Schade, "Die Entwicklung des Zolltarifes der Bundesrepublik Deutschland bis zum EWG Außentarif" (Ph.D. diss., Eberhardt Karls University, Tübingen, 1963), 40-41.

policy strategy for European trade cooperation, we shall first have to examine these tariff schedules in more detail.

MEASURING TARIFF PROTECTION

In the previous sections and chapters we described national tariff schedules in terms of such seemingly clear qualifications as relatively "high" or "low," without indicating what these concepts implied for the actual tariffs imposed, or for their protective impact. This terminology will now have to be clarified, first by comparing tariff structures in nominal and effective terms, and second, by analyzing several complaints about high tariffs which the OEEC received during the 1950s. Given the drawbacks of working with tariff averages and the constraints involved in comparing national tariff schedules, the data chosen here represent a large cross-section of actually applied tariff rates. (For Italy, the tariff rates refer to the legal tariff schedule, the rates of which are on average about 10 percent higher than those actually imposed.) In 1951, the GATT Secretariat collected rates for most of the 570 items of the five-digit Standard International Trade Classification (SITC) of 1950. This enables us to reconstruct a fairly detailed picture of European tariff rates.[23] The figures include the tariff cuts imposed *after* the Torquay round of 1950–early 1951. Therefore, they slightly underestimate the extent of the high tariff problem on the eve of the Trade Liberalization Program. On the other hand, they have the great advantage of being comparable and of incorporating all the major tariff revisions in France, Italy and West Germany. Here we will summarize the main conclusions from this data set by looking at the frequency distribution of national tariff rates over ten major tariff intervals: zero ad valorem rates, rates of 1-5, 6-10, 11-15, 16-20, 21-25, 26-30, 31-35, 36-40 percent and, finally, rates higher than 40 percent ad valorem. Further details of these findings are presented in graphs in the appendix at the end of this book.

The first observation worth making when comparing rates for the different SITC sections and countries is that tariffs in SITC zero (food and foodstuffs) are among the highest for all countries except the United Kingdom, which has only one agricultural rate higher than 20 percent. That country's highest duties are concentrated in sections five (chemicals) and seven (machinery and transport equipment). The frequency distribution of tariffs within section zero shows a wide divergence in national levels. Danish tariffs are by far the lowest, even compared with the rest of Scandinavia and Benelux, whereas Italy's are by far the highest rates; almost one-third of its rates fall in a range of 26-40 percent. France has 37 items of 26 percent or more, compared to 25 for West Germany.

Tariffs in SITC two (inedible crude materials, fuels excluded) have the characteristic frequency distribution of rates on raw materials used as inputs. The tariffs listed here are usually very modest, ranging from 1 to 10 percent. Swedish, Danish, Norwegian and Benelux duties are among the lowest, followed by Italian and German ones. Again, though, the British pattern in this section is somewhat different: it has a comparatively large concentration of items in the interval 6-10 percent.

SITC three (mineral fuels, lubricants and related materials) shows a tariff pattern similar to that of section two, with the difference that it consists of only 13 items equal or below 10 percent (except in Italy and France). For Italy these rates include tariffs imposed on cokes, crude or partly refined petroleum and lubricating oils, for France they include tariffs levied on cokes only. Tariffs for animal and vegetable oils and fats (SITC four) are again much lower in Denmark, Norway and Sweden than in the United Kingdom, France and Italy. Benelux and West Germany occupy the middle ground between these extremes, with most of their tariffs concentrated in the interval 6-10 percent.

In SITC four (animal and vegetable oils and fats) Italy and France levy the highest tariff rates and Denmark and Sweden the lowest. Ten of the French total of seventeen tariff items are concentrated in the interval 16-20 percent, while Italy has six items in the same interval. By comparison, all the Danish and Swedish rates are concentrated in the first three intervals. In Benelux and West Germany the distribution by interval is similar, with most tariffs concentrated within 6-10 percent. The United Kingdom has comparatively many rates between 11 and 15 percent, but it does not levy any higher than 15 percent.

Chemicals (SITC five) comprise a much larger part of each national tariff schedule than the total of 42 tariff positions of the SITC would suggest. The reason is that by 1951 most European states had reclassified and refined their chemicals divisions to incorporate a wide variety of new items. The SITC division nonetheless provides the main trends in European duties on chemical imports. It shows a very large gap between the low tariffs of Benelux, Denmark and Sweden on the one hand, and the mostly very high tariffs of West Germany, France, Italy and the United Kingdom on the other.

SITC six (manufactured goods classified chiefly by materials) is a comparatively large section which shows a marked divergence between the levels of Denmark and Sweden and those of France, Italy, West Germany and the United Kingdom. Italy clearly has the highest duties: 72 of a total 162 tariff items are equal to or above 26 percent. French rates are heavily concentrated in the intervals of 16-25 percent, and the British and German rates in those of 11-20 percent, although the latter two also levy a substantial number of tariff items between 21 and 25 percent. The most striking feature of this section is the Benelux duties. Unlike those Benelux rates levied in other sections, these manufacturing duties frequently range within the higher intervals of 6 to 20 percent.

In SITC seven (machinery and transport equipment) Danish tariffs are unmistakably the lowest among the eight countries, whereas Italian and French ones again come out as fairly high; 52 of the total of 62 French tariff items fall in the interval 16-30 percent, and no fewer than 25 Italian items reach levels of 31 percent or higher. German and British tariffs are mostly clustered in the range of 11-20 percent, but there are differences between these two tariff structures. Whereas almost half of the British rates fall between 16 and 20 percent, those of West Germany are more heavily concentrated within the interval 11-15 percent. Both countries also levy several high rates of between 26 and 40 percent. The majority of Benelux duties in the machinery and transport sector can be found one interval below that, although some fall in the 16-25 percent range.

Finally, SITC eight (miscellaneous manufactures not elsewhere specified) is not characterized by the usual large disparity between French, Italian and British rates on the one hand and those of Sweden,

Denmark and the Netherlands on the other. In this case, the latter three also rely on tariff protection, in particular for their textiles industries. Most of the Benelux rates fall within the 11-25 percent range, while Danish duties vary from 16 to 25 percent, with the exception of some relatively high ones of 26-30. The West German and British tariff structures in this section are fairly similar, since both countries levy rates between 16 and 25 percent.

Generally, this overview of national tariff schedules confirms the existence of a rift between high- and low-tariff countries that was so often discussed in postwar European trade fora. The difference between the nominal tariff levels imposed by Denmark, Sweden and Benelux and those levied on virtually identical products by France, Italy, West Germany and the United Kingdom formed a major issue in all campaigns and plans for tariff reductions after 1947. The assumption was that in the absence of other trade impediments, high nominal tariffs were more restrictive to imports than low ones and their protective impact was therefore larger. By the 1960s, however, economists began to challenge this assumption on theoretical as well as empirical grounds. They introduced effective rates of protection as a more adequate measure for assessing the restrictive impact of tariffs.

The problem is that most assessments of effective tariffs do not relate to levels of protection in the 1950s, nor do they allow for comparisons across European countries. The only way to use the concept for our period is to rely on calculations made by Herbert Grubel and Harry Johnson, which are based on the input-output tables for 1959 of France, Italy, West Germany, Belgium and the Netherlands. Although these are far from ideal, they can be used as additional indicators of trends in tariff protection in the 1950s. After all, West European tariffs remained fairly stable between the Torquay round of 1950-1951 and the first tariff changes for the Common Market's tariff alignment in 1960. Even the GATT round of 1956 did not result in major modifications.[24]

The Grubel-Johnson estimates suggest that in France, Italy and Belgium the simple unweighted averages of their effective rates were higher than the nominal ones, whereas this was the opposite in the Netherlands and Germany. The figures in table 3.4 indicate that in some Dutch and German sectors the nominal tariff levels did not keep pace with the value added contents of the products. Presuming that these rates are indeed correct, they suggest that the usual practice of "cascading" tariff rates to protect end products did not outbalance the overall cost-increasing effects of tariffs on intermediate products. This is expressed

TABLE 3.4

Simple Average Nominal and Effective Tariff Rates in EEC Countries, 1959

	Nominal rate	Effective rate
France	30.4	36.4
Italy	18.2	27.4
Belgium	14.0	17.7
West Germany	7.3	1.9
Netherlands	6.3	4.7

Source: H. Grubel and H. Johnson, "Nominal Rates, Indirect Taxes and Effective Rates of Protection: The Common Market Countries, 1959," *The Economic Journal* (1967): 761-76.

in the negative rates of effective protection calculated by Grubel and Johnson for Dutch and German manufacturing sectors.[25] What is also striking is the difference between Dutch and Belgian levels of effective protection. Not only did the Dutch have far more negative rates per sector but also their positive rates were usually within the range of 4 to 17 percent, whereas the Belgian ones frequently reached levels between 15 and 30 percent. Apart from these negative tariff rates, the results of this study are not all that different from a comparison of nominal levels. If one is mainly interested in relative rather than absolute tariffs, it appears valid—as several experts have argued—that nominal rates are good indicators of effective rates (see table 3.4).[26] Grubel and Johnson's nominal and effective duties both point at high protection levels in France and Italy, low levels in the Netherlands and Germany and average ones in Belgium. In the country ranking for nominal and effective levels, the only difference occurs in the Dutch and German positions. The latter rank lower than the former, if effective tariffs are used. This may well be the impact of Germany's unilateral and temporary reductions of 1956 and 1957, which give its figures a downward bias.

Now that we have examined the tariff structure of several European countries, it is time to look at some other qualitative data assessing the effects of the gradual return to tariff protection in Western Europe. This will be done by analyzing the tariff inquiries that the OEEC undertook in the 1950s, after heavy pressure from its low-tariff members.

THE OEEC'S TARIFF INQUIRIES

The Organization for European Economic Cooperation held two investigations, one in 1950 and one in 1955. In both cases, it ruled that all

TABLE 3.5

Distribution of Tariff Complaints by SITC Section, 1950

SITC Section	Number of complaints
6 manufactured goods classified chiefly by materials	71
5 chemicals	61
0 food and live animals	39
7 machinery and transport equipment	20
8 miscellaneous manufactured articles	17
2 inedible crude materials, except fuels	14
4 animal and vegetable oils and fats	5
3 mineral fuels, lubricants and related materials	1
1 beverages and tobacco	0
9 commodities and transactions not classified according to kind	0
Total	228

Source: See chap. 3, note 27 and 28.

those members filing complaints should be able to show that high tariffs (rather than other factors such as lack of competitiveness, supply bottlenecks, transport costs, etc.) had caused a drastic drop in their exports and had limited their benefits from the Trade Liberalization Scheme. The countries "accused" would have the right to refute this evidence before the results would be summarized in a final report to the Council.[27]

At the first inquiry of 1950, which was made before the Germans presented their new tariff schedule, the OEEC received 493 complaints, 297 of which were furnished with exports data. Its final report to the Council avoided a close scrutiny of these cases, but the archives provide additional data that can be used for a more detailed analysis.[28] To allow for a comparison, the 297 complaints have been reclassified according to the five digits of the UN's revised SITC of 1960. There are no large differences between the general distribution of tariff complaints by countries accused and the distribution by complaining countries. France ranks in first position for complaints made by the Netherlands, Denmark and Sweden; Italy is in second position, or for Belgium/Luxembourg, in first.

The breakdown of tariff complaints into SITC sections provides more interesting results (see table 3.5). This breakdown shows a large concentration of complaints within sections five and six (chemicals and manufactured goods classified by materials) and a much smaller number within sections zero, seven, eight, and two (respectively food, machinery and transport equipment, miscellaneous manufactures and inedible

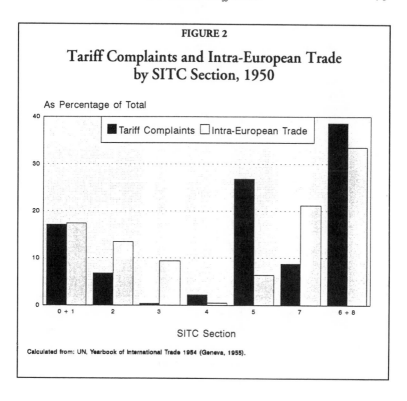

FIGURE 2

Tariff Complaints and Intra-European Trade by SITC Section, 1950

As Percentage of Total

■ Tariff Complaints □ Intra-European Trade

SITC Section

Calculated from: UN, Yearbook of International Trade 1954 (Geneva, 1955).

crude materials). Negligible or absent are tariff complaints within sections four, three, one and nine. Since each section varied quite substantially in its importance to trade, a more accurate indicator is the degree to which complaints by section were over-represented compared to their weight in intra-European trade.[29] The results of this exercise are presented in figure 2.

Figure 2 confirms the dominance of complaints in the chemical sector, which are about four times as high as one could reasonably expect from the sector's weight in intra-European trade. The other overconcentration of complaints occurs in the sections six and eight. (It seems fair not to attach any value to the overrepresentation of section four, because this received five tariff complaints only.) We should now take a closer look at the products within these sections to see whether one product group or export market stands out as a notorious source of tariff complaints.[30]

Starting with the complaints in the chemicals sector, we can immediately single out the Netherlands and Denmark as those responsible for the disproportionately large number of cases in SITC section five. Their complaints were mainly directed against France and Italy, although several of the Danish cases also involved Benelux. Within chemicals, Danish problems largely concerned dyestuffs, paints and varnishes, pharmaceuticals and plastics. The Dutch cases, by contrast, focused on organic and inorganic chemicals (SITC numbers 512-514). Complaints referring to sections six and eight were more evenly divided over complainants and commodity groups. Still, there was a noticeably larger amount in division 68, nonferrous metals. Most of these cases were put forward by Belgium and Luxembourg and were directed against Italy, France and the United Kingdom.

Before we formulate any hypotheses on the nature of the tariff problem, it is worth comparing these findings with those from OEEC's second inquiry of 1955, in which West Germany participated fully. Again, the OEEC asked its members whether the existing tariff disparity in Europe hampered their efforts to remove quantitative restrictions, and again it asked for clear evidence of damage.[31] Unlike the previous examination, however, the complainants no longer specified their complaints by country "accused." Therefore, we can only present a distribution of tariff cases by complaining country (see table 3.6). The total number of complaints in 1955 is much smaller than in 1950. It is all the more striking that a different country sample (i.e., with Austria present as a complainant and West Germany fully represented as a country accused) shows results that are similar to those from the inquiry of 1950 (see tables 3.5 and 3.7). As in the first inquiry, tariff cases in SITC five and six and eight are heavily overrepresented in relation to their weight in international trade and once again, Danish and Dutch complaints about chemicals dominate. The only clear difference between the results of both inquiries is that complaints within sections six and eight are more overrepresented in 1955. This is due mainly to a larger number of cases in section six (45 percent of total complaints in 1955, compared to 31 percent in 1950). Unlike in 1950, complaints in division 68 (nonferrous metals) hardly played a role. Instead, many cases concerned paper and paperboard (division 64) and textile yarn and fabrics (division 65).

How should we explain the dominance of chemicals within the inquiry? It seems there is a combination of factors at work here. First, France and Italy levied comparatively high tariffs on most chemical products, whereas the United Kingdom and West Germany both

TABLE 3.6

Distribution of Tariff Complaints by Country Complaining, 1955

Complainant	Number of complaints
Austria	51
Benelux	27
Sweden	15
Denmark	9
Norway	9
Total	111

Source: See chap. 3, note 31.

applied their highest available tariffs to the chemical sectors. In West Germany, chemicals had the highest share of tariff items of 35 percent (the maximum tariff within the German schedule). These rates had been introduced to allow producers to step their capital investments rapidly by charging high prices on the protected domestic market. This safe domestic basis would enable producers to re-conquer simultaneously (via lower export prices) the foreign markets they had lost to British, Swiss, French and American competitors.[32] In Britain, most chemical products fell under the category of goods that, for strategic reasons, held very high tariffs of between 33.3 and 50 percent. Compare these French, German and British tariffs with those of Benelux, Denmark and Sweden and it is plain that chemicals represent an almost classical case of European tariff disparity.

Second, Denmark and the Netherlands, unless they maintained quantitative import restrictions or were involved in international cartels, could not reserve their markets for domestic producers because their tariff barriers were too low. Furthermore, the size of their markets was too small to benefit from large-scale production and standardization. In the case of plastics, for instance, where high levels of investments in R&D were crucial for developing and maintaining competitive strength, exporting to large markets such as West Germany and France was considered essential to Dutch and Danish producers.[33] Only then could such individual firms undertake the production expansion and investments in technology that could lead to lower cost prices.[34]

Swedish, Norwegian and Austrian producers of paper and paperboard or Belgian and Danish producers of textiles and nonferrous metal

TABLE 3.7

Distribution of Tariff Complaints by
SITC Section, 1955

SITC section	Number of complaints
6 manufactured goods classified chiefly by materials	50
5 chemicals	32
7 machinery and transport equipment	9
8 miscellaneous manufactured articles	8
0 food and live animals	7
2 inedible crude materials, except fuels	5
Total	111

products faced problems similar to those of Danish and Dutch chemical exporters. Competing with large scale foreign producers required mass production and standardization. Mass production required export outlets but high tariffs formed an impediment. In a situation of high demand and economic growth such as existed in the second half of the 1950s, the impact of such barriers could be modest, and this may well explain why the number of tariff complaints was lower in 1955 than in 1950. However, it was in times of surplus capacity, overproduction and economic recession that tariff barriers were likely to hit hardest.[35] Producers knew this only too well and that is why their complaints dominated the tariff inquiry and why their governments began a crusade against tariff disparities. Before examining these attempts, though, it is worth discussing the actions of the accused countries. The case of the chemical industry will illustrate some of their considerations for maintaining high tariffs.

TARIFFS AND QUOTAS: THE CASE OF CHEMICALS

In Britain, the rumors of an OEEC attack on quantitative restrictions had caused a wave of unrest among industrialists in the chemical sector, particularly among dyestuffs manufacturers. Before the war, most fine chemicals and dyestuffs had been protected against imports either under the Safeguarding of Industries Act or under the Dyestuffs Act. These acts had assured the products' duty free import under license, in quantities determined by representatives of the British chemical industries (in effect Imperial Chemicals Industries, ICI) in coordination with the board of trade. Additional imports beyond these quantities were automatically subject to high customs duties of 33.3 or sometimes 50 percent. This protection system had been largely responsible for establishing Britain's fine chemical industry, which in turn had given incentives to many innovative developments in pharmaceuticals. Like all other import legislation, the Dyestuffs Act had been suspended during the war, but by 1946 the Association of British Chemical Manufacturers (ABCM) urged for its reintroduction. Initially, the government did not respond to this pressure and departed from the prewar system by offering France an import quota worth 200,000 pounds sterling. When in 1949 it offered similar quotas to Switzerland and Belgium, however, representatives of the ABCM increased their pressure on the board of trade for a change in policy. Their greatest fear was lack of time to adjust and prepare for a competitive market situation. Once the OEEC's new rule of the nondiscriminatory application of quotas came into force, it seemed there would be no way of stopping what were considered more aggressive German chemical manufacturers from entering the British domestic market. Moreover, the tariff of 33 percent that Britain had negotiated at the GATT round in Geneva could not keep out competitors. Producers still feared that the British market would be flooded by foreign companies facing overproduction.[36] As an intermediate solution, the government agreed to continue its policy of issuing individual licenses only for some types of dyestuffs, until a new tariff legislation had been drafted. It would justify this system to the OEEC authorities on strategic grounds. Although this was hardly an elegant solution, British officials hoped it might persuade the industry to accept tariff protection instead of quotas. And once the industry had accepted the tariff, they would also assist government officials with the cumbersome task of determining new tariff classifications for chemicals.

Yet by the summer of 1950 the board of trade realized that the system of individual licensing linked to a further refusal of new quotas was causing too much friction with Britain's OEEC partners. Already France and the Netherlands threatened with retaliatory measures. By continuing to violate the new OEEC rules, Britain also provoked similar violations of OEEC rules by its partners. This, the board concluded, could irreparably damage Europe's trade and payments system. In future occasions, British industry therefore would have to learn to rely on tariffs rather than quotas.[37]

When German tariff experts decided upon the levels of tariff protection for chemicals, they agreed with the representatives of industry that this sector was severely handicapped by war damage, Allied production limits, lack of capital and dependence on foreign patents. The prospects for a complete recovery were considered very bleak indeed. Germany would probably never regain its leading position among the world's largest chemical producers.[38] In September 1949, industrialists were told that the government would increase under license its chemical imports from the Netherlands and Switzerland. As a result, the industry immediately began insisting on a rapid introduction of the new tariff schedule. Swiss competition on the domestic market, they claimed, would be stronger than ever before because Switzerland's former markets in the Eastern Zone of Germany had been eliminated. Moreover, other main competitors in the United Kingdom and France would flood the market once they had restored their prewar production capacity. This would lead to a price fall on the German market and a lack of capital investments that would merely accentuate domestic producers' relative weakness. By 1952, as Marshall aid would come to an end, the chemical industry would be unable to fulfill its traditional role of foreign currency earner.[39]

Such scenarios of doom clearly influenced Germany's new tariff rates. Many individual sectors within the industry received the status of infant industry, which meant that they could count on tariffs of between 35 and 40 percent.[40] Yet it soon turned out that the chemical sector recovered much more easily and also much faster than anticipated. By 1950, even before the new tariffs came into force, the industry's overall production already equaled that of 1936, and some specific sectors surpassed it. Exports, a major force in the production boom, approached 13 percent of total German exports. Throughout the 1950s (with the exception of 1952), this share would remain more or less constant, thereby keeping pace with the fivefold increase in the value of total German exports.[41] By mid-1953, both the government and the leading representatives of the chemical industry recognized that the competitive situation had changed so drastically in Germany's favor that many high tariffs had become obsolete and could easily be cut. However, rather than opting for unilateral tariff reductions as they had done for some raw materials, they wanted multilateral tariff reductions. These would improve export opportunities without reducing bargaining strength. Indeed, the government promised not to impose any unilateral tariff cuts until the various schemes for tariff reduction under discussion within GATT, the OEEC and the Council of Europe assured that Germany obtained reciprocal tariff concessions.[42]

France was another major target for complaints from chemicals exporters. Danish manufacturers traditionally exported small quantities of organic compounds under a quota issued by a *Comité des Matières Colorantes*. This body of civil servants and experts of industry adopted similar criteria for determining imports as did British dyestuffs manufacturers under the Dyestuffs Act. By the end of 1948 and into early 1949, once chemical duties were reintroduced, Danish exports faced tariffs ranging from 25 to 30 percent. Moreover, by 1950, France further tightened its grip on chemical imports. In March, the government installed another technical committee of industrialists from the pharmaceutical industry to control foreign supplies. Similar bodies in other sectors soon followed when the OEEC decided upon new liberalization requirements. The result was the almost complete disappearance of Danish paints on the French market and a drastic fall in French imports of Danish pharmaceuticals and different types of organic compounds. That this was not due to Danish producers' uncompetitiveness can be concluded from the steady growth of their chemical exports in hard currency markets such as the United States and Switzerland.[43]

These practices within the European chemical industries illustrate that there existed a direct link between the reintroduction of tariff protection and the start of the OEEC's Trade Liberalization Program. They also indicate that the transition from quotas to tariffs could cause major shocks to individual producers and exporters. It did not necessarily mean an immediate improvement in their export opportunities. Sometimes they saw entire export markets disappear because tariffs reappeared. Admittedly, governments could only increase duties which they had not consolidated during the GATT rounds in Geneva and Annecy. Usually, though, they had been careful enough to secure their freedom to raise tariffs on sensitive items. Moreover, tariff consolidations under GATT lasted contractually only three years. And if that offered still not enough flexibility, governments could and did also change their nomenclatures in such a way as to create new, frequently discriminatory tariff barriers. Countries such as the Netherlands, Denmark and Sweden, traditionally reliant upon quotas solely for protection and trade bargaining, formed the exception. By 1951, they had bound more than 80 percent of their tariffs under GATT. As we shall see below, they found themselves in a weak negotiating position, since quotas eventually had to be abandoned under the postwar trade rules of the OEEC and GATT. Tariffs, meanwhile, had made a full return as accepted commercial policy instruments.

The OEEC's inquiry of 1950 had no direct impact on the tariff policies of member states "on trial" for applying high or prohibitive rates. If anything, these states became more belligerent toward members' complaining. France, the United Kingdom and Italy vetoed changes in the Liberalization Code and any other concrete measures by the Organization to solve the tariff dispute. After turbulent debates, the complaining countries managed to extract just one concession. The Council would review its decision to move toward the 75 percent target if the GATT conference in Torquay failed to make "satisfactory progress" in reducing high tariffs.[44] This was a Pyrrhic victory, since the opponents of drastic tariff cuts held an even stronger position within GATT, where they had developing nations on their side. Nonetheless, the low-tariff countries continued pushing schemes for tariff alignments. One such plan, launched within the OEEC but inspired by the Schuman Plan, was a Dutch initiative for sectoral integration known as the Stikker Plan.

THE STIKKER PLAN

The Dutch had anticipated a disappointing outcome to the OEEC inquiry and had therefore also examined other ways to avoid the unconditional removal of quota barriers. The appointment of their own minister of foreign affairs, Dirk Stikker, as the OEEC's Political Conciliator offered a different and perhaps more successful route for action. But what form should such action take? One tentative suggestion by the ministry of economic affairs involved a scheme for preferential European tariff reductions in several predetermined stages.[45] Another proposal started with a plea for "equalizing competitive conditions" and ended in a litany of complaints about the OEEC's trade liberalization method. By June, the Dutch ministry of foreign affairs had cast all these tariff grievances in a more positive mold by proposing a sectoral attack on trade barriers. The "Stikker Plan of Action" was born only days after Schuman had announced his plan for pooling the French and German coal and steel sectors.[46]

The new plan was said to aim at creating a strong and balanced European internal market by gradually removing tariffs, quotas and other trade impediments in all those sectors that would benefit from a gradual transition to free intra-European trade. It would start with "the basic industries, agriculture and those processing industries which can offer a particular contribution, by their specialization, to the viability of Europe and whose products are important for international trade, in Europe as well as inter-continentally."[47] An integration fund would provide extra financial means to modernize individual firms and, where necessary, to reallocate labor made redundant because of productivity increases. Which sectors would be chosen depended on the OEEC's Council of Ministers. It should decide by three-quarters majority rather than by unanimity, as was usual. Undoubtedly, Stikker's visit in April to the ECA in Washington had been a source of inspiration. He subsequently embraced European integration as the panacea for trading problems, not in the least because he felt that France, Italy and Britain would surely think twice before openly rejecting a European initiative that received official American support. This tactic, though, only briefly made an impact. Stikker's sudden conversion into a prophet of European integration left most officials surprised, if not skeptical. Only two months earlier, Dutch ministers had threatened to raise their tariff walls and to adopt an "active trade policy" of imposing quota barriers in retaliation for high tariffs.[48] They had even threatened to block the OEEC's Trade Liberalization Program within the Council. It is no surprise, therefore, that Stikker's arguments for a sectoral approach to economic integration appeared rather unconvincing. Moreover, his real concern, the OEEC's Liberalization Scheme, still surfaced in the last version of his plan. This stated that European integration "seems impossible to realise . . . by uniformly raising the liberalisation percentage."[49] The American State Department expressed appreciation for Stikker's devotion to European integration but secretly doubted his motivations. Could his plan really provide the first step toward a European market, as he claimed? Or would it simply give the Europeans yet another excuse for postponing further quota relaxation?[50] One thing was clear: if they really wanted to remove impediments to intra-European trade, there would be few sectors upon which members would agree. More likely, many governments would settle for an incomplete and partial attack on trade restrictions in one or more sectors, thereby allowing vested protectionist interests to survive very easily. In that case, sectoral integration might even encourage private producers to regulate European markets through international cartel agreements.

While the Americans stayed in the background after Stikker's announcement, Italy and France took little time to respond. Still in June, the Italian minister for Marshall Plan affairs, Giuseppe Pella, presented an alternative plan for economic integration. Instead of aiming at the complete elimination of all obstacles to intra-European trade, he envisaged tariff reductions through multilateral negotiations within GATT among OEEC member states. In contrast to normal GATT procedures, these European countries would consolidate the outcome of negotiations among themselves for ten years, conditional upon two further measures. The first measure was a further automatic reduction of their mutual tariffs, for example by 15 percent in three stages of each three years. The second measure entailed reopening negotiations among OEEC members for additional preferential tariff cuts. [51] This was a polite but firm way of indicating that Italy considered tariffs legitimate, even essential measures of protection against more competitive countries. Italy might suggest moderate tariff reductions on a *quid pro quo* basis, but it rejected any action to reduce tariff disparities. In July 1950, three days before a meeting of the OEEC's Ministerial Council, the French government presented a third plan. It proposed establishing a European Investment Bank financed partly by Marshall funds, private capital and government subscriptions as well as by a loan from the International Bank for Reconstruction and Development (IBRD). The Bank could help carry out the most capital-intensive investments needed to improve Europe's industrial competitiveness toward third countries in general and the United States in particular. [52] To indicate their views on the Stikker Plan, French officials did not even mention tariffs in their proposal. Their priorities lay with transforming French firms into modern, internationally competitive and viable units, and not with dismantling the protective barriers that had allowed these firms to survive.

At the Council Meeting, all three plans were passed on to a special Working Party No. 6 for further study, while technical experts began examining which sectors would be most suitable for economic integration. Already at that stage, the Dutch proposal rapidly lost ground. West Germany, for one, felt that its new tariff schedule had to cushion the impact of quota relaxations on those domestic industries whose productive capacity still lagged behind that of their European competitors. Therefore, it did not yet consider joining tariff cuts. [53] In Britain, the cabinet committee on European economic cooperation unanimously agreed that Stikker's concealed attempt to impede the elimination of quotas could not be tolerated. The government had already publicly committed itself to removing most quota restrictions and to securing adequate tariff protection. [54] A subsequent study by the board of trade concluded that Pella's plan would be a lesser evil because it allowed Britain to maintain "a reasonable level of protectionism for the general run of . . . industries."[55] British representatives to the Working Party thus received instructions to reject any such dangerous plans for economic integration or preferential tariff reductions. They played along with the Working Party's sectoral studies without committing themselves to anything concerning the Stikker, Pella or Petsche Plans.[56]

This tactic proved successful. As long as the national experts were studying the sectors that were of interest to each of the member states, their governments would not have to voice openly their misapprehension of the scheme. The Dutch realized this too and, by the end of October 1950, decided to throw all their weight behind a compromise between their own plan and the Pella and Petsche initiatives. Before this could happen, though the French government gave the discussions an unexpected turn. It linked its original proposal for a European Investment Bank to a more solid and above all more convincing attempt at economic integration. Convincing, that was, in the eyes of the American administration, which at this precise time considered easing France's defense burden by increasing its dollar aid to that country. In November 1950, the French representatives to the OEEC swung around by openly advocating preferential European tariff reductions. They even proposed a scheme for five annual tariff cuts of 10 percent each, covering 80 percent of total intra-European trade. Thus, a maximum of 20 percent of intra-European trade could be exempted from such cuts. To reduce the existing tariff disparity, member states should respect "floor levels" of between 5 and 10 percent, below which they would not cut their tariffs. In addition, they should unilaterally bring down most of their high tariffs to "ceiling levels" of 35 to 45 percent.[57] This scheme eventually gave the final blow to the Stikker plan because it met active opposition from Italy and the United States.

The Italian government refused to consider anything but very modest automatic tariff cuts. Any further reductions, it claimed, should be negotiated within GATT. For their part, the Americans saw with growing anxiety how this French plan for a preferential European tariff zone violated GATT's nondiscrimination principle. It also failed to meet the requirements for customs unions or free trade areas. Furthermore, they knew that while the Dutch continued pushing for more drastic tariff cuts than those suggested by France, they, too, would gladly accept a preferential tariff zone in Europe. By the end of 1950, not even the most flexible officials in the U.S. Administration would consider confronting

Congress with a discriminatory European trading zone that lacked any supranational dimensions and that violated GATT's norms and regulations.[58] When France and the Netherlands received this message, they abandoned the discussions on tariff schemes and allowed Working Party No. 6 to run aground.

THE LOW-TARIFF CLUB

Despite the failure of the Stikker Plan, the low-tariff states in Europe continued pressing their case. Since their balance of payments situations remained precarious and their industries experienced growing competition at home and abroad, reducing tariff disparities and obtaining reciprocal export opportunities remained high on their policy agenda for the OEEC. A breakdown of the customs duties imposed on their main export products illustrates the scale of their demands. Table 3.8 compares the customs duties that low-tariff states levied (Group I) with the duties they encountered in their main European export markets, West Germany, the United Kingdom, France and Italy (Group II). The selection of export products has been made by calculating from the UN trade statistics all those export products (subdivided up to five SITC digits) each of which accounted for more than 1.5 percent of the total exports of at least one low-tariff country.

The disparity in tariff levels within agriculture (SITC zero) is quite striking. Denmark, Sweden and to a lesser degree also the Benelux countries levied tariffs that were far below those imposed in France, West Germany and Italy. Norway breaks the pattern of these countries in Group I by levying one very high tariff (of 53 percent) on cream and another of almost 22 percent on fresh vegetables. In Group II, British agricultural tariffs were clearly below the average, even compared to Benelux tariffs.

Not surprisingly, Danish exporters were likely to suffer most from high agricultural tariffs. Almost 70 percent of their export products in 1952 was concentrated in SITC zero, and of that more than 52 percent consisted of meat, dairy products and eggs (SITC numbers 01 and 02). The Netherlands (whose agricultural exports were 30 percent of its total exports) faced similar problems for its supplies of dairy products, meat and fresh vegetables. For Norway, exports of fish and fish meal (SITC number 03) made up 18 percent of its total exports. These were hampered by rates of between 9 and 34 percent. It is also worth considering here that state trade, a frequently used device to avoid quota liberalization

TABLE 3.8

Tariffs on Main Exports of Low-Tariff Countries, 1951

SITC no.	Group I				Group II			
	Benelux	Denmark	Norway	Sweden	France	FRG	Italy	UK
0								
012-01	12.0	0.0	-	3.0	37.0	26.0	33.0	5.0
013-02	28.0	7.0	3.0	6.0	30.0	23.0	25.0	9.0
022-01	17.0	-	-	3.0	15.0	33.0	19.0	7.0
022-02	17.0	-	53.0	1.0	19.0	20.0	19.0	9.0
023	15.0	-	-	-	25.0	25.0	30.0	5.0
025-01	3.0	0.0	4.0	1.0	18.0	15.0	11.0	7.0
025-02	3.0	0.0	6.0	-	18.0	7.0	8.0	10.0
031	3.0	1.3	-	2.7	19.0	13.0	16.7	9.3
032	24.0	3.5	10.5	8.5	25.5	28.5	34.0	9.3
054	6.0	1.3	21.7	8.8	17.8	14.8	11.0	9.0
061-02	22.0	9.0	18.0	8.0	110.0	45.0	5.0	-
2								
251	0.0	0.0	-	0.0	16.4	5.4	4.8	4.0
262	0.2	0.0	2.8	0.0	0.5	0.6	2.1	4.4
262-01	0.0	0.0	-	0.0	0.0	0.0	9.0	5.0
272	2.5	0.2	0.0	0.0	4.5	2.3	2.2	7.8
281-01	0.0	0.0	0.0	0.0	0.0	0.0	0.0	0.0
292-06	0.0	10.9	9.0	0.7	23.0	17.0	11.0	22.0
3								
311-01	0.0	0.0	-	0.0	2.0	5.0	0.0	10.0
313-03	0.0	0.0	-	0.0	3.0	-	5.0	-
5								
541	6.4	0.0	0.6	1.6	17.2	17.6	22.6	20.4
561	0.0	0.0	-	0.8	4.3	15.5	8.0	12.3
6								
641	13.8	4.2	5.7	3.7	22.0	17.5	26.3	18.3
651	6.3	2.5	7.0	4.5	17.1	11.5	21.9	15.3
652	15.0	4.5	16.0	5.0	22.0	19.5	21.5	21.0
657	23.0	10.0	33.7	8.9	35.0	26.5	31.3	19.0
661-02	3.0	0.0	31.0	4.0	10.0	5.0	25.0	8.0
664	10.2	4.8	20.1	9.6	20.1	20.3	32.2	15.6
664-03	8.0	6.0	23.0	19.0	20.0	25.0	32.0	15.0
672-02	0.0	25.0	0.0	0.0	14.0	2.0	4.0	0.0
681	4.2	0.8	3.4	3.8	16.5	16.2	22.7	21.2
681-04	3.0	0.0	-	5.0	17.0	16.0	24.0	27.0
681-05	4.0	0.0	-	6.0	17.0	21.0	23.0	29.0
682	3.0	0.5	1.0	2.0	8.0	6.0	10.5	10.0
684	3.0	2.5	-	2.5	21.0	14.5	36.0	12.5
687-01	3.0	0.0	-	0.0	0.0	0.0	2.0	10.0
699	12.3	2.8	9.4	5.4	21.1	14.3	29.4	20.7
699-12	5.0	1.0	19.0	4.0	18.0	15.0	26.0	16.0
7								
716	8.1	3.9	15.4	9.5	18.1	11.4	27.8	20.2
716-14	6.0	1.0	20.0	10.0	27.0	20.0	27.0	20.0
721	11.7	6.2	12.7	7.8	20.8	12.1	31.1	17.8
731	11.6	4.6	22.0	9.5	16.9	13.9	22.9	29.6
735	1.7	0.0	7.0	3.0	5.0	0.5	10.7	10.0
735-02	0.0	0.0	-	0.0	0.0	0.0	11.0	10.0
8								
841	22.3	10.8	18.8	9.1	24.0	23.1	25.5	23.2
842	13.0	3.0	7.5	10.5	19.3	18.3	23.7	16.3
9								
921	5.0	0.0	15.0	4.5	15.0	5.0	7.5	2.5

0 = food and foodstuffs. 2 = crude materials. 3 = minerals, fuels, lubricants. 5 = chemicals. 6 = manufactures of one main material. 7 = machinery and transport equipment. 8 = miscellaneous manufactures. 9 = manufactures not elsewhere specialized

Calculated from: UN, *International Trade Statistics, 1951*, and Weighted incidences of customs tariffs by sectors. 14 July 1953. PRO. BT 11/4901.

measures within agriculture, was less common in low-tariff countries than in France, the United Kingdom, West Germany or the OEEC as a whole.[59] By the end of 1953, more than 9 percent of total intra-OEEC trade went through governmental channels. The low-tariff countries therefore argued that they were extra handicapped by the OEEC's lack of attention for trade impediments other than quotas on private imports.

In section two (crude materials) most states in Group I had either zero or very low rates, whereas those rates levied in Group II were also below average. Yet there were two important exceptions. First, tariffs on flower bulbs, a Dutch export product, varied between 11 and 23 percent. Second, France imposed tariffs on pulp and waste paper (SITC 251) of more than 16 percent on average. Norway and Sweden, whose exports in this sector amounted to some 14 and 19 percent respectively of their total exports, were hit hardest by these duties.

Although the export interests of the low-tariff countries in chemicals (section five) were not particularly large if expressed as shares of total exports, we have already seen that the tariff disparity within this dynamic and fast-growing sector aroused much concern.[60] The Netherlands and Denmark, in particular, were in the process of expanding their relatively young chemical and pharmaceutical industries. As long as their own producers had difficulties holding their own in the domestic market and faced high tariff walls in the British, French, German and Italian markets, they insisted on maintaining quota protection.

Like the agricultural sector, manufacturing goods classified by materials (section six) contained many separate product groups for which tariff disparities between Groups I and II were prominent. Again, however, it should be noted that the Norwegian tariffs formed the exception because these were comparatively high in textiles. Benelux also had some fairly high rates within this sector. One may assume that Sweden and Norway would gain substantially from tariff cuts for paper, paper board and newsprint (SITC 641), in which more than 8 and 10 percent of their respective exports were concentrated. The Norwegians could also expect large benefits from tariff cuts for ferro-alloys and aluminum, of which the share in total Norwegian exports exceeded 10 percent. French, German, Italian and British duties on these products ranged between 12.5 and 36 percent.

Within section seven (machinery and transport equipment), the Netherlands, Sweden, Denmark and the BLEU held substantial export interests in electrical machinery and appliances (SITC 721), a fast growing sector that Italy, the United Kingdom and France protected by tariffs of between 17 and 31 percent. Norway, however, whose export interests within section seven were heavily concentrated in ships and boats (SITC 735), seemed better placed within the group of "high-tariff" countries. Its tariffs ranged between 7 and 22 percent, to protect Norwegian machinery industries from their main competitors in Sweden and West Germany. The group of other machinery (SITC 716), a major export sector in Sweden and Denmark, shows a large difference in rates imposed by the Benelux countries, Sweden and Denmark on the one hand and France, Italy and the United Kingdom on the other.

The last group of main export products worth examining in some detail is that of miscellaneous commodities (section eight). Here the division between high- and low-tariff states is clearly not applicable since all countries except Sweden levied high tariffs. For Benelux in particular, tariff protection in textiles represented a blemish on their carefully cultivated free trade image. These tariffs served partly as shelter for Belgian industries, which contributed more than 4 percent of Belgium's total exports and which struggled to meet international competition. Danish textile producers, a small but politically vocal pressure group, also received tariff protection above standard levels in Denmark.

This breakdown of tariff barriers levied on low-tariff states' major export products confirms once more that some sectors and therefore some economies were more likely be damaged by high tariffs than others. It also shows that the professed low-tariff countries sometimes also imposed high tariffs to protect specific domestic industries. As a rule, however, these small states were too dependent on cheap imports to resort to general tariff increases. To them, a more balanced distribution of the gains and losses from the Trade Liberalization Program required reductions in high tariff barriers. With this in mind, they created a joint lobby that soon acquired fame as the Low-Tariff Club.

Although the club of low-tariff states had joined forces on and off since 1949, the starting point of their systematic, concerted action was early 1952, shortly after the United Kingdom reintroduced quotas after a run on the pound sterling. It was then that the secretary-general of the OEEC, Robert Marjolin, reported that the Organization could no longer ignore the disparity in European tariffs because "some small countries" deliberately maintained quotas in retaliation for high tariffs imposed against their exports.[61] Despite opposition from France and Britain, the Council subsequently instructed the OEEC's Steering Board for Trade, a specialized OEEC body, to study the matter.[62]

The Steering Board would examine two aspects of the tariff issue: first, to what extent trade liberalization during the previous two years had been accompanied by rises in tariffs, and second, to what extent new tariff rates impeded further progress in quota liberalization.[63] It took almost a year before the Board produced a number of ambiguous and vague conclusions.[64] The report to the Council stated that tariff cuts seemed "indispensable" to the advancement of the Trade Liberalization Scheme. However, to pacify the Italian, British and French delegations, it was quick to add that:

> The Steering Board for Trade does not mean by this that the existence of customs duties is incompatible with the idea of a European market, the reason for the establishment of a customs tariff not being purely commercial but financial, economic and social. It is the existence of high customs duties on certain commodities, and great disparities between the tariffs of Member countries that would render a common market less effective.[65]

Although the report stated that GATT should remain the appropriate forum for tariff negotiations, it also suggested that OEEC countries should first draft a so-called commodity, or common, list consisting of products with high tariffs and then examine ways of reducing these rates. Despite their disappointment about the report, the low-tariff states at least secured the Council's official recognition of a link between tariff disparities and the Trade Liberalization Program.[66] This was crucial because it allowed them the chance to make further quota elimination conditional upon progress in the field of tariffs. In addition, they could now launch their own plans for tariff cuts within the OEEC. Before examining such initiatives, though, we must turn to a major new policy change that Britain had adopted meanwhile. Its so-called Collective Approach had a large impact on the OEEC's tariff debate.

THE COLLECTIVE APPROACH

In December 1952, shortly after the Commonwealth Economic Conference, the British government announced a plan for sterling convertibility.[67] This plan, promoted as a Collective Approach to Freer Trade and Convertibility, aimed at creating a worldwide system of multilateral trade and payments by a joint move toward convertibility in Britain, the sterling area, and possibly a nucleus of European countries. A precondition was that the Americans supported this move by backing sterling reserves and by adopting a "good creditor policy" that also involved cutting its most restrictive tariffs.[68] Once this one-world setting was established, the regional, discriminatory trade and payments system of the EPU and OEEC would cease to exist, and a rewritten, strengthened GATT would guarantee nondiscrimination.

A release from GATT's no-new-preference rule (see chapter 1) was considered an essential part of the Collective Approach. Sterling convertibility would only be meaningful if Britain removed its quantitative restrictions to trade, including its restrictions toward the dollar area. However, if quotas had to be abandoned, tariffs would become the main instruments of protection; it was here, the British argued, that their problems started. The Ottawa agreements of 1932 committed their country to guarantee duty-free or preferential tariff treatment on a wide range of imports from Commonwealth countries. In return, it received guaranteed preferential treatment for a number of important export products to Commonwealth markets. As a contracting party to GATT, however, Britain was also committed to observe the ban on rises in preferential margins. This meant that if a British government wanted to increase the tariff on a commodity on which rested a contractual Commonwealth obligation to observe duty free entry (or a preferential tariff margin), it had only two options. The first one was to impose a tariff rate on the Commonwealth good that used to be imported duty free (or, if it concerned a preferential tariff, to increase that preferential tariff by the same extent as the "normal" tariff increase). The second option was simply to accept the automatic increase in the margin of preference that this entailed. Either option meant that Britain would violate a contractual obligation; in the first case, it would break its contractual obligations with the Commonwealth country in question, and in the second case it would violate GATT's no-new-preference rule. In the eyes of the British government, the combined impact of both international agreements severely and unjustly restricted its freedom in tariff policy matters and, by implication, its scope for removing quotas. It was therefore determined to release itself from the no-new-preference rule.

An announcement to this effect had a profound impact on OEEC members. Until the end of 1952, most European governments had been left in the dark on the details of Britain's convertibility plans, and they merely had been able to speculate on the if, how and when of such an operation. Some feared that ending the EPU's system of clearing and automatic credits could have a disastrous impact on intra-European trade liberalization. For, once sterling was made convertible, the British would probably be forced to reimpose new quantitative restrictions to prevent Europeans from hoarding sterling for conversion into dollars. Quotas would thus be re-erected, bilateralism would return and European trade and employment would plunge into a downward spiral.[69] Furthermore, even if its quotas returned only temporarily, what else could British insistence on more tariff freedom imply but a wish for higher duties?

The French took the lead in criticizing the British plans by pointing at their negative consequences for the Trade Liberalization Program. Given that they had dismantled hardly any of their own quotas and had firmly relied on highly protectionist measures, this was more than a little ironic. Still, the stakes were high for France. Sterling dominated its trade and payments transactions with Europe, and the EPU allowed it to run large deficits with the sterling area and with other European members. Liquidating these arrangements would mean that France would lose these easy credit arrangements and that it would have to write off the gold it had already paid to the Union.[70] Italy, too, rejected the plan. Its balance of payments, although not suffering any structural problems, had been severely hit by British and French import restrictions. Since its trade with the EPU countries accounted for more than 65 percent of total Italian trade, it preferred renewing—and possibly strengthening—these payments arrangements.[71]

Belgium and Germany both seemed torn between the financial and the trade consequences of a move toward convertibility. As the Belgian debate of 1952 on the EPU's renewal had shown, banking circles and the treasury pushed toward restoring convertibility of the franc because it would allow Belgium to pay its dollar deficits by using its surplus with European countries. However, a majority in the cabinet decided that Belgian overall interests in maintaining the present trading system in Europe outweighed financial considerations and therefore took sides with the French and Italians.[72] The German government also faced this dilemma. About 60 percent of German exports went to the OEEC countries. For most German industrialists, breaking up the EPU and risking trade stagnation seemed too great a gamble.[73] Others, however, such as cabinet ministers Ludwig Erhard and Franz Blücher, believed that the economy was best served by reducing its dependence on the European market and by expanding toward overseas markets in South America, Africa and the Commonwealth area.[74] They enthusiastically supported the Collective Approach and regularly claimed that the German government would be "just one step behind" the British in going convertible. The government's official stance on convertibility nevertheless remained cautious. This stressed the need for temporarily maintaining the EPU and the Trade Liberalization Program to avoid the collapse of European trading.[75]

For the low-tariff countries, commercial interests and hence the EPU's maintenance still overshadowed any other considerations.[76] The Dutch government insisted on averting the risk that convertibility would force debtor countries to reintroduce quotas. They wanted to maintain the Union during an interim period in which rules for debtors would be strengthened and members should gradually approach internal convertibility and expand trade liberalization. This would be their first step toward establishing external convertibility.[77] Danish officials were also highly critical of the British plan, since it could seriously damage the larger part of their exports. They claimed that further progress toward freer trade and currencies depended on British and French willingness to remove quotas and eliminate high tariffs. By 1953, they even hinted that a sudden move toward convertibility might well force Denmark into a common market with the Six.[78]

British officials tried to ease suspicion that their government would go it alone but without much success. A memorandum of January 1953 promising European governments "ample time and opportunity" to examine possible changes in the payments system failed to convince the skeptics. Their suspicions seemed to be confirmed just two months later, when the British discussed the issue with the American administration without first consulting the Europeans.[79] France and Italy reacted by threatening with reprisals if Britain failed to relax quotas and expand imports in the near future. They subsequently received support from the OEEC's Steering Board for Trade, which singled out Britain as the key country determining the pace of liberalization in Europe.[80]

Yet already by mid-March, British plans for a rapid return to convertibility with American financial support were shattered. The new American administration under Eisenhower had no intention of facing Congress with the burdens of a convertibility operation that could disrupt the OEEC's Trade Liberalization Program, destroy the EPU and endanger European integration. Nor was prepared it at this stage to table proposals for tariff reductions as part of the "good creditor policy," which the British considered essential to their Collective Approach. The British thus came back empty-handed, consoled only by an American invitation to clarify their complaints on U.S. import policies.[81] To avoid embarrassing questions and further criticism from the Europeans, the British changed tactics after the American "no." While carefully hiding the "secret elements" of the Collective Approach (involving flexible exchange rates, convertibility for nonresident sterling and financial support),[82] their statement to the OEEC's Council at the end of March 1953 was ostensibly European in tone. They promised to cooperate on the convertibility issue and to safeguard intra-European trade liberalization. Moreover, they agreed to renew the EPU for another year, to increase their own liberalization percentage from 44 to 58 percent and to raise their tourist allowance.[83] Foreign secretary Anthony Eden and chancellor Butler later concluded that "the Europeans were so pleased . . . that they did not press us unduly on this delicate subject."[84] However, both ministers underestimated the discontent among members of the Low-Tariff Club.

The OEEC's Secretary-General answered the British statement with the promise of a liberalization offensive that should enable the Organization to regain its momentum and increase the overall liberalization level far beyond the 75 percent target. This "new look" lost some of its vigor because OEEC members refused to accept new targets until France and the United Kingdom had re-liberalized.[85] With convertibility and further quota liberalization still in the air, moreover, the Low-Tariff Club agreed to harden their tariff demands.

EUROPEAN COMMODITY LISTS

We have already discussed one of the Club's OEEC initiatives, the inquiry of 1955 into the impact of high tariffs. Another initiative involved cutting tariffs imposed on commodities of a common list, and there are two reasons for examining this closer.[86] First, it dominated most tariff discussions within the OEEC and GATT during the 1950s. Second, it represented an attempt at tackling not just the tariff problem but also another major obstacle to the OEEC's program, namely lack of reciprocity in countries' liberalization efforts. In theory, the commodity list approach to tariff cuts worked as follows. Members would draw up a list of commodities that were predominantly "European," in the sense that no less than 80 percent of these imported products came from within the OEEC area. They could then cut tariffs on such products in conformity with GATT rules on a most-favored-nation basis without losing much bargaining power to non-European competitors such as the United States or Canada.[87] These competitors might be tempted to join the tariff cuts if they so wished. If successful, the approach could also be introduced in the process of quota removal to promote a larger degree of reciprocity among countries with widely varying trade structures.

No matter how ingenious in theory, the commodity lists had considerable practical drawbacks. For instance, they gave rise to endless discussions on the precise selection criteria and classification systems used for collecting genuinely "European" commodities. It also proved impossible to agree upon the final list if no prior agreement existed on the method and extent of the tariff cuts. Furthermore, there were always some governments complaining that the list failed to provide a balanced picture of reciprocal export interests among OEEC members. It is doubtful whether that was possible, especially since some export products that proved vital to certain states did not meet the criterion of covering 80 percent of intra-European imports.

Yet the main political reason why tariff reductions in the short term did not stand a chance was British opposition. The original British motives for joining the OEEC's exercises in 1952 had been to ease fears that Britain's planned move toward convertibility might be paralleled by an upward revision of its tariffs. On previous occasions, when these exercises had threatened to turn into full-blown plans for preferential European tariff cuts, British delegates had escaped by demanding noncommitting studies of product lists, which had usually ended up in some bottom drawer. In the course of the 1950s, however, when the dismantling of quotas increasingly revealed high tariff barriers, low-tariff states also turned to their other bargaining weapons. They tried to maintain quotas and block the Trade Liberalization Program. It was then that Britain began to grasp the danger of the tariff issue.[88]

By the end of 1954, Denmark threatened to veto the OEEC's move toward 90 percent quota liberalization if the Organization refused to impose binding measures against high tariffs and state trading.[89] The Danish government clearly had not forgotten the painful experience of liberalizing up to 75 percent of its imports, a step that had been taken at high costs to domestic spending and employment. Further liberalization would expose its infant industries to competitors—mostly German— who would undercut domestic prices, take over parts of the Danish market, cause unemployment and damage industrialization efforts. Therefore, it wished to stall the new 90 percent commitment and demanded guarantees for increased export opportunities.[90]

Some safeguards were eventually provided. In January 1955, the Council adopted the 90 percent stage for a trial period of 18 months, but tariffs and state trade found to be restrictive could no longer be excluded from the national quota lists. Any member suffering from a rise in tariff disparities could withdraw liberalization measures beyond 75 percent to compensate for the damage caused to its exports (provided it could substantiate such claims). Such retaliatory measures would be subject to regular review by the OEEC. Members were also bound by decision to prepare for a new worldwide tariff round.[91] Thus, the OEEC found temporary relief from tariff debates while the burden of this issue shifted toward GATT.

The Danish case, but also the plight of the entire Low-Tariff Club, plainly showed that the Trade Liberalization Program had reached its limits. Ultimately, after the termination of the EPU agreement, GATT would have to take over responsibility for simultaneously removing all trade barriers: quotas, tariffs, state trading and subsidies. Yet the problem remained that several European countries held grave doubts about GATT's competencies, if only because the organization's adequate functioning depended so heavily on the economic policies of its two major sponsors, the United States and Britain. The Benelux states even concluded that effective, long-term commercial and economic arrangements could only be found in smaller, supranational frameworks of a more binding nature. When, one year later, they relaunched the plan for a common market of the six ECSC members, the British were finally forced to embrace a new European policy. Tariff cuts, they now argued, provided the sole remedy to avoid the creation of an economic bloc in Europe. Commodity lists, partial free trade areas and mutual preference systems suddenly all received serious cabinet scrutiny. As we shall see in chapter 5, the eventual outcome of Britain's u-turn was Plan G, a proposal for an industrial free trade area in OEEC Europe. These initiatives did not emerge, however, until European tariff initiatives within GATT were also exhausted.

FOUR

European Tariff Plans in GATT

In the previous chapter we examined several early postwar initiatives for tariff reductions among the European states within the OEEC. These efforts provided only one perspective on the drive toward preferential tariff reductions and customs unions. Even though the first attempts had been made within the ECUSG and the OEEC, it was certainly not obvious at the time that such cuts would automatically take place on an exclusively European basis. After all, the first postwar tariff reductions took place within GATT. That was the worldwide agreement specifically designed to organize tariff rounds and to deal with tariff disputes. It was also the instrument with which the United States hoped to achieve ultimately a global system of multilateral trading under a set of fixed rules. And more important still from the European angle, GATT was the only framework in which European states could challenge American protectionism and bargain for cuts in U.S. customs duties.

Soon after 1945, expanding sales into the American market became a major target for European exporters. West Germany and the United Kingdom in particular were keen to increase their export shares in consumer durables and capital goods to that vast overseas market. These states had products that could compete directly with American domestic goods and they could expect valuable dollar gains from cuts in U.S. tariffs. Their tariff policies therefore focused on obtaining favorable concessions from the United States during successive GATT rounds. On the same grounds, they also resisted the early attempts by the Benelux states, Denmark and Sweden to present the tariff disparity issue as an exclusively European problem that required European solutions. If high tariffs were to be reduced, they argued, this required a major American contribution in return. To this end, several schemes for European tariff reductions were launched within GATT. It is to that setting that we will therefore turn.

GATT'S NEGOTIATING PRINCIPLES

The 23 states that had signed GATT in November 1947 had accepted a negotiating framework with rules and provisions quite different from the GATT we know now.[1] Surprising as this may seem, the "old" GATT of the 1940s and 1950s could not compel countries to engage in tariff conferences. Such an obligation had been scrapped from the draft ITO text because of opposition by the less developed countries. The same happened to a British proposal, pushed during the Anglo-American talks in 1944, for multilateral, linear tariff reductions of a fixed percentage. This never reached the Suggested Charter for the ITO because the American government thought it would raise problems with Congress. The eventual rules stipulated that trade negotiations be conducted "on a reciprocal and mutually advantageous basis."

Reciprocity was in fact a key element of tariff bargaining in GATT, and not only because Congress demanded this.[2] One argument for reciprocity is that it enables countries to balance their mutual, potential gains from tariff cuts, whether these be defined in terms of trade values, monetary flows or domestic employment. For instance, for each increase in imports there may be an equivalent increase in exports, and for each fall in employment in the domestic-oriented industry there may be an increase in employment in the export-oriented industry. Linked to this is the political consideration that reciprocal concessions will more easily receive political endorsement from domestic interest groups.[3]

Even though reciprocity was considered a key principle, the General Agreement's articles were deliberately and sufficiently vague to leave the interpretation of what could be considered reciprocal or equivalent to the discretion of each country individually. The only indication of meaning offered was the principle that binding a low duty was normally accepted as equivalent to reducing a high one. This principle would accommodate the needs of low-tariff countries, which had very small negotiating margins and would be in relatively weak bargaining positions in relation to high-tariff countries. In practice, however, most states cherished their tariff weapons far too much to comply with a nonformalized guideline that contested deep-seated commercial practices of tough tariff bargaining and that neither the GATT nor the U.S. nor any of the low-tariff countries could enforce.[4]

The first six tariff rounds that took place between 1947 and 1962 were characterized by the so-called "bilateral-multilateral" method of tariff negotiating.[5] The first stage, when the principal suppliers of a commodity requested tariff reductions from their main importing partners, was essentially a bilateral affair involving long and cumbersome item-by-item negotiations. Only the last stage was really multilateral in nature, since the reciprocal requests and concessions were all disclosed simultaneously. This allowed the negotiators to take stock of all the concessions received, including those obtained indirectly (from other countries' bilateral negotiations) under the MFN clause. The concessions finally agreed to were framed in a separate agreement that also committed Contracting Parties not to raise their new tariff rates for a predefined period, usually lasting only three years. When this phase expired, they could either withdraw their concessions or renegotiate them with their original bilateral partner or with any other country that held a substantial interest in the tariff item in question.[6]

EVALUATING GATT'S TARIFF CUTS

So far, only a handful attempts have been made to evaluate the impact of the first GATT rounds on levels of tariff protection. Those few studies available are either of poor quality or almost exclusively concerned with reductions in the American schedule.[7] This stems partly from the difficulties involved in assessing the value and impact of concessions negotiated and partly also from Contracting Parties' unwillingness to disclose such delicate information. What we do have, however, are figures of concessions exchanged in the first six tariff rounds, and their trade coverage, as well as an assessment of average tariff cuts for manufactures during this period (see table 4.1).

During the first round in Geneva in 1947, tariff concessions reached a record of 45,000, while the average depth of the cuts for manufactures amounted to 19 percent. After that, both the number of concessions and the depth of the cuts fell drastically. They reached an all time low with the Geneva round of 1955-56, only to rise again with the first across-the-board reductions of the Kennedy round of 1963-67. The Torquay round seems to break the downward trend in concessions exchanged, but

TABLE 4.1

Total Number of Concessions Exchanged (I),
Their Trade Coverage in Millions of U.S. dollars (II)
and the Average Depth of Tariff Cuts in Percent Ad Valorem (III),
in the First Six GATT Rounds, 1947–1967

Tariff Round	Year		I	II	III
Geneva	1947		45,000	$ 10,000	19
Annecy	1949		5,000	n.a.	2
Torquay	1951		8,700	n.a.	3
Geneva	1956		2,700	$ 25,000	2
Geneva	1961	'Dillon'	4,400	$ 49,000	7
Geneva	1967	'Kennedy'	8,159	n.a.	35

n.a.= no comparable figures available. * tariff cuts in percent ad valorem

Sources: H. Mayrzedt, *Multilaterale Wirtschaftsdiplomatie zwischen westlichen Industriestaaten: Instrument zur Stärkung der multilateralen und liberalen Handelspolitik* (Bern: Lang, 1979), 369; J. Finger, "Trade Liberalisation: A Public Choice Perspective," in *Challenge to a Liberal International Trade Order*, R. Amacher, G. Habeler and Th. Willet, eds. (Washington, D.C.: American Enterprise Institute for Public Policy Research, 1979), 450; Curzon, *Multilateral Commercial Diplomacy: An Examination of the Impact of the General Agreement on Tariffs and Trade on National Commercial Policies and Techniques* (London: Joseph, 1965), 81.

that observation is misleading. Its results are quite poor if account is taken of West Germany's and Austria's accession during this round. According to GATT's normal procedures, both countries had to pay their "entrance fee" to obtain all the concessions swapped by the Contracting Parties during previous rounds. As a result, West Germany alone was responsible for more than 1,180 concessions, i.e., 14 percent of the total granted in Torquay.[8]

While the average depth of the tariff cuts negotiated in 1947 stands out quite favorably compared to those of the subsequent rounds, the reductions themselves hardly affected levels of protection. Many rates still contained "extra margins" that could easily be cut without changing effective protection levels. Once such margins were negotiated away and the cuts threatened to have a real impact on domestic protection, progress stagnated. After the first Geneva round, the share of tariff consolidations increased noticeably, at the expense of tariff reductions. Again, the Torquay round formed the exception owing to the large number of West German cuts. Other states offered mainly consolidations.

These quantitative indications of a stagnation in the early 1950s are supported by qualitative evidence based on research into national tariff policies.[9] In 1949, the developing nations among the Contracting Parties had already indicated that they had reached the limits of their abilities to cut tariffs because they relied heavily on tariff revenue for their state budgets. Elsewhere, too, pressure for tariff protection had worked against further successes. As we saw in chapter 3, France and Italy had tested GATT by entering the Annecy conference with completely redrawn bargaining schedules. In 1950, West Germany followed their example in Torquay, whereas the United Kingdom was exploring the scope for tariff increases to compensate for its loss of quota protection. Furthermore, the American government faced Congressional pressure to avoid new cuts.[10] In this climate of tariff proliferation, the OEEC's Council had adopted a resolution calling for concerted European action to reduce import duties during the Torquay round. It threatened to relax the 75 percent liberalization target if the GATT conference failed to produce satisfactory progress. In this way, the Torquay round became a debating forum on European tariff problems and a testing ground for GATT's effectiveness.

THE TORQUAY CONFERENCE

At the start of the new round in October 1950, delegates of Benelux, Scandinavia and France and the United States entered talks on new methods for cutting tariffs.[11] Although Benelux took the initiative for the meeting, it expected concrete proposals to come from the French delegation since their ministry of foreign affairs earlier had proposed stage-wise tariff reductions covering the OEEC's common list of key products in intra-European trade.[12] France therefore seemed likely to play a significant role in the tariff talks. Still, it turned out to be a role that was different from the one the Benelux governments anticipated. The French ministry of industry blocked these proposals after receiving a flood of complaints, in particular from its machinery producers, about increased competition from Germany. The cabinet reacted by agreeing to limit tariff concessions to an absolute minimum and to withdraw several tariff concessions on machinery, transport equipment and rubber products. In this way, the ministry of industry regained the freedom to raise these duties, if necessary. The French delegation received contradictory instructions from rivaling ministries throughout the negotiations and lost control completely when the Americans demanded far more concessions than the ministry of industry wanted to grant in return for the French withdrawals. Compromise was not in sight until January, when just before his official visit to the United States the French president René Pleven finally decided to arbitrate the ministerial conflicts.[13]

These controversies took place in an atmosphere of growing domestic economic instability. Like other European countries, France had to cope with rapid inflation following the Korean war boom. It faced additional financial burdens from the war in Indochina and American pressure for larger domestic defense efforts. As political unrest over higher prices built up, the search for a better policy began. Minister of Finance Maurice Petsche, a member of the left wing of the center-conservative cabinet, tried to fight inflation by increasing imports and by breaking price-fixing agreements between producers.[14] Hoping to secure further long-term American financial support after Marshall aid had ended, he argued that without it the confidence and stability needed for industrial competitiveness, productivity rises and price reduction would be lacking. Despite the intense opposition of protectionist forces in his cabinet, Premier Pleven followed Petsche's line. During his visit with President Truman in Washington he agreed to make tariff concessions in exchange for additional American aid. Only a week after, however, Pleven had to resign. As interim ministers, Petsche and Robert Buron managed to push the promised tariff reductions through cabinet, but French participation in a tariff reduction plan seemed more remote than ever.[15]

The Benelux partners, having waited more than two months for the French cabinet to endorse the plan for tariff reductions in stages, decided at the end of January to go it alone. A "Memorandum on European Tariff Disparity" summarized the deficiencies in GATT's negotiating method from their point of view. The gist of their argument was that the predominantly bilateral conduct of negotiations put low-tariff countries at a disadvantage. They were usually unable to qualify as principal suppliers, and so had no means of obtaining substantial concessions from their larger, high-tariff neighbors. To reinforce their action, they launched a direct attack on GATT and the OEEC:

> It is clear that in the present circumstances the low-tariff countries could only increase their limited bargaining power by drastic action. Not only could they decide—collectively or not—to abstain from concluding further tariff agreements with high tariff countries who are not willing to meet them on the road to better equilibrium, but they might also refuse to reconsolidate their existing schedules. This would increase their possibility to raise their tariffs. Moreover the resolution of the Council of O.E.E.C. of 27 October 1950 points in the direction of quantitative restrictions. It is however highly desirable that such drastic action should be avoided.[16]

Direct multilateral tariff negotiations between the industrial nations of the OEEC, the United States and Canada, they suggested, could offer the only way out. To transfer an "OEEC problem" to a worldwide framework where the American voice was so strong was to open a new set of dilemmas. From the outset of the informal talks that began in October the American government maintained that preferential intra-European tariff reductions short of a customs union were unacceptable.[17] It contended that the economic benefits of strictly European cuts could not balance the economic and political disadvantages. Depicting a preferential tariff agreement as a dangerous precedent, the United States warned that it would harden Commonwealth resistance to reductions in Imperial Preference, in turn fueling British calls for a release from GATT's no-new-preference rule. The American government also faced domestic opposition to Europe's restrictions on dollar imports. It was fighting an intense battle with Congress over the extension of the Reciprocal Trade Agreement Act (RTAA). European tariff reductions that did not benefit the United States could tip the balance in favor of the protectionists in Congress and weaken the administration's efforts to strengthen the powers of GATT. The State Department and the ECA knew, however, that without a solution to the European tariff problem their European trade policy was at risk. The Trade Liberalization Program had almost reached an impasse. Yet hope remained; various OEEC members seemed committed, as the American secretary of state, Dean Acheson, put it, "to develop [the] best case that can be made of [a] discriminatory low tariff club" without directly opposing American policy toward GATT and Europe.[18]

This is precisely what the Benelux states had tried to do in their memorandum on European tariffs. They had suggested separate multilateral negotiations among the OEEC members of GATT, while hinting that the tariff problem endangered further, worldwide liberalization and also European economic integration. They had also gone out of their way to stress that their nondiscriminatory negotiating method complied with GATT rules while, of course, also recognizing that quotas imposed for dollar-saving purposes offered convenient limits to American and Canadian competition. They professed strict compliance to GATT's own article 28 (which recognized that reducing a high tariff was equivalent to consolidating a low one), but also added that this rule had not cut tariff disparities. All this suggested that Benelux would table a regional plan within the OEEC once GATT's nondiscriminatory item-by-item negotiations had stalled.[19] Only then would France and Italy cooperate, and only then could Benelux achieve its aim of linking the removal of quotas with tariff cuts.

THE CRAZY GANG

Between January and April 1951, a group of eleven OEEC members, soon baptized as the Crazy Gang, held several unofficial meetings with the American and Canadian delegates to discuss European tariff disparities. Since the RTAA would lapse in June, the American government insisted on immediate so-called rehearsals of linear tariff cuts to judge their effectiveness.[20] Benelux, France, West Germany, Norway, Denmark, Austria and Sweden subsequently produced a short list of high-tariff products important to their trade. The tariff rehearsals could start.[21] Before discussing their outcome, it is worth considering how other European countries reacted to this sudden turn in the GATT talks. Having rejected the tariff issue within the OEEC, they now discovered that it threatened to reappear there through skillful manipulation of GATT.

A new and potentially powerful trading partner, West Germany was vital to the success or failure of any tariff operation. It figured prominently in Benelux attempts at reducing tariff disparities. By 1950, the Federal Republic had, like prewar Germany, become the largest single trading partner of the Netherlands and Belgium. It came prepared to enter GATT with a carefully composed bargaining tariff that under the item-by-item negotiating method would require years of haggling to eliminate its excess protection. The French and Italians, had, moreover, imposed their schedules in anticipation of powerful new German competition on the European market. All this suggested that West Germany would play a role in tariff policy commensurate with its strength.

The German government expected immediate export opportunities from multilateral action in GATT. Even after Torquay, many of its tariffs would retain an extra bargaining margin that could be cut without serious repercussions to domestic producers. Agriculture was the only real impediment to Germany's participation. Earlier bilateral negotiations with the Dutch, Danes and Italians on agricultural duties had almost failed because of Germany's meager offers.[22] When a proposal for multilateral tariff cuts emerged, German farmers successfully lobbied for agriculture's exemption, even though this sector was still heavily protected by rigid quotas, high duties and subsidies.

Of the other main European countries, neither Britain nor Italy supported the Benelux proposals in their existing form. The British were annoyed about the new initiative. They had come to the Torquay conference to extract American tariff reductions, preferably without having to cut Commonwealth preferences. The government wanted to improve export performance in the dollar area and also to stifle the Conservative opposition at home, which feared that the Labor government was selling out on imperial preference just as quantitative import restrictions were being relaxed.[23] The board of trade therefore had no interest in multilateral negotiations with the low-tariff countries.[24] Hoping to block the initiative by proving that complaints about low-tariff countries' weak positions were totally unfounded, it decided to offer Benelux and the Scandinavian countries several few attractive concessions. These low-tariff countries, however, were determined to reject these favorable concessionary offers to strengthen their case for preferential cuts outside GATT, whereupon the British were forced to block the talks quite openly. New tariff schemes promised new and embarrassing challenges to Britain's levels of tariff protection, its system of Imperial Preference and its policy on Europe. These had to be ignored or, if necessary, crushed.

The Italians had protectionist motives for opposing the pilot study. They had fulfilled their liberalization obligations to the OEEC and expected to rely mainly on tariffs to protect their industries. Unlike the British, they were interested in the attempts by Benelux to push the tariff issue to a preferential framework. There, under the rubric of "European integration," the Italians as usual introduced bargaining tariffs in order to extract concessions on free movement for their underemployed labor force.[25]

Less than a fortnight after the start of the pilot study, the Dutch delegation leader hinted that the tariff rehearsal had stalled; of all tariff items proposed for multilateral cuts, only three had received general approval.[26] He then made a plea for automatic tariff reductions within the OEEC, allegedly to assist integration and to strengthen the European economy. The existing tariff disparities should be eliminated, he argued, by bringing down high tariffs. They were to reach the lowest, "base," levels prevailing among the main European producers by means of successive automatic annual cuts of 25 percent of the difference between the high tariffs and these base levels. After three years their impact would be examined to consider whether special circumstances justified exemptions from the fourth and final tariff cuts.[27]

Even though Italy and France had previously disputed both the notion of tariff leveling and the suggestions for automatic tariff reductions, they joined Benelux in requesting a shift toward the OEEC. There, without American delegates, European preferential arrangements could be discussed more freely.[28] The Americans became painfully aware that the tariff rehearsals had been a "perfunctory exercise" and a mere playground for a preferential European tariff scheme.[29] They desperately wanted to avoid any impression of GATT's incompetence in dealing with the tariff problem and demanded its continuing involvement in the European talks. The British instantly joined them, claiming that GATT was, and should remain, the only appropriate forum for tariff issues. As a result, the European countries had to settle for a compromise. They agreed to study the tariff disparity problem in a special Intersessional Working Party of GATT, which would keep in close contact with the OEEC. To meet British demands, half of its members would consist of representatives of non-European countries.

Against all odds, the French, not Benelux, took the initiative in the new Working Party. Their delegate, de Montremy, tabled a new scheme for reducing tariff disparities similar to the Benelux proposals of January 1951,[30] that envisaged leveling duties for products of the OEEC's common list (see chapter 3) and allowed for exempting sensitive products. The plan clearly intended to give governments full control over the timing and the extent to which weaker sectors had to face European competition. It also implicitly criticized the Dutch and Scandinavians for demanding rigid automatic reductions of tariff disparities under international supervision, as well as for refusing to raise their quota liberalization percentages out of fear of domestic pressure groups.[31]

Like previous tariff schemes of French origin, this new proposal had not received cabinet endorsement. Most ministers were too preoccupied with the forthcoming elections of June 1951 to become involved in departmental clashes over tariff policy. There appeared to be no real coordination on tariff matters, whether among departments or across successive French governments. What remained as a constant factor throughout the postwar years was fear of even small tariff cuts if introduced on a worldwide basis. Preferential European tariff reductions provided the only means of limiting American competition and of regulating, or at least tempering, the impact of European competition on the French economy.

PFLIMLIN'S TARIFF PROPOSAL

It is hard to think of a more radical policy shift than the launching, at the sixth GATT session in September 1951, of a French plan for multilateral worldwide tariff reductions. The proposal recommended making them in annual cuts of 10 percent, spread over three years. Instead of applying these reductions to individual tariff items, they would be spread over the weighted average levels of five major sectors: raw materials, semimanufactures, foodstuffs, equipment and industrial consumer goods. France invited all Contracting Parties to join and provided exemptions for developing countries.

The new French minister of foreign trade Pierre Pflimlin, who initiated the plan, described it as meeting three essential conditions for tariff action. It promised substantial and fast progress, was flexible enough to avoid severe economic disruptions, and could parallel other actions in the field of economic integration in Europe and the rest of the world.[32] How should one explain the sudden arrival of this nondiscriminatory French tariff scheme? It was in fact an ill-prepared stunt by an incoming minister eager to clear the unresolved burden of his predecessor's domestic and foreign commitments. The French elections of June 1951 had brought to power a rightwing cabinet of mainly Radicals and Conservatives, with some members of the Mouvement Républicain Populaire (MRP). Pflimlin had moved from the ministry of agriculture in the old cabinet to the ministry of foreign commerce in the new one. Unofficially, though, he had remained in charge of some agricultural issues, including among these the so-called Green Pool negotiations.[33] While the cabinet was taking office in mid-August, civil servants of the foreign ministry's directorate of economic relations had met with Benelux colleagues in Paris to discuss a joint initiative for European tariff reductions. The two parties then had agreed to resume the talks in September on the basis of de Montremy's earlier suggestions for reductions covering the common list. The French delegates were to present the results at the forthcoming GATT session, thereby insisting on the need for action in a preferential European framework.[34]

On September 6, the Benelux group sent a memorandum with new, more detailed tariff suggestions to the ministry of commerce. Then, without notifying Schuman, Pflimlin called for an interdepartmental meeting of tariff experts to discuss de Montremy's scheme. On that occasion, an official of the ministry of industry suggested reducing the average tariffs weighted by products groups. Pflimlin immediately agreed. Two days later, French tariff experts had drafted the text for a new plan for progressive, automatic reductions of European tariffs. Then, during the night of September 13, Pflimlin suddenly insisted on a revised text, changing the European scheme into a plan for general, worldwide tariff reductions in GATT.[35] One day later, French ministers approved the plan. Pflimlin himself, as leader of the French delegation to GATT, personally launched the initiative at the opening of the sixth session, at which most members of the French delegation heard the proposal for the first time.[36]

There are strong indications that Pflimlin's intervention sprang from the wish to answer often contradictory demands from the Americans, Benelux officials and domestic pressure groups for a change in French tariff policy. Just a few weeks earlier, the American administration had promised up to 500 million U.S. dollars in import support in exchange for a "realistic" import program and new tariff cuts and suspensions.[37] Although the French government tried to fulfill these conditions, it could not overcome the opposition of those domestic producers that felt unable to meet the growing German and Belgian competition.[38] In addition, it encountered a rapidly growing balance of payments deficit, which gave the parliamentary opposition further reason to demand tighter import quotas. If this were not enough, the new cabinet also inherited the legacy of prior French tariff cooperation with Benelux, which had been led to believe that a joint reduction scheme could surface at any moment. By launching a plan for worldwide tariff action in GATT, Pflimlin answered to their calls for action while shifting responsibility for future cuts to the United States. Coming so shortly after the failure of the Torquay round, the Americans might have welcomed a multilateral tariff plan in GATT. However, they had either to join it or, as appeared more likely, take the blame for its failure, if Congress rejected substantial automatic reductions.[39] This strategy was not anti-American, Pflimlin later assured the Dutch; it merely served to impress upon the Americans that if they kept demanding tariff cuts, they would have to take the lead.[40]

It was not accidental that the method for tariff cuts had been devised at the ministry of industry and had found staunch support from a former minister of agriculture. By using average tariff levels, France could impose cuts below 30 percent or even make totally exempt uncompetitive and 'political' products, including agricultural goods. The only requirement was that by the end of each year, average tariff levels covering each of the five groups were cut by at least 30 percent. The method also sidetracked the notion of tariff leveling, which nearly all French departments considered potentially dangerous because it gave low-tariff countries a free ride.

The plan was received coldly at the ministry of foreign affairs. Its officials unsparingly criticized it as impractical and they tried to push the French delegation to GATT back onto the old, preferential course. They argued that the other GATT delegates would regard the Pflimlin plan as a mere attempt to torpedo tariff cuts. After all, France itself had always claimed that tariff action was only possible in a European framework. By obstructing progressive tariffs cuts in Europe—in the words of one official, a "precondition of European integration"—France undermined the very policy it had advocated.[41] As for Pflimlin's role in this, a civil servant at the ministry concluded, "Monsieur Pflimlin declares in his plan that its measures should be reconciled with the plans for regional integration. But this is simply impossible, because one cannot reconcile what is contradictory."[42] In other words, the worldwide approach of GATT would ultimately clash with European demands for preferential trading schemes.

THE GATT PLAN

If the Benelux partners expected Pflimlin's plan to stall, they were gravely disappointed. It remained firmly on GATT's agenda, and by the end of 1953 reemerged with several practical guidelines for implementation. It contained little of the original plan's simplicity and flexibility. In two years of technical negotiations, the composition and the number of tariff groups as well as the depth of the tariff cuts had all undergone major changes. A consensus had nonetheless emerged on the following measures:

(1) three annual cuts of ten percent each of the average tariffs for each of eleven sectors.

(2) the calculation of these average tariffs based on the ratio of import values and total duty collected.

(3) a "decapping" procedure for individual tariffs above a ceiling level and an exemption from tariff cuts for average tariffs per sector below a floor level.[43]

The number and composition of sectors mentioned in (1) would largely determine the depth of the cuts. If tariffs were to be divided into just four or five sectors, as the British, French and Italians suggested, the scope for excluding sensitive items from the 30 percent cuts was much larger than if the weighted average tariff for each of the 52 SITC sectors had to fall by 30 percent. Or to take another extreme, if a country's sensitive products were all concentrated in one small sector, it had to make many more painful tariff cuts than if those products were spread over several larger sectors. Countries therefore wanted to subdivide further all those product groups that would bring them large export gains. For the same reasons, they wanted to tuck away their "weaker" sectors in some corner of a large group.[44] The provisional version of the plan that GATT published in 1953 envisaged ten different sectors of widely different import coverage. The smallest sector, for fish and fish products, covered less than one percent of participating countries' total imports. By far the largest were the sectors IV (petroleum products) and I (primary products for food excluding fish), comprising 15.4 and 39.8 percent respectively.

The GATT plan's third principle introduced a difference between the cuts imposed on high and low tariffs. For each of the ten sectors, it calculated a "demarcation line" based on the average tariff levels among the Working Group's eleven countries (see table 4.2).[45] If a country's weighted average tariff in a sector lay below this demarcation line (see item (2) of list), it did not have to cut rates within that sector by the full 30 percent but only by a proportion of it, the exact cut depending on the tariff's distance from the demarcation line.[46] Tariffs more than 50 percent below this line were exempted altogether, but they had to be consolidated for at least five years. Before the end of the third year, all high tariffs on individual SITC items had to be reduced to so-called ceiling levels, which varied according to four product groups. For raw materials, the ceiling was 5 percent, for agricultural products 27 percent, for semimanufactures 15 percent and for manufactures 30 percent.

The notion of floors and ceilings had been used during the negotiations for the Stikker-Pella-Petsche plan. The Swedish economist and Council of Europe delegate Bertil Ohlin had incorporated it into his "Low-Tariff Club" plan that, in December 1951, had reached the Council's Assembly in a modified form. The scheme proposed reducing tariffs above 35 percent before a specified date and imposing maximum levels of 5, 15 and 25 percent for raw materials, semimanufactures and manufactures respectively. During the first year, each country would impose these maximum levels on tariffs covering 70 percent of its imports. In the second and third years, this would be extended to import coverages of 80 and 90 percent respectively. By the end of the third year, countries would have to decide on the fate of tariffs covering the remaining 10 percent.[47]

TABLE 4.2

Weighted Average Tariffs (in percentage)* and Demarcation Lines (D) Calculated for Tariff Cuts under the GATT Plan, 1953

Sector	D	Aust	Ben	Canada	Den	Fran	FRG	Italy	Norway	Swed	UKt	USA
I	7	30	1	4	1	1	11	27	2	5	3	2
II	11	21	5	7	1	9	21	23	3	3	6	10
III	8	1	14	9	0	9	15	19	1	2	8	6
IV	2	1	0	2	0	2	2	2	1	0	1	4
V	8	9	4	7	1	17	15	20	6	3	8	6
VI	6	10	10	11	4	15	14	21	8	5	10	2
VII	14	21	13	14	4	18	18	22	13	6	14	18
VIII	7	11	4	10	1	6	10	22	3	3	4	6
IX	11	23	10	9	4	16	12	23	6	10	18	6
X	12	11	9	11	5	14	8	20	13	6	19	16

Contents of the sectors:

I	primary products for food excl. fish
II	manufactures products for food excl. fish
III	fish and fish products
IV	petroleum products
V	chemicals other than pharmaceutical products, pharmaceutical and cosmetic products
VI	semifinished products of leather, rubber, wood and cork
VII	textile yarn and thread, textile fabrics incl. clothing
VIII	base metals and manufactures of base metals
IX	machinery and transport equipment
X	miscellaneous manufactured products

* the tariffs were weighted by the value of imports.
t since the United Kingdom refused to furnish data on its weighted tariff averages, its figures were not available to members of the subgroup and are not included in the demarcation lines. The British did make the calculations for their own tariffs, though. These U.K. rates were found in: Effects on the United Kingdom tariff of participating in a plan for automatic tariff reductions, Annex B, Comparison of average incidence of duty with those of other countries, BT 205/14.

Source: GATT, Basic Instruments and Selected Documents, Second Supplement (Geneva, 1954), 87-89.

Ohlin originally intended to create a preferential area in Europe, but the Council of Europe's revised proposal was more cautious, vaguely suggesting extending the European tariff cuts to other GATT members in exchange for "equivalent" tariff concessions. This ambiguity meant that some parliamentarians saw it as a preferential European tariff scheme, others as the first stage of a European customs union. Several British and French members even considered it a stepping stone for a system of overlapping preferences between Western European economies and their former overseas colonies, a proposal they formalized in the so-called Strasbourg Plan of 1952.[48] Although most national governments ignored the Ohlin Plan, the Council eventually succeeded in transferring it to the GATT Working Party examining the Pflimlin Plan, where Germany strongly supported it. German tariff experts considered its ceiling levels a valuable compromise between the Danish-Dutch demands for drastic reductions of high tariffs and the French-Italian refusal to differentiate between high and low rates.[49]

The special measures proposed for cutting high tariffs meant that the Working Party needed to calculate a comprehensive and comparative overview of actual rates within each national tariff schedule. In June 1952, this was finally completed, listing the national tariffs for each of the 570 SITC items and their demarcation lines, which indicated the impact of the proposed decapping procedure.[50] It showed for instance that in the SITC divisions 711 and 712, where the ceiling level for end products was 30 percent, Italy would have to bring down five legal tariffs, and Austria and the Federal Republic each only one (see table 4.3). Exempting low tariffs meant that Denmark would not have to cut any of its tariffs within this division since their weighted average incidence fell more than 50 percent below the demarcation line, whereas Benelux, Canada, Norway, Sweden and the United States would all have to reduce tariffs by less than 30 percent. Not surprisingly, the rules for "high" and "low" tariffs belonged to the GATT plan's most complex and controversial rules: complex because they required extensive calculations to find out the number and depth of the cuts, and controversial because decapping meant that governments could no longer exempt any politically sensitive tariffs. By assuming that high tariffs had to be cut more than low tariffs, it also brought the European tariff disparities issue right back on the European political agenda where earlier, Pflimlin had tried to take it off.[51]

The French ministry of industry instantly insisted on bringing back Pflimlin's version of the plan, demanding an official cabinet statement condemning the decapping procedure.[52] It had only accepted Pflimlin's original scheme because it replaced the earlier, more drastic Benelux proposal and also restated France's right to protect uncompetitive industries in the face of German competition.[53] The decapping procedure envisaged in GATT's revised Pflimlin Plan, it argued, again contested this right. Yet the ministry of foreign trade decided not to block GATT's latest version altogether, fearing this would lead to accusations of French sabotage and even more radical tariff proposals by the low-tariff countries. This turned out to be a wise move, since the pressure on France gradually diminished and attention switched to the United States. In the course of 1953 and 1954, the main issue was no longer exactly what the GATT plan would look like, but whether the Americans would join.

TABLE 4.3

Ad Valorem Tariffs of Member Countries in SITC Groups 711
(Power Generating Machinery, Excl. Electric Machinery)
and 712 (Agricultural Machinery)

SITC no.	Aus	Ben	Can	Den	Fra	FRG	Ita	Nor	Swe	UK	USA	A
711-02	25	6	20	1	20	10	35	20	14	18	-	16.9
-02	11	6	-	-	22	10	37	2	11	18	-	14.6
-03	5	6	13	5	19	18	35	20	10	20	13	14.9
-04	-	6	5	0	15	40	20	12	13	20	15	14.6
-05	14	9	14	4	22	20	32	11	13	21	12	15.6
-09	17	9	14	5	23	12	33	20	10	20	15	15.6
712-01	43	6	0	3	15	11	24	11	9	15	0	12.5
-02	25	6	0	0	16	18	26	10	10	14	0	11.4
-03	0	6	0	2	15	11	21	17	8	15	5	9.1
-09	8	6	1	4	15	12	25	10	15	18	0	10.4

* A = average tariff; - = no tariff levied

Source: GATT, Subgroup of the Working Party on reduction of tariff levels. Data furnished by members of the subgroup pursuant to Annex F of IW.2/15, June 1952, BT 11/4901.

THE AMERICAN DIMENSION

What were the plan's chances of implementation? Would the Atlantic trading nations really accept the 1953 draft, loopholes and ambiguities included? To answer this question we must first examine the political climate. The Working Party had only presented the draft hoping to persuade the American government to adopt a clear stand on automatic tariff cuts, not to suggest its full acceptance in Europe. The American delegate to GATT's Working Party had kept a low profile because his government lacked the legal powers to join a new tariff action. That premise might have changed after the American election campaign in the autumn of 1952. The Democratic candidate, Adlai Stevenson, promised to ease access to the American market and forsake strict reciprocity. There were also rumors that the State Department would embark on automatic tariff cuts instead of item-by-item negotiations under the RTAA.[54] The European delegates in the Working Party had agreed among themselves that they would only join a worldwide, nondiscriminatory tariff plan if the United States imposed large tariff cuts. Britain, West Germany, France, Sweden, Norway, Denmark and Italy had repeatedly stressed this while the Benelux partners had explicitly written this down in their own memorandum of January 1951.[55] Naturally, the Torquay debate had already suggested various ways in which America's refusal to join could serve Europeans interests. They could exploit it as an excuse either for launching discriminatory plans or resisting further tariff cuts. Whatever their motivations, though, the United States would not have endorsed a GATT plan without a positive response from Europe. After the American elections, France, Benelux, Germany and Denmark therefore agreed to present their joint plan to the new administration as a European initiative for worldwide tariff cuts.[56] Britain refused to support their venture.[57]

In March 1953, meanwhile, the British government embarked on a secret mission to the new American government in the hope of receiving support for its Collective Approach (see chapter 3).[58] It urged Washington to adopt a "good creditor" policy: the unilateral reduction of high American tariffs, the liberalization of customs procedures and the abolition of the notorious "Buy American" policy. Eisenhower nevertheless feared that it was still too early in his presidency to confront Congress with demands for tariff reductions. A month later, he appointed a special committee under the chairmanship of the acclaimed free trader Clarence B. Randall to undertake a review of American foreign economic policy. Major commercial policy decisions awaited the results of the Randall Committee's investigations.[59]

In the British board of trade, the rumors of U.S. participation in across-the-board tariff cuts triggered an internal debate on the pros and cons of joining the GATT plan.[60] It could hardly have been otherwise, since the United States was Britain's prime target in trade bargaining for export expansion. Some early estimates had suggested that if the United States were to reduce all its high tariffs, at least ten of the twenty major British export products would expand considerably their share of the U.S. market. There were several more high-performing British export products that hardly entered the American market, such as electrical appliances, motor cars, textile machinery and paints, which together covered 787 million U.S. dollars. Since the American market absorbed less than 46 million U.S. dollars of that total, the British, rightly or wrongly, argued that this was due to restrictive American import measures.

No one imagined that the Eisenhower administration would undertake the unilateral tariff cuts that the British had demanded in their Collective Approach. If the Americans subscribed to the GATT plan, however, it would guarantee drastic reductions of all the very high American tariffs that had obstructed British exports since the 1930s. Officials like the second secretary of the board of trade Edgar Cohen saw this as a decisive argument for British participation. They also maintained that the first stage of bilateral negotiations with the United States usually put far more pressure on them to lower tariffs than the multilateral, across-the-board approach to reductions. The tiresome and highly politicized bilateral confrontations with the United States during the Geneva and Torquay rounds seemed to prove this. If both governments accepted the new method, Britain would be on par with the other industrialized contracting parties, and American pressure on Britain for large concessions would ease. A precondition for the success of this procedure was a simple and straightforward scheme that left little or no room for special cases or exemptions. The GATT plan would therefore have to be stripped of its "phoney mathematical measurement."[61] Not everyone in the board of trade, however, accepted this interpretation. Other tariff experts denied that Geneva and Torquay had been failures because of unevenly heavy American pressure on Britain. They also doubted whether the benefits from American cuts would really exceed the costs for domestic industries and whether the Americans accepted across-the-board tariff cuts. Despite all the rumors of a new U.S. trade policy on Europe, they noted that nothing had happened so far, and the Eisenhower administration seemed increasingly keen to shelve the subject. By December 1953, most board of trade officials ended the debate, agreeing merely to wait and see.

Britain was certainly not the only country where attention focused on American trade policy. Throughout 1953 and 1954, other European states also discussed the impact of American import restrictions on their export performance and balance of payments. Fears of cutbacks in defense spending and of a coming American economic recession fueled such debates. The U.S. administration faced increasingly loud calls for higher barriers against European exports. The American Tariff League, renowned for its protectionist sentiments, initiated a powerful campaign against imports from what it stigmatized as "high tariff" Europe. It also attacked the Public Advisory Board for Mutual Security for its appeal for a new, more liberal tariff act and for the simplification of customs procedures.[62]

Between July 1953 and September 1954, American producers requested the investigation of more than eighteen cases of serious damage (compared to just eleven between 1945 and 1953). under the so-called escape clause. This clause gave domestic industries the right to demand an independent inquiry into the effects of tariff changes. If the U.S. Tariff Commission decided serious damage would result, it could demand the return of the old tariffs. Some commodities under study covered large shares of total exports of individual European countries to the United States. In 1954, for example, more than 36 percent of Swiss exports to the United States consisted of watches. In one other extreme case, more than 68 percent of total Icelandic exports were codfish fillets to the United States.[63] While most peril point claims were rejected, the threat of protectionism deterred individual exporters to the United States, enhanced European insistence on new American import legislation and reinforced opposition to U.S. competition in European markets.[64]

It is difficult to assess to what extent American tariff barriers really damaged Europe's export performance in the United States. The British assessments mentioned earlier illustrate that the evidence deployed to demonstrate their impact usually only amounted to a set of comparatively high American nominal tariff rates with matching, low export figures. Several American experts made other, more elaborate qualitative studies by industry, suggesting that the impact of tariff cuts depended on their timing, depth and speed and on the product.[65] The Randall Committee's final report mentioned that if all the American tariff rates of 1951 had been suspended, imports would have been raised by 800 million U.S. dollars and 1,800 million dollars over three to five years. This equaled an increase in European exports of between 7 and 18 percent, approximately the total sum of direct U.S. military aid granted to Western Europe in 1951.[66] Yet experts' findings also indicated that many of these tariffs could easily have been cut without serious injury to domestic producers.

The trade figures show that in 1953, Italy, Norway and the BLEU partners each exported around 10 percent of their total exports to the United States. Following the American recession in 1954 these percentages dropped. The British, German, Dutch and Danish shares varied at around 6 or 7 percent in both years, while French export shares were only around 4 or 5 percent (see table 4.4). The United Kingdom was by far the largest exporter to the United States, followed by West Germany, the BLEU, France and the Netherlands.

However, before drawing tentative conclusions from these export figures, it is worth mentioning some details of European countries' manufacturing exports to the United States. Machinery and transport equipment took the largest share in British exports to the American market, and within that section motor vehicles (SITC 732) and metalworking, mining and other industrial machinery (714-716) dominated. Textiles (266, 65 and 84) ranked second, followed by miscellaneous manufactures (8). For Germany, the ranking was somewhat

TABLE 4.4

Exports of Raw Materials and Foodstuffs (I) and Industrial Products (II) for Main European Countries Exporting to the United States, 1953–1954

(in millions of dollars at 1950 prices)

Exports		I	II	I and II as % of total exports	I and II as % of total exports
		1953	1954	1953	1954
U.K.	I	140.6	126.6	6.3	5.7
	II	234.5	235.3		
FRG	I	66.1	67.5	6.9	5.7
	II	181.9	182.2		
BLEU	I	103.5	68.7	10.1	8.3
	II	97.1	113.5		
France	I	82.2	66.7	5.0	3.9
	II	79.1	80.6		
Netherlands	I	74.8	93.5	7.7	6.6
	II	78.3	56.1		
Italy	I	51.1	53.5	9.2	7.5
	II	69.2	51.4		
Sweden	I	53.4	36.0	6.5	4.6
	II	18.3	19.6		
Denmark	I	47.6	49.9	6.7	7.6
	II	6.7	15.0		
Norway	I	37.2	31.6	10.8	7.0
	II	7.9	8.1		

Source: Economic Commission for Europe. *Economic Survey of Europe in 1956* (Geneva, 1957) Tables VIII and IX. Annex.

different. Its exports to the American market consisted largely of so-called miscellaneous manufactures, in particular precision instruments. Machinery and transport equipment occupied a second position, largely as a result of high exports of metal working and industrial machinery. Textile products figured more prominently in British than in German exports, whereas this situation was the reverse for chemicals. Textiles took up a large share of Italian and French exports to the United States. In Belgium they ranked in a strong second position, after miscellaneous manufactures. Machinery and chemicals were also fairly strong Italian exports, while their importance in French exports was negligible. Chemicals, however, occupied a firm third position in French manufacturing exports. Dutch manufacturing exports to the American market differed distinctly, comprising large quantities of chemicals and electrical appliances. Textiles ranked third, but at a considerable distance. Scandinavian exports also formed a group in themselves, consisting mainly of Norwegian and Swedish paper and pulp and Danish and Norwegian foodstuffs. Manufacturing exports were relatively insignificant. In Swedish exports, metalworking and other industrial machinery were the only group of manufactures that stood out as fairly large. For Norway, chemicals took a larger-than-average share in manufactured exports, whereas Denmark's exports into the U.S. market were evenly spread over most sections.

American tariff expert Harry Piquet's calculations for 1951 estimated that if U.S. tariffs were totally eliminated, the greatest increases in imports would take place in textile fibers, textile manufactures, machinery, vehicles and inedible animal products. The smallest increases would occur in wood and paper products. These findings would suggest that the United Kingdom, Germany and to a lesser extent Belgium and Italy had most to gain from American participation in the GATT plan. There are, moreover, other reasons for assuming *a priori* that Britain and the Federal Republic of Germany would gain most in absolute and relative terms. They were the only countries whose shares of manufacturing exports exceeded those of raw materials and agricultural exports. Since American raw material tariffs tended to be low and many agricultural products fell under a quota regime, the potential gains from tariff cuts were highest for exporting countries with an industrial bias. In addition, income and price elasticities of demand for imported manufactures were higher than for raw materials and agricultural products, which also favored industrial exporters.

Throughout the 1950s, European governments often complained that they could expand market shares quite drastically, if only the Americans would cut their high tariffs. Their assumptions were usually not based on thorough assessments of export shares and competitive strength, but on simple comparisons of average "European" and American nominal tariff levels. If we make such a comparison by presenting all of the 570 American manufacturing SITC tariffs that exceeded an average of British, French, Italian and German rates, the picture in table 4.5 emerges.[67]

The figures in table 4.5 indicate that American tariffs in textiles, manufactures of ferrous and nonferrous metals, many miscellaneous manufactures (SITC 899, including products such as basketwork, brooms, umbrellas, matches, candles, buttons, combs and smoking pipes) were often much higher than European ones. Peril point goods, such as watches and clocks, scientific and precision instruments also figure on this list. Several case studies of these "high tariff" sectors indicate

TABLE 4.5

List of American Tariffs on Manufactures That Exceeded the Average of British, German, French and Italian Tariffs

SITC No	Description	American tariff in %
5		
531.0	Synthetic organic dyestuffs	45
533.3	Prepared paints	25
551.2	Synthetic perfumes	26
581.1	Products of polyester	27
581.9	Other artificial plastics	29
6		
631.2	Plywood, including veneered panels	23
631.2	Other articles of wood	28
641.4	Cigarette paper in bulk, rolls or sheets	23
651	Textile yarn and thread	20-43
652.1	Cotton fabrics, woven, other than grey	24
653	Textile fabrics, woven, other than cotton fabrics	27-40
654	Tulle, lace and embroidery	34-63
655	Special textile fabrics and related products	18-89
662.2	Nonrefractory ceramic bricks	32
663	Mineral manufactures, n.e.s.	18-43
664.2	Optical glass and elements thereof	50
664.8	Sheet or plate glass, coated with metal	30
664.9	Glass, n.e.s.	29
665.2	Glass tableware and other glass for households	30
666	Pottery	47-60
677	Precious and semiprecious stones	8-17
681	Pig iron	17
682	Copper and alloys	6-16
687	Tin and alloys	22
689.3	Magnesium, wrought	25
698	Household equipment of base metals	34
7		
715.2	Metalworking machinery other than machine tools	17
716.6	Paper mill and paper pulp machinery	23
729.2	Electric lamps	23
731.5	Railway and tramway coaches	23
735.9	Ships and boats, n.e.s.	11
8		
897	Jewellery and goldsmiths' and silversmiths' ware	49-57
812	Sanitary plumbing and heating	23-35
821	Furniture	30
841	Clothing of textile fabric	28-62
851	Footwear	25
861	Scientific, medical, and optical measuring instruments	31-37
864	Watches and clocks	37-51
891.1	Phonographs, tape recorders	29
892	Printed matter	8-19
899	Manufactures articles, n.e.s.	18-44

Compiled from: GATT, Subgroup of the Working Party on reduction of tariff levels. Data furnished by members of the subgroup pursuant to Annex F of IW.2/15. June 1952. PRO.BT 11/4901.

that labor intensive American industries, such as glassware, pottery, watches, optical instruments, some types of textiles such as embroidery, woollen and worsted, cotton hosiery and footwear were most vulnerable to tariff cuts. Large scale producers of capital-intensive, standardized products in the chemical, metalworking, machinery, iron and steel sectors were fairly immune to foreign imports and no longer needed high import duties. Again others, such motor cars and other vehicles, experienced rising competition, but could still rely on large after-sales service networks to maintain domestic market shares.[68] Piquet estimated large benefits for European producers of cars, other motor vehicles, machinery and textiles, but the importance of Canadian and Japanese exporters in the U.S. suggests that their gains would certainly be larger.[69] Japan's gains would certainly outweigh European gains in textiles, electrical lamps, miscellaneous rubber products and toys (SITC 899), pottery and footwear, all export sectors that were already rapidly gaining ground in U.S. markets.

Simple comparisons of absolute tariffs can only hint at who gained from American liberalization, but they nonetheless played a prominent role in European negotiating strategies. Most items presented in table 4.5 kept returning to the lists requesting tariff reductions that British and German trade officials presented to their American counterparts.[70] These also covered several products of infant industries that relied on quotas on dollar imports for their protection from American competitors. These products included agricultural machinery, electrical household equipment, some types of machine tools, pharmaceutical products, industrial chemicals, chemical plastics, rayon and rayon manufactures and motion pictures. This created additional economic and political pressures on European governments to take a tough line in trade bargaining with the Americans.

THE RANDALL REPORT

In January 1954, the Randall Committee produced the results of its policy study.[71] It singled out the weak elements in American foreign trade policy but suggested few constructive remedies. While criticizing the negative influence of protectionist measures such as the escape clause, peril point procedures and customs administration methods, the study did not propose radical changes. Its main tariff recommendation, the extension of the RTAA for three years, ended hopes for a comprehensive revision of American policy. The committee suggested giving the president the power to reduce overall tariff rates by up to 5 percent annually over three years.[72] He would also be empowered to cut high tariff rates in effect since January 1945, unilaterally by 50 percent instead of the 5 percent tariff cuts. Moreover, since the escape clause and peril point provisions survived, the U.S. Tariff Commission in investigating complaints could still rally protectionist members of Congress against the proposed tariff cuts. Theoretically, the president could reject the Tariff Commission's advice on peril points if he considered a tariff reduction to be in the national interest. However, once the Commission signaled a peril point, even a determined president would see his room for maneuver shrink.[73] As for the escape clause, even the slightest threat of reimposing a high tariff usually destroyed foreign exporters' hopes of expanding sales in the U.S. market.

While national governments in Europe were generally disappointed with the Randall Report, GATT's secretariat did its utmost to avoid an atmosphere of total pessimism. It still maintained that:

> . . . the French Plan has had a very definite influence on the framing of the tariff proposals embodied in the Randall Report, and we know from reliable sources that this proposal made a very favourable impression on the minds of certain members of the Randall Commission. These proposals are going to be fought very bitterly by the protectionist forces in the USA, and any statement that may give the impression to these forces that there are very serious defects in the Plan would certainly imperil the chances of bringing about tariff reductions in the USA.[74]

Such information was misleading. Even in the State Department, Eisenhower's March 1954 message on foreign economic policy (which was based on Randall's recommendations) was seen as "constructive but relatively cautious and lacking in boldness." Deputy assistant secretary for economic affairs, Thorsten Kalijarvi, criticized the Administration's record of "inaction at best or retreat."[75] Secretary of State John Foster Dulles supported this view, arguing that America had lost credibility after its recent use of various protectionist measures such as quotas, subsidies and peril point procedures. At a cabinet meeting in mid-March, however, such opinions were smothered. Randall and Sinclair Weeks, the secretary of commerce, convinced Eisenhower that major changes would arouse massive opposition and would threaten even the smallest policy modifications. Two months later, after agreeing to drop still more of the Randall Report's recommendations, Eisenhower asked for and received from Congress a one-year extension of the Trade Agreements Program. The current mood of Congress—"a combination of election year caution, uneasiness due to local employment, and general feeling that the already overcrowded timetable is not the best setting for a extremely controversial subject like tariff reductions"—left no other alternative.[76] With that decision, any remaining hopes for the GATT plan were dashed.

In the previous chapters we saw that the Benelux countries, Sweden and Denmark saw the existing tariff disparity in Europe as a major impediment to the full and stable expansion of their exports. These states aimed at drastically reducing tariff barriers in the United Kingdom, France, Italy and West Germany before opening their domestic markets, still partially protected by quotas, to the full force of European competition. What this chapter on European tariff schemes in GATT adds is the evidence that tariff protection in Europe also had a very significant American dimension. The United Kingdom, West Germany and to a lesser extent also France and Italy all expected large potential economic gains from expanding exports into the American market. They were concerned with the formidable challenge of meeting American competition, not just within the United States but increasingly also on their domestic market and their neighboring markets in Europe. This is one main reason why these states would not support a plan for nondiscriminatory, across-the-board tariff reductions unless it promised a drastic scaling-down of American duties. It meant that U.S. tariff cuts would have to offer substantial and above all long-term export benefits that were likely to outweigh any sacrifices such as reduced domestic employment, increased dollar expenditure or damage to infant industries. It is clear from what we have discussed so far that the domestic constraints on U.S. foreign trade policy and also the lack of tariff stability within GATT offered very few prospects for such long-term benefits.

While the United Kingdom, West Germany, France and Italy can be singled out as the European nations whose trade policy was particularly fixed on maintaining their bargaining strength toward the United States, it should be stressed that their interests in the GATT plan (or in any other plan for linear tariff cuts) and hence their positions during the discussions were not completely identical. The considerations of each of these countries therefore require some explanation.

British exports were expected to gain most from large, across-the-board cuts in the American tariff, but Britain also had a lot to lose from joining such tariff cuts. Its tariff levels were comparatively high, in particular on engineering equipment, chemicals, motor cars and precision instruments, for which German competition on the domestic market was already very strong. Britain's attitude toward the GATT plan suggests that this fear of German competition continuously worked against Britain's participation in any plan for tariff reductions, with or without large American concessions. This is why U.K. delegates received instructions to obstruct the GATT plan, as they did with all other tariff plans. Nonetheless, some signs of change were already visible. The board of trade's assessments of the pros and cons of participation indicated a growing awareness of the pressures upon Britain to change its policy. In the next chapter we will see that these pressures eventually resulted in a British initiative for across-the-board tariff cuts in GATT.

France and Italy both had less to gain from American participation than Britain, even though they had specific export industries that were keen on opening up American markets. These may well have exerted some pressure on the government to join the GATT plan if the Americans participated. However, their governments' persistent demands for U.S. participation served as a mere excuse for avoiding any commitments to reduce tariffs. They were not prepared to reduce their levels of protection toward competitors within or outside Europe if all they received in return were tariff cuts. They needed safeguards against economic and social dislocations and larger, more visible and immediate economic benefits in exchange.

It is fair to say that West Germany was the motor behind the GATT plan. It desperately needed a more effective method of tariff reductions, not merely because it needed export outlets but also because by 1953 it came under growing European pressure to reduce its excess bargaining rates and its balance of payments surplus. While such pressure was mainly restricted to OEEC members, the German government and the industrial organizations insisted on worldwide reductions in GATT rather than on preferential European cuts. They knew that many producers expected large advantages from freer access to American markets. When U.S. participation eventually appeared impossible in 1954, they grudgingly accepted the failure of their original bargaining tactic, and were forced to undertake unilateral tariff cuts (see chapter 6). However, so deeply rooted was this notion of tariff bargaining that they would only impose these cuts temporarily, to avoid losing bargaining strength in future tariff rounds. This underlines the validity of Lawrence Krause's statement that Europe's postwar history of dismantling trade barriers was "a story of careful horse-trading in which no concession was given without extracting one of equal value."[77]

The American governments of the 1950s could not offer drastic tariff concessions nor linear cuts. Even if they tried, they faced too much domestic opposition to widespread, across-the-board tariff reductions. This is far from surprising, given that throughout the period many

European countries had been allowed to maintain quantitative restrictions on dollar imports. After 1953, therefore, U.S.-European tensions over tariff policy intensified. This was partly due to the American recession of 1953-1954, which only had a very mild impact on the European economies and which helped European producers reduce further the productivity gap with their American competitors. Yet its main cause lay in the fast growth rates achieved by the European economies. By 1953, Europe had radically expanded its production and exports. Most countries had thus been able to reduce their dollar shortage and to start gradually eliminating their quota restrictions on dollar imports. This meant that tariffs gained in importance as instruments for protection and bargaining in trading relations between the United States and Europe.

GATT's failure in the 1950s drastically to reduce tariff barriers was in essence the mirror image of America's declining grip on Europe. The bilateral-multilateral method of the first tariff conferences had been designed by U.S. negotiators with the assumption that as the principal suppliers of most products, they would take the lead in offering large tariff reductions. This would invite a spillover effect in concessions to other countries and minimize the opportunity for free riding. However, this scenario underestimated the impact of the economic and political business cycle in American trade policies, which rendered tariff rates inherently unstable and which made the game of tariff negotiating increasingly precarious. It also underestimated the impact of West Germany's return as a large economic power and, in turn, the effect of German recovery on the economic potential of Europe as a whole. These changes would gradually alter the balance of forces from a situation where the United States had dictated the rules of the world trading system to one where the United States and Europe had to meet on an almost equal footing. Nothing would express this shift more clearly than the formation in 1958 of the European Economic Community. It gave a decisive push toward preparations for genuinely multilateral, across-the-board tariff negotiations during the Kennedy round of 1963-1967.

FIVE

Tariffs and the Six:
The Beyen Plan and the
Common Market

So far, the tariff issue in postwar Europe has led us along several very different initiatives: a customs union for 16 OEEC members, a preferential trading agreement including France, Italy, the Benelux states and, possibly eventually, Germany, a scheme for OEEC-wide sectoral integration inspired by the Schuman plan and still other, equally ill-fated plans for linear tariff reductions within the OEEC and the GATT. Their persistency throughout the 1950s reflects European governments' long-term ambitions to obtain freer, stable and secure market access for exports to neighboring economies. Nowhere was this policy rooted deeper than in the Benelux states. As members of the Gold bloc in the 1930s, Belgium, the Netherlands and Luxembourg had been in the vanguard of states condemning competitive devaluations and retaliatory tariff policies. They had sought to conclude an international tariff truce and had subsequently in 1932 launched the so-called Ouchy Convention for a preferential trading area with "like-minded" Norway, Denmark and Sweden. Even though Sweden had not endorsed this initiative because Britain had condemned it sharply, the initiative had shown Belgian and Dutch determination to advance regional solutions to the twin threats of economic instability and widespread protectionism.[1] As we discussed in chapter 2, in the immediate aftermath of the war, regional economic integration was just one of several important means available for promoting a more stable, open trading environment. Once economic recovery was underway, however, and the OEEC and GATT proved increasingly incapable of satisfying small countries' demands for reciprocal market access and tariff stability, the Netherlands and Belgium again played their regional card. The Dutch Beyen Plan of 1953 and the joint Benelux Memorandum of 1955 set in motion the negotiations that eventually culminated in the creation of the Common Market of the Six. The Netherlands' historical experiences of trading with Germany help to explain this country's high profile.

GERMANY'S ROLE IN DUTCH POLICIES FOR EUROPEAN INTEGRATION

As the futile talks in the European Customs Union Study Group of 1948 had shown, Germany was destined to play a pivotal role in any Dutch regional strategy. In the first postwar bilateral trade agreements for Germany, the Allied Occupation Authorities had made a rigid distinction between essential and "normal," or nonessential, imports. Since virtually all Dutch imports had been listed as essential products and the bulk of their exports to Germany (including exports of services) had been labeled normal or nonessential, they had paid large amounts of hard currency and had received weak deutschmarks. Many of the traditional Dutch horticultural products had not even been allowed entry into Germany because their caloric value had been considered too low to justify being imported. The Netherlands had thus been forced to supply some of its horticultural production as government loans to the Bizone.[2] As a result of these arrangements, Dutch-German economic transactions had expanded only very slowly between 1946 and 1947. Naturally, The Hague had greeted the bilateral treaty of 1949 with outright euphoria since it had committed the American authorities to remove quotas on virtually all Dutch exports to Germany and also to clear all restrictions on German exports to the Netherlands (with the exception of limitations on coal, iron and steel exports), in return for additional Dutch imports of some German nonessential manufactures. Compared to the previous year, the new bilateral trade agreement of 1949 had envisaged a threefold rise in the value of Dutch exports to Germany.[3] Actual export expansion had soon progressed beyond all expectations, even dwarfing the growth rate of German exports to the Netherlands. By November 1949, Germany had already risen from sixth to first in the ranking of Dutch export markets, leaving Britain behind in third position. Germany had liberal-

TABLE 5.1

Liberalization of German Imports From Various OEEC Countries, 1949

(AS PERCENTAGE OF IMPORTS IN 1948)

	December 1949
Denmark	84
Netherlands	77
Sweden	71
United Kingdom	54
Norway	39
Italy	34
France	28
OEEC average	55

Source: Wemelsfelder. *Het herstel van de Duits-Nederlandse economische betrekkingen,* 37 (see chap. 5, note 2).

TABLE 5.2

Countries' Percentage Shares in Total German Imports, 1928, 1938, 1949, 1950

	1928	1938	1949*	1950
Netherlands	5.1	4.0	3.5	12.6
Sweden	2.3	4.8	4.5	5.7
France	5.3	2.6	0.9	4.2
Italy	3.3	4.5	4.5	4.0
Denmark	2.5	3.1	1.7	4.0
U.K.	6.4	5.2	2.4	3.8
OEEC average	51.1	54.5	37.0	21.1

* before liberalization

Source: Wemelsfelder. *Het herstel van de Duits-Nederlandse economische betrekkingen,* 48 (see chap. 5, note 2).

ized 77 percent of total Dutch imports in 1948, a relatively high percentage in view of the weighted average of 55 for the OEEC countries (see table 5.1).

Germany's first trade liberalization measures do not entirely explain this drastic expansion of Dutch imports because Denmark and Sweden had also obtained high liberalization percentages, but their exports to Germany had grown less fast. Whereas Denmark's share in Germany's total imports had risen from 1.7 percent before liberalization to 4.0 percent after liberalization, the Dutch share had gone up from 3.5 to 12.6 (see table 5.2). This rise can be attributed almost entirely to the agricultural sector, which had managed to fill the gap left by agricultural producers in the Eastern Zone.[4] The 1949 agreement had in fact intensified trading links with Germany to a level that surpassed even that of the late 1920s. Naturally, the Dutch had recognized that this unbalanced, preferential bilateral arrangement would be temporary, but they had been determined to defend their open, stable export outlets in Germany against the international threats that soon became all too apparent: the Fritalux initiative and the OEEC's Trade Liberalization Program.

Since the Fritalux initiative had excluded Britain and Germany and could have caused a drain on gold and hard currency reserves, Dutch negotiators had demanded a customs union including Germany from the outset. This proposal would force countries to remove all barriers to their intraregional trade, not just the quotas mentioned in the early French and OEEC proposals for trade liberalization. It also had the added advantage of forcing the French government to treat Germany on equal terms or to shelve Fritalux altogether.[5] As we have seen, early in 1950 Fritalux had indeed fallen over France's German stumbling block.

The OEEC's Trade Liberalization Program had also become a potential danger to the Netherlands' newly acquired position on the German market. One problem had been its exclusion of state trade from the liberalization targets, which indirectly hampered Dutch agricultural exports.[6] The scheme had also had unfavorable side effects for Dutch exports to Germany; whereas some 73 percent of their exports had received free access under the favorable bilateral trade agreement of 1949, this figure had threatened to drop to 29 percent.[7] The nondiscrimination rule and the use of 1948 as a base year for calculating the amount of trade that had to be liberalized had implied that once Germany had met the overall target of 60 percent, it would in fact tighten quotas on imports from the Netherlands. This shock had been compounded by Germany's payments difficulties (see chapter 3). By partially suspending trade liberalization measures in 1951, major exports flows had been cut off from the German market, causing Dutch payment positions to deteriorate.

By 1950, faced with protectionist threats and economic instability and challenged by possibilities for unprecedented trade expansion, the contours of Dutch policy on Europe had become apparent. In June, the Netherlands had launched the Stikker Plan. Although apprehension about the OEEC's Trade Liberalization Program had been a driving force, it had marked the start of an active search for a European framework that offered long-term economic security and stability for trading relations with Germany. When this sectoral approach had failed, doomed partly by the inconsistencies inherent in its design, a new Dutch minister had been ready to launch a second regional integration initiative relying on a different strategy and forum.

THE BEYEN PLAN

One of the more intriguing aspects of the Stikker Plan had been its attempt to change the OEEC's purely intergovernmental decision-making procedure. By allowing the Council to decide by three-fourths majority rather than by unanimity on which sectors to integrate, it had hoped to prevent Council members from blocking integration with their veto right. Under this new procedure, member states that had voted against removing quotas and tariffs in one particular sector were free to opt out while the others went ahead, and thus Stikker had expected to avoid the Council's veto. It is not hard to see why the logic underlying this assumption proved flawed. In the unlikely event that member states indeed would have abandoned their veto right to allow a majority to go ahead, integration in each individual sector would have involved a constantly changing group of OEEC countries. Instead of integrating European markets it would have fragmented them by creating an entire range of intra-European sectoral preferential zones.[8] Building on this, the new Dutch foreign minister who took office in September 1952, Johan Willem Beyen, concluded that integration by sector and the trade liberalization within the OEEC failed to meet Dutch commercial needs.[9] These could only be satisfied within a more restricted group and only if participants committed themselves in advance to a rigid and automatic timetable for creating the customs union. When the occasion arose in the form of the European Political Community (EPC), he launched a Dutch proposal along exactly those lines.[10]

The Treaty for the EPC was linked to the attempts since 1950 to form a European army in which German units were integrated to promote Western defense efforts. The explosion of the Russian atomic bomb in 1949, the outbreak of the Korean war in June 1950 and subsequent American pressure on European governments to increase their defense contributions and accept the involvement of West German army divisions in NATO produced a new French integration initiative. Known as the Pleven Plan, it tried to control a revived German army through its integration into one large European army under supranational control.[11] In May 1952, the Six members of the ECSC signed the Treaty for this European army, officially called the European Defense Community (EDC). After ratification in the national parliaments, a newly formed assembly would assume political control over the EDC.

Before signing, the French foreign minister Schuman, the Italian prime minister Alcide De Gasperi, and the German chancellor Konrad Adenauer unfolded proposals in the Council of Europe for constructing a European community with political competencies. Without delay, federalists in the Council jumped at the occasion, calling for a genuine political union controlled by a parliamentary assembly. At a meeting in September 1952, the Six ECSC ministers agreed to bring the ECSC and the EDC under a supranational European authority. They charged an ad hoc assembly with drafting the constitution for a European Political Community. At the same meeting, Beyen successfully demanded that they also examine the prospects for economic integration. Again, the Dutch created an opening to push their case for a customs union.

Beyen presented his plan early in 1953, when Ohlin's Low-Tariff Club proposal, Pflimlin's worldwide plan and the OEEC's commodity list were still being discussed. To avoid entering a purely political community with extensive supranational powers but without economic competencies, Beyen presented a detailed customs union proposal, committing governments to remove internal tariffs and to create the common external tariff within a strictly defined period through automatic, linear tariff reductions. These measures had to be written into the EPC Treaty, to prevent governments from delaying or blocking the project. A European fund would provide financial assistance to countries that experienced economic problems from implementing the plan.[12] The Dutch thought that a proposal addressed to the Six and attached to the EPC Treaty could provide far more political and economic leverage than a similar initiative in taken in GATT or the OEEC. As they would soon discover, however, the EPC negotiations incorporated a unique constellation of political and military interests that could have also seriously restricted their economic proposal. A short overview of national standpoints will illustrate this.

REACTIONS TO THE BEYEN PLAN

As one of the initiators of the EPC, Italy saw the Treaty as a great federalist achievement which national governments should present in its original form to the national parliaments. Prime Minister De

Gasperi, who staunchly supported the European constitution and also needed a pre-electoral success, did not want to delay its conclusion by entering in lengthy economic debates. His political successor, Giuseppe Pella, was more willing to talk about economic clauses, but he rejected the rigid and technical arrangements proposed by the Dutch. In his view, Italy's interests lay with a flexible program for building the union that took account of investment requirements for underdeveloped regions and the need for access to member countries' labor markets for unemployed workers.[13] Throughout the negotiations, the new government therefore demanded that the new community's institutions, not the ministers, draft and approve a customs union proposal. This position effectively ruled out active Italian participation in the Beyen Plan discussions.

France's position in the EPC deliberations was as always more complex and ambiguous. Still in 1952, Schuman had presented the plan for political organization as a big leap toward European unity. In January 1953, however, when a new French government under René Mayer took office and George Bidault replaced Schuman, the last minister to defend the EPC Treaty left the cabinet.[14] Mayer's cabinet condoned an EPC because it filled the existing democratic gap by fusing the EDC and ECSC assemblies, but it did not back proposals for transferring the executive authorities of both communities to an all-embracing political authority. It also rejected Beyen's scheme for a European customs union as going beyond the EPC's scope. Officially, France maintained that economic provisions could be discussed, provided they would be laid down in a separate protocol requiring separate ratification. Like Italy, however, it was hardly up to serious customs union discussions.

In February 1952, the French government had had to suspend all import liberalization commitments in the OEEC because of severe balance of payments problems. One month later, a new cabinet had taken office and its minister of finance, Antoine Pinay, had tried to suppress inflation and improve France's external economic position. A representative of the liberal right, he had used a mixture of moral persuasion of employers and small entrepreneurs, price controls and tax advantages to keep down prices and to raise savings and exports.[15] Exporters of industrial products had received a special rebate of fiscal and social charges while import restrictions had continued to protect them from foreign competitors. In 1954, Pinay's successor, Edgar Faure, extended these policy instruments by decree into a vast system of price regulations, investment premiums and export subsidies.[16]

By August 1952, cost of living had dropped 4 percent and wholesale prices more than 5 percent, there remaining fairly stable until 1955. This result, however, had not yet seen a significant export rise because the tax relief had mainly benefited agricultural producers with only limited export outlets and many small, inefficient businesses at the expense of efficient, internationally competitive industries. Moreover, the export prices that did fall were insufficient to close the gap with foreign prices.[17] The balance of trade recovery that took place between the second half of 1952 and the beginning of 1954 was thus almost entirely due to a fall in imports.[18]

The French government had for a long time refused to relax the import quotas it had introduced in 1952 for balance of payments reasons. By the autumn of 1953, however, it faced unprecedented pressure from OEEC governments, who warned that they would not accept new liberalization commitments unless France finally met the Trade Liberalization Program's old 75 percent target.[19] In October, the OEEC's Council forced its members to submit formal explanations justifying their remaining quotas as part of a general resolution demanding further trade liberalization and calling upon France to meet the 75 percent target before March 1954. From that moment on, the prospect of dismantling protective quotas threatened the French economy like the sword of Damocles. The government subsequently raised its official liberalization effort to 18 percent (see table 5.3),[20] but it refused participation in the OEEC's justification procedure to avoid an embarrassing international showdown of French protectionism.[21]

It took another two months before the government, in the wake of strong international pressure, took further action. Early in February 1954, it charged a committee of leading industrialists and experts known as the Nathan Committee with performing a study of the disparity between French and foreign price levels. One solution it considered was a devaluation. This was rejected, first because it would not tackle the causes of France's weak competitive position and second because it might fuel inflation by increasing the costs of raw material imports.[22]

While most cabinet ministers agreed that a devaluation would be politically impossible to defend, their views on France's future liberalization policy parted entirely. Minister of Finance Edgar Faure appeared anxious to reach a 60 percent target, but his colleague Jean Marie Louvel at the Ministry of Industry rejected this as far too drastic. He insisted on reaching just 30 percent, followed by an extension to 75 percent only after a transitional phase of at least 18 months during which the

TABLE 5.3

French Liberalization Percentage with the OEEC, 1951–1955

Date	Percentage
13.05.1951	75
4.12.1952	suspended
1.10.1953	8
1.12.1953	18
21.04.1954	53
26.10.1954	63
6.11.1954	67
4.01.1955	72

Source: G. Marcy, "Libération progressive des échanges et aide à l'exportation en France depuis 1949." *Cahiers de l'Institut de Science Economique Appliqué*, série P, no. 2 (1959): 2.

government would help industries to adjust to growing foreign competition.[23] A true defender of industrial interests, he also demanded that other OEEC countries harmonize social policies.

Supporters of social harmonization argued that France's advanced welfare legislation left producers with social charges that were higher than anywhere else in Europe. French industries were said to suffer from unfair cost disadvantages which added greatly to their inability to compete internationally. They argued that other OEEC members should eliminate this unfairness by raising social charges to the French level, in exchange for which France would then relax quota restrictions and, by 1958, eliminate all quotas. This logic contradicted the Nathan Report's recommendations, which stressed that high social and fiscal charges could hardly be blamed for France's weak competitive position in Europe. Most industrial representatives, however, wholeheartedly endorsed Louvel's strategy. The Federation of Machine Industries for instance was one of many organizations to incorporate his proposals in their policy recommendations to the government.[24] In March 1954, the cabinet finally accepted a compromise on import liberalization, agreeing to meet an initial target of 53 percent and to impose by decree a so-called special temporary compensatory tax. Soon notorious in international circles as the French "super tariff," this extra 10 percent duty initially covered one third of all imports.[25] It served to cushion the shocks of further import liberalization for domestic industry. The extra revenue, moreover, went into a special fund for reducing raw material prices and for modernizing marginal firms. France could hardly have expressed more clearly that it rejected surrendering its tariffs, which was the essence of Beyen's Plan.

Unlike the French, the Germans became active supporters of the EPC's economic clauses. From the very beginning they had welcomed the EDC as a way of rearming and integrating Germany into a Western defense system based on equality. Minister of Economic Affairs Ludwig Erhard and Vice-chancellor Franz Blücher also wanted broad economic tasks for the new community, and they praised the Dutch for having abandoned the narrow, sectoral approach. In their view, however, a joint move toward convertibility among several larger OEEC countries should precede the removal of internal tariff barriers. These countries should meanwhile also tackle "real" market distortions such as capital restrictions, export subsidies and cartels, since a mere customs union could easily be dominated by protectionist forces, thereby also damaging joint British-German efforts to restore convertibility.[26]

Until the start of the ECSC's Council of Ministers meeting in September 1953, however, this view did not enter the debate because Chancellor Konrad Adenauer determined Germany's negotiating position. In need of a political success just before the elections in September, he initially insisted on quickly wrapping up the EPC discussions and postponing the economic discussions, but when that tactic stranded on French opposition, he lost interest in the EPC. Erhard could thus push his own, rather different views on economic integration, provided that Germany's core policy aim, the EDC, survived unharmed. From then on, the German delegation staunchly supported Dutch claims that an EPC without economic clauses was useless. At the bottom line, though, Adenauer would force them toward a compromise with France, which held the key to the EDC's success.[27] This position left the Netherlands and Belgium as the only states to consider a political community where economic competencies were acceptable.

As the initiators of the customs union, many Dutch policy-makers were moderately optimistic about its effects on the national economy. A subcommittee of the ministry of economic affairs had made some promising forecasts, based on the assumption that the union's future common external tariff levels were between 8 and 13 percent.[28] On the positive side was a fall in import prices worth some 90 million Dutch florins, following the removal of internal tariffs. Since almost 56 percent of Dutch nonagricultural products (in SITC 2-9) came from outside the area of the Six, the negative price effect of the upward adjustment of Dutch tariffs toward outsiders was considered fairly modest, about 350 million Dutch florins. This would bring the total increase in import prices to 3 percent of total Dutch imports. Other, more complete calculations using similar methods confirmed this positive outcome. One assessment of 1953 made at the Ministry of Economic Affairs suggested that trade diversion toward member countries amounted to 4 or 5 percent of total Dutch imports, but the effect of an upward tariff adjustment on cost of living would only be 2 or 3 percent. Moreover, if the removal of internal quota restrictions was also taken into account, Dutch exports would rise by between 3 and 7 percent.[29]

Somewhat less optimistic calculations made in 1952 by the Dutch econometrician Peter Verdoorn had suggested that in the short and long run the impact from the creation of the internal market might be disappointing. Assuming that none of the members would appreciate their currencies, the balance of payments would improve by 80 million U.S. dollars. Dutch manufacturing exports would initially increase by 5 percent, thereby raising employment by 30,000 to 50,000 jobs. In the short run, the removal of quotas would mainly benefit exports in agriculture and food and feeding stuffs, but in the long run this would mean permanently surrendering protection in chemicals, metals and machinery which the Dutch had imposed to promote industrialization. Given their weak competitive position on the internal market of the Six, this might cause long-run damage to these industries.[30] Interestingly, it was mainly in the nonquantifiable political impact of the customs union that Verdoorn saw advantages for the Netherlands; the customs union would probably strengthen its negotiating position, avoid bilateral negotiations with member countries (where the Dutch generally found themselves in a weak position) and allow for collective negotiations toward third countries.[31]

Although Verdoorn's estimates were by no means generally accepted by policy-makers, they clearly show that the government's position on customs unions was more complicated than one might expect from a simple glance at the Netherlands' trade dependence or tariff levels. One of the most common worries was that the country's economy would be locked into a high-cost area, an opinion that Prime Minister Willem Drees frequently voiced. He argued that since low price levels were the key to competitiveness, it was dangerous to underestimate the inflationary impact of tariff harmonization. He also sincerely doubted the usefulness of further Dutch participation in the EPC because he felt that with the exception of the customs union, which stood little chance of being accepted, the community had little to offer. Instead of trusting their fate with a small, politically unstable framework that was likely to suffer from unsound French economic policies, he argued, the Dutch should keep relying on the OEEC to improve their position. Since Drees threw his political weight behind this position, Beyen received little negotiating room. His credo throughout the negotiations became "no political integration without economic integration."[32]

The Belgians were more concerned with the community monetary and social aspects than with its commercial ones. Prime Minister Paul van Zeeland early on supported Beyen's attempts to solidify the EPC's tariff clauses, but he also stressed that social and monetary policy coordination was just as important. Since Belgium had a massive surplus on its EPU account which it could only draw upon for soft, nonconvertible currencies, it wanted proposals to solve this imbalance. Moreover, it demanded provisions for freedom of capital movements and for coordinating salaries.[33] Without these provisions, Belgian delegates argued, the Six would be signing little more than an extended Benelux arrangement, ruled by escape clauses and special exemptions.[34]

THE ROME CONFERENCE

Given the widely varying negotiating positions, the outlook for the Rome conference was decidedly bleak. By October, the ministers' deputies finished a report that summarized their mostly conflicting positions on general issues, without tackling whether and how the economic community should be formed. Instead of Beyen's customs union, the report now explicitly mentioned the need to free not only goods but also capital, labor and services. It also stressed that members of this common market had to accept positive economic integration by coordinating monetary and social policies.[35] However, the Dutch were merely prepared to give the community the right to propose coordinating measures, whereas both the Germans and the Belgians wanted to go much further. If governments accepted the Beyen Plan, they argued, governments would invoke safety clauses as soon as eliminating trade barriers caused economic shocks, thereby effectively halting the entire internal market project. Only if the future community's independent supranational authority could make recommendations and take binding decisions on coordination, could they avoid a unilateral return to trade barriers.

Opinions were even more divided on the issue of the transitional stages leading to the Common Market. Even the BLEU partners failed to reach a common stance. Luxembourg delegates, always quick to point out their country's vulnerable economy and precious national identity, did what the French could not do openly; they declared they would support any method for creating the Common Market provided Luxembourg could keep its protective measures. The French were rather negative, stressing the risks involved in creating a common market and insisting on permission to use the entire arsenal of economic policy instruments, including quotas and tariffs to protect strategic and infant industries. They also rejected fixed automatic stages to eliminate internal trade barriers, which other delegates wanted laid down in the Treaty.[36] As for the common external tariff, a cosmetic formula masked the wide gap between high- and low-tariff countries' positions. The conference report stated that external customs duties had to be "as liberal as possible" and had to avoid a rise in prices within the community.[37] This looked like a concession to Benelux and Germany, but what these two countries considered "possible" differed widely from the Italian or French interpretation. Moreover, they knew that the openness of the Common Market also depend on the community's handling of nontariff matters such as escape clauses, special regimes, restrictive practices and common trade policies.

The Rome Report's impact was felt when the experts resumed work in Paris. The French delegation leader Olivier Wormser immediately rejected it as a basis for discussion. Whereas previously he was willing to exchange views, he reverted now to a strategy of tacit noncooperation, thus effectively limiting the talks to an entirely noncommittal exchange of views. These talks are nevertheless worth following, because for the first time since the creation of the European Customs Union Study Group in 1948 tariff experts systematically reexamined the problems involved in creating an internal market.

The experts began by discussing the elimination of internal tariffs and by working out a variety of proposals that, if dealt with at a ministerial level, could offer room for compromise. For a short while, the Beyen Plan steered the discussion on whether to follow GATT's article 24, which stipulated that interim agreements toward a customs union should be formed "within a reasonable timespan" and according to a "plan and a schedule" (see chapter 2). Almost everyone agreed that if the Six went ahead they needed the flexibility of a waiver from the GATT rules.[38] The Beyen Plan's automatic reductions were thus replaced by more flexible methods of tariff cutting, some of which were inspired by the Pflimlin and GATT plans. To introduce further flexibility in the scheme, some delegates proposed deciding in advance on the method for imposing the first 50 percent of all tariff cuts and allowing the community's authority to decide on the second 50 percent.

Over a ten-year transitional period members could thus adjust the speed of their cuts to progress made in monetary and social policy coordination or they could gradually decrease the scale of tariff reductions to compensate for the growing competition that industries would encounter after each stage of tariff cuts.[39] Another way of creating more flexibility was to impose the cuts on weighted average tariffs, not on actual levels, or to cut tariffs by commodity groups, as suggested in the GATT plan. Customs duties would then be divided into groups and their average (weighted or arithmetic) levels in each group eliminated in subsequent stages.[40] Within these commodity groups, members were free to chose which rates to cut first and to what extent. Belgium also suggested adopting the floors and ceilings of the GATT plan, so that the lower Benelux rates could initially come down at a slower pace than higher French, Italian and German rates.[41]

Ironically, France's attempts to avoid radical, linear reductions through the Pflimlin plan clearly backfired, since the plan suddenly resurfaced as a method for achieving a customs union. What could the French do? Apart from opposing the plan, very little. At one time, the French representative suggested by way of counter proposal that the Six accept an obligation to conclude with eachother preferential purchasing agreements as a gesture of mutual European solidarity. But since this would force the other five to buy France's high-cost agricultural imports, they immediately rejected it as totally unacceptable.[42]

The talks on the common external tariff were equally cumbersome, but after a while several alternatives to Beyen's automatic method emerged that might be accepted. Again, the Pflimlin and GATT plan methods surfaced, as did a proposal for a tariff standstill agreement of three years, during which each of the Six would remain in charge of their own tariff. After that period, they could impose cuts via the GATT plan method or via GATT's normal bilateral-multilateral negotiating procedure, allowing countries to take maximum advantage of their high tariffs in bargaining with third parties.[43] The Germans brought up this bargaining option because they were keen to secure access to markets outside the community for their rapidly expanding industrial exports. Tariff bargaining seemed ideally suited to these aims, since it not only reduced rates in third countries but it would also indirectly bring down the community's future external tariffs by reducing the average rates individually levied by the Six. The other delegates, though, were skeptical of this approach. France and Italy refused to reduce protection against outside competitors under any circumstances. Moreover, they thought it unlikely that third countries would offer concessions once it became known that the Six would eventually reduce their tariffs anyway. Benelux complained that the GATT plan would reduce their low duties even further whereas Germany could keep considerable protection simply by imposing the cuts on its higher, legal tariffs. Belgium in particular feared that some domestic industries would be ruined by German competitors even before all its internal tariffs were eliminated. It therefore insisted on "decapping" all high rates before cutting the normal ones.[44]

Whatever proposals were launched, however, the economic talks had reached a complete stalemate. Even the Dutch knew they were fighting a lost battle.[45] Germany, Belgium, Luxembourg and Italy at least shared an interest in some aspects of the economic clauses, although their demands had rapidly developed far beyond the original Dutch customs union proposal. For France, by contrast, the economic clauses in the Rome Report did not seem to hold a single redeeming feature. The French government would never abandon its national modernization policy and surrender economic sovereignty for the mere sake of market competition and integration.[46] Nor was it convinced by the argument that Germany's competitive force could best be contained in a community structure, with resources that only the community could muster.[47]

Continuing the economic talks in fact merely represented a political holding operation for what was becoming increasingly unlikely: France's ratification of the EDC. The French government had initially tried to win time to rally support for the Treaty, which for a wide variety of reasons had become increasingly controversial and unpopular.[48] When the government under Pierre Mendès-France finally presented it to the National Assembly in August 1954, parliamentarians rejected it. The EPC Treaty and the economic clauses attached to it thus were also lost.

THE "RELANCE EUROPÉENNE"

While the EDC catastrophe crushed federalist hopes for a political community, ideas for relaunching "Europe" along different routes were back on the table as soon as the creation of the Western European Union (WEU) solved the problem of German rearmament. Two different approaches dominated the talks. The first one, favored by a circle of committed "pro-Europeans" close to Jean Monnet and the Belgian foreign minister, Paul-Henri Spaak, aimed at creating an entirely new, supranational institution for energy, and in particular nuclear energy.

This sector, a most promising but still underdeveloped field for economic expansion, should become the driving force for European integration.[49]

The second approach, pushed by the Dutch government, was based on the Beyen Plan. After the fall of the Mendès-France government in February 1955, Beyen suggested resuming the negotiations on his plan where they had been left off in August 1954. He was convinced that supranationality was a precondition for success because "intergovernmental economic cooperation [had] reached the limits of what [was] possible and offer[ed] few guarantees for real cooperation in times of economic recession."[50] He now fully acknowledged that the Six should not merely aim for a customs union but should work toward a common market, for which a customs union would lay a solid foundation. Sectoral economic integration on the other hand could not do so, since it would solve problems in one sector at the expense of productivity and price levels in others.[51] As he saw it, the talks in the EPC's Economic Committee had shown a general consensus among five of the six ECSC states on eliminating internal trade barriers. The Six should therefore pursue this road toward general economic integration, thereby also defending supranationality against the dangers of resurgent Franco-German bilateralism.[52]

While the Dutch still saw Beyen's scheme as the basis for a common Benelux proposal to the Six, and while Spaak and Monnet clearly pushed sectoral integration, some ministries within the Belgian government were exploring their own alternatives to recapture the momentum. In October 1954, the ministries of trade and economic affairs were unpleasantly struck by the ever closer economic cooperation between France and the Federal Republic.[53] These states had conducted bilateral talks on mutual investment projects in French North Africa and, by the end of a month, concluded an agreement to extend mutual trade, investment and cultural cooperation within Europe and the French Affiliated Territories.[54] Belgian producers had tried for years to obtain a foothold in French overseas markets, which were heavily protected by a system of preferential quotas, subsidies and exchange controls. They now feared that German competitors might succeed in obtaining preferential access.

This suspicion grew once they learned of talks for a bilateral trade agreement allowing France to sell part of its agricultural surplus to West Germany. Although such deals were not uncommon in agriculture, the fact that Germany's protectionist agricultural ministry had clearly been overruled hinted at substantial benefits for German industrial exporters.[55] The Belgian ministry of economic affairs certainly interpreted this as a warning. Its director general, Jean van Tichelen, later recalled:

TABLE 5.4

Annual Growth Rates (in percentage) of Exports From Selected European Countries into West Germany, 1953–1955

Exporting country	1953/54	1954/55
Norway	28.3	18.7
Netherlands	26.9	21.1
France	24.9	42.8
United Kingdom	19.3	9.0
Denmark	18.8	45.0
Sweden	14.5	17.3
Italy	10.9	26.5
Switzerland	10.6	17.8
Belgium/Luxembourg	5.7	47.0

Source: United Nations, *Yearbook of International Trade Statistics, 1955* (Geneva, 1956).

Soon it transpired that France made large efforts to strengthen its economic ties with the Federal Republic. Of course, this was also in the interest of peace, but the mutual opening up of French and German markets to each others' products threatened to damage the Benelux countries. The figures confirmed our worries. French trade with West Germany was growing faster than ours. We had to react.[56]

France's exports into Germany indeed grew faster, in particular between 1953 and 1954, the year on which the Belgian officials based their assessments. Whereas BLEU exports rose by 5.7 percent, French exports increased by almost 25 percent in this period (see table 5.4).[57] By way of comparison, Italian exports to Germany rose by 10.9 percent and British and Danish exports by 19.3 and 18.8 percent respectively. Only Dutch exports grew faster than those of France, by almost 27 percent. During the following year, by contrast, all countries except the United Kingdom would experience a drastic spurt in their exports into Germany.

The economic ministries were alarmed by Belgium's comparatively weak export performance in the German market and by the extraordinary intensity of the French export boom. Within the scope of a few months, they considered several different scenarios for a joint Benelux initiative to resume multilateral talks on European economic cooperation. One plan, put forward in October 1954, directly responded to their fears of preferential trade deals that excluded Benelux. It entailed a free trade area between the Six and their overseas territories.[58] Another, more widely discussed proposal suggested creating a European free trade area that excluded agriculture and the affiliated territories. It would provide countries the freedom to exclude those manufacturing industries that were clearly uncompetitive because of differences in factor costs.[59]

Both schemes apparently aimed at obtaining freer access to the French and German markets while protecting Belgium's weaker sectors. Agriculture was one such sector. Already during the Beyen Plan discussions the ministry of agriculture had rejected this sector's inclusion in a customs union or common market, even if its formation underwent a long transition period.[60] Chemicals was another sector demanding special treatment and there, too, the scheme would serve Belgian interests. Belgian coal was still higher in price than coal elsewhere (despite the working of the ECSC), with the result that the predominantly coal-based chemical industry had difficulty competing with German, French and Dutch producers. Claiming that its chemical industry suffered from unevenly high factor costs, the Belgian government insisted on maintaining some form of protection in this industry.

The economics ministry's plans were never put to the test, partly because Spaak and Monnet convinced the Belgian and Luxembourg governments that there was more hope for sectoral integration and partly also because the Dutch still preferred the general integration approach. By the end of April 1955, Monnet and the three foreign ministers of Benelux decided to present the sectoral as well as the general common market approach as two parallel strategies for further integration. In a joint memorandum addressed to the Six, the Benelux governments called for an economic community under a common authority and for sectoral integration in the field of classical energy, transport and atomic energy. While their proposal was deliberately vague on the character of this common authority, it specifically mentioned the need for harmonizing social policies, since that would certainly appeal to the French.[61]

How did the other three governments respond to the Benelux proposals? The German position cannot be explained without mentioning the departmental struggles within the government. Chancellor Adenauer cautiously welcomed the relaunching of economic integration initiatives, not because he was skeptical of Germany's entering a common market but because he feared it would meet French opposition and could hamper European political integration.[62] However, once the discussions on the Common Market were underway and made substantial progress, he pushed very hard for their quick and successful conclusion.

Within the German ministry of economic affairs, two groups were fighting for a decisive say in the negotiations. The ministry's Schuman Plan Department welcomed the Benelux initiative as beneficial for Germany and Europe. Its head, Hans von der Groeben, took great pains to play down the outspoken criticism of Ludwig Erhard, who argued that the Benelux Memorandum was based on purely political considerations.[63] Erhard warned of a gradual sliding into a small "dirigiste" and protectionist club of Six, which would hinder Germany's trading links with non-European countries and its sound financial policies. Insisting on a liberal and outward-looking common market, he urged the Six to ban all forms of trade discrimination and unfair competition, such as subsidies and cartel agreements. If a supranational institution would help to enforce community rules, so much the better. However, if it served other, purely political or protectionist purposes, wider economic cooperation within GATT and the OEEC would be preferable to a common market of the Six.[64]

The French government's reaction was cooler still. Earlier in 1954, Mendès-France had again indicated that securing France's economic modernization and international viability were his priorities. Economic integration could always be discussed at a later stage. This policy remained almost unchanged after the shift in government in February 1955. Edgar Faure became prime minister, but continuity was assured with Pierre Pflimlin taking over at the ministry of finance. Faure insisted very early on that France's interests stretched no further than European cooperation in nuclear energy and transport.[65] His government would not commit itself to anything "European" before the elections in the spring of 1956, least of all to projects involving tariff cuts. France's uphill struggle to raise the liberalization percentage was causing already more than enough political agony. It also prompted further pressure for a rise in tariff protection. Nevertheless, there were clear signs of an improvement in France's external economic performance. Since May 1955, it experienced a period of remarkable production and export expansion while prices remained stable. GNP at market prices rose by 4.8 percent in 1954 and by 5.8 in 1955. The balance of payments improved drastically and the trade deficit shrank from more than 413 billion francs in 1952 to 86 billion in 1955. The percentage of imports covered by exports rose from 87 percent in 1954 to 93 the following year. Gold and currency reserves also increased steeply.[66]

A breakdown of French exports by country of destination shows a sharp exports expansion toward the European countries (see table

TABLE 5.5

Annual Growth Rates (in percentage) of French Exports to Main Markets, 1953–1955

Destination	1953/54	1954/55
Switzerland	32.6	30.7
Italy	26.9	12.8
West Germany	24.9	42.8
Belgium/Luxembourg	20.9	14.6
Netherlands	16.2	37.0
Total Continental Western Europe	22.9	26.5
United Kingdom	13.3	46.4
United States	-14.4	31.6
French overseas areas	9.2	5.3

Source: United Nations, *Yearbook of International Trade Statistics, 1955* (Geneva, 1956).

5.5). Exports to continental Western Europe increased steadily at annual rates of well over 20 percent between 1953 and 1955, compared to rates below 10 percent for exports into the French overseas areas. This formed a striking contrast to previous years, when exports had been largely absorbed by the preferential markets of the Franc Zone. As we saw earlier, West Germany was one of its fastest growing export markets, absorbing the largest share of France's exports to Europe (see table 5.6). By 1953, it had overtaken the BLEU as France's largest European export market and one year later it took just over 8 percent of total French exports. France also improved its position in the Swiss market. In 1954, Switzerland had overtaken Italy, the United States and the United Kingdom in the ranking of major French export markets.

   This period of high export growth paved the way for a changing attitude toward market integration among various French producers. A new generation of more outward-looking entrepreneurs was discovering the advantages of new and faster growing sales opportunities abroad. They had tasted the fruits of market expansion and began pressing for a reorientation toward Europe. Agricultural producers also demanded export outlets for their growing production of wheat, sugar, wine and dairy products.[67] Already in 1951, the then minister of agriculture, Pflimlin, had tried to solve France's surplus problem by launching a proposal for sectoral integration in agriculture that became know as the Green Pool. This involved a product-by-product organization of the

TABLE 5.6

Destination of French Exports to Main Markets, 1953–1955

(AS PERCENTAGE OF TOTAL EXPORTS)

	1953	1954	1955
French overseas areas:	32.3	31.8	29.2
Algeria	12.0	11.4	11.8
French West Africa	4.9	5.6	4.7
West Germany	7.4	8.2	10.4
Belgium/Luxembourg	6.4	6.6	7.0
United Kingdom	5.6	5.8	7.3
USA	4.8	3.7	4.2
Italy	3.4	3.9	3.8
Switzerland	3.2	6.5	5.1
Other	36.9	33.5	33.0

Source: United Nations. *Yearbook of International Trade Statistics, 1955* (Geneva, 1956).

European market by guaranteeing markets and prices for European farmers.[68] Like so many schemes of this kind, the Green Pool had failed to materialize and agricultural exporting countries had been left to rely on bilateral deals. If a European common market were to come about, however, agricultural producers would finally acquire safer export outlets for their growing surplus.

Obviously, there were still major pressures on the government to preserve import controls. Some sectors of the economy coped with low productivity levels and high production costs. This is why they were internationally uncompetitive and wanted to preserve import protection.[69] The economy as a whole also still suffered from demand inflation caused by large military expenditure. The government was therefore reluctant to abandon its arsenal of regulatory policy measures such as export incentives, import taxes, quantitative restrictions and multiple exchange rates. Both considerations shaped French policy toward European economic integration. A new French government considering joining the Common Market would insist on special treatment during a period of readaptation, giving domestic industries exclusive rights to maintain protection against member countries. It would also demand a harmonization of social charges in the direction of French levels in exchange for trade liberalization. Lastly, it would require export outlets for its agricultural surplus within the framework of an organized market.

THE SPAAK REPORT

Although the political climate in France remained unsettled, the foreign ministers of the ECSC countries meanwhile agreed to discuss the Benelux Memorandum at an intergovernmental conference in Messina on June 1–3, 1955. Apart from sectoral plans, they discussed both the removal of barriers to the trade in goods and the freeing of services, capital and labor. In addition, they explored the possibilities for the harmonization of social, economic and financial policies, the application of safeguard clauses and the creation of a readaptation fund. Despite numerous French and German reservations, the talks ended with a final resolution calling for further study of the sectoral and common market proposals among a group of governmental experts.

Until November 1955, a Brussels study conference of experts chaired by Spaak subsequently tested the ground for the negotiations. The results of these discussions were outlined in the Spaak Report of April 1956. This concluded that of all the initiatives mentioned in Messina, only sectoral integration in nuclear energy and general economic integration through a common market required further examination. For trade and tariff matters, the report drew heavily from the Beyen Plan negotiations and the GATT plan. It summarized the steps toward the creation of the Common Market and described the most promising methods for eliminating internal tariffs and for creating the external tariff. Since these methods were to form the starting point for the governmental negotiations, we shall discuss its recommendations in the tariff field.[70]

The Spaak Report considered a customs union the core of the future Common Market. It urged for an open, outward-looking arrangement that complied to GATT's article 24 on interim agreements toward a customs union. The union would be created according to a twelve year schedule with a maximum extension of three years. This transitional period would be divided into three stages of four years each. In the first stage, all tariffs close to the future common external tariff level would be reduced by 10 percent and all other tariffs by 30 percent. In the second stage they would be cut by another 30 percent and in the last phase the remaining ones would be removed completely.

To meet French demands for more flexibility in this automatic approach, the authors of the Spaak Report turned to a method resembling that of the Pflimlin Plan. Tariffs were arranged in broad groups according to their actual levels. Rates below 10 and above 50 percent would be divided into groups with a range of 5 percent each. Rates between 10 and 50 percent would be divided into groups with a 2.5 percent range. Each government would be free to decide which individual tariff lines to cut first, provided it met the overall reductions required per group. The tariff averages per group were defined as the actual tariffs applied during the period 1953-1955, weighted by the quantity of imports from third countries in this period.

Further flexibility was introduced by giving the community's supranational authority or Commission (supported by a majority in parliament and a qualified majority in the Council of Ministers) powers to change the tariff cutting procedures. After the first two stages, the commission could prolong the transition period by three more years. Upon approval by the Commission, a country facing special difficulties could also temporarily postpone cuts of "sensitive" tariff items, provided that imports under these items did not exceed 5 percent of its total imports.

The Spaak Report was far less detailed on the procedure for establishing the external tariffs. Just as during the Beyen Plan discussions, it proved simply too difficult to work out a compromise between French demands for the highest possible level acceptable to GATT and Dutch calls for a tariff similar to that of Benelux. In the end the authors suggested three different ceiling levels for raw materials, semimanufactures and end products. Just as in the Ohlin and Pflimlin Plans, the existing rates above these ceilings would have to be decapped before gradually adapting to the common level.

The external tariff levels would be calculated by taking the arithmetic average of the French, Benelux, German and Italian customs duties that were actually applied on all the products of the Brussels Nomenclature of 1955.[71] A decapping procedure would be imposed for raw materials, semimanufactures and manufactures, but the ceiling levels for each of these groups were left unspecified. To minimize the risk of trade deflection, the schedule for forming the common external tariff had to follow that outlined for the internal market. After the first 10 percent cuts in internal tariffs, those rates within a range of 15 percent of the future external tariff would be adapted immediately. The others would be brought in line with the external rates in steps of 30 percent, to be taken after each stage in the transitional period.

The method for removing quantitative restrictions was also an issue of bitter debate. The French preferred to follow the slow pace of the OEEC's Trade Liberalization Program. The others favored a separate scheme that would speed up their removal and tighten escape clauses. The Spaak Report had neither taken sides nor offered compromises. It merely stated that in the last phase of the transition toward the Common Market, quotas could only be applied in concerted action, after common agreement and for a maximum period of one year after completing the removal of internal tariffs. The abolition of quotas would be irreversible, except in cases where the Treaty's safety clauses applied.

BRITAIN'S REACTION TO THE COMMON MARKET

So far we have left out Britain's stance on the Common Market, which well until mid-1955 had been characterized by benign neglect of things happening in Brussels. By the end of that year, however, the British government began to reverse its policy of abstention, developing a new course that would fundamentally influence the policy choices of the Six. Below, we shall examine this new policy and its consequences for the Common Market negotiations. To appreciate its origins, it is worth briefly recalling the tariff events leading up to it.

The United Kingdom had always turned its back on European tariff initiatives, whether in the form of customs unions, sectoral integration or simply tariff reduction schemes. Not since Foreign Secretary Bevin's flirtations in 1948 with a European customs union had it seriously considered joining tariff reductions that differed from the traditional bilateral-multilateral procedure of GATT. Whenever the tariff issue was raised, British delegates received instructions to reject low-tariff countries' complaints within the OEEC and to discourage new tariff cutting methods within GATT. All this changed by the end of 1954. The Low-Tariff Club threatened to block the OEEC's 90 percent liberalization target, to employ import quotas in retaliation for high tariffs and to undermine the convertibility discussions (see chapter 3). In view of these threats, the British cabinet reluctantly approved the option of multilateral, across-the-board tariff reductions in GATT.

The first British tariff initiative was conceived during the special session for the review of GATT rules that began at the end of 1954. Based on the Havana Charter's old article 17, it entailed a commitment to the Contracting Parties to enter into tariff negotiations. This commitment was one of several Low-Tariff Club demands for changes in the GATT rules. It also referred to the possibility of using across-the-board tariff cutting schemes such as the Pflimlin or GATT plans.[72] The British negotiators intended to present their blueprint to the low-tariff countries at the OEEC's next Council meeting in January 1955. Naturally, they planned to explain that they could only participate in such a scheme on equal terms. It would then be up to the Europeans to insist on American participation. Yet before they could table their draft article, it became clear that the Americans could never accept such a commitment since Congress would simply reject it. Consequently, the British simply withdrew their proposal, relieved that the Low-Tariff Club was settling for much less. The revised GATT article on tariff negotiations explicitly recognized only the principle previously unwritten, that binding a low-tariff was equivalent to reducing a high tariff.[73]

A second British proposal emerged in July 1955, after GATT's secretariat tried to devise alternatives to the GATT plan which had failed so clearly in 1954.[74] Still heavily based on the old GATT scheme, the secretariat's new scheme suggested exchanging lists of tariff requests and maximum concessions on a multilateral basis. GATT's trade negotiating committee would examine these lists for their fairness, giving special regard to low-tariff countries. It would also stress the need to decap tariffs higher than 50 percent.[75] Since the European and even the American delegates gave this scheme the benefit of the doubt, the British delegate suddenly stood alone in opposing it. Faced with complete isolation and pressure by the OEEC, the president of the board of trade, Peter Thorneycroft, and the chancellor, Butler, instructed their delegate to submit an alternative tariff scheme that would take off the pressure.[76] This suggested multilateralizing the traditionally bilateral stage in GATT negotiations by agreeing to take 15 percent tariff cuts as general negotiating targets. Moreover, it recommended imposing ceiling and floor levels of 50 and 10 percent respectively. If the principal supplier of a product refused to negotiate on that basis, such a product would be excluded from the operation.[77]

Although the British delegate to the OEEC lobbied hard for its acceptance, it failed to satisfy Danish and Dutch demands for drastic reductions in European tariff disparities.[78] Italy, Sweden and Germany were more positive, but they realized only too well that the plan's fate ultimately depended on the Americans. Indeed, in August 1955, the die was cast. American diplomats announced that the British proposal was unacceptable. The official justification was that since the U.S. was forced to exclude its specific and revenue duties (which made up a relatively high share in its schedule), the Contracting Parties presumably would never agree to join the scheme. While this may have played a role, it was even more obvious that the U.S. government disliked setting tariff reduction targets. This practice would be interpreted at home as unwarranted international pressure on the president to exploit his new negotiating mandate under the Trade Agreements Extension Act.[79] Even though the British initiatives in GATT still failed to satisfy low-tariff countries, the fact that they were launched at all shows the U.K. government's growing awareness that the tariff issue formed a threat to its European policy. In the course of 1955, officials recognized that the OEEC's new quota liberalization effort would end in "a flop" due to the Low-Tariff Club's obstruction and delaying tactics.[80] Britain still faced the Club's tariff inquiry and their scheme for a European commodities list. This would again be discussed before mid-1956, when the 18 months trial period for the OEEC's 90 percent target was due to end. Added to all of this were now also the Messina proposals for a common market and for sectoral integration in energy.

Initially, the Messina plans did not arouse major worries within the British government. It accepted the invitation of the Six for the experts' conference, but it was convinced their project would eventually strand on French objections.[81] By sending a representative, the government simply wanted to show its goodwill. Moreover, its spokesman, the under-secretary of the board of trade Russell Bretherton, might steer the discussions toward a more modest form of economic cooperation within the OEEC that would also meet some of the Low-Tariff Club's grievances.[82] Indeed, the Messina proposals initially seemed less embarrassing to Britain than the OEEC's tariff schemes. When the issue of close cooperation with the Six was raised, Britain could easily point at its dislike of supranationality and its special links with the Commonwealth as the major barriers toward participation. Within the OEEC, however, it had no easy, standard policies available when low-tariff countries put British protective tariffs within the spotlights.

In November 1955, the government decided not to join the Common Market. This decision was based on the conclusions of a study by a working party of officials from all the departments concerned.[83] This group started from the assumption that if Britain were to join, it would almost certainly be followed by Ireland, the three Scandinavian countries, Switzerland and Austria. Further, it raised the specter of the Common Market embracing the Scandinavian countries (who were negotiating their own customs union at the time) as well as the Six, in the face of British aloofness. In this form, the area would absorb almost 26 percent of total British exports (see table 5.7).

In an ambiguous summary, the report concluded:

TABLE 5.7

British Exports to the Six, Scandinavia, Ireland, Switzerland and Austria, 1955
(AS PERCENTAGE OF TOTAL BRITISH EXPORTS)

The Six	12.9
Denmark, Norway and Sweden	8.3
Ireland	3.7
Switzerland	0.9
Austria	0.4

Source: United Nations, *Yearbook of International Trade Statistics, 1955* (Geneva, 1956).

We do not feel able to predict with any certainty whether or not the ultimate results of entering a common market would be beneficial to the United Kingdom economy (once the adjustments necessary in the transition period had been made), as compared with the situation in which no common market of any kind was established. In the long run, the benefits for the United Kingdom economy as a whole would show themselves in the form of higher productivity and output in this country, as a results of a more efficient use of resources in Europe generally.[84]

It explained that the United Kingdom might lose or benefit from the change in trading patterns in Europe and the Commonwealth. After pointing at the benefits from cheaper supplies outside the Commonwealth and the costs of a loss in Commonwealth preference, the report greatly added to the confusion by stating: "We feel obliged, however, to conclude that, on balance, the net long run effects on the United Kingdom of any weakening of the Commonwealth Preference System which resulted from our entry into a common market would be adverse: it is uncertain whether these adverse effects would offset the gains to be expected from United Kingdom participation in a common market."[85]

Despite these uncertainties, the report settled for a negative net impact from joining. One main reason was that adopting the common external tariff would automatically reduce the margins of preference that Commonwealth countries enjoyed in the British market over non–Common Market countries. Again, the no-new-preference rule played a role in this. The margin of preference would shrink for goods receiving a lower common external tariff, whereas it was not allowed to rise for products obtaining a tariff higher than the British, since that would violate GATT's rules. Another consideration was that preliminary sectoral studies gave a rather gloomy picture of the impact on industries of Britain's participation in the Common Market and its loss of preferences. The studies predicted that on the losing side would be horticulture and most other sectors within agriculture and fishing, the optical industries, the woolen textile producers, and producers of pharmaceutical products, dyestuffs, hard tools and some types of electrical equipment.

The problem with these sectoral analyses was that they were so biased against joining that even the authors of the final report expressed sincere doubts about their validity. They noted that:

> . . . there is a noticeable tendency for practically every report on a sector or industry to suggest that the United Kingdom industry would most probably lose from free competition with the industries of other potential common market countries in the area of the continental common market plus United Kingdom (quite apart from any additional losses arising from reduced preferences in Commonwealth markets). This is not logically easy to accept, and is not borne out by our experience in export markets such as the U.S.A. and Switzerland—where the United Kingdom competes with continental Europe on fairly equal terms.[86]

In comparison, the sectoral studies were curiously optimistic on the impact of staying aloof.

Shortly after cabinet's decision against joining, the Americans insisted that the British withdraw from the Messina conference.[87] The Eisenhower administration strongly endorsed the efforts of the Six for closer integration and was anxious to avoid negative British interference.[88] Still in November, therefore, the British withdrew their delegation. Rather than face accusations of trying to sabotage the Common Market they would "let it collapse of its own weight."[89]

As the project developed, however, some British cabinet ministers began looking for ways to influence it in Britain's favor. Thorneycroft, for instance, warned of its damaging effects on British trading interests.[90] Earlier, in 1952, he had advised participation in a scheme for tariff reductions and quota elimination on the basis of the OEEC's common list. At the time, cabinet colleagues had ignored his recommendation but now, almost four years later, he received support from his colleague at the treasury, Harold Macmillan. Even though most other ministers still firmly believed the Six would fail, they agreed that Britain should "pick up the pieces" and regain the initiative.[91] Thorneycroft and Macmillan should therefore develop a counter-proposal that could be presented to the Six.

But what options were available? By the beginning of 1956, British officials considered two alternative schemes, one for the creation of a European preferential zone within the OEEC and another for the automatic reduction of tariffs covering goods on the OEEC's commodity list. Both plans had tariff reductions as their central element because, as one treasury official warned his superior, "The key to this is tariffs. If we can offer nothing on tariffs, the rest would be of little value to Europe."[92] In the following months, four other proposals reached the mutual aid committee, thereby bringing the final list to six plans.[93] They entailed the following policy initiatives:

A. Active cooperation in tariff initiatives within the OEEC, to placate the low-tariff countries and to bring the Liberalization Program back on course.

B. Merging the OEEC and the Council of Europe, to create a framework for limited but "real initiatives" in the field of economic cooperation.

C. A European commodities tariff scheme involving a 20 percent tariff reduction covering all goods on the OEEC's European commodities list. It also suggested a decapping procedure for tariffs above 40 percent and a floor level of 10 percent below which tariffs were exempted from reductions. The reductions made among the OEEC countries would be extended to GATT countries in return for reciprocal tariff reductions.

D. A free trade area for steel, allowing Britain to cut its steel tariffs to 10 percent and to be associated with the ECSC.

E. An industrial free trade area with OEEC Europe, involving the elimination of intra-OEEC tariffs and quotas for all products except those of interest to Commonwealth exporters. This would allow Britain to preserve its margins of preference with the Commonwealth countries and its own tariffs toward third countries.

F. A "Strasbourg type" system of mutual tariff preferences between Britain and the Commonwealth and Europe and its overseas territories.[94]

The ministers agreed that option F was not feasible. It violated GATT's no-new-preference rule and accentuated the tensions already existing between Britain's worldwide approach to freer trade and payments and its system of Commonwealth Preference. Moreover, as the Collective Approach had shown, several Commonwealth countries (in particular Canada) were critical of extending preferences since it might damage their trading links with the United States. Finally, European governments might object to opening their markets to Commonwealth products just when they were throwing up trade barriers against the influx of Japanese products.[95]

Plan D, a free trade area for steel, would require a waiver from GATT but it would be feasible if British producers were assured of strict rules against dumping and unfair competition. On the other hand, it would hardly be received as an attractive alternative to a common market. The same was true for options A and B, which were therefore kept in reserve.

This left plan C and E, both involving tariff cuts. The first one, the European commodities list, had the disadvantage that it would almost certainly affect a range of sensitive, uncompetitive British industries without providing a convincing alternative to Messina. The Benelux countries would probably consider it a mere gesture that could neither solve the European tariff disparity issue nor come close to the attractions of the total and permanent elimination of tariffs. Furthermore, the impact of these cuts on each country's export opportunities and import growth depended on which products were put on the list. It would be extremely difficult to agree to a definitive list of commodities which balanced the cost and benefits for the United Kingdom. Plan E, by contrast, presented a full-blown British answer to Messina, while still preserving the essentials of Commonwealth Preference. Commonwealth goods could continue to enter the British market duty free and they could keep their preferential treatment toward countries outside the free trade area. Furthermore, British producers could keep most of their preferences in Commonwealth markets. If it excluded agriculture, plan E's impact could thus be positive for Britain.[96]

The British government had only just agreed to pursue a further study of the industrial free trade area (by now renamed plan G), when in May 1956 the Low-Tariff Club launched a new tariff reduction method. Presented within the OEEC, it looked—in the words of Bretherton—"uncomfortably similar" to Britain's Plan C.[97] It also suggested automatic tariff cuts covering the goods of the European commodities list. The cuts would amount to 25 percent and would be extended unilaterally to all GATT members, since their relevance to nonparticipants was limited.

Ironically, the impact of the Low-Tariff Club's scheme on British tariff protection would be less than that of Plan C, since the first excluded tariffs below 20 percent and the second did not.[98] On the other hand, the Club announced these cuts as a first step only, which the British government found unacceptable so soon after the GATT round of 1955-1956.[99] The government now faced a new dilemma. It was ready to block the Club's proposal but: "if we go no further, there may well be a complete deadlock . . . and the effects could well be deplorable. The tariff issue has come to be widely regarded as a test of the efficacy of the OEEC as an instrument of European cooperation, a patent failure at this point might leave the Messina Group as the focus of further activity in Europe."[100] The British delegation was therefore forced to launch its most promising alternative, plan G, even though this existed only as a preliminary draft proposal that still required cabinet and parliamentary approval. In July 1956, the OEEC created a study group to examine Britain's proposal for associating the Common Market of the Six with the other OEEC members.[101] An obvious way to accomplish such an association would be through a free trade area, and indeed this is what the study group immediately found itself discussing. This maneuver gave the cabinet breathing space until November, when parliament eventually endorsed the negotiations for an OEEC-wide free trade area.

The Six regarded this British move as a fresh attempt to thwart the Common Market. The French felt that the British demanded the best of both worlds by trying to obtain free access to the internal European market while keeping their own market closed to Europe's agricultural exports. Benelux representatives to the OEEC were also infuriated since they had hoped to secure the European commodities scheme as an extra safeguard against French efforts to obtain a high external tariff. The British maneuver had sidetracked their scheme and with it, they feared, the chance to cut European tariffs of 20 percent or more.[102]

THE SIX ON THE ROAD TO ROME

Although France's attitude would remain a constant worry for the Common Market supporters, the French elections of January 1956 undoubtedly improved the project's chances of acceptance. The new government under the socialist Prime Minister Guy Mollet was more positive than its predecessor, and it could rely on a favorable economic and political climate. True, the proposed European Atomic Energy Community (or Euratom) appealed much more to the French public than the Common Market, but the government realized early in 1956 that the latter could become crucial to France's economic future. Its fast industrial expansion depended on ever increasing imports of raw materials and semimanufactures. This in turn required it to step up exports by improving international competitiveness and by acquiring outlets for French agricultural produce. Economic liberalization was therefore unavoidable. Provided certain safeguards were obtained, the internal market of the Six would form a relatively safe environment in which French industries could adapt to these new requirements.[103]

After the National Assembly debate on Euratom, the French government obtained clearance to negotiate on the Common Market and it then formulated six conditions for joining.[104] It demanded that the decision to enter from the first to the second stage in the transition toward the internal market be taken by unanimity within the Council of Ministers. In addition, it insisted on harmonizing social costs, inclusion of its overseas areas, permission to maintain tariffs and export subsidies for balance of payments reasons and the right to reintroduce exchange controls during balance of payments problems. Last, it demanded an exceptional status within the future community. The government thus went for maximum safeguards in the process of creating the Common Market.[105]

The first and last conditions were closely linked. If France obtained a special status, its industries would almost immediately profit from the reduction in trade barriers while still being spared the potentially negative effects of increased competition on the domestic market. This would give the country a temporary preferential position that could smooth the process of internal and external economic liberalization. However, if it failed to obtain a special status and encountered severe economic difficulties, it could still delay or halt the transition by a using a veto within the Council of Ministers. The other demands were also designed to safeguard the French position within the Common Market. They should have satisfied those French industrialists who were prepared to support a common market that combined export opportunities with built-in safeguards against unfettered competition.

Although the compromise that was worked out at a special summit failed to meet all the French demands, it provoked storms of protest, particularly in Germany and the Netherlands. Eventually, however, these countries also agreed that the Council of Ministers would need a unanimous vote if it were to proceed without delay. Failing that, it could take up to two years before the Council was allowed to decide by qualified majority to enter the second stage. France received a special status during the transitional phase and the right to preserve its export subsidies and special import tax, but only under specifically defined circumstances and during a strictly limited period. It could also resort to special measures to remedy balance of payments problems.

Before the Six could turn to the remaining internal market issues, the French tabled a new demand. Their foreign minister, Maurice Faure, stated that participation of the French overseas areas was a *sine qua non* to his government. The Six should provide exporters within the overseas areas with free access to the Common Market. They should also assist in the economic development of these areas by contributing to an investment fund and by concluding long-term preferential contracts for agricultural imports. In exchange, the Six would receive free access for their own exports into these areas, once the transitional period had ended.[106]

Both within and outside France, these proposals caused widespread controversy. In France, they met staunch opposition from traditional "colonial" French producers who had always considered the French Union as their rightful, preferential export market. They strongly criticized the government's plan to increase competition within the French zone and saw it as the beginning of the French Union's demise.[107] Others argued that "Eurafrica" offered the only way of strengthening the strained links between France and its mostly African territories. Apart from political difficulties—which certainly dominated the debate— there existed strong economic tensions within the Union. France faced the ever increasing burden of financial aid, price support schemes and investments in the overseas areas. These areas in turn suffered under the high prices of imports from the mother country, which according to some assessments lay about 40 percent above world market prices. Already in 1954, a subcommittee of the *Commissariat au Plan* had urged a break of this vicious circle of preferential, high-cost trade that fueled inflation in both areas. Yet it had also decided in favor of strengthening economic ties within the Union. In its view: "The future of France, a former world power on the map but not according to the statistics of production and standard of living, does not merely depend on the efforts of the center and the sound development of the overseas areas but on its coherent development as a unity."[108]

These efforts had started with the ratification in 1954 of the Treaty for a Franco-Tunisian customs union agreement. A customs union with

Morocco had been planned as a further step toward one large customs union comprising the entire French Union. If France were to participate in a European common market it would be cumbersome and difficult to keep European products outside this Union by maintaining a discriminatory trading regime. French officials at the ministry of foreign affairs indeed concluded that at some stage these two aims of the European Common Market and the separate economic advancement of the French Union were bound to collide.[109] They therefore opted for a solution that associated their African overseas areas with the Common Market.

Apart from Belgium, which shared the wish to include Belgian Congo, there were few enthusiasts for the French proposals. The other governments felt uneasy at the prospects of being drawn into French colonial problems and of sharing the financial burden of investment programs and purchasing arrangements. Eventually though, they gave in. By the end of February 1957, agreement was reached on the size of their investment contributions. The overseas areas would enjoy all the advantages of the tariff reductions within the European Community. In return, the Six would benefit from the progressive abolition of customs duties by the associated areas, except when these areas needed their duties to "meet the needs of their development and industrialization or produce revenue for their budgets."[110]

Well before the "Eurafrican" controversy was solved, the Six agreed on the method and schedule for removing internal trade barriers. At French requests they abandoned the Spaak Report's method of cutting tariff averages by product groups, and they turned to a less complicated procedure that combined linear reductions with a certain flexibility (see table 5.8).[111] France's support for this linear method did hold a price tag. It demanded and obtained a safety clause in the Treaty allowing members to halt temporarily the tariff cuts in production lines that experienced severe difficulties from increased competition.

The Treaty articles defined the rates subject to reductions (or "base rates") as those duties in force in each member country on January 1, 1957. During the first year, members would cut all their duties by 10 percent. Further reductions of 10 percent would follow 18 months after the end of the first, and the third at the end of the fourth year. Unlike the first, these second and third cuts would not be imposed on each tariff item individually but in a way that would reduce total customs receipts by 10 percent.[112] Tariffs above 30 percent, however, would each be reduced by at least 10 percent of the base rate. By the end of the first four-year stage, each member should have lowered all its base duties by at least 25 percent.

During the second stage of four years, there would again follow three reductions, each consisting of a 10 percent cut in total customs receipts (with a minimum of 5 percent for each individual item and a compulsory 10 percent for all rates above 30 percent). The first cut would be made 18 months after the beginning of the second transitory stage (i.e., half way through the fifth year), the second 18 months later and the third 12 months after the second. By the end of this four-year stage at least 50 percent of the base duties would have been cut. Finally, in the third and last stage all remaining tariffs would be eliminated according to a procedure determined by the Commission and approved in the Council of Ministers by qualified majority.[113] The removal of quantitative restrictions would take place by gradually increasing the total value of imports under the quotas in steps of minimum 20 percent a year, with at least 10 percent for each individual quota. Beforehand, all bilateral quotas open to any of the members would be converted into global, nondiscriminatory ones.

By January 1957, the Six had dealt with the most essential decisions relating to the internal market for commodities. One major problem remained, however, and that was agriculture. The Spaak Report had confirmed the decision to include this sector in the Common Market on the condition that it would receive special transitional measures. These should mitigate the impact of eliminating protection and should guarantee a minimum standard of living for European farmers. The type of measures and the extent of support remained a matter for debate. Germany and Luxembourg, whose producers were most likely to suffer from increased competition in agriculture, heavily opposed agriculture's inclusion in the Common Market. Luxembourg fell back on its usual tactic of first demanding an exemption status and then keeping a low profile. The Germans wanted to keep their own agricultural organization in charge of imports, price fixing and subsidizing, believing it would provide more safety against competition than any common policy ever could.[114] The Netherlands and Italy rejected this because part of their gains from joining the Common Market would come from expanding agricultural exports to Germany. France occupied the middle ground; it also aimed at opening up the German market for its surplus, but on three conditions only. First, it insisted on maintaining its own system of market organization and price regimes for at least another eight years into the transitional period. Second, it demanded that member countries

TABLE 5.8

Schedule for the Removal of Tariffs Within the Common Market, 1957

Stage	Year	Period for new cuts (months)	Tariff cuts	Other requirements
I	1	12	10% of all basic tariff items	Cuts minimal 25%
	2½	18	10% of (basic tariffs x value of imports	
	3			
	4	18	10% of (basic tariffs x value of imports	
II	5½	18	10% of (basic tariffs x value of imports	Cuts minimal 50%
	6			
	7	18	10% of (basic tariffs x value of imports	
	8	12	10% of (basic tariffs x value of imports	
III	9		Elimination of remaining tariffs.	
	10		Procedure decided by qualified majority	
	11		in the Council of Ministers.	
	12			

Compiled from: European Communities. *Treaties Establishing the European Communities: Amending Treaties: Other Basic Instruments* (Luxembourg. 1983).

conclude preferential purchasing contracts, thus forcing them to buy French products above market prices. Third, it wanted a high common external tariff for agriculture, a system of guaranteed minimum prices and subsidies on exports to third countries.

The Dutch, the only ones not relying on border controls for agricultural protection, insisted that agriculture fall under the same transitional regime as the other sectors. They wanted firm treaty regulations that committed all members to removing protectionist frontier controls within the Common Market. Only then could they avoid being pulled into a common policy that either upheld existing restrictions and forced members to buy overpriced surplus production, or that lacked any common agricultural policy. By the end of the negotiations, the Dutch faced a combination of both evils. Agriculture was included in the schedule for the customs union, thus assuring progress toward the elimination of tariffs and quotas. However, designing the arrangements for a common agricultural policy was left to the Commission. Until members reached agreement on such a policy, national market organizations would remain in existence and agricultural trade would have to be developed further through long-term purchasing agreements.[115]

THE COMMON EXTERNAL TARIFF

The other decisions that were partially postponed until after the Treaty's conclusion concerned the common external tariff. The procedure for its formation was quickly determined since there were no objections to the method outlined in the Spaak Report. Tariff headings within a range of 15 percent of the common tariff should be leveled toward the common external tariff before the end of the first four-year phase. For all other customs duties, the margin of difference with the common tariff would be reduced gradually in two steps of at least 30 percent each, one taken after the first transitional stage and the other after the second. A final step would follow in the third and last phase.

Determining the exact external tariffs was by far the greater problem. As we have seen, the Spaak Report had suggested a calculation method based on the arithmetic average of the rates imposed by the Six, whereby the Benelux partners were counted as one customs area. It had also proposed a decapping procedure with three ceiling levels each for raw materials, semimanufactures and end products. This method raised two problems, one related to selecting the ceiling levels and the other to determining the composition of these three groups. Both difficulties still had to be solved when the Six entered the stage of governmental negotiations.

The national positions on this issue mirrored those adopted during the Beyen Plan discussions. West Germany and Benelux demanded a low external tariff to avoid a rise in the price of their imports and to limit the danger of retaliation by third parties. France and Italy on the other hand pressed for higher rates closely corresponding to their own tariffs. Shortly after the start of the negotiations, the French government handed in a long list of raw materials and semimanufactures that it wished to see classified as end products in order to raise their decapping ceiling and keep out competitors from third countries.[116] Behind such obvious divisions on the Common Market's average levels of tariff protection, there also surfaced numerous other, more complex clashes of interest once it came down to determining the rates on individual products. The German government, although not insisting on one particular calculation method, demanded full knowledge in advance of all the individual duties within the common external tariff schedule. It argued that this knowledge would be indispensable for preparing its domestic producers for the advent of the Common Market. For this reason, each country agreed to select 300 tariff positions for which experts, by using two alternative sets of decapping ceilings, would calculate the future common rates; one low-tariff alternative involved ceilings for raw materials, semimanufactures and manufactures of 5, 10 and 20 percent respectively, and one high-tariff alternative was based on ceilings of 15, 20 and 40 percent respectively.[117]

As the Dutch had explicitly stated in their reaction to the Spaak Report, the external tariffs would be an issue crucial to their economic welfare. They wanted the future levels fixed in advance, but unlike Germany they firmly supported Spaak's choice of using unweighted arithmetic averages of the existing tariffs as a basis for calculation. The reason was that average rates weighted by the volume of imports worked against them, since these tended to give much larger weight to high tariffs (whose effect it is to limit or prohibit imports) than to low ones. Their greatest fear was that the negotiations would lead to an agreement to fix the precise levels only after the Treaty was signed, and that the community would adopt a protectionist policy in international negotiations. For this reason, they were keen to ensure that the supranational Commission would be given the leading role in future common tariff negotiations with third countries.[118]

The Belgian government showed much more flexibility on this point. While it had joined calls for low tariffs at an earlier stage, it now seemed quite willing to strengthen its bargaining position toward third countries with a common tariff schedule that surpassed Benelux levels. Belgian negotiators suggested determining a so-called fighting tariff that would be higher than normal average levels but not so high as to violate GATT rules. This should strengthen the Common Market's position in multilateral negotiations with other GATT partners. Much to the annoyance of the Dutch, they also suggested creating a separate product group for agricultural products which would be given a ceiling level of 27 percent. This position received immediate support from the Italians and Germans, who also favored higher agricultural tariffs toward third countries. Unusually, the French sided with the Dutch on this matter. They argued that tariff levels would not really matter once the Six had created an organized market for agriculture.[119]

In December 1956, around 2,000 rates of the hypothetical external tariff schedule had been calculated for both the high and low decapping ceilings. By that time, the delegations agreed to abandon the Spaak method in order to break the deadlock. They reached a settlement on a ceiling of 3 percent for raw materials, 10 percent for semimanufactures and on an arithmetic average for end products. They also agreed that tariff levels covering a maximum of 2 percent of each member's imports in 1956 would be put on a separate list, called list G. Their precise levels would be negotiated after signing the Treaty, before the end of the second year of its implementation.[120] Until a settlement was reached, members were allowed to apply a system of tariff quotas.

This compromise only solved part of their problems. The exact division of products by raw materials, semimanufactures and end products was still undecided, as was the role of agricultural products, fiscal tariffs and the French and Italian legal rates in determining external tariffs.[121] Moreover, France now argued that its approval of decapping meant that Benelux would benefit at the expense of members in need of protection. It laconically claimed that: "Without making an appeal to complex weighing methods, it would be logical to exclude the zero or low duties from the calculations for the common external tariff."[122] And with that statement a new conflict developed.

If these French demands were met, and if rates of 3 percent or lower were to be excluded, tariffs would rise quite drastically for sectors such as organic and inorganic chemicals, petroleum products, synthetic dyestuffs, and nonferrous metals and metal manufactures.[123] The Dutch and Belgian chemical industries used many of these goods as intermediary products, a reason why their tariffs did not exceed 7 percent. Yet French negotiators insisted that they could go no lower than a 15 percent ceiling because their chemical industries would only survive with adequate protection against outside competitors. Germany and Italy were prepared to accept a compromise rate of between 7 and 15 percent, but the Dutch were not. Eventually, only a new set of intricate rules could break the deadlock. The French conceded that as a rule, the common external tariff should be based on the arithmetic average of tariffs effectively applied on January 1, 1957. The Italians were allowed to define their applied tariff as the legal schedule, i.e., without the temporary 10 percent reductions made in 1949.[124] The other solutions all represented exceptions to the general principle of using an arithmetic average. The French received a special list of 73 of their normally suspended tariff positions (list A) for which their higher, legal rates would be used for calculating the external tariff. The Franco-Benelux dispute over tariffs equal or below 3 percent was solved by raising such rates on organic chemicals, dyestuffs and plastics (list E) up to a floor levels of 12 percent before calculating the external tariff. At the same time, these products were given ceiling levels of 25 percent, which the common tariffs should not exceed.[125] The ceilings for manufactures (list B) and semimanufactures (list C) had remained the same, i.e., 3 and 10 percent respectively.

These compromises were intertwined with an agreement on ceilings for inorganic chemicals (list D), which had provided the other major Franco-Benelux stumbling block. Benelux accepted a ceiling of 15 percent, in exchange for an assurance that the Commission received authority to grant tariff quotas at a reduced rate to members whose traditional imports largely depended on third countries and who would face a shortage within the Common Market.[126] Moreover, tariff quotas could also be given to countries importing goods on lists E and G, if changes in supply sources or shortages would damage their processing industries. Finally, another list of some 25 tariff positions (list F) included goods for which the tariff levels had to be determined in separate negotiations after signing the Treaty. Many of these products received tariff levels below those obtained from calculating regular arithmetic averages in order to lower the costs for members importing from outside the community.[127]

On March 25, 1957, the Treaty establishing the European Economic Community was signed in Rome. Its articles on the customs union, in the Treaty's language the foundation of the Community, were the direct outcome of almost two years of intensive and protracted negotiations between the Six. Yet its shape owed much to the tariff negotiations that had taken place during the previous years. It contained several of the provisions worked out earlier during the discussions on the Pflimlin, Ohlin and Beyen plans, such as flexible tariff reductions spread out over groups of tariff items, stage-wise tariff cuts of 10 percent and also the decapping of high tariffs and the use of floor rates. Furthermore, its tariff articles clearly reflected the disparity problem: over 80 percent of tariff items on list G (for which the members failed to reach agreement before signing the Treaty) covered chemicals. These were the same products that had been a bone of contention to "low-tariff" Benelux, Sweden and Denmark and that had figured so prominently in the OEEC's tariff examinations in 1950 and 1955. And many other items that ranked high on these lists of tariff complaints (again chemicals, but also base metals, paper and paperboard etc.) had found their way onto the special lists A to E annexed to the Treaty.

For the Netherlands and Belgium, the two Low-Tariff Club members joining the EEC, list G represented a large element of insecurity about the impact of the Common Market, since their import-dependent industries could be damaged if they failed to secure low external tariffs for these products. Dutch policymakers were keenly aware that both list G and the general formula for the external tariff could at least in the short run have a negative impact on their economy. Prime Minister Drees in particular appeared extremely pessimistic about the economic prospects. Only one month after signing the Treaty, he concluded that the Dutch were about to enter "a relatively small, protectionist combination."[128] However, most others felt that the short-term disadvantages did not outweigh the long-term advantages from a permanent solution to tariff problems. The EEC did after all offer a large internal market free from tariffs and quantitative import restrictions, permanent free access to the rapidly expanding German market, a strong position in negotiations with the United States, Britain and Japan, as well as a safe haven for an extensive system of agricultural protectionism.

In Germany, it was the ministry of economic affairs that had strong objections to the Treaty of Rome. Erhard infuriated many of his colleagues within the government by publicly announcing in France that his country had joined for purely political reasons. The Common Market itself, he argued, was "economic nonsense."[129] Germany's commercial interests, although not as "worldwide" as Erhard liked to believe, indeed went far beyond the framework of the Six. They were particularly strong in the remaining small European economies of Scandinavia, Austria and Switzerland. However, there was little doubt that Erhard's concept of worldwide economic integration did not lay within the range of possible compromises. One reason was that, at least until the mid-1950s, the persistent dollar shortage had forced most European countries to discriminate against imports from the dollar area. This strengthened protectionist tendencies and increased the pressure for a common European policy of hard bargaining toward the United States. Furthermore, it was only in exchange for concessions outside the tariff sphere that France and Italy were prepared to surrender part of their tariff barriers.

Only a European solution could accommodate these compromises and this is what happened when the Six concluded the Treaty of Rome. The experiences of previous, aborted tariff plans had shown the need for Benelux and West Germany to accept a common market with a sufficiently high external tariff and with special arrangements for France.

Not surprisingly, though, many critics of the Treaty within Germany, Belgium and the Netherlands refused to see the trading framework of the Six as their final aim. They became vigorous supporters of Britain's attempts in the late 1950s to bring the Six and the remaining OEEC members together within a wider free trade area.

SIX

European Tariff Plans and National Tariff Policies: The Cases of Germany, Britain and the Netherlands.

A recurring theme in this book is that governments inspired, molded and shaped tariff plans for national policy aims. Their policies have been explained in terms of their perceived national interests, whether these were economic, financial or political. By focusing on national states as actors in the international network of economic and political relations, we have thus assumed that commercial policies are the outcome of a governmental or intergovernmental decision-making process, and that what is expressed at lower levels within governments and societies requires no direct explanation. When examining the behavior of European states within the OEEC, the GATT and the ECSC, for instance, we abstracted from decision making and bargaining at the sectoral, parliamentary or party elite levels.[1]

Even though one chapter cannot possibly offset this limitation in perspective, this last part will try and highlight some of those aspects of domestic decision making that can be shown to have influenced European tariff schemes.[2] It will trace how governments in Germany, Britain and the Netherlands coped with various domestic opportunities and constraints and how, and to what extent, such influences impeded or stimulated tariff reductions in Europe. It will also discuss some of the implications of closer international trade cooperation for national economic policies. One aspect of particular interest in this context is the link between domestic pressure upon governments to retain quotas and international pressure by the OEEC and GATT for their elimination. Everywhere in Europe the compulsory switch from quotas to tariffs affected special interest groups within the economy that feared international competition and had a strong interest in preserving the relative safety of quota protection. A closer look at this process may offer further insights into the interaction of domestic interest groups, national governments and international organizations in shaping commercial policy choices.

THE DOMESTIC DEBATE IN WEST GERMANY

West Germany is an unmistakably interesting starting point for such a case study because successive governments were so obviously and openly divided on commercial policy and economic integration. The proverbial clashes between the foreign ministry and the economics ministry under Erhard on the wider Free Trade Area seem to ridicule any notion of a monolithic decision-making process. Another, more compelling reason for starting in Germany is the country's importance for the entire Western world. The Americans saw it as a key player in the future liberal economic order and wanted it to be a forerunner of trade liberalization within the OEEC and GATT, while the Europeans knew that Germany's economic position directly influenced their national economic welfare. During the discussions in 1948 for the OEEC-wide European customs union, it had been Germany's absence that severely impeded attempts at integrating the European market. In all other plans that followed, its role only increased because it was becoming Europe's fastest growing economy and largest trader. Free access to the German market thus became an economic objective for Benelux, France and Italy alike, since this would guarantee rapid growth of their economies. As we shall see, these countries closely watched domestic German forces in favor of and against trade liberalization and adapted their national commercial policies accordingly. A closer look at the German domestic scene will therefore also contribute to a better understanding of other countries' policies and of the motives for European-wide tariff reductions.

In chapter 3 we already touched upon West Germany's new tariff schedule of 1951 and the country's accession to GATT. It had entered the negotiations in Torquay with a "bargaining tariff," which it had partly reduced to levels considered necessary for protecting domestic industries. The German government had successfully withstood Allied pressure for widespread modifications of its draft schedule. In addition, it had obtained a favorable balance of concessions that offered good prospects for the expansion of traditionally strong export sectors, such as machinery, optical and electro-technical instruments and chemicals. However, this bargaining tactic also carried some serious disadvantages that constrained the government's future tariff policy. By allowing pressure groups and parliament from the start to assist in defining bargaining rates, it had restricted its freedom to maneuver previously regained from the Allies. The result was that once the OEEC's Trade Liberalization Program increased foreign competition on the domestic market, import-competing producers in the textile, rubber and paper industries and some sections of the pharmaceutical and metalworking industries insisted on preserving the 1951 rates.[3] Throughout the 1950s, moreover, the agricultural lobby persistently undermined Erhard's trade liberalization policy.[4]

Immediately after the Torquay negotiations, the German government decided to suspend and reduce several mainly agricultural tariffs likely to cause sharp rises in consumer prices.[5] Other high rates on basic consumption goods were preserved, however fierce the protests from trade unions, consumer organizations and foreign exporters. The high new customs duties on potatoes, pork and eggs, for instance, almost caused a breakdown in Germany's bilateral negotiations with Denmark and the Netherlands. The butter duty even became a cabinet matter, since the Danes, Swedes and Dutch had threatened with retaliatory measures against German industrial exports because the existing tariff prevented them from filling their bilaterally negotiated butter quotas. Furthermore, the Social Democratic Party (SPD) had launched a new campaign against high tariffs on essential foodstuffs. In March 1952, German ministers therefore decided to examine the impact of cutting the 25 percent rate to 15 percent. Upon examination, however, Chancellor Adenauer and the agricultural minister rejected this proposal, fearing that it would cause a parliamentary debate on import duties that would damage the government.[6]

A look at some temporary individual tariff cuts imposed between 1951 and 1953 confirms the impression that the cabinet wanted to stabilize consumer prices and cut input prices for processing industries, usually after consultations with the industries concerned.[7] The impact of these cuts on overall levels of protection remained small. The only drastic reductions that were imposed in this period resulted from bilateral negotiations with Switzerland in September 1951, just before the new tariff schedule was introduced.[8]

By the end of 1951, prompted by OEEC countries' complaints about the new German tariff schedule, the ministry of economic affairs insisted on raising Germany's official quota liberalization percentage for manufactures and agricultural products.[9] Officially, these quotas were in place to safeguard the country's precarious balance of payments position, but unofficially, as even some German officials admitted, the critics were right. In their efforts to shelter weak industries from the Trade Liberalization Program's first impact, civil servants had gone much too far; they had excluded almost the entire textile sector from the list of liberalized imports and had maintained the system of state trading in agriculture. Even though the OEEC only took account of restrictions on *private* trade when it calculated members' official liberalization percentages, Germany had not yet met the 60 percent target within agriculture.[10]

Erhard managed to improve Germany's record by putting several textile products on Germany's new list and by raising the official liberalization percentage up to 51 percent for foodstuffs and to 60 percent for raw materials and manufactures. He would have liked to liberalize still more, but producers convinced him that industry needed guarantees that other OEEC members did not impose export restrictions on scarce raw materials and that France, West Germany's fastest growing export market, would also improve its record.[11] When France failed to to do so, however, Germany had to relax its import restrictions unilaterally in the course of 1952. By April 1953, after the interdepartmental committee on trade policy reassured producers once more that the existing import duties were high enough to protect weaker industries, the government liberalized imports by up to 90 percent.[12]

Most industrial producers supported the cabinet's decision to rely almost entirely on tariff protection. They needed freer access to European markets and expected to achieve this by taking the lead in removing quota restrictions and reducing tariffs. During the international discussions on the Pflimlin and Beyen Plans, for instance, major industrial organizations such as the *Bundesverband der Deutschen Industrie* (BDI), the *Deutscher Industrie und Handelstag* (DIHT) and the German section of the International Chamber of Commerce regularly issued statements expressing the need for further tariff cuts in Europe. Together with their government they argued that the Pflimlin Plan, because of its worldwide scope, deserved the most attention, provided that all important industrial nations would participate.[13]

The first rumors of temporary *unilateral* German tariff reductions caused a storm of negative reactions from domestic industries.[14] A tentative discussion at the end of 1953 showed that Erhard and the German OEEC delegation preferred linear, across-the-board reductions since these could increase imports and domestic prices much more effectively than a limited number of individual tariff cuts. They received support from a variety of political parties and organizations, but were condemned by a coalition including the ministry of agriculture, farmers' organizations, the parliamentary committee for agriculture and many Christian Democratic politicians, as well as import-competing manufacturers in the textile, paper, leather and toys branches. Several internationally competitive industries also argued against unilateral linear tariff cuts, urging instead for a concerted German diplomatic effort to get the GATT plan accepted.

In view of this opposition, Erhard was eventually forced to back down in cabinet and abandon across-the-board cuts. Ministers agreed to study plans for cutting individual rates, relaxing quotas in industry and agriculture and loosening capital restrictions.[15] They appointed a tariff committee made up of representatives from government, industry, agriculture and the trade unions. This group decided that tariffs were recommended for cuts if at least one of three criteria applied: the bargaining margin originally imposed for the Torquay round had been left intact, the protected industries concerned had outgrown the need for heavy tariff protection or the reduction would contribute to a more harmonious tariff structure. This last criterion referred predominantly to sectors where previously tariffs had been cut at the insistence of manufacturing industries using them as inputs. As a result, these industries had actually experienced increases in *effective* levels of protection.[16]

A recurrent theme in virtually any German debate on trade policy was the privileged position of farmers. So it proved to be this time. Should agriculture be excluded once more from tariff reductions and quota relaxations, thus shifting the full burden to industry? That the cabinet did not exclude this sector in advance of the committee's investigations was a small miracle in itself. Earlier, the agricultural lobby had complained bitterly about import liberalization beyond the OEEC's 60 percent target, and it strongly opposed such measures in combination with tariff cuts. The reason why the government still tried to include the sector regardless of such opposition was that industrialists saw it as a precondition for support for unilateral tariff cuts.

Faced with this new threat to farmers, the ministry of agriculture meanwhile tried to win time. Having started its own examination of unilateral tariff cuts in December 1953, it claimed to need at least until the end of March 1954 to conclude talks with the agricultural organizations.[17] However, these discussions appeared to be concerned with new, rather than fewer, protective measures. Much to Erhard's horror, the ministry of agriculture and the farmer lobbies together embarked on a campaign for so-called sliding scale tariffs, the incidence of which moved in the reverse direction of price levels. These would assure stable prices on the domestic market, once quotas were relaxed. On January 1, 1954, the ministry indeed introduced its first sliding scale tariff on brewing malt, for an experimental one-year period. This product originally held a 20 percent ad valorem tariff, but domestic producers and their suppliers, the wheat growers, had complained that this level was too low once foreign producer prices started dropping.[18] Raising the ad valorem tariff was in itself not effective if prices abroad continued to fall, but a mixed, sliding scale tariff would now neutralize the drop in the price of imported malt with a rise in tariff incidence. As usual, consumers paid for this sophisticated protection measure, since the tariff modified only the downward price movements, not the upward ones.[19]

Even though this system suited only fairly homogenous products (i.e., bulk-produced raw materials and agricultural products), its introduction troubled foreign exporters. Shortly after introducing the new tariff on malt, the minister of agriculture suggested extending the experiment to eggs. He also managed to convince several tariff experts at Economic Affairs of the tariff's effectiveness as an anti-dumping measure against Japanese industrial exports. In the absence of adequate legislation, his argument ran, sliding tariffs were highly suitable as retaliatory measures.[20] This clearly worried the Danes and Dutch, who headed the protests within the OEEC and GATT since they feared that Germany would revert to widespread use of sliding tariffs once it had to raise the official OEEC trade liberalization percentage for food and feeding stuff.[21]

The agricultural ministry's operation was a successful maneuver to ditch unilateral tariff cuts in agriculture. When the cabinet insisted on a restricted use of sliding scales, the ministry gave way but also seized the opportunity to block further tariff cuts, accepting the decision to remove quotas on some agricultural products ostentatiously "only under protest," and only in exchange for the sector's exclusion from any unilateral tariff reductions.[22] Once again, the agricultural lobby had gotten its way.

By April 1954, the committee for tariff reform formulated some preliminary advice, proposing cuts for 700 of the total of 3,650 tariff positions in the German schedule. The depth of most cuts varied between 10 and 33.3 percent, apart from a few rare cuts of 50 percent. Almost all tariffs of 40 percent (in total 42 positions) were recommended for 30 percent cuts. Of the 44 positions of 35 percent, the committee suggested cutting 42 of them by between 5 and 30 percent. All cuts had to be imposed temporarily, until the end of June 1955, when the consolidation period for GATT's tariff concessions expired. The exception to this rule concerned customs duties of 40 percent, which existed primarily within the chemical sector. These rates were recommended for permanent cuts.

The committee had clearly tried to temper fears of excessive foreign competition on the home market and diminished international bargaining power. It stressed that the cuts only involved those tariffs that had proved unnecessarily high and that bargaining purposes had received due consideration.[23] Nevertheless, some industries protested vehemently against individual tariff cuts, even where these amounted to only a few percent. To give just one example: In September 1954, a producer of woolen blankets sent a letter to Erhard, requesting him to reject the recommended tariff reduction of 2 percent (from 18 to 16 percent) for his product. Erhard promised to pass on the request to the president of the parliamentary committee on foreign trade. This committee eventually rejected the proposed tariff cut.[24] In truth, the government no longer expected the cuts to result in an import surge. Some 60 percent of total imports covered under the cuts were raw materials and semi-manufactures imported duty free or at modest tariff levels. Any major contribution to rising imports therefore had to come from the proposed tariff cuts ranging between 10 and 33.3 percent on manufactures, which represented a mere 15 percent of total imports. As a positive gesture to OEEC members, however, these reductions would do quite nicely.

The cuts were planned for September 1954, but after receiving cabinet approval in June, they still had to pass all the legislative stages. It took until January 1955, almost one year after the OEEC had told Germany to moderate its excessive creditor position within the EPU, before the Bundestag finally approved the cuts with some minor amendments.[25] By that time, Ludwig Erhard had become so concerned with the steep rise in domestic prices that he saw the cuts as too little and too late. He and his colleague at finance warned the cabinet of an overheated economy, urging for action "with all possible economic policy means," including radical quota liberalization and drastic tariff cuts.[26] Up to then, they argued, this policy had never materialized because the government had always been forced to follow a parliamentary route that delayed and watered down proposals, forcing policymakers to use general monetary and credit policy measures that were less effective and heavily disliked by the business community.[27] To secure liberalization measures in the existing situation, the two ministers suggested asking the Bundestag for an empowering act covering all chapters of the German tariff schedule (including agricultural and revenue duties) without any limits on the depth of the cuts. Since this act enabled the government to reduce tariffs without prior parliamentary approval, it isolated the tariff machinery from direct interference by interest groups and transformed tariffs into flexible economic policy instruments.

The joint ministerial proposal received mixed reactions. Vice-chancellor Franz Blücher admitted the need for strengthening governmental powers over tariffs, but he and his colleague at agriculture insisted on exempting the agricultural sector while other ministers doubted the proposal's feasibility. Already in 1952, Erhard had asked parliamentary approval for a change in the tariff law that would authorize modifications without prior consent, but parliamentarians had firmly rejected his request. Since the cabinet felt that a second similar defeat had to be avoided at all costs, it decided to move very carefully by first examining the political climate of support.[28] As talks during the following months indicated, it was wise not to move too quickly. No matter how slow and inadequate the existing legislative procedures were, parliamentarians overwhelmingly refused to surrender their role in tariff-making. Erhard was thus left to pursue his "counter-cyclical and psychological policy" by issuing some thirty different laws for temporary tariff cuts on basic materials and a few agricultural products.

The attempts in Germany to strengthen the government's grip on tariffs were far from unique. Everywhere in Europe, governments increased their influence over the national economy, trying to expand the range and effectiveness of policy instruments. In the field of trade policy this resulted in attempts to transform tariffs from quasi-permanent, almost constitutional constructions into flexible, quickly adaptable administrative policy measures.[29] Hence the use of a two-column tariff based on legal and applied tariffs in Italy, the introduction of sliding-scale duties in West Germany and the emergence in 1954 of a temporary levy or "super tariff" in France. What seem to have been special circumstances in Germany of the 1950s were the rapidly changing economic realities underpinning the tariff system and the system's incapacity to cope with fast changes. Germany's unprecedented economic recovery since 1947 turned the 1951 tariff schedule into an anachronism almost on the day it was implemented. It was, moreover, the outcome of overrated reparation and war damage estimations, and of exaggerated expectations from tariff bargaining coinciding with a short-lived balance of payments crisis that had prompted calls for high tariffs. Two years on, most German industrialists could happily live with lower duties, indeed wanted a tariff scheme that reduced German rates in exchange for more access to foreign export markets. Their political backing, together with the general public's endorsement of a constructive international role for Germany helped Erhard to pursue an active trade liberalization policy within the OEEC and GATT. These frameworks for international economic cooperation also offered the Federal Republic a solid base to accomplish its broader foreign policy goals of political rehabilitation and integration within the Western world.

The growing network of international agreements and obligations sometimes limited rather than increased governments' freedom to maneuver. In the 1950s and 1960s, when European governments all promoted foreign exports and common trade rules to generate higher domestic economic welfare and stability, interdependence increased to unprecedented levels. Many governments initially experienced great difficulties in assessing the costs and benefits from these forms of international organization. This was partly because, in the short run at least, such arrangements almost always reduced the scope for autonomous commercial policy actions, and partly also because they represented unknown and untested constructions susceptible to turbulent international and domestic change. The British case discussed below offers some further insights into the linkage between international and domestic constraints on commercial policies. It singles out the internal economic and political considerations that shaped British attitudes toward international tariff cooperation within GATT, the OEEC and the Six.

BRITISH POLICYMAKERS AND THE TARIFF

After the war, the British Labor government had rejected any major revision of its prewar tariff schedule. Consequently, throughout the

1950s British policymakers had to cope with a complex, historically grown set of different, often overlapping tariff provisions specifically designed for the extraordinary economic conditions of the 1930s.[30] In addition to the Import Duties Act of 1932, which imposed a general 10 percent tariff on all goods (except those charged under other tariff acts), there were special provisions for beef and veal, silk and artificial silk, and for so-called key industries. Naturally, there also existed a whole range of exemptions and reductions for Commonwealth countries, imposed under the Ottawa Agreements.[31] The only major institutional difference with the prewar period was that the board of trade, rather than the Import Duties Advisory Committee (IDAC), had gained responsibility for tariff modifications.

This soon became a heavy task, since the old tariff system assumed a freedom to maneuver that the new postwar government no longer possessed under its freshly accepted international commitments. Various key industries, for instance, had become used to high tariffs as well as quota protection against foreign imports, even though these import quotas clashed with GATT principles.[32] Some domestic lobbies also worked against preserving the traditional tariff system, such as industrialists demanding protection against Commonwealth imports that entered Britain duty free under Imperial Preference. Under these circumstances, the government needed skillful maneuvering to accommodate vested interests depending on the old system, and to promote internal and international trade liberalization. As one official at the board of trade complained during one of the OEEC's tariff examinations:

> . . . as individual United Kingdom industries have for the past years been accustomed to these [pre-war] duties, which were not originally chosen to any special reference to the problems of any of them, it is presumably fair to say the industries are now adapted to the duties rather than the duties adapted to the industries, and this is bound to make it all the more difficult to reach any useful conclusion in discussions of any particular item.[33]

In 1948, the president of the board of trade, Harold Wilson, tried to increase the scope for modifying tariffs. Unlike his Conservative colleague Peter Thorneycroft later in 1954, he did not seek a waiver from GATT's no-new-preference rule but opted for loosening the U.K.'s tariff commitments toward the Commonwealth. To avoid widespread political protests within his own party and from the opposition, he concluded a confidential gentlemen's agreement with Commonwealth countries enjoying contractual rights to duty free entry into the U.K. This would enable signatory partners to re-negotiate those preferential commitments preventing the imposition or raising of MFN rates. Any requests for such renegotiations would receive "sympathetic consideration" and would, in principle, be granted if they caused no material damage.[34]

The purpose of this gentlemen's agreement was twofold: to increase Britain's bargaining strength at the forthcoming GATT round in Annecy, and to allow the board of trade to investigate demands for tariff increases on items for which Britain had preferential obligations. Horticultural producers united in the National Farmers Union (NFU) and several manufacturing industries had earlier expressed an interest in raising some duties on Commonwealth imports. The board of trade had subsequently singled out more than 20 items (covering an import value of 50 million pounds) that were sensitive to pressure for tariff increases.[35]

When informing cabinet of these protective pressures, Wilson stressed the need for a tactful approach. The most direct way of solving the problem, he wrote, was to present a new tariff bill in parliament that covered all previous tariff laws and that outlined Britain's future tariff policy. This approach, however, had major drawbacks. Under the existing economic situation it was absolutely impossible to assess industries' future needs for protection or to present a long-term perspective on the role of tariffs and quotas in governmental policy. Even if a major tariff act were ready in time to deal with requests received thus far, parliamentary approval still seemed questionable. Another option was to draft only a minor tariff bill formalizing the gentlemen's agreement and leaving out any related policy issues. This solution, Wilson argued, was in itself quite attractive since the government might be able to sneak the bill in for approval during the parliamentary debate on the ITO. However, if it attracted excessive attention to the no-new-preference rule, it could also undermine support for the highly disputed ITO agreement. A final option, then, was to seek governmental powers in the finance act of 1949. This method, which had been frequently used in the past as a quick way of amending existing tariff legislation,[36] was eventually presented to the cabinet. The finance act might allow ministers to respond to the NFU's pressures just in time before the general elections of 1951.[37]

Yet the cabinet's economic policy committee was not impressed by their suggestion. A majority of ministers feared they would be exposed to heavy criticism from parliament and public opinion if they agreed to raise horticultural tariffs. In the existing situation of import restrictions, food rationing and price and wage restraints, they found it hard to defend tariff increases that would push up consumer prices. Retail prices for fruit and vegetables had been high for many years, and public opinion would undoubtedly strongly disapprove of a policy that deprived people of more variety against lower prices merely to satisfy the horticultural lobby. Ministers therefore turned down the proposal and summoned Wilson to present further information on commodities likely to receive requests for tariff increases, and to give alternative policy suggestions.[38]

A further development compounding pressures for tariff increases was the British government's proposal for trade liberalization within the OEEC. With the Americans pressing for moves toward sterling convertibility and British participation in closer European cooperation, the government wanted a new initiative to keep control over future developments.[39] By the end of March 1949, the treasury and the board of trade presented the outlines of a British proposal for import relaxations. In their view, the government should aim at minimizing obstacles to free trade, within the limits of maintaining an overall, as well as a dollar, surplus on the overseas accounts. Initially, relaxing import controls would be limited to soft currency sources, leaving Britain free to discriminate against imports from the dollar area.

For all their talk of commitments to freer trade, however, they took careful notice of domestic calls for protection:

> However strong we have said in the past that import licensing is not imposed for protective purposes, there is no doubt that our own producers have been protected and have come to feel that they are entitled to such protection. And apart from the simple protective argument (which we must reject though its rejection would be easier if we had greater freedom of manoeuvre on our own tariff . . .), there are more specious types of protective argument which can be put forward.[40]

Put differently, the straightforward protective argument in favor of quotas was clearly unacceptable in the light of the U.K.'s international role, but there was no reason that should prevent the government from using quantitative restrictions in individual cases where tariffs could not offer adequate protection. Balance of payments motives, strategic reasons or the existence of controls on the domestic market would suffice to justify these remaining restrictions. Which import quotas could be relaxed and which needed preserving was investigated in a confidential interdepartmental inquiry.[41]

At the board of trade level, this inquiry was conducted by a special Working Party on Import Licensing Relaxations.[42] Its record provides interesting insights into the assessed competitiveness of various economic sectors, and the arguments for and against quotas and the extent to which tariffs should replace quotas. One of the general guidelines given to the Working Party was that import quotas could not be relaxed until domestic sales restrictions were lifted. Competitiveness and the existing degree of tariff protection were other important factors guiding the decision to relax quotas. The engineering and scientific instruments industries, for instance, were two major sectors requiring additional protection against import competition. The ministry of supply recommended excluding engineering products from open general license because the industry had to meet high export targets without being able to satisfy domestic demand. Once West Germany became a soft currency country within the OEEC scheme, Britain could not exclude competing German engineering exports for long. As a result, British industries would probably divert production back to the home market.[43] Expert assessments for the scientific instrument industry were more pessimistic because even the existing, high-key industry duties could not provide sufficient shelter against German competitors. Tariffs of 50 percent or more might meet the needs of some individual producers, but since many rates were bound under GATT, the scope for imposing these high tariffs was very limited.[44] The Import Licensing Committee therefore recommended keeping the most important strategic items off the product list proposed for open general license, and a special study would meanwhile determine what additional methods of protection could be introduced.[45]

The Working Party's discussions show that usually the underlying debate was not whether British industries could compete in the face of domestic governmental controls, but rather whether they could compete at all once the sellers' market disappeared.[46] Cabinet ministers were torn between the advantages from international action liberalizing quotas on intra-European trade and the disadvantages for domestic employment. In the end, they tried to solve this dilemma by reintroducing previously suspended tariffs and by imposing additional duties.[47] Their final proposal of October 1949 for unilaterally removing quotas left the most sensitive, uncompetitive sectors comfortably sheltered behind quotas. For the time being, restrictions toward Germany would be maintained and all horticultural products subject to tariff appeals were excluded from open general license.[48]

It may be true, as some observers have argued, that the Labor government's trade liberalization operation stemmed from a genuine belief in exposing industry to healthy competition, improving economic efficiency, reducing prices and limiting bilateralism to a necessary minimum.[49] It is certainly hard to dispute that quotas were essential if raw material scarcity or governmental export targets undermined industries' domestic position. Nevertheless, if one leaves these constraints aside and looks at the arguments in favor of and against freer trade, what remains is a clear British reluctance to face the consequences of trade liberalization on domestic employment. This explains the rather ambiguous policy of combining proposals for European-wide quota relaxation with attempts to replace such quotas by protective tariffs and, when that failed, keeping import quotas for specific industries. Quite a few of these quotas eventually survived the OEEC's regular investigations into protective import restrictions and, by the end of the 1950s, were identified as "hard core" protection.

The Conservative government that replaced Labor after the general elections in October 1951 presented itself as highly committed to multilateral trade and payments and less sensitive to industrial pressure for tariff increases. However, it appeared heavily constrained by political party sentiments supporting Imperial Preference. The activities of a small group of British Conservatives within the Council of Europe, for example, proved downright embarrassing. In their view, the British government had been misguided in refusing to join the Coal and Steel Community, and had also been mistaken in assuming that closer integration with Europe and preserving traditional ties with the Commonwealth were irreconcilable policies. In their Strasbourg plan of 1951, some of these party members advocated stronger ties between Britain, the Commonwealth and Europe and its overseas territories as an appropriate answer to Continental calls for European economic cooperation.[50] They felt this could reduce Britain's economic and political dependence on its much cherished "special relationship" with the Americans, who after all had forced Britain to sell out Imperial Preference in exchange for Lend-Lease and additional dollar aid.[51] The ideas of these party members illustrate that five years after the heated debate on Britain's accession to GATT, fervent pro-Commonwealth and anti-GATT sentiments were still quite common within the Conservative Party and could influence governmental decision making.

In May 1952, the Foreign Office brushed the Strasbourg plan aside, but it resurfaced during Working Party talks on the review of British commercial policy in preparation for the Conservative Party conference and the Commonwealth economic conference.[52] Two of the trading systems under consideration were a closed sterling-Commonwealth block on its own and a similar area in association with OEEC countries and their overseas areas. The Working Party ruled out the first option because the sterling area was far from self-sufficient. Imports from the outer sterling area tended to be more essential than exports to this area, and even the Strasbourg plan's rigorous development policy could never entirely eliminate import requirements. An association with OEEC countries and their overseas territories could reduce the area's dependence on vital raw materials, but given Western Europe's limited dollar earning capacity, the area would presumably end up with a dollar gap even larger than that of the sterling-Commonwealth area on its own.[53] This left only a third Commonwealth option, a system of extended, interlocking Empire preferences with Europe. Of all the policy options under discussion, this turned out to be the most controversial one.

As we saw in previous chapters, margins of preferences could theoretically rise if the MFN rates were raised or if preferential tariffs were reduced, but GATT's no-new-preference rule prevented this in practice. Even without this limitation, the scope for extending preference was small; independent Commonwealth countries that were rapidly industrializing refused to expand preferences for British exporters competing with their domestic producers, even in return for larger preferences in the U.K. market.[54] Moreover, since Britain already admitted most of its Commonwealth imports duty free, the only way to increase preferential margins was to raise MFN duties and risk retaliatory action in export markets outside the Commonwealth. Allowing European countries and their overseas territories to join the preferential area would reduce this risk, but Canada would certainly object very strongly, as would Commonwealth producers, who would then have to share their preferential export markets with European competitors. And since it also involved general tariff cuts toward Europe, British farmers would also oppose the plan.[55]

Despite the practical problems, the government insisted on obtaining a release from the no-new-preference rule.[56] Clearly, political pressure for tariff rises had increased, but no member of a Conservative government was prepared to share political responsibility for a gradual and simultaneous erosion of Imperial Preferences. Thorneycroft's statements prove this. He argued that "the practical importance of extending preferences to the Commonwealth might be limited, but its symbolic and political meaning were very important indeed."[57] The Commonwealth countries had already earlier criticized the proposal, but Britain still went ahead, because "the United Kingdom should not be the first to turn their backs on the system of Imperial Preference."[58]

How could the government reconcile this policy move with commitments to establish multilateral trade and payments? The answer is simple: it could not. Its review of external economic policy concluded that a system of multilateral trade and payments was the only sound policy aim. This was also the assumption underlying the Collective Approach to introduce convertibility. Government officials claimed that a release from the no-new-preference rule would assist their Collective Approach because it would facilitate a switch from quotas to tariffs. Yet such a switch would have been much easier and more convincing if the government had allowed preferential margins to decrease automatically. The decision to escape the no-new-preference rule was thus ultimately a party political one, designed to silence the critics within the Conservative Party. Lord Cherwell, Churchill's closest adviser, admitted that the decision in favor of a multilateral and against a preferential trading system could "prove very unpalatable to many members of our party. But they may be reconciled by the view, which seems to be accepted, that we should try to get rid of the 'no new preference rule' in the G.A.T.T. and to resume greater freedom in tariff policy."[59] In 1954, at a special session for reviewing GATT rules, the government therefore asked for a waiver.

These awkward policy maneuvers did not end after Britain received a waiver allowing for an increase in several horticultural tariffs without having to impose duties on Commonwealth imports. During the same review session, Britain insisted on strengthening the rules on the use of quantitative restrictions in preparation for the move to convertibility, but it maintained its own protective import quotas to shelter chronically uncompetitive industries.[60] As in many other countries, agricultural quotas had also survived under the dubious label of "balance of payments" restrictions directed mainly against American and Canadian competitors on the home market. Britain's Import Licensing Committee had scrutinized many of these quotas in 1949 and 1950, when it had been asked to assess protected industries' future competitive strength. Often they had passed the test because of their importance as dollar savers, as was the case with several types of machinery, tractors, refrigerators, X-ray apparatus and portable powered tools. After the war, in the absence of strong American and German competition, such industries had drastically expanded investments in productive capacity, and by 1953 their total production value amounted to some 240 million pounds, at least 31 percent of which was exported. Removing import quotas on these products might cause export to drop by 18 percent and it could endanger more than 15,000 jobs located in so-called development areas,[61] where successive British governments had stimulated the settlement of new industries with cheap loans, capital grants and, of course, import quotas.[62]

Tighter rules on quotas could only come about if the government reconsidered its entire tariff policy or accepted the political and social costs of a permanent loss of protection. Admittedly, a waiver of GATT rules for "hard core" quotas—which many other countries would doubtless also request—might absorb instant pressure for tariff increases. However, it could neither meet the needs of all those industries demanding protection, nor offer the sort of long-term protection that chronically uncompetitive industries needed. An additional problem was that eliminating all quotas would again force the issue of duty free entry for the Commonwealth back into the spotlights. Since "politically vocal" industries were already demanding further protection against low-cost consumer goods imported from Pakistan, India and Hong Kong, their continued pressure would further compromise the government's policy for freer trade and payments. Officials at the board of trade realized this only too well. Shortly before the review of GATT, they spelled out the dilemmas of Britain's tariff policy with a profound frankness:

> This is a serious situation. Individual problems can sometimes be met by various devices. But we cannot meet all our problems by improvisation. Our difficulties really stem from the fact that we are trying to please everybody; to pacify the protectionists and to remain on terms with free traders; to sign up with the multilateralists but to raise our hat respectfully to the system of Commonwealth Preference and Commonwealth Free Entry. When we meet two of our ill-assorted friends simultaneously—as we sometimes do—we rely on our agility and speed of mind and foot to extricate us from embarrassment. It is not a restful policy.[63]

However, it was also obvious that in the near future, a policy change would be politically impossible:

> Short of a major calamity no-one in an election year is going to put an

Act in the Statute Book to tax Commonwealth entry. And certainly we are not going to walk out of the G.A.T.T. So we shall have to make the best of things . . . The fact that convertibility has receded gives us more time and enables us to live with the difficulties a little longer. This side of convertibility our problems over the tariff are manageable, the other side they are not.[64]

Again, therefore, the government opted for maintaining the status quo. Within the space of one year, however, it would be confronted with regional integration initiatives on the Continent that would dictate a drastic review of its commercial policy.

What this episode in British tariff policy indicates is that while the government's longterm commercial policy goals were directed toward establishing worldwide convertibility and multilateral trade, its tariff policy in particular met several constraints that hampered its realization. On the domestic side, the government had to cope with the burden of the 1930s, a mishmash of tariff laws and preferential arrangements for Commonwealth countries that made Britain ill-equipped for the international tariff negotiations of the 1950s. More importantly, Conservative policymakers were 'forced to perform a careful balancing act between strong party sentiments in favor of Imperial Preference, their commitments toward the multilateral trading system embodied in GATT, their special provisions for development areas and growing pressure from domestic industry for protection against cheap Commonwealth exports.

This move was far from successful. Not only were policymakers unable to appease these party members, their desperate attempts to do so undermined the policy of raising industrial competitiveness. Since tariffs were considered a politically sensitive issue, ministers constantly postponed creating more effective tariff machinery, thereby preserving a system that clashed with pledges for freer trade and convertibility. It was not so much that tariff protection and convertibility were mutually exclusive policy aims, but rather that the tariff system invited many different, competing protectionist pressures which undermined Britain's credibility as a champion of freer trade and convertibility. When policymakers finally realized this and tried to adapt the tariff system to the U.K.'s own, long-term commercial aspirations and developments in Europe, it was rather late in the day. Their responses, expressed in schemes for linear tariff cuts within GATT, an OEEC-wide free trade area and a European Free Trade Association (EFTA), were defensive, intent on avoiding economic isolation and preserving commercial independence toward countries outside Europe.

While Imperial Preference caused problems specific to British policymakers, those associated with abandoning quota protection were not. Nor were they confined to Europe's larger economies, which faced a much wider variety of domestic interests and policy concerns than smaller, relatively open economies such as Denmark or the Netherlands. The latter were more inclined to strengthen their economic position by obtaining tighter rules for international trade policy, but they, too, assessed the costs and benefits of limitations forced upon their national economic policies. And like other states, they felt the tension between domestic economic reconstruction policies and international commitments to freer trade and payments. This will be highlighted by examining some episodes of Dutch postwar commercial policy.

TARIFF DILEMMAS IN THE NETHERLANDS

"A simple return to the prewar situation was unthinkable in 1945."[65] This textbook stereotype accurately describes a widespread conviction of Dutch contemporaries after the war. It was not just that the war had brought more damage to the Netherlands' productive capacity and trade relations than to almost any other European economy. It also reflected a general understanding that its existing postwar economic and social problems were really of a structural nature, rooted in the 1920s and 1930s. Therefore, reconstruction rather than recovery prevailed in the Dutch vocabulary.

What were these deeply rooted economic problems that dictated a new, postwar economic strategy for the Netherlands? One key feature of the country's successful economic performance had been interdependence with the world economy through highly specialized, import-dependent industries and wide-ranging, competitive export sectors. Agriculture, which employed almost 20 percent of the total labor force, had increasingly looked to foreign markets.[66] The rising international demand in the 1920s for Dutch meat, dairy products, fruit and vegetables had given a further impetus to efficiency improvements introduced since 1900, coinciding as it did with growing imports of fertilizers and agricultural machinery from Germany and Britain. Both developments increased the sector's interdependence with foreign economies. Equally, earnings from trade and services had reached extremely high levels and had offered employment to 23 percent of the labor force. However, a considerable part of Dutch transit trade had relied on two pillars: colonial and Rhine trade. The first had proved highly vulnerable to cyclical price fluctuations in primary produce (such as rice, tin, copper and oil), whereas the second had been founded upon access into Germany.

What had long seemed to be the strong pillars of the Dutch economy, policymakers in 1945 increasingly interpreted as structural weaknesses. They saw the declining importance of capital income from the Dutch East Indies and of transit trade with this area as signs of growing competition from Asian countries, even though it was in fact a direct consequence of the Dutch refusal to devalue the guilder. A second indicator of structural problems was the slowdown of growth rates in agriculture, in particular, arable farming. This implied still more specialization in intensive dairy produce and horticulture and raised the need to find employment in industry for redundant agricultural labor. Furthermore, the Dutch economy's increasing vulnerability to economic and political changes in Germany emerged as a weakness. The events of the 1930s had taught that Germany's attempts to create an autarkic system of bilateral trading agreements with Eastern Europe greatly damaged Dutch economic welfare. They had initially pushed the Netherlands closer to the United Kingdom, but even this did not solve Dutch commercial problems.

All these problems explain why a return to the prewar situation seemed unthinkable and undesirable. But what were the policy alternatives? We can discern two directions in Dutch policymaking, both of which became part of the same strategy for economic reconstruction. One was the industrialization drive, an essential element in reforming the prewar economic fabric and in coping with acute problems such as war destruction, dollar shortages, the temporary loss of Germany and the collapse of international trade and payments. The other instrument involved a reorientation of foreign economic policy. Interdependence with the world economy accounted largely for the Dutch economic success but also for its extreme vulnerability to international economic fluctuations. By grasping a more active role in European economic affairs, the Netherlands met the quest for greater economic security and stability. These economic strategies of industrialization and active European involvement through national and Benelux channels characterized all Dutch commercial policy actions in the 1940s and 1950s.

After Germany's defeat in 1945 and the release of the Potsdam plan for its de-industrialization, the Dutch ministry of economic affairs, cooperating closely with private industry, had started planning for the rapid development of new industries to substitute products formerly supplied by Germany and, in the long run, take over parts of Germany's former export markets. Appropriately called the "baby package," the program would direct about 75 percent of its financial resources to the domestic market and 25 percent to export markets.[67] At the time of its inception, the ministry had deplored this heavy emphasis on import substitution, but private industry had left it with no real alternative, since industrialists risking participation in it had made it plain that they wanted the stability and safety of secured domestic demand for their infant products.[68] The joint investment and research efforts were concentrated in metallurgy, machinery, chemicals (all three dominated by the Koninklijke Hoogovens IJmuiden), pharmaceuticals and electronics. The products receiving specific mention were metal thread and cables, steel pipes, iron casting work, several types of agricultural machinery, lorries, aluminum products, nylon, nitrogenous, phosphoric and sulfuric fertilizers, plastics, detergents, transformers and telephones. For some products, among which were automobiles, tires, fittings, twist drills and typewriters, the government had also managed to secure research and investment cooperation with foreign companies.[69] In exchange for industry support, the government was committed to providing temporary quotas on competing imports. By the beginning of 1950, therefore, when the OEEC increased pressure on governments to improve their trade liberalization performance, many of these infant industry products emerged on lists recording quota protection. This pressure, occurring while the Netherlands' own international crusade against tariffs was still in full swing, even forced Dutch civil servants to raise tariffs on some aluminum products.[70]

Domestic insistence from the more outward-looking directorate general for foreign economic relations, in combination with international pressure by the OEEC and GATT, eventually led to a gradual dismantling of most of these quotas.[71] The improved Dutch payments position clearly assisted this liberalization process, since it ensured that states could no longer easily disguise protective quotas as balance of payments safeguards. In 1950, for instance, the Netherlands had still managed to cover up all its infant industry quotas with GATT's escape clause for balance of payments, but in 1956 this was impossible.[72] By this stage, GATT's rather strict quota examinations even elicited a joint Benelux suggestion to revive prewar international cartels as a way of solving the "hard core" quota problem.[73]

The evidence is hard to trace, but there are indications that the Dutch government sometimes sanctioned and even supported private business agreements if, for various reasons, public policy tools were considered less suitable. Its policy toward the international rayon cartel offers a case in point. Dominated by the American DuPont company and the British Imperial Chemicals Industry (ICI), this cartel carved up international markets through restrictive licensing agreements in combination with quota and price arrangements. The Dutch license holder Algemene Kunstzijde Unie (AKU) had been assigned to exclusive production for the domestic market and had to steer clear of foreign markets. Shortly after the war, the government had used an import quota to support this market division, but at the end of 1953 it replaced the quota with an import tariff to meet international commitments under the OEEC's Trade Liberalization Program.[74]

The government's involvement with international cartels did not always result in smooth settlements, and in at least one reported case involving metal fittings it caused an international trade dispute. The Dutch government's foreign investment and cooperation program for the machinery industry had led to the establishment of a Dutch-American Fuse Company (NAF), which held a domestic monopoly and participated in a large network of international cartels. In 1953, the Dutch government forced the NAF to terminate participation in the cartel, subsequently prompting the minister of economic affairs to put a complete halt on fuse imports because a strong Swedish-German coalition of cartel participants allegedly threatened to flood the home market and ruin the Dutch-American company. This measure caused a complete deadlock in tariff negotiations with the Swedes, who threatened to retaliate by restricting Dutch agricultural exports. By 1954, the ministry yielded to the cartel's force, allowing the NAF to rejoin the international cartel agreement, and advised the cabinet to accept its production quotas, price and market sharing practices. It kept import quota in place, however, as a double safeguard against Swedish and German exports to the domestic market.[75]

Like British policy for the development areas or Germany's agricultural policy, Dutch industrialization policy and the nontariff barriers it entailed often clashed with international rules and regulations. Dutch pleas for reducing European tariff disparities were therefore not always convincing, if only because elsewhere tariffs were considered legitimate instruments of trade policy. Moreover, their traditional preference for quotas as retaliatory and protective devices clashed with

Belgian trade policy. At times, this also impeded an effective, joint Benelux policy on European economic cooperation.

Officially, the Benelux states had conducted a common tariff policy from the moment they entered the Annecy negotiations of 1948 with a unified, common Benelux tariff. In practice, however, their tariff policy was little more than the sum of their often diverging national and sectoral economic interests. In March 1950, for instance, the Dutch had threatened to maintain and reintroduce quantitative restrictions as retaliatory measures against high European tariffs, despite strong Belgian warnings that such actions violated the GATT rules and undermined Benelux's authority as a promoter of multilateral trade in Europe.[76] The Belgian delegation to GATT had subsequently presented a separate statement distancing itself from the Dutch on this matter.[77] At the tariff negotiations in Torquay, tensions between the Benelux partners remained high because several Belgian experts suggested withdrawing concessions to strengthen their bargaining position in future GATT rounds and satisfy sectoral domestic pressures for more protection.[78] The Dutch, however, insisted that Benelux had to offer generous concessions if it wanted to avoid accusations of deliberately obstructing the negotiations. Tariff increases, they claimed, had not only proved to be less effective in curbing the flow of specific imports, but they were also "contradictory to the spirit of the Torquay negotiations."[79]

Throughout the 1950s, opportunistic and tactical arguments continued to dominate the internal Benelux debate on trade policy instruments. Illustrative are the talks on the Pflimlin Plan, during which the Dutch and Belgians clashed over the number and composition of agricultural products. The Belgian ministry of agriculture refused to accept Dutch and Danish proposals dividing this sector into several products groups, since that reduced tariff protection for Belgian farmers.[80] The dispute had to be solved at the highest level of Benelux decision making, where delegates received instructions to the effect that "the Belgians will keep quiet when the Dutch delegation come up with their proposal for four [agricultural] sectors." The Belgians would agree to this provided that, to quote again the instructions, "it was already clear that [the Dutch] proposal would not stand a chance anyway."[81] Dutch negotiators were thus forced to accept a common stance that left no room for direct benefits from agricultural tariff cuts. Benelux meanwhile had to keep a low profile during the Pflimlin Plan discussions because it could not present a convincing common stand against other countries' protectionist proposals.

Benelux reactions to the Ohlin Plan were equally split. The Dutch delegates considered its "decapping" procedure the most interesting aspect, as it meant that Benelux tariffs would hardly be affected whereas other countries would have to impose substantial tariff cuts.[82] Even so, they had decided not to push too hard for its incorporation into the Pflimlin Plan, under the assumption that the Belgian government was no longer prepared to support yet another plan for tariff reductions. With hindsight, however, this assumption was mistaken. As a Dutch delegate later recalled, "You may remember that, at the time, we had to ask our mission in Paris not to push the matter because "our Belgian colleagues" showed so little enthusiasm for a really drastic solution to the tariff problem. Meanwhile, they obviously have discovered that the Ohlin plan's effect is to exempt Benelux tariffs. Hence their enthusiasm. We saw no reason to dampen their emotions."[83] What such incidents indicate is that the existence of a common tariff in itself did not guarantee a coordinated, common tariff policy. Even Benelux's common fight for European tariff cuts within the OEEC and GATT and during the Beyen Plan negotiations suffered from internal disagreements over tariff policy. Each partner wanted to pursue its own objectives, which were often rooted in different prewar commercial policies.

Dutch trade policy traditionally employed low tariffs, quotas for balance of payments protection, for retaliation against restrictive and discriminatory import policies abroad, and after 1945 also for temporary infant industry protection. In agriculture, however, it had already developed a wider-ranging system of guaranteed minimum prices and state trade. As a result, protective quotas hardly played a role in Dutch agricultural policy. Belgium and Luxembourg, however, had always used tariffs to protect domestic industries, to retaliate and to bargain for trade concessions. They did not normally use quotas for infant industry protection, but they did use them for the agricultural sectors. Benelux' trade policy record shows that the three partners lacked a common vision on the relative importance and use of tariffs and quotas. Obviously, different traditions in trade policy only partly explain why, throughout the 1950s, the Benelux partners failed to coordinate their trade policies effectively. Their diverging economic experiences since 1945, so strikingly reflected in respective balance of payments situations, were more crucial still. Until 1951, the Dutch balance of payments situation was fairly weak, but thereafter it improved quite drastically. Belgium's balance of payments followed a reverse course, being very strong until the beginning of 1952 and showing volatile movements and deficits in the following years. After 1951, moreover, Belgian governments increasingly faced industrial pressures to raise tariffs because many of the old, heavy Belgian industries had difficulties withstanding European competition. The Dutch government, however, which at this stage saw the first successes of its industrialization efforts, wanted to keep down import prices and promote export expansion through tariff negotiations. Obviously it was unreasonable to assume, as some policymakers did in 1953, that in such divergent economic circumstances a protocol for a common trade policy could guarantee a coordinated Benelux trade policy.[84] By 1955, when the Netherlands was unmistakably the strongest of the three economies, it saw the advantages of a common trade policy. As one civil servant explained, "Now that we have reached agreement on the common liberalisation list, we will have to make a start with a common policy for Benelux in trade negotiations. In negotiations with countries such as France, where the Netherlands lacks bargaining weapons, it is important to operate as a Benelux unity."[85] Belgian officials, though, feared that the gains from a coordinated, common trade policy could not outweigh the loss of freedom to protect vulnerable industries. The structural, economic and political differences between their economies proved too large to overcome within the small, intergovernmental framework of Benelux.

The construction of the EEC eventually removed the need for a common Benelux trade policy within Europe. In that wider framework, Belgium and the Netherlands proved only too willing to surrender part of their national decision-making power in trade matters to the European Commission. Somewhat ironically, during the EEC negotiations all three Benelux partners insisted that the future European Commission, after consultations with the Council of Ministers, be solely responsible for tariff negotiations with third countries. Their negative experiences within Benelux had taught them that intergovernmental decision-making on the basis of unanimity would inevitably lead to inertia and inefficiency in trade policy.

Conclusion

The title of this book is *Tariffs, Trade and European Integration, 1947–1957*. Its central argument is that the early history of postwar European economic integration can only be understood if it embraces a comprehensive analysis of the trade and tariff questions facing the states involved both individually and collectively. The decade between the announcement of Marshall aid and the birth of the Common Market witnessed a wide range of European proposals for regional trade integration, varying from schemes for multilateral tariff reductions among a limited group to plans for preferential reductions, free trade areas and customs unions. These schemes represent a continuous search for economic stability and welfare that eventually culminated in the creation in 1958 of the European Economic Community.

To sum up the analysis, we will go through the main empirical findings on tariff policies and European integration that help to address these questions and explain this specific institutional outcome. We will then deal with the book's further argumentation on the interaction between international institutions and national policies operating in trade policy areas.

During the relatively short phase of postwar economic recovery up to 1950, European countries managed to restore industrial output and productivity above prewar levels and were well on their way to rapid economic expansion. European trade, however, initially recovered only slowly because the Depression and the war had fundamentally changed intra-European trading relationships and trading links between Europe and the rest of the world. The absence of crucial supplies from and exports to West Germany and Eastern Europe, the loss of foreign property holdings, the disruption of triangular trade with the colonies and the initial impossibility of expanding invisible earnings all resulted in a staggering dependence on dollar imports and a relatively late and imbalanced trade recovery.

The early American insistence on restoring sterling-dollar convertibility to facilitate the return to free, worldwide multilateral trade was therefore premature. So large was dollar hunger that millions of pounds were immediately exchanged for dollars and payments restrictions had to be reinstalled. The Marshall Plan was subsequently launched as an altogether different regional route toward solving Europe's structural economic problems. By supplying dollar aid over a period of four years, the Marshall Plan provided European countries with essential raw materials, capital goods and agricultural products and helped to expand production and investments, while it also greatly assisted national reconstruction programs by allowing national governments to maintain high levels of investment without having to curtail domestic consumption.

With the launching of Marshall aid, the U.S. government temporarily abandoned its nondiscriminatory worldwide approach to trade and payments recovery and began to foster regional trading groupings among the member countries of the OEEC. On one level, this policy change reflected an awareness that the interwar and wartime import controls which had pushed trade toward bilateral and regional preferential channels could only be abandoned at great economic, political and social costs. Indeed, preferential trading blocs such as those of Britain and France and their former colonies and bilateral trading agreements might be greatly disliked in the United States for their discriminatory and trade distorting impact, but they did reduce dependency on dollars and initially also facilitated trade expansion in Europe. On another level, U.S. support for regional agreements was based on the assumption that European industries could only benefit from free trade if their levels of productivity and technological development did not lag too far behind those of their American competitors. This explains why the Truman government accepted the OEEC countries' temporary discrimination against American exports.

In the early recovery period up to 1949, the American appeal for an OEEC-wide customs union to strengthen Europe's economic, political and military cohesion met with a cautious reception. As the deliberations within the European Customs Union Study Group showed, governments were generally wary of increasing competition on the European market, especially while economic uncertainty prevailed. In 1948, domestic industries still faced so many supply bottlenecks and price and currency controls that any assessment of their competitive position within the future internal market was necessarily speculative. Added and linked to this were uncertainties on the customs union's membership and its common external tariff. France rejected Germany's inclusion on equal terms, but Benelux and may other OEEC states insisted on it because of their traditional dependence on trade with that country. Until the autumn of 1948, the British role was also unclear. Early on there were doubts whether the British would surrender part of their preferential access to Commonwealth markets in exchange for participation within the customs union. Few countries were willing to reveal their policy before they knew the British verdict.

Most European governments then were initially reluctant to join a large, OEEC-wide customs union, and they could easily justify their reluctance with mainstream economic arguments. As we have seen, neither contemporaneous tariff theory nor integration theory (that was still maturing in these years) provided a strong economic case for customs unions and common markets. So why then did customs unions gradually obtain such a high profile in the postwar period, and why did initiatives such as Fritalux, the Schuman and Stikker Plan all emerge within such a relatively short period of time? Our examination of their shape, timing and origins suggests that their underlying motivation varied substantially.

Paradoxically, part of the answer to these questions lies in the fact that those initiatives did not all constitute plans for "pure" customs unions along the lines envisaged by the Americans and subsequently analyzed by economists and embodied within GATT's article 24. Rather, they all deviated quite fundamentally from the ideal type. In its original concept, Fritalux aimed at removing quotas only in particular sectors, leaving tariff barriers unharmed. The Stikker Plan was a scheme for sectoral elimination of quotas and tariffs that fell far short of a customs union, whereas the ECSC represented a common market limited to the coal, iron and steel sectors. The Pella Plan merely aimed at the reduction of European tariffs and not at their complete elimination. Even Benelux, which was often cited at the time as a textbook example of a customs union on its way to becoming a full economic union, for a long period fell short of achieving the free movement of goods within the internal market. Quantitative restrictions and cartel agreements initially survived and agriculture remained entirely exempt from the free operation of market forces. Moreover, when in 1960 the Benelux countries finally ratified the treaty for the economic union, their primary motivation was to consolidate bargaining power towards EEC partners.

It is important to remember, therefore, that the customs union concept in fact became shorthand for all sorts of initiatives for preferential European trade cooperation. Not only did these often fail to meet the official GATT requirements, they also thwarted early American ambitions for a large, OEEC-wide union that would underpin Europe's political entity. When in 1949 American ECA officials coined the phrase "European integration" and gave their blessing to smaller regional groupings, they accepted this reality. Europe's nations would clearly only enter arrangements of their own design, at their own pace and serving their own perceived national interests.

France's trade policy initiatives illustrate this very well. The Conseil Tripartite with Belgium, the Netherlands and Luxembourg was mainly designed to strengthen France's political and economic weight toward Germany. Fritalux was originally launched as a monetary agreement that deliberately excluded Germany, but when American and Benelux demands fundamentally changed this proposal, it could no longer guarantee French safety with regard to Germany. The French government therefore abandoned the initiative and, forced by Germany's imminent return to the coal and steel market in Europe, put forward the Schuman Plan to embrace Germany in a supranational sectoral agreement that satisfied French economic and military safety needs.

The Dutch integration initiative that followed so shortly after France's Fritalux and Schuman Plan was certainly inspired by the sectoral approach, but its aims were rather different from those of Schuman. Stikker's scheme expressed a concern to preserve the Netherlands' trade expansion into Germany and to halt or at least modify the OEEC's Trade Liberalization Program. It favored those domestic sectors that depended on European export markets while leaving other, infant industries temporarily protected. Moreover, it was the first of many preferential regional plans designed to turn the rising tide of tariff protection, coinciding with the removal of quantitative barriers to intra-European trade.

This brings us to the wide range of tariff plans launched after 1949: the Benelux Memorandum, the Pflimlin Plan and the British tariff proposals tabled in GATT; the Stikker and Petsche plans, the European Commodity Lists and Plan G launched in the OEEC; the Ohlin Plan within the Council of Europe. At their peak between 1952 and 1954, tariff plans were being discussed within each of these three institutions simultaneously, whereas the Six also examined the Beyen Plan for a customs union. What are we to make of all these proposals? Three conclusions can be derived from them. First, the tariff disparity issue was instrumental to their conception. The driving forces campaigning against tariff disparities were not the six future members of the ECSC and the EEC but rather the Benelux countries, Denmark and Sweden, while Switzerland and Germany occasionally also offered support. As we have seen, the French Pflimlin Plan, the Italian Pella Plan and the two British schemes were fundamentally different. In essence, they tried to "control" the potential damage to domestic industry that a tariff alignment might entail. Second, the countries united in this Low-Tariff Club did not seek to establish supranational ways of tackling tariff protection. Instead, they tried to table the issue in every relevant international forum and on every possible occasion. This leads to the third observation, that the European tariff plans reflect a process of trial-and-error. Only as a result of their negative experiences within the OEEC and the GATT and positive experiences with ECSC supranationality did the Low-Tariff Club's Benelux members begin to perceive the Six as a potential solution to their problems.

Even in the Netherlands—the country often seen as the "brain" behind supranational customs unions because of its role in the Beyen Plan and the relance européenne—support for a supranational customs union among the Six was still not overwhelming in 1952. Active Dutch participation in all kinds of tariff reduction plans, falling short of a customs union, suggests that such a union was neither considered an end in itself nor the only means to that end. Indeed, one could speculate whether the Dutch would have supported the Common Market of the Six had they achieved drastic tariff cuts within the OEEC or GATT. Their fear of being locked into a closed, high-tariff club dominated by French protectionists and interventionists was so fundamental that it may have outweighed the perceived advantages of an internal market free from tariffs and quotas. It is certainly illustrative that throughout the Common Market negotiations, they continued pushing for OEEC-wide tariff cuts to bring down the Market's future CET. After signing the Treaty of Rome, moreover, they took great pains to bring the United Kingdom into the new Community.

The flaws of trade liberalization within the OEEC and GATT gradually drove the Benelux countries toward proposing supranational frameworks for market integration. There were, however, more important conditions favoring customs unions to straightforward tariff reductions, whether preferential or nondiscriminatory. By combining internal free trade with outward protectionism, a supranational customs union was far more likely to offer the stable and secure compromise between high- and low-tariff countries. The fate of the Beyen Plan indicates that a customs union may have been a necessary but certainly not sufficient condition for a successful compromise. When discussed in 1953, it could not bridge the gap between, on the one hand, liberal Benelux and West Germany, and on the other, protectionist Italy and France. Italy insisted on freedom of movement for its redundant workers whereas France demanded social harmonization and guaranteed outlets for high-priced, agricultural exports. Belgium and West Germany also insisted on policy coordination since they felt that internal tariff elimination alone could not guarantee the customs union's realization and long-term stability.

The Beyen Plan discussions set in motion a learning process that greatly contributed to the success of the EEC negotiations. This time, the Six managed to formulate a crucial package deal that satisfied French economic and political needs. Apart from the obvious "bonus" of Euratom, France received economic concessions it could not have obtained within a simple customs union: the prospect of a common agricultural policy, an investment fund to develop overseas areas in Africa, concessions on the harmonization of social legislation and a special transitional arrangement to adapt the domestic economy to competitive market conditions. In exchange, France had to dismantle protective tariff and quota barriers toward member countries and accept a tariff alignment toward common external levels. This meant that it would finally have to open up domestic markets for industrial exports from the Benelux countries, Italy and Germany.

While France was obviously indispensable to the Common Market, Germany's role was more crucial still. In the years 1949-1954, this country's rapid economic expansion had greatly benefited its traditional trading partners. The fear that these benefits might be at least temporarily lost through resurging protectionism, bilateralism or balance of payments restrictions explains these countries' eagerness to enter a regional trading framework with Germany. Indeed, the EEC's package deal neatly integrated Germany within the internal market. The country's extraordinary trading performance strengthened support for a common market that could solidify mutual trading gains. The OEEC's Trade Liberalization Program and the European Payments Union further enhanced the trend toward regionalism in Europe by institutionalizing discrimination toward the United States. Although initially supported by the United States as a temporary measure to facilitate European recovery, dollar discrimination gradually promoted permanent forms of preferential trading. Quotas on dollar imports were originally introduced in the late 1940s to protect industries that saved dollars and promoted economic modernization and regional employment. Under the Trade Liberalization Program, these industries could expand within the European market without American competition. When the Americans began demanding a liberalization of dollar imports, several European governments decided to maintain dollar restrictions under GATT's "hard core" provisions or replace quota restrictions by high tariffs. Quite a few of the Common Market's high external tariffs were indeed deliberately aimed against the United States, offering sensitive European industries a welcome shelter.

The EEC's creation epitomized the end of the European tariff disparity issue and the beginning of a new tariff debate on disparities between the Common Market and the United States. After the Six had unified their national tariffs into a common external tariff, negotiations started with the United States during the Dillon round of GATT. Those familiar with the European tariff disparities debate of the 1950s will recognize the arguments in the debate between the EEC and the United States in the decades that followed. By 1961, the Six, acting as a unity, insisted that American nominal tariffs were unacceptably high and distorted normal competitive conditions. They also pressed for a new method of large scale, linear tariff negotiations within GATT and threatened to retaliate by preserving quotas on dollar imports. A debate on the global dismantling of protection thus replaced the debate on regional tariff disparities. Now, as then, economists stress the virtues of free trade, but they also admit that neomercantilist policies often prevail.

Market loss and market access were key policy concerns in the 1950s, although they often surfaced under slightly different labels, such as export losses and gains, fair trade or reciprocity. Reciprocity has been problematic for students of the postwar trading framework brought up in the classical economic tradition, since the assumption that traders will only exchange "a dollar's worth of increased exports for every dollar's worth of increased imports" seems to undermine the theory of the gains from unilateral free trade.[1] The reciprocity requirement in fact reflects a preoccupation with welfare defined in Keynesian terms of collective production, employment and external balance, not with economic welfare defined as private consumption levels. Whereas classical economics assumes that unilateral tariff cuts will raise welfare levels and that tariffs will only pay off if they improve the terms of trade or protect infant industries, Keynesian models suggest that a tariff is imposed to maintain or increase domestic employment levels and to improve the balance of trade.[2]

In the postwar GATT rounds that we have studied, trade policy debates continuously centered on the reciprocity requirement, reflecting this concern for conquering export markets and maintaining employment. From the very first round in Geneva, low-tariff states complained that genuine reciprocity was not guaranteed if equal norms were applied to high and low tariffs. Essentially, they wanted to change the accepted reciprocity norm by formalizing the principle that reducing a high tariff was equivalent to consolidating a low rate, but to no avail. All their other attempts after 1949 to obtain linear tariff cuts and alignments within GATT stemmed from the same desire to raise bargaining power and improve export opportunities.

Reciprocity was also a key problem in trade disputes within the OEEC, where Low-Tariff Club members complained that reciprocal market access was absent as long as tariffs cuts and quota liberalization were not negotiated or discussed in tandem. Even though the interconnectedness of tariff and quota protection was obvious, the OEEC's practice of focusing on quotas and leaving tariff cuts to GATT's cumbersome item-by-item procedures favored protectionist forces in Europe. It indirectly encouraged high tariff countries to re-activate their customs schedules and slowed down progress within GATT. It also inspired low-tariff countries to maintain quota restrictions by retarding the OEEC's Trade Liberalization Program.

In Europe's external trading relations a similar reciprocity issue emerged with an important American dimension. The United States' superior productivity levels and competitive strength made European negotiators extra keen to obtain large, stable and long-term export gains in exchange for tariff concessions. The U.S. government, however, could only negotiate on an item-by-item basis and was bound by law to bargain for strictly reciprocal market access. The architects of GATT expected that the United States, as principle supplier of many products, would play a leading role in the exchange of large tariff concessions, which would then spill over to other states but without causing free riding. Yet their scenario overestimated the U.S. government's freedom to maneuver in trade negotiations, its ability to withstand protectionist domestic forces and also the complexity of worldwide tariff negotiations. By 1950, negotiations between the United States and its industrialized trading partners made increasingly little headway and tariff reductions stagnated.

The problem grew worse when protectionist lobbies reintroduced escape clauses and peril point procedures. Both measures could damage European export shares directly but also indirectly by increasing the insecurity under which exporters had to operate within the American market. The official American refusal in 1954 to join the linear tariff cuts of the GATT plan convinced many European governments that substantial and permanent tariff cuts required preferential European frameworks. Not only would this maximize their mutual export increases, it would also increase their weight in trade bargaining toward the United States.

The centrality of reciprocal trade bargaining, the slow pace of trade liberalization and widespread state intervention suggest that neither the United States' powerful position nor the acceptance of a free trade ideology was sufficient to establish a smoothly working liberal trading order. The GATT system lacked the degree of multilateralism and the ability to adapt to economic changes. Moreover, U.S. foreign economic policy sometimes failed to pursue a well-defined policy supporting GATT, thus accentuating the system's structural weaknesses and stimulating the formation of other regional trading blocs.

The reasons why some trade liberalization eventually came about, and why in Europe this occurred within a regional common market, are in fact far more complex than theories of hegemonic stability or dominant free trade ideas and ideologies would suggest. National policies in the 1950s reveal that over time and depending on the issue, governments responded differently to domestic and international constraints on trade policies. In Britain, for instance, the government felt so inhibited in its attempts to protect horticultural producers and silence die-hard Commonwealth supporters within the Conservative Party that it tried to change the GATT's no-new-preference rule. Yet that same government also demanded tighter GATT rules on quotas to support its long-run policy for convertibility and to restrain domestic opposition against quota liberalization. In Germany, the government's freedom in tariff policy matters was far less restrained by early Allied supervision than by the American Bizone authorities' decision to give the Bundestag a large say in tariff policy. The Americans considered Germany an essential player in Europe's transition toward freer trade and payments, but ironically the Bundestag effectively blocked Erhard's proposals for unilateral, linear German tariff cuts and faster trade liberalization in agriculture. Just as in the United States, parliament was initially biased toward protectionism while the government favored trade liberalization.

What all national governments had in common was the ambition to increase influence over tariff making, often by obtaining emergency powers to change tariffs without prior parliamentary approval. Furthermore, the reluctance of interventionist France and Italy and free trade-minded Denmark, the Netherlands and Germany alike to surrender quantitative restrictions indicates that within due course, tariffs would be less relevant. The Depression and the war had taught free traders and protectionists that nontariff barriers to trade and direct state intervention held the future. If a new depression hit their economies, more sophisticated forms of protection and control would emerge. In the long run, therefore, the gradual tariff rounds of GATT and the creation of regional frameworks such as the EEC and EFTA accelerated and accentuated the advent of new forms of protectionism.

Appendix

Comparing European Tariff Levels by Main SITC Section, 1951

A decision one needs to make before comparing tariff levels is whether to use unweighted or weighted tariffs. In the late 1940s and the 1950s, both approaches were quite commonly used and often produced markedly different results.[1] In 1957, for instance, an extensive comparison was made of unweighted average rates applied by the Common Market countries for 1,100 four-digit tariff lines of the Brussels Tariff Nomenclature (BTN) of 1955.[2] The main deficiency of this method is that it attributes equal weight to rates on products whose importance to trade vary widely. To meet this problem, one can weigh the tariff headings by, for instance, import values, domestic production or consumption values. The method of weighing by import value was commonly applied in the 1950s, even though low-tariff countries criticized it since it gives high tariffs—which tend to be related to low levels of imports—less weight than low tariffs and it excludes prohibitive tariffs altogether.[3] Similar problems can occur if production or consumption are used to weigh rates, since both are, at least indirectly, influenced by the tariff's protective impact.[4]

Since the late 1950s, economists have used effective protection as a more adequate measure of the tariff's restrictiveness. It is based on the assumption that since the protection of value added, not of final products, is of primary concern to producers, duties on raw materials and intermediate and final products all have to be counted. Generally, the higher the tariff on the inputs of the final product, the higher the production costs and the lower the level of effective protection. Although there is no doubt that effective protection offers useful insights into the mechanisms of protection, there are considerable difficulties involved in its practical use.[5] Since the effective rate of protection is defined as the difference between the value added during a production process that is protected and a production process under free trade, one needs information on the input coefficients in both situations. "Free trade" data were usually not available, however, and some economists therefore estimated these by substituting input coefficients of countries with low levels of protection, or by assuming that free trade prices were equal to protected prices minus their tariff rates.[6] Another way of circumventing the problem altogether is to ignore the possible impact of the tariff and of technological changes on the factor coefficients by assuming that input coefficients have remained unchanged.[7] Whatever method chosen, though, comparing effective protection rates inevitably relies on reliable figures of nominal tariff rates. The tariff comparisons in this book are made on the basis of data derived from calculations made in 1951 for most of the 570 five-digit tariff lines in the SITC of 1950, which have the advantage of covering a wide range of European countries, the United States and Canada, and of providing a broader product range than most other comparisons available for that period.[8]

To maintain a general overview of rates by country or product group, the national tariffs items within each SITC section are displayed in a bar diagram giving each country's frequency distribution by major tariff interval. The divisions 1 (tobacco and beverages) and 9 (miscellaneous manufactures not elsewhere specified) are omitted because they represent only a fraction of the total number of tariffs and include many revenue duties. The first interval (indicated as n.a., not available) represents goods that were not charged with a duty. The second includes all tariffs with a zero rate. All subsequent intervals are 5 percent, except in the categories with the highest tariff rates, i.e., above 30 percent.

SITC 0
Italy and West Germany

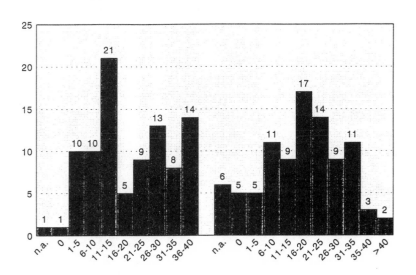

SITC 0
United Kingdom and France

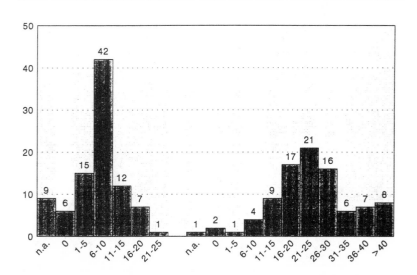

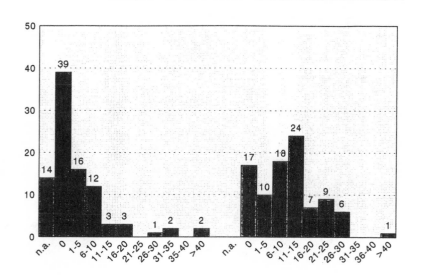

SITC 0
Denmark and Benelux

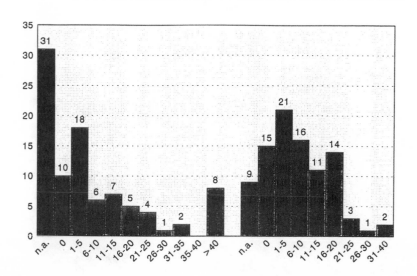

SITC 0
Norway and Sweden

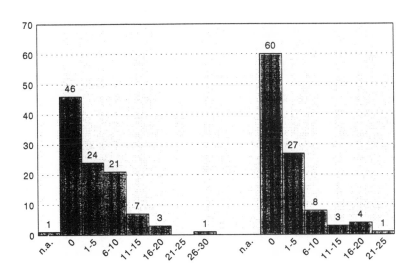

SITC 2
Italy and West Germany

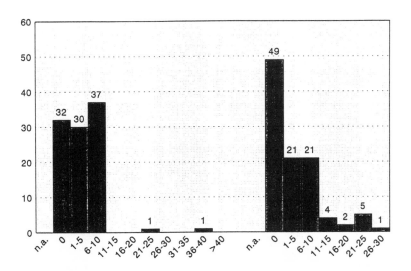

SITC 2
United Kingdom and France

SITC 2
Denmark and Benelux

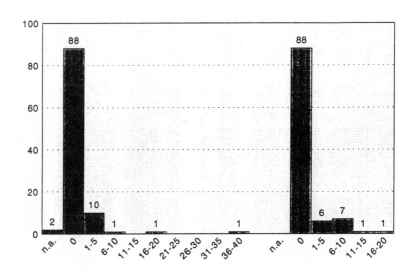

SITC 2
Norway and Sweden

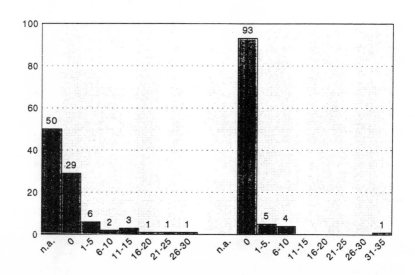

SITC 3
Italy and West Germany

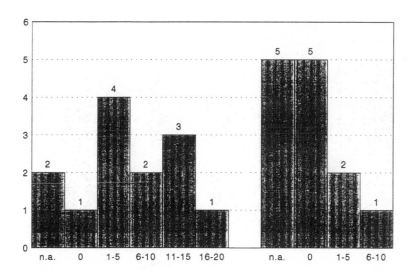

SITC 3
United Kingdom and France

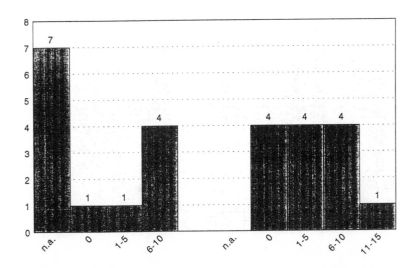

SITC 3
Denmark and Benelux

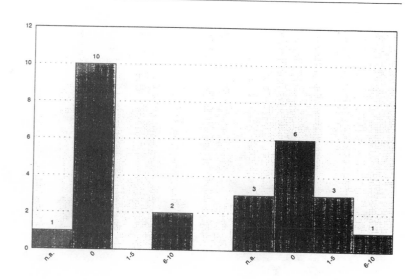

SITC 3
Norway and Sweden

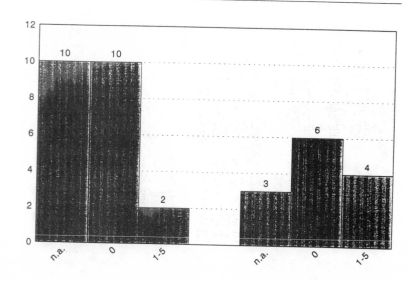

SITC 4
Italy and West Germany

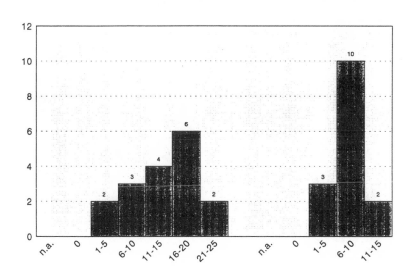

SITC 4
United Kingdom and France

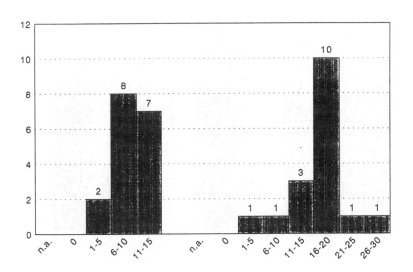

SITC 4
Denmark and Benelux

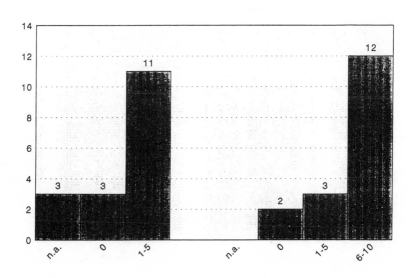

SITC 4
Norway and Sweden

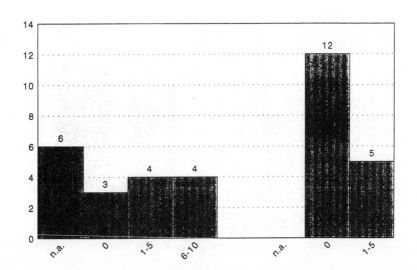

SITC 5
Italy and West Germany

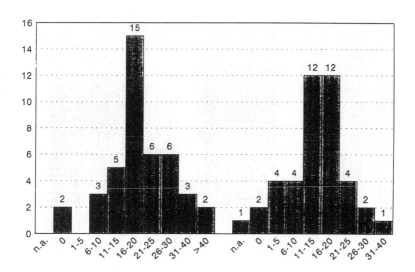

SITC 5
United Kingdom and France

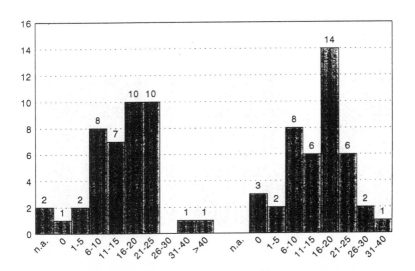

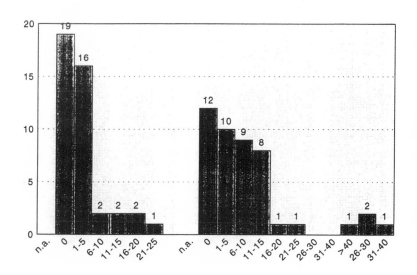

SITC 5
Denmark and Benelux

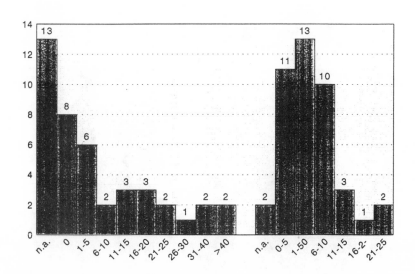

SITC 5
Norway and Sweden

SITC 6
Italy and West Germany

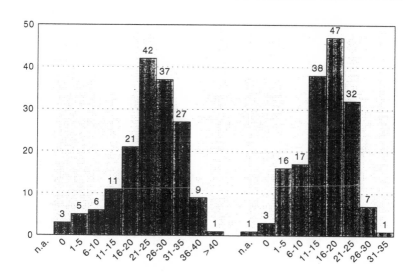

SITC 6
United Kingdom and France

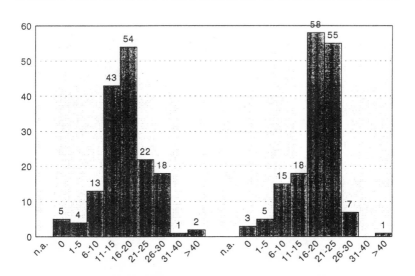

SITC 6
Denmark and Benelux

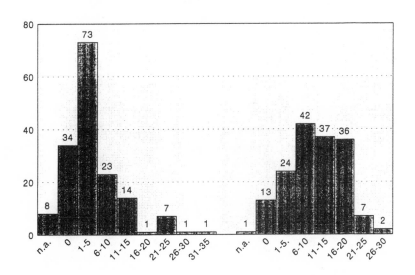

SITC 6
Norway and Sweden

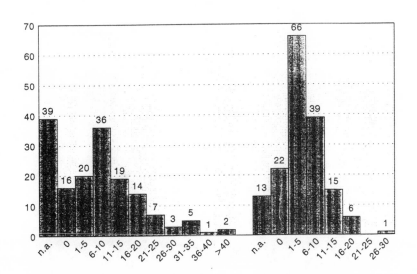

SITC 7
Italy and West Germany

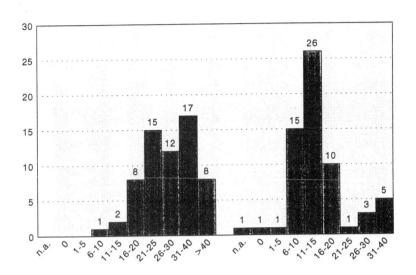

SITC 7
United Kingdom and France

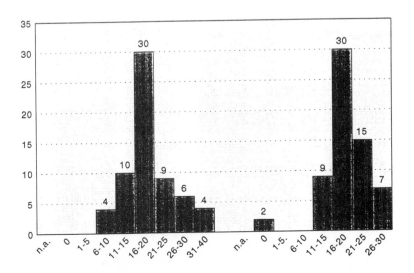

SITC 7
Denmark and Benelux

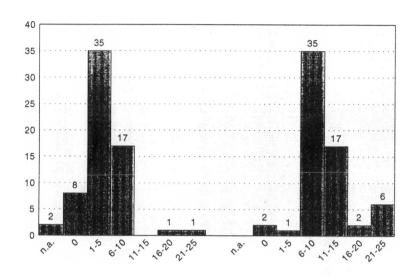

SITC 7
Norway and Sweden

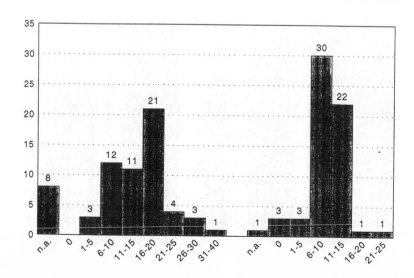

SITC 8
Italy and West Germany

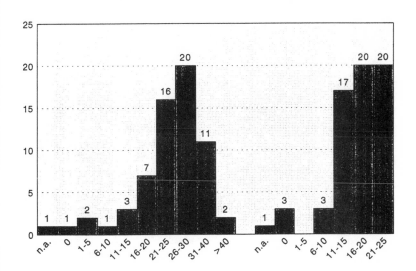

SITC 8
United Kingdom and France

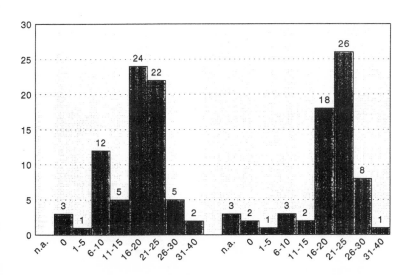

SITC 8
Denmark and Benelux

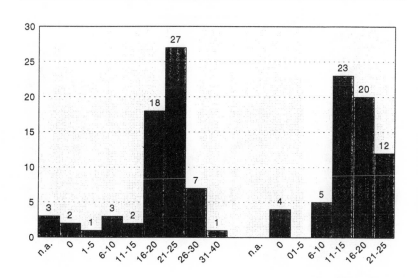

SITC 8
Norway and Sweden

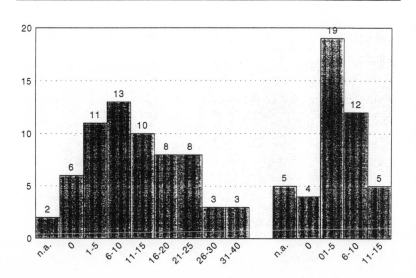

Notes

Introduction

1. The classics on regional trade and tariff issues of this period are: G. Curzon, *Multilateral Commercial Diplomacy: An Examination of the Impact of the General Agreement on Tariffs and Trade on National Commercial Policies and Techniques* (London: Joseph, 1965); W. Diebold, Jr., *Trade and Payments in Western Europe: A Study in Economic Cooperation, 1947-1951* (New York: Harper and Brothers, 1952); K. Kock, *International Trade Policy and the GATT, 1947-1967* (Stockholm: Almquist and Wiksell, 1969); G. Patterson, *Discrimination in International Trade: The Policy Issues, 1945-1965* (Princeton: Princeton University Press, 1966); E. Thorbecke, *The Tendency Towards Regionalization in International Trade* (The Hague: Martinus Nijhoff, 1960). See also for a contemporary analysis of regional trade issues: S. Dell, *Trade Blocs and Common Markets* (London: Constable, 1963) and J. Meade, H. Liesner, and S. Wells, eds., *Case Studies in European Economic Union: The Mechanics of Integration* (London: Oxford University Press, 1962). Two useful accounts from the 1970s are: O. Hieronymi, *Economic Discrimination Against the United States in Western Europe (1945-1958): Dollar Shortage and the Rise of Regionalism* (Geneva: Droz, 1973), and H. Mayrzedt, *Multilaterale Wirtschaftsdiplomatie zwischen westlichen Industriestaaten: Instrumente zur Stärkung der multilateralen und liberalen Handelspolitik* (Bern: Lang, 1979).

2. A selection of archival-based studies that also focus on aspects of trade policy: W. Asbeek Brusse, "The Stikker Plan," in *The Netherlands and the Integration of Europe, 1945-1957,* R. Griffiths, ed. (Amsterdam: Nederlands Economisch Historisch Archief, 1990), 69-92; W. Bührer, "Erzwungene oder freiwillige Liberalisierung? Die USA, die OEEC und die westdeutsche Außenhandelspolitik, 1949-1952," in *Vom Marshall Plan zur EWG: Die Eingliederung der Bundesrepublik in der westliche Welt,* L. Herbst, W. Bührer, and H. Sowade, eds. (München: Oldenbourg, 1990), 139-63; R. Griffiths, "The Abortive Dutch Assault on European Tariffs," in *Modern Dutch Studies: Essays in Honour of Peter King, Professor of Modern Dutch Studies at the University of Hull on the Occasion of his Retirement,* M. Wintle, ed. (London: Athlone, 1988), 186-91; R. Griffiths and F. Lynch, "L'Échec de la 'Petite Europe': les négociations Fritalux/Finebel, 1949-1950," *Revue Historique* 274 (1985): 159-93; R. Griffiths and F. Lynch, "L'Échec de la 'Petite Europe': Le Conseil Tripartite, 1944-1948," *Guerres Mondiales et Conflits Contemporains* 252 (1988): 39-62; P. Guillen, "Le projet d'union économique entre la France, l'Italie et le

Benelux," in *Histoire des débuts de la construction européenne, mars 1948–mai 1950 (Origins of the European Integration, March 1948–1950)*, R. Poidevin, ed. (Paris: Libraire général de droits et de jurisprudence, 1989), 143-64; H.-J. Küsters, "Zollunion oder Freihandelszone? Zur Kontroverse über die Handelspolitik Westeuropas in den fünfziger Jahren," in *Wirtschaftliche und politische Integration in Europa im 19. und 20. Jahrhundert*, H. Berding, ed. (Göttingen: Vandenhoeck und Ruprecht, 1984), 296-308; A. Milward, "The Committee of European Economic Co-operation (CEEC) and the Advent of the Customs Union," in *A History of European Integration*, vol.1, *1945-1947: The Formation of the European Unity Movement*, W. Lipgens, ed. (Oxford, Eng.: Clarendon, 1982), 507-70; A. Milward, *The Reconstruction of Western Europe, 1945-51* (Cambridge, Eng.: Methuen, 1987); A. Milward, *The European Rescue of the Nation-State* (London: Routledge, 1992); A. Milward, F. Lynch, F. Romero, R. Ranieri, and V. Sørensen, *The Frontier of National Sovereignty: History and Theory* (London: Routledge, 1993); R. Ranieri, "L'Espansione alla prova del negoziato—l'industria italiana e la comunita' del carbone e dell' acciaio, 1945-1955" (Ph.D. diss., European University Institute, Florence, 1988).

3. See for instance: H.-J. Küsters, *Fondements de la Communauté économique européenne* (Brussels: Editions Labor, 1990), 360-62. An earlier, extended version of this work has been published in German under the title *Die Gründung der europäischen Wirtschaftsgemeinschaft* (Baden-Baden: Nomos, 1983).

4. Most studies therefore tend to discuss protectionism and trade liberalization in the 1950s by examining quantitative restrictions to trade. To mention just some of the literature: W. Abelshauser, "Der Kleine Marshallplan: Handelsintegration durch innereuropäische Wirtschaftshilfe, 1948-1950," in *Wirtschaftliche und Politische Integration In Europa im 19. und 20. Jahrhundert*, H. Berding, ed. (Göttingen: Vandenhoeck & Ruprecht, 1984), 212-24; G. Bossuat, "La politique française de libération des échanges en Europe et le plan Schuman (1950-1951)," in *Die Anfänge des Schuman-Plan: Beiträge des Kolloquiums in Aachen, 28. -30. Mai 1986*, K. Schwabe, ed. (Baden-Baden: Nomos, 1988), 319-332; J. Clerx, *Nederland en de liberalisatie van het Europese handels- en betalingsverkeer* (Groningen, Netherlands: Wolters-Noordhoff, 1986); A. Fleury, "La situation particulière de la Suisse au sein de l'Organisation européenne de cooperation économique (OECE)," in *Histoire des débuts de la construction européenne, mars 1948–mai 1950 (Origins of the European Integration, March 1948-1950)*, R. Poidevin, ed. (Paris: Libraire général de droits et de jurisprudence, 1989), 95-117; P.-H. Laurent, "America's Ally, Britain's Opponent: Belgium and the OEEC/EPU Debates, 1947-50," *Millennium: Journal of International Studies* 16 (1987): 453-66; H. Möller, "The Reconstruction of the International Economic Order After the Second World War and the Integration of the Federal Republic of Germany into the World Economy," *Zeitschrift für die gesammte Staatswissenschaft* 137 (1981): 344-66; H. Pohl, ed., *Die Auswirkungen von Zöllen und andere Handelshemnissen auf Wirtschaft und*

Gesellschaft vom Mittelalter bis zur Gegenwart (Stuttgart: Steiner Verlag, 1987); H. Schmieding, "How to Fill a 'Dollar Gap'?: Observations on the Liberalisation of West Germany's External Trade and Payments, 1947-1958," working paper no 291, Institut für Weltwirtschaft, Kiel, Germany, 1987.

5. For example: C. Buchheim, "Einige wirtschaftspolitische Maßnahmen Westdeutschlands von 1945 bis zur Gegenwart," in *Wettbewerbsbeschränkungen auf internationalen Märkten: Referate und Diskussionsbeiträge des 10: Wissenschaftlichen Symposiums der gesellschaft für Unternehmersgeschichte am 25.–27. September 1985 in Lüneburg,* H. Pohl, ed. (Stuttgart: Steiner Verlag, 1988), 213-26.

6. Early empirical work on the impact of the preferential customs areas was done by Kreinin, "On the 'Trade-Diversion' Effect of Trade Preference Areas," *Journal of Political Economy* 67 (1959): 398-401. The classical works on the impact of the EEC are: L. Krause, "European Economic Integration and the United States," *American Economic Review,* Papers and Proceedings 53 (1963): 185-96; E. Thorbecke, "European Economic Integration and the Pattern of World Trade," *American Economic Review,* Papers and Proceedings 53 (1963): 147-74; and B. Balassa, "Trade Creation and Trade Diversion in the European Common Market," *The Economic Journal: The Journal of the Royal Economic Society* 77 (1967): 1-17. The following two articles give a critical discussion of contemporaneous literature on trade creation and trade diversion in customs unions: W. Sellekaerts, "How Meaningful Are Empirical Studies on Trade Creation and Trade Diversion?" *Weltwirtschaftliches Archiv* 109 (1973): 519-53; J. Pelkmans, "Effects of the Community's Customs Union: Revision and Extension of Conventional Theory," in *Integrationskonzepte auf dem Prüfstand,* R. Bieber et al., eds. (Baden-Baden: Nomos, 1983), 49-67.

7. Among these, for instance: Political and Economic Planning, *Atlantic Tariffs and Trade* (London: Political and Economic Planning, 1962); R. Bertrand, "Analyse du tarif douanier francais par industries," in *Cahiers de l'Institut de Science Economique Appliquée* série R, Etudes et Materiaux pour le Marché Commun, no. 2 (1958); Idem, "Comparaison statistique du niveau des tarifs douaniers des pays du Marché Commun," *Cahiers de l'Institut de Science Economique Appliquée,* série R, Etudes et Materiaux pour le Marché Commun, no. 2 (1958); E. Lerdau, "On the Measurement of Tariffs: The U.S. Over 40 Years," *Economia Internazionale* 10 (1957): 232-47; R. Cooper, "Tariff Dispersion and Trade Negotiations," *Journal of Political Economy* 72 (1964): 597-603.

8. There are exceptions, but these usually focus rather heavily on security considerations of European trade policies. See for instance: J. Grieco, *Cooperation Among Nations: Europe, America, and Non-Tariff Barriers to Trade* (Ithaca, NY: Cornell University Press, 1990) and D. Verdier, *Democracy and International Trade: Britain, France and the United States, 1860-1990* (Princeton:

Princeton University Press, 1994), 201-41, which singles out the years 1940 to 1962 as those of the "creation of the Cold War trading regime."

9. This problem of assessing the impact of tariffs on overall levels of trade and growth is widely discussed. See: F. Capie, *Tariffs and Growth: Some Insights from the World Economy, 1850-1940* (Manchester, Eng.: Manchester University Press, 1994). A summary of views on the interwar period is provided in Hentschel, "Zur Politik internationaler Wettbewerbsbeschränkungen in der Zwischenkriegszeit-Maßnahmen und Wirkungen: USA, Grossbrittanien, Deutschland und Frankreich," in *Wettbewerbsbeschränkungen auf internationalen Märkten: Referate und Diskussionsbeiträge des 10: Wissenschaftlichen Symposiums der gesellschaft für Unternehmersgeschichte am 25–27. September 1985 in Lüneburg,* H. Pohl, ed. (Stuttgart: Steiner Verlag, 1988), 110-61; Bhagwati briefly discusses the issue for the postwar years in his *Protectionism* (Cambridge, MA: MIT Press, 1988), 3-10.

10. For an explanation of the various uses and meanings of integration, see: F. Machlup, *A History of Thought on Economic Integration* (London: Macmillan, 1977).

11. There are many looser definitions of integration, such as "the creation and maintenance of intense and diverse patterns of interaction among previously autonomous units." See: W. Wallace, introduction to *The Dynamics of European Integration* (London: Pinter, 1992), 9.

12. I have used the concepts applied in J. Pelkmans, *The Process of Economic Integration* (Tilburg, The Netherlands: Tilburg University Press, 1976), 70.

13. During the 1950s, the word *liberalization* became synonymous with the removal of quantitative restrictions, not tariffs. Throughout this thesis, liberalization will be used in that meaning when the context refers to the OEEC's Trade Liberalization Program.

14. The source material used for reconstructing tariff plans and policies is largely derived from governmental archives in Britain, Germany, the Netherlands, France and Belgium. For further details, see the list of archival references at the beginning of this book.

15. See for a classic treatment of this issue: B. Balassa, "Tariff Protection in Industrial Countries: An Evaluation," *Journal of Political Economy* 73 (1965): 573-94.

Chapter 1

1. H. Shutt, *The Myth of Free Trade: Patterns of Protectionism Since 1945* (Oxford, Eng.: Basil Blackwell, 1985), 9. Following Borchardt, Wolfram Fischer has argued that even in the 1980s, when the New Protectionism gained ground, some 70 percent of professional economists adhered to free trade. W. Fischer, "Swings between Protection and Free Trade in History," in *Free Trade in the World Economy: Towards an Opening of Markets,* H. Giersch, ed. (Tübingen: Mohr, 1987), 30. However, as Anne O'Krueger has pointed out, international

trade thinking since 1945 developed differently in developing countries, where the infant industry argument for protectionism was more widely accepted. A. O'Krueger, "Theory and Practice of Commercial Policy: 1945-1990," working paper no. 3596, National Bureau of Economic Research, Cambridge, MA, 1990, 2.

2. F. Capie, *Tariffs and Growth: Some Illustration from the World Economy, 1850-1940* (New York: St. Martin's Press, 1994), 8.

3. J. Hagelstam, "Mercantilism Still Influences Practical Trade Policy at the End of the Twentieth Century," *Journal of World Trade* 25 (1991): 99; Capie, *Tariffs and Growth,* 12; B. Cohen, "The Political Economy of International Trade," *International Organization* 44 (1990): 261.

4. This section is limited to broad approaches that each offer a somewhat different, long-run overview of trends in international trade and protectionism. No attempt is made to present the full range of interpretations and arguments. Historical approaches are provided by Fischer, "Swings Between Protection and Free Trade in History," 20-32. A summary overview of different political economy approaches is provided by D. Lake, ed., *The International Political Economy of Trade,* vols. 1 and 2 (Aldershot: Edward Elgar, 1993).

5. This overall picture is based on Capie, *Tariffs and Growth,* 8-12; Fischer, "Swings Between Protection and Free Trade in History," 20-32; S. Pollard, *European Economic Integration, 1815-1970* (London: Thames and Hudson, 1974), 109-70.

6. J. Cuddington and R. McKinnon, "Free Trade versus Protectionism: A Perspective," in *Tariffs, Quotas and Trade: The Politics of Protectionism,* W. Adams et al., eds. (San Francisco: Institute for Contemporary Studies, 1979), 5-6.

7. Capie, *Tariffs and Growth,* 14; J. Black, "Arguments for Tariffs," *Oxford Economic Papers* no. 2 (1950): 194-95.

8. J. Pelkmans, *Vrijhandel of protectionisme: Een Europa dat openstaat voor de wereld* (The Hague: Stichting Maatschappij en Onderneming, 1985), 77; R. Lipsey, *An Introduction to Positive Economics,* 4th ed. (London: Weidenfeld and Nicholson, 1975), 795.

9. J. Eatwell, M. Milgate, and P. Newman, eds., *The New Palgrave: A Dictionary of Economics* (New York: Stockton Press, 1987), 586.

10. Pelkmans, *Vrijhandel of protectionisme,* 72.

11. Eatwell et al., eds., *The New Palgrave,* 586.

12. Capie, *Tariffs and Growth,* 14.

13. Black, "Arguments for Tariffs," 205. Unlike tariffs, however, subsidies have to be paid directly from the government's budget.

14. J. Bhagwati, *Protectionism* (Cambridge, MA: MIT Press, 1988), 105-6.

15. A fuller explanation of this new trade theory is provided by G. Grossman and J. Richardson, *Strategic Trade Policy: A Survey of Issues and Early Analysis,* Special Papers in International Economics, no. 15 (Princeton, NJ: Princeton University Press, 1985), 1-34. See for an application of strategic trade policy, H. Milner

and D. Yoffe, "Between Free Trade and Protectionism: Strategic Trade Policy and a Theory of Corporate Trade Demands," *International Organization* 43 (1989): 239-72.

16. These judgments on the practical applicability of strategic trade policies have not only been stressed by ardent free trade economists as Bhagwati and O'Krueger, but recently also by other economists such as Helpman and Krugman. Bhagwati, *Protectionism*, 106-7; O'Krueger, *Theory and Practice of Commercial Policy*, 23-25. In a concise overview of these trade policy issues, Pomfret arrives at a similar conclusion: "As a general rule for trade policymakers, the case for free trade is enhanced rather than diminished by the introduction of scale economies and imperfect competition analysis. . . . The conclusion remains, therefore, that multilaterally agreed upon free trade is the optimal policy." R. Pomfret, *International Trade Policy with Imperfect Competition*, Special Papers in International Economics, no. 17 (Princeton, NJ: Princeton University Press, 1992): 48-49.

17. Bhagwati, *Protectionism*, 108.

18. Economists' debate on this matter is not entirely over but it seems to shift toward the consensus that free trade policies and multilateral trade liberalization measures still have the best papers. P. Krugman, "Is Free Trade Passé?" in *International Economics and International Economic Policy: A Reader*, P. King, ed. (New York: McGraw-Hill, 1990), 105.

19. O'Krueger, *Theory and Practice of Commercial Policy*, 17.

20. Capie, *Tariffs and Growth*, 17-19. This explanation of protectionism is generally known as the Stolper-Samuelson theorem.

21. See for an early discussion of these empirical studies: B. Frey, *International Political Economics* (Oxford, Eng.: Basil Blackwell, 1984), 42-60.

22. D. Lake, introduction to *International Political Economy of Trade*, vol. 1, (Aldershot: Edward Elgar, 1993), xiv-xv.

23. Capie, *Tariffs and Growth*, 19-22; O'Krueger, *Theory and Practice of Commercial Policy*, 20-21.

24. Lake, introduction to *International Political Economy of Trade*, xiii.

25. See for example: Charles P. Kindleberger, "The Rise of Free Trade in Western Europe," *Journal of Economic History* 35 (1975): 20-55; See also Capie, *Tariffs and Growth*, 22-24.

26. Bhagwati, *Protectionism*, 22-24; Fischer, "Swings Between Protection and Free Trade in History," 33.

27. J. Ruggie, "International Regimes, Transactions, and Change: Embedded Liberalism in the Postwar International Economic Order," *International Organization* 36 (1982): 379-415.

28. W. Thompson and L. Vescera, "Growth Waves, Systemic Openness, and Protectionism," *International Organization* 46 (1992): 505.

29. Fischer, "Swings Between Protection and Free Trade in History," 28.

30. This argument is made in S. Strange and R. Tooze, eds., *The International Politics of Surplus Capacity: Competition for Market Shares in the World Recession* (London: Allen and Unwin, 1981).

31. A critical analysis of the hegemonic stability theory gives D. Lake, "Leadership, Hegemony, and the International Economy: Naked Emperor or Tattered Monarch with Potential?" *International Studies Quarterly* 37 (1993): 459-89.

32. See: C. Kindleberger, *The World in Depression, 1929-1939* (Berkeley, CA: University of California Press, 1973); S. Krasner, "State Power and the Structure of International Trade," *World Politics* 28 (1976): 317-47. A further theoretical refinement of hegemonic stability theory is provided by David A. Lake, who demonstrates that hegemonic stability theory is really composed of two distinctly different theories, i.e., leadership theory, which is concerned with explaining patterns of international economic stability, and hegemony theory, which tries to explains patterns of international economic openness. Lake, "Leadership, Hegemony, and the International Economy," 459-89.

33. Kindleberger, *The World in Depression*, 305.

34. Krasner, "State Power and the Structure of International Trade," 322-23.

35. Krasner, "State Power and the Structure of International Trade," 337. Another study by Krasner and Webb on international economic openness and the role of the United States since 1945 also stresses that economic openness increased from American hegemony, even though the authors observe a significant decline in American power resources. M. Webb and S. Krasner, "Hegemonic Stability Theory: An Empirical Assessment," *Review of International Studies* 15 (1989): 183-98.

36. Krasner, "State Power and the Structure of International Trade," 328-29.

37. T. McKeown, "Hegemonic Stability Theory and 19th Century Tariff Levels in Europe," *International Organization* 37 (1983): 87-88.

38. For the period up to 1960, the countries included in the study were those of North America and Western Europe. During the period 1960-1985, Japan, Australia and New Zealand were added. The author focuses on imports rather than exports or total trade because, in his own words, "the political effects of increased imports are generally viewed as more disruptive than those of increased exports." See: T. McKeown, "A Liberal Trade Order? The Long Run Pattern of Imports to the Advanced Capitalist States," *International Studies Quarterly* 35 (1991): 151-72.

39. McKeown, "A Liberal Trade Order?" 163-65.

40. McKeown, "A Liberal Trade Order?" 158.

41. One could, moreover, criticize McKeown's (and Krasner's) use of Simon Kuznetz's national income statistics.

42. H. Schwartz, *States versus Markets: History, Geography, and the Development of the International Political Economy* (New York: St.Martin's Press, 1994), 10-41. An elaborate account of this process is provided in C. Tilly, *Coercion, Capital, and European States* (Cambridge, MA: Basil Blackwell, 1990).

43. P. Kenen, *The International Economy,* 3rd ed. (Cambridge, Eng.: Cambridge University Press, 1994), 5-6. As Magnusson argues, it is an oversimplification to consider mercantilism a coherent school of thought with narrowly defined principles. The mercantilism mentioned here is in fact the "mercantile system" that Adam Smith and his followers described and criticized. See: L. Magnusson, *Mercantilism: The Shaping of an Economic Language* (London: Routledge, 1994), 98.

44. A concise explanation of Dutch and British economic growth in this period can be found in A. Maddison, *Dynamic Forces in Capitalist Development: A Long Run Comparative View* (Oxford, Eng.: Oxford University Press, 1991), 33-40.

45. McKeown, "Hegemonic Stability Theory and 19th Century Tariff Levels," 82.

46. A. Kenwood and A. Lougheed, *The Growth of the International Economy, 1820-1980: An Introductory Text* (London: Allen and Unwin, 1987), 75. However, average import duties remained above 50 percent and increased up to 60 percent in the year 1921-22, since the drop in prices increased the relative weight of the duties, which were mainly specific rather than ad valorem. R. Fremdling, "Die Zoll- und Handelspolitik Großbritanniens, Frankreichs und Deutschlands vom späten 18. Jahrhundert bis zum ersten Weltkrieg," in *Wettbewerbsbeschränkungen auf internationalen Märkten: Referate und Diskussionsbeiträge des 10. Wissenschaftlichen Symposiums der gesellschaft für Unternehmersgeschichte am 25-27. September 1985 in Lüneburg,* H. Pohl, ed. (Stuttgart: Steiner Verlag, 1988), 29-30.

47. Cuddington and McKinnon, "Free Trade versus Protectionism," 12.

48. Kindleberger, "The Rise of Free Trade in Western Europe," 33.

49. McKeown, "Hegemonic Stability Theory and 19th Century Tariff Levels," 560.

50. Pollard, *European Economic Integration,* 111-12.

51. Pollard, *European Economic Integration,* 114-18. On the tariff and trade policy of the Zollverein, see: R. Dumke, *The Political Economy of German Economic Unification: Tariffs, Trade and the Policies of the Zollverein Era* (Ph.D. diss., University of Wisconsin, 1977).

52. It took advantage of protectionist pressures within Austria and of the Austrian government's dependence on high tariffs for revenue purposes. See: McKeown, "Hegemonic Stability Theory and 19th Century Tariff levels," 87.

53. P. Bairoch, *Economics and World History: Myths and Paradoxes* (New York: Harvester Wheatsheaf, 1993), 32.

54. Maddison, *Dynamic Forces in Capitalist Development,* 40.

55. This link between the growth cycle and protectionism is, of course, subject to different interpretations. See for a more elaborate discussion for the nineteenth century: Capie, *Tariffs and Growth,* 26-37.

56. Bairoch, *Economics and World History,* 46.

57. For France, Britain and Germany this process is analyzed by Fremdling, "Die Zoll- und Handelspolitik," 25-62.

58. Capie, *Tariffs and Growth,* 8-9.

59. Bairoch, *Economics and World History*, 50-51.
60. See also: J. Foreman-Peck, *A History of the World Economy: International Economic Relations Since 1850*, 2d ed., rev. (New York: Harvester Wheatsheaf, 1995), 113-19.
61. Kenwood and Lougheed, *The Growth of the International Economy*, 86-87.
62. Kenwood and Lougheed, *The Growth of the International Economy*, 90-110. A detailed analysis of the multilateral system of trade and payments is provided by S. Saul, *Studies in British Overseas Trade, 1870-1914* (Liverpool: Liverpool University Press, 1960), 58. For a good description of the international trading system in this period: Foreman-Peck, *A History of the World Economy*, 90-119.
63. G. Hardach, *The First World War, 1914-1918* (London: Allen Lane, 1977), 254-82.
64. Pollard, *European Economic Integration*, 132.
65. W. Ashworth, *A Short History of the International Economy Since 1850*, 3rd ed. (London: Longman, 1975), 231.
66. A reconstruction of interwar tariff policies and tariff levels in Europe and the United States is provided by B. Simmons, *Who Adjusts? Domestic Sources of Foreign Economic Policy During the Interwar Years* (Princeton, NJ: Princeton University Press, 1994), 174-218.
67. W. Brown, *The United States and the Restoration of World Trade: An Analysis of the ITO Charter and the General Agreement on Tariffs and Trade* (Washington, DC: The Brookings Institution, 1950), 36.
68. Quoted in: League of Nations, *Commercial Policy in the Inter-war Period* (Geneva: League of Nations, 1942), 37.
69. Cuddington and McKinnon, "Free Trade versus Protectionism," 14.
70. Kindleberger, *The World in Depression*, 281-82.
71. These countries could only spend their Reichsmark balances on the German market.
72. R. Hogg, "Belgium, France and Switzerland and the End of the Gold Standard" in *The Netherlands and the Gold Standard, 1931-1936: A Study in Policy Formation and Policy*, in R. Griffiths, ed. (Amsterdam: Nederlands Economisch Historisch Archief, 1987), 193.
73. See: League of Nations, *International Currency Experience: Lessons of the Interwar Period* (Princeton, NJ: Princeton University Press, 1944).
74. Kenwood and Lougheed, *The Growth of the International Economy*, 210-11.
75. For example, if Germany had concluded a clearing agreement with Belgium, German importers of Belgian products would pay marks into an account at the German central bank where they would be credited to the account of the Belgian clearing agency. German exporters to Belgium would be paid from this account, and the marks would be debited to the Belgian account. In Belgium, the reverse process would take place for Belgian exporters to and importers from Germany, who would pay and be paid in francs.
76. Pollard, *European Economic Integration*, 148.

77. D. Aldcroft, *From Versailles to Wall Street, 1919-1929* (London: Allen Lane, 1977), 296-313; Kindleberger, *The World in Depression*, 281-82.

78. A. Milward, *War, Economy and Society, 1939-1945* (London: Allen Lane, 1977), 99-131.

79. R. Gardner, *Sterling-Dollar Diplomacy: The Origins and the Prospects of Our International Economic Order*, rev. and enl. ed. (New York: McGraw-Hill, 1969) provides a detailed account of the negotiations and terms for Lend-Lease.

80. W. Ashwort, *A Short History of the International Economy Since 1850*, 3rd ed. (London: Longman, 1975), 266-67.

Chapter 2

1. R. Solomon, *The International Monetary System, 1945-1981* (New York: Harper and Row, 1982), 12-13.

2. J. Bhagwati, *Protectionism* (Cambridge, MA: MIT Press, 1988), 22-24.

3. D. Calleo and M. Rowland, "Free Trade and the Atlantic Community," in *International Political Economy: Perspectives on Global Power and Wealth*, J. Frieden and D. Lake, eds. (New York: St. Martin's Press, 1987), 340.

4. Cordell Hull to Henry A. Wallace, 26 December 1934, Cordell Hull Papers, 50:118, Roosevelt Study Center, Middelburg, Netherlands.

5. American delegate to Acheson, Welles and Cordell Hull, 4 August, 1941, CHP, 51:118, RSC.

6. A total of 56 countries accepted the invitation by the United Nations for the Havana Conference and sent official representatives. The Soviet Union, Albania, Rumania, Finland, Bulgaria, Hungary and Yemen declined the invitation. In the end, 54 countries signed the Final Act. The most elaborate account of these events is: W. Brown, *The United States and the Restoration of World Trade: An Analysis of the ITO Charter and the General Agreement on Tariffs and Trade* (Washington, DC: The Brookings Institute, 1950).

7. R. Gardner, *Sterling-Dollar Diplomacy: The Origins and the Prospects of our International Economic Order*, rev. and enl. (New York: McGraw-Hill, 1969), 364.

8. These 50 percent tariff cuts would be imposed on the levels prevailing in 1945.

9. G. Curzon, *Multilateral Commercial Diplomacy: An Examination of the Impact of the General Agreement on Tariffs and Trade on National Commercial Policies and Techniques* (London: Joseph, 1965), 32.

10. Gardner, *Sterling-Dollar Diplomacy*, 349-60.

11. Curzon, *Multilateral Commercial Diplomacy*, 32. Among the groups rejecting the Charter because of its escape clauses for the use of quotas were the American Chamber of Commerce, the National Association of Manufacturers and the National Foreign Trade Council. Those supporting the Charter were the National Council of American Importers, several organizations defending

consumer interests and the Committee of Economic Development of the National Planning Association.

12. P. Gerbet, *La construction de l'Europe*, rev. ed. (Paris: Imprimerie Nationale Éditions, 1994), 60-61.

13. Gardner, *Sterling-Dollar Diplomacy*, 379; B. Kaufman, *Trade & Aid: Eisenhower's Foreign Economic Policy, 1953-1961* (Baltimore: Johns Hopkins University Press, 1982), 14-15.

14. A. Milward, *The Reconstruction of Western Europe, 1945-51* (Cambridge, Eng.: Methuen, 1987), 49-52, 220.

15. Western Europe is here defined as comprising Austria, Benelux, France, Italy, West Germany and Switzerland, together covering some 80 percent of Europe's trade.

16. R. Griffiths, "Creating a High Cost Club: The Green Pool Negotiations: 1953-1955," in *The Green Pool and the Origins of the Common Agricultural Policy*, R. Griffiths and B. Girvin, eds. (Bloomsbury: Lothian Press, 1995), 21-50.

17. There is a vast body of literature on the American initiative of 1947, much of which is archival based. The works used in this short description are: M. Hogan, *The Marshall Plan: America, Britain and the Reconstruction of Western Europe, 1947-1952* (New York: Cambridge University Press, 1987); Milward, *The Reconstruction of Western Europe*; I. Wexler, *The Marshall Plan Revisited: The European Recovery Plan in Economic Perspective* (Westport, Conn.: Greenwood Press, 1983).

18. Milward, *The Reconstruction of Western Europe*, 68-69.

19. N. Owen, *Economies of Scale, Competitiveness and Trade Patterns within the European Community* (Oxford: Clarendon, 1983), 2-4; S. Dell, "Economic Integration and the Example of the United States," *The Common Market: Progress and Controversy*, in L. Krause, ed. (Englewood Cliffs, NJ: Prentice Hall, 1964), 76-81. See also: L. Herbst, "Die zeitgenössische Integrationstheorie und die Anfänge der europäischen Einigung, 1947-1950," *Vierteljahrshefte für Zeitgeschichte* 34 (1986): 161-205.

20. Hogan, *The Marshall Plan*, 427. Hogan, though, has criticized the view that American politicians used the concept of European integration to sidetrack opposition by the isolationists in Congress, who rejected large-scale American involvement in Europe.

21. Quoted in: Brown, *The United States and the Restoration of World Trade*, 307.

22. Herbst, "Die Zeitgenössische Integrationstheorie," 178-79. J. Viner, *The Customs Union Issue* (New York: Carnegie Endowment for International Peace, 1950). First published in 1950, this was one of the pioneering theoretical works on customs unions and free trade areas, offering an analytical framework for assessing their—static—effects on world trade and the trade of individual member countries. Before the war, however, other studies had also hinted at the potentially negative impacts of customs unions on trade.

23. J. Pelkmans, *The Process of Economic Integration* (Tilburg, Netherlands: Tilburg University Press, 1975), 68, 76-78.

24. S. Dell, *Trade Blocs and Common Markets* (London: Constable, 1963), 62.

25. Note by the Board of Trade, Customs Union for Western Europe, 30 June, 1947, Public Record Office, Foreign Office 371: 62552.

26. G. Patterson, *Discrimination in International Trade: The Policy Issues, 1945-1965* (Princeton, NJ: Princeton University Press, 1966), 16.

27. Ibid.

28. J. Mayall, "The Institutional Basis of Post-War Economic Cooperation," *International Institutions at Work*, P. Taylor and A. Groom, eds. (London: Pinter, 1988), 55.

29. Dell, *Trade Blocs and Common Markets*, 76-77.

30. Brown, *The United States and the Restoration of World Trade*, 156. Curzon, *Multilateral Commercial Diplomacy*, 261.

31. Viner, *The Customs Union Issue*, 125.

32. Both phrases are quoted in: K. Kock, *International Trade Policy and the GATT, 1947-1967* (Stockholm: Almquist and Wiksell, 1969), 74.

33. K. W. Dam, *The GATT: Law and International Economic Organization* (Chicago: University of Chicago Press, 1970), 278-79.

34. Dam, *The GATT*, 90-91.

35. See for a more elaborate account: W. Lipgens, *A History of European Integration*, vol. 1, *1945-1947: The Formation of the European Unity Movement* (Oxford: Clarendon Press, 1982). A useful, short overview of the various postwar federalist movements is provided by Gerbet, *La construction de l'Europe*, 51-59.

36. The motivation behind the formation of the Benelux customs union is discussed in A. Boekestijn, "Een nagel aan Adam Smiths doodkist: De Benelux-onderhandelingen in de jaren veertig en vijftig," in *Het Benelux-effect: België, Nederland en Luxemburg en de Europese integratie, 1945-1957*, E.S.A. Bloemen, ed. (Amsterdam: Nederlands Economisch Historisch Archief, 1990), 143-68.

37. Quoted in: R. Griffiths, "The Strangehold of Bilateralism," in *The Netherlands and the Integration of Europe, 1945-1957*, R. Griffiths, ed. (Amsterdam: Nederlands Economisch Historisch Archief, 1990), 13.

38. Ibid., 15.

39. More details of this Conseil Tripartite are given in: R. Griffiths and F. Lynch, "L'Échec de la 'Petite Europe': Le Conseil Tripartite, 1944-1948," *Guerres Mondiales et Conflits Contemporains* 152 (1988): 39-62.

40. Griffiths and Lynch, 'L'Échec de la 'Petite Europe': le Conseil Tripartite," 63; S. Peters-Godts, "La politique européenne du Gouvernment Belge, septembre 1944–mai 1950" (Ph.D. diss., European University Institute, Florence, 1987), 56-61.

41. G. Kurgan-van Hentenryk, "La Belgique et le relèvement économique de l'Allemagne 1945-1948," *Relations Internationales* 51 (1987): 355.

42. Its member countries were: Austria, Belgium, Denmark, France, Greece, Ireland, Iceland, Italy, Luxembourg, the Netherlands, Portugal, the United Kingdom, Switzerland and Turkey, while Norway and Sweden sent observers but later joined as full members. Four British Dominions sent observers to the Study Group. General Secretary, "Report on the activities of the Study Group—November 1947–December 1948," 1 December 1948, Algemeen Rijksarchief, Archieven van het Ministerie van Economische Zaken, Directoraat Generaal voor Buitenlandse Economische Betrekkingen, 1125.

43. F. Knipping, "Que faire de l'Allemagne? French Policy toward Germany, 1945-1950," in *France and Germany in an Age of Crisis, 1900-1960: Studies in Memory of Charles Bloch,* H. Shamir, ed. (Leiden, Netherlands: Brill, 1990), 73-75; Gerbet, *La construction de l'Europe,* 97.

44. Telegram, U.K. Delegation in Paris to the Foreign Office, 2 August 1947, PRO, FO 371:62552.

45. In January 1947, he proposed a study of the pros and cons of a full customs union or any other economic link either with Metropolitan France, the French Union or Western Europe (including the western zones of Germany). However, this "French option" was never seriously dealt with by the economic departments. Memorandum by the Secretary of State for Foreign Affairs, "Proposal for a study of the possibilities of close economic co-operation with our western European neighbours," 18 January 1947, CP(47)35, PRO, Cabinet Papers 129:16.

46. See for a more detailed survey of the departmental differences within the British government: Hogan, *The Marshall Plan,* 46-47, 109-11; Milward, *The Reconstruction of Western Europe,* 237-50.

47. Memorandum by the Secretary of State for Foreign Affairs, "Proposal for a Study of the Possibilities of Close Economic Co-operation with Our Western European Neighbours," 18 January 1947, CP(47)35, PRO, CAB 129:16.

48. Minutes of the Cabinet Economic Policy Committee, 10 September 1948, PRO, CAB 134:216.

49. First Report of the European Customs Union Study Group, March 1948, ARA, MEZ, BEB 1125.

50. General Report of the Economic Committee of the European Customs Union Study Group, October 1948, ARA, MEZ, BEB 1126.

51. Ibid.

52. Minute to Robert Burns, 11 June 1948; Telegram, Board of Trade to Washington, 24 November 1949, PRO, Board of Trade 64:494.

53. R. Griffiths and F. Lynch, "L'Échec de la 'Petite Europe': les négociations Fritalux/Finebel, 1949-1950," *Revue Historique* 274 (1985): 161.

54. W. Diebold, Jr., *Trade and Payments in Western Europe: A Study in Economic Cooperation, 1947-1951* (New York: Harper and Brothers, 1952), 358.

55. Griffiths and Lynch, "L'Échec de la 'Petite Europe': les négociations Fritalux/Finebel, 1949-1950," 161.

56. Griffiths, Lynch, "L'Échec de la 'Petite Europe': les négociations Fritalux/ Finebel, 1949-1950," 164.

57. M. Camps, "Comment," in *From Marshall Plan to Global Interdependence: New Challenges for the Industrialized Nations,* Organization for European Cooperation and Development, ed. (Paris: Organization for European Cooperation and Development, 1978), 31.

58. Milward, *The Reconstruction of Western Europe,* 208-9.

59. F. Machlup, *A History of Thought on Economic Integration* (London: Macmillan, 1977), 13.

60. Stafford Cripps to Harold Wilson, 14 June 1948, PRO, BT 11:3883.

61. R. Poidevin, "Le facteur Europe dans la politique allemande de Robert Schuman," in *Histoire des débuts de la construction européenne (mars 1948–mai 1950): Actes du colloque de Strasbourg, 28–30 novembre 1984,* R. Poidevin, ed. (Paris: Librairie général de droits et de jurisprudence: 1988), 318.

62. Gerbet, *La construction de l'Europe,* 65, 90.

63. Poidevin, "Le facteur Europe," 315.

64. European Customs Union Study Group, "General Report of the Economic Committee," vol. 1, October 1948, ARA, MEZ, BEB 1126.

65. "Treaty Establishing the European Coal and Steel Community," 18 April 1951, *European Communities: Treaties Establishing the European Communities: Amending Treaties: Other Basic Instruments,* Article 2. (Luxembourg: 1983).

66. Over the last five years, archival studies on the Schuman Plan have become abundant. One of the most wide-ranging books in the field is: K. Schwabe, ed., *Die Anfänge des Schuman-Plans 1950/51: Beiträge des Kolloquiums in Aachen, 28–30. Mai 1986* (Baden-Baden: Nomos, 1988). See also: J. Gillingham, *Coal, Steel and the Rebirth of Europe, 1945-1955: The Germans and French from Ruhr Conflict to Economic Community* (Cambridge, Eng.: Cambridge University Press, 1991).

67. Milward, *The Reconstruction of Western Europe,* 366.

68. W. Bührer, *Ruhrstahl und Europa: Die Wirtschaftsvereinigung Eisen- und Stahlindustrie und die Anfänge der europäischen Integration, 1945-1952* (München: Oldenbourg, 1986), 165-166.

69. F. Lynch, "The role of Jean Monnet in Setting Up the European Coal and Steel Community," in *Die Anfänge des Schuman-Plans, 1950/51: Beiträge des Kolloquiums in Aachen, 28–30. Mai 1986,* K. Schwabe, ed. (Baden-Baden: Nomos, 1988), 120.

70. Gerbet, *La construction de l'Europe,* 96.

71. Gerbet, *La construction de l'Europe,* 91-94.

72. R. Bullen, "The British Government and the Schuman Plan, May 1950–March 1951," in *Die Anfänge des Schuman-Plans: Beiträge des Kolloquiums in Aachen, 28–30 Mai 1986,* K. Schwabe, ed. (Baden-Baden: Nomos, 1988), 201.

73. Bullen, "The British Government and the Schuman Plan," 204-7.

74. A. Milward, "The Belgian Coal and Steel Industries and the Schuman Plan," in *Die Anfänge des Schuman-Plans 1950/51: Beiträge des Kolloquiums in Aachen, 28–30. Mai 1986*, K. Schwabe, ed. (Baden-Baden: Nomos, 1988), 437.

75. Calculated from Economic Commission for Europe, *Economic Survey of Europe in 1951* (Geneva, 1952), 161 (which assesses the Belgian employment figure at 153,000 for the coal mines) and Ibid., 47 (with an estimated employment in steel-related industries of 611,000).

76. E. Krier, "L'industrie lourde luxembourgeoise et le Plan Schuman," in *Die Anfänge des Schuman Plans, 1950/51: Beiträge des Kolloquiums in Aachen, 28–30. Mai 1986*, K. Schwabe, ed. (Baden-Baden: Nomos, 1988), 357.

77. Milward, "The Belgian Coal and Steel Industries," 347.

78. R. Griffiths, "The Schuman Plan," in *The Netherlands and the Integration of Europe, 1945-1957*, R. Griffiths, ed. (Amsterdam, Nederlands: Economisch Historisch Archief, 1990), 117.

79. R. Ranieri, "The Italian Steel Industry and the Schuman Plan Negotiations," in *Die Anfänge des Schuman Plans, 1950/51: Beiträge des Kolloquiums in Aachen, 28–30. Mai 1986*, K. Schwabe, ed. (Baden-Baden: Nomos, 1988), 346.

80. W. Diebold, Jr., *The Schuman Plan: A Study in Economic Cooperation, 1950-1959* (New York: Praeger, 1959), 141.

81. Economic Commission for Europe, *Economic Bulletin for Europe* 2 (Geneva, 1950), 29.

82. J. Meade, H. Liesner and S. Wells, *Case Studies in European Economic Union: The Mechanics of Integration* (Oxford: Oxford University Press, 1962), 215.

83. Meade et al., *Case Studies*, 343.

84. Ranieri, "The Italian Steel Industry," 347.

85. Bührer, *Ruhrstahl und Europa*, 168.

86. R. Griffiths, "The Schuman Plan Negotiations: The Economic Clauses," in *Die Anfänge des Schuman-Plans, 1950/51: Beiträge des Kolloquiums in Aachen, 28–30. Mai 1986*, K. Schwabe, ed. (Baden-Baden: Nomos, 1988), 54.

87. Verslag inzake de besprekingen betreffende het Plan Schuman, 17 January 1950, ARA, MR 586.

88. Griffiths, "The Schuman Plan Negotiations," 56.

89. Milward, "The Belgian Coal and Steel Industries," 442-43.

90. Griffiths, "The Schuman Plan Negotiations," 61.

91. Compte Rendu de la réunion restreinte concernant le Plan Schuman du lundi 4 septembre, 4 September 1950, Ministère des Affaires Étrangères, (Ministerie van Buitenlandse Zaken), Brussels, 5261. The German delegate had been the only one favoring an approach in stages, in the hope that it would keep the transitional production levies to a minimum.

92. Ranieri, "The Italian Steel Industry," 352-55.

93. Diebold, *The Schuman Plan*, 203.

94. Milward, "The Belgian Coal and Steel Industries," 445.

95. Griffiths, "The Schuman Plan," 51-52.

96. These maximum tariffs comprised the regular ad valorem Benelux tariffs plus two percent.

97. A. Boekestijn, "The Formulation of Dutch Benelux Policy," in *The Netherlands and the Integration of Europe, 1945-1957,* R. Griffiths, ed. (Amsterdam: Nederlands Economisch Historisch Archief, 1990), 27-48; T. Mommens, "Agricultural Integration in Benelux," in *The Netherlands and the Integration of Europe, 1945-1957,* R. Griffiths, ed. (Amsterdam: Nederlands Economisch Historisch Archief, 1990), 49-69.

98. R. Griffiths and D. Barbezat, "The European Integration Experience," in *Promoting Regional Cooperation and Integration in Sub-Saharan Africa* (Brussels: Global Coalition for Africa, 1992), 91.

99. The ECSC's approval in GATT is discussed in Patterson, *Discrimination in International Trade,* 125-39.

Chapter 3

1. W. Diebold, Jr., *Trade and Payments in Western Europe: A Study in Economic Cooperation, 1947-1951* (New York: Harper and Brothers, 1952), 216. From an economic theoretical viewpoint, this distinction between quotas and tariffs may seem dubious, especially given that textbook economics (at least until the mid-1960s) usually insisted that they were—or in any case could be interpreted as—equivalent with regard to their influence on import volumes, domestic prices, output and consumption levels. Seen from the perspective of policy-makers and tariff negotiators at the time, however, this equivalence held little practical significance in the real world of market imperfections. Indeed, as Bhagwati subsequently demonstrated, it is only on very rare occasions when competitive international and domestic market structures prevail that tariffs and quotas have a similar protective impact. The equivalence theorem thus rests on the assumption that supply and demand schedules are given. Early statements on the difference between tariffs and quotas are provided by: League of Nations, *Quantitative Trade Controls: Their Causes and Nature* (Geneva, 1943); H. Arndt, *The Economic Lessons of the Nineteen-Thirties: A Report* (London: Oxford University Press, 1944) and C. Wilcox, *A Charter for World Trade* (New York: Macmillan, 1949). See for a further analysis of economic thinking on this issue: J. Eatwell, M. Milgate, and P. Newman, eds., *The New Palgrave: A Dictionary of Economics* (London: Macmillan, 1987), 33-34; P. King, ed. *International Economics and International Economic Policy: A Reader* (New York: McGraw-Hill, 1990).

2. K. Dam, *The GATT: Law and International Economic Organization* (Chicago: University of Chicago Press, 1970), 148-49. Always assuming, of course, that tariff rates are not so high as to be totally prohibitive.

3. Italics mine. Quoted in: A. Milward, *The Reconstruction of Western Europe, 1945-51* (Cambridge, Eng.: Methuen, 1987), 304.

4. Quoted in: F. Boyer and J. Sallé, "The Liberalisation of Intra-European Trade in the Framework of OEEC," *International Monetary Fund Staff Papers* 4 (1955): 179.

5. There were exceptions to this unanimity rule. A member could voluntarily withdraw from the voting procedure if its interests were not directly involved in a particular decision. The Council could also exclude a member that no longer fulfilled its obligations under the OEEC Convention, but this occurred rarely. M. Blacksell, *Post-War Europe: A Political Geography*, 2d ed. (London: Hutchinson, 1981), 41.

6. For West Germany the base year for calculating the liberalization percentage was 1949, and for Austria 1952.

7. The formulation of this Code had been delayed by the negotiations for the EPU, the European payments system sustaining the transition toward multilateral trade (see chapter 2).

8. The time limit for a waiver of liberalization measures on balance of payments grounds was later shortened to 12 months. For an extensive treatment of the Code's provisions see the various volumes of the *European Yearbook* dealing with the OEEC, in which basic texts, resolutions and agreements are given: Council of Europe, *European Yearbook*, various volumes.

9. O. Hieronymi, *Economic Discrimination Against the United States in Western Europe (1945-1958): Dollar Shortage and the Rise of Regionalism* (Geneva: Droz, 1973), 106.

10. This is explored further in chapter 4.

11. Ministère des Finances, "La politique commerciale et douanière de la France et d'Allemagne occidentale," *Statistiques et Etudes Financières*, supplement 113, (1958): 495-628.

12. OEEC Trade Committee, Special Session (August 1950), "Memorandum by the Secretary General on the examination of certain import duties," 24 August 1959, TC(50)74, Annex 3: France, Bundesarchiv, Koblenz, Germany, Bundesministerium für Wirtschaft: 7535.

13. This is also discussed in G. Bossuat, *La France, l'aide américain et la construction européenne, 1944-1954* (Paris: Imprimerie nationale, 1992).

14. M. Cavalcanti, *La politica commerciale italiana, 1945-1952: Uomini e fatti* (Naples: Edizione Scientifiche Italiane, 1984), 189.

15. This was constructed by applying for each commodity a tariff that was calculated as the legal tariff plus 11 percent and divided by two. It only concerned tariffs above 11 percent.

16. Widerstände gegen die Inkraftsetzung des Italiänischen Generalzolltarifs, 16 June 1952, Bundesarchiv, Koblenz, Bundesministerium für den Marshall Plan: 128.

17. R. Ranieri, "L'espansione alla prova del negoziato—l'industria italiana e la comunita' del carbone e dell' acciaio, 1945-1955," (Ph.D. diss., European University Institute, Florence, 1988), 151-52.

18. The German minister of economic affairs, Ludwig Erhard, and most Germans with him considered this unilateral granting of MFN status an intolerable discrimination.

19. F. Jerchow, "Außenhandel im Wiederstreit: Die Bundesrepublik auf dem Weg in das GATT, 1949-1951" in *Politische Weichenstellungen im Nachkriegsdeutschland, 1945-1953,* A. Winkler, ed. (Göttingen, Germany: Vandenhoeck und Ruprecht, 1979), 271.

20. Beschluß der Bundesregierung über die Vorbereitung einer deutschen Zolltarifreform, 11 October 1949, BA, B 102:702. The comparisons of average tariff rates including the United Kingdom and the United States can be found in Betr. Internationale Zolltarifverhandlungen in Torquay, Entwurf, August 1950, B 136:1277.

21. Bericht über den Verlauf und Ergebnis der Internationalen Zoll- und Handelskonferenz der GATT Staaten, 19 April 1950, Bundesarchiv, Koblenz, Bundeskanzleramt: 1277, (Vierte Tagung vom 23.2 bis 3.4.50 in Genf).

22. Vergleichzollsätze, n.d., BA, B 102:7279; P. Schade, "Die Entwicklung des Zolltarifes der Bundesrepublik Deutschland bis zum EWG Außentarif," (Ph.D. diss., Eberhardt Karls University, Tübingen, 1963), 37; Jerchow, "Außenhandel im Wiederstreit," 278-79. The German government was in such a strong bargaining position because the Torquay conference was due to start in three weeks. Since GATT only allowed fully sovereign states to participate in the tariff negotiations it meant that increased pressure from the Allied High Commission would put Germany's accession to GATT at risk.

23. GATT Subgroup of the Working Party on Reduction of Tariff Levels, June 1952, PRO, BT 11:4901 (Data furnished by members of the subgroup pursuant to Annex F of IW.2/15).

24. The German tariff schedule forms the major exception. It underwent two unilateral tariff cuts in 1956 and 1957 of, on average, 25 percent each. Therefore, as indicators of Germany's effective protection, the figures for 1959 must be handled with extreme caution.

25. As Grubel has pointed out, negative rates of effective protection may sometimes be the outcome of measurement errors, but it is difficult to distinguish them from "genuine" negative rates. H. Grubel, "Effective Tariff Protection: A Non-Specialist Guide to the Theory, Policy Implications and Controversies," in *Effective Tariff Protection: Proceedings of a Conference Sponsored by the General Agreement on Tariffs and Trade and the Graduate Institute of International Studies,* H. Grubel and H. Johnson, eds. (Geneva: GATT, 1971), 7-8.

26. S. Guisinger and D. Schydlowsky, "The Empirical Relationship Between Nominal and Effective Rates of Protection," in *Effective Tariff Protection,* Grubel and Johnson, eds. (Geneva: GATT, 1971), 270.

27. Betr: Untersuchung für die OEEC, 31 March 1950, BA, B 102:56347; Customs Tariffs: Method of examination proposed by the Trade Committee,

6 April 1950, B 102:7536; Kurzbericht über die High-Level Sitzung des Handelsausschusses, 22–24 March 1950, B 102:913.

28. The OEEC's tariff inquiry has been traced via the OEEC documents in the German Bundesarchiv in B 102:7535. It is worth stressing that several deficiencies render this examination unsuitable for reconstructing a fully accurate or complete picture of the scope of the European tariff problem. One reason is that the Federal Republic hardly figures in the tariff inquiry because only Norway and Belgium complained about the old German schedule. Every other country decided to wait for the new schedule with which Germany would enter the forthcoming tariff negotiations in Torquay. Secondly, Germany itself reserved its final judgement of the new Italian schedule because it could not furnish (yet) statistical indications of its restrictiveness. Others, though, more than compensated for this by assuming that Italy's unusually high tariff levels were simply bound to be restrictive. Thirdly, the OEEC did not receive any tariff complaints from the Scandinavian states against the United Kingdom, since they clearly felt a political commitment to avoid a potentially embarrassing confrontation with their closest political ally and most important European trading partner. Similarly, for purely political motives, the Federal Republic of Germany did not present a case against prohibitive French tariffs. Its tariff negotiators received instructions not to trouble the French in any way with this matter.

29. Of course, this still leaves us with the familiar problem that the value of trade in each commodity group is likely to be influenced by trade barriers.

30. Belgium/Luxembourg and Sweden and Norway had 12, 3 and 2 complaints respectively.

31. The same method of standardizing the number and classification of complaints is used as that adopted earlier for the inquiry of 1950. The data of the OEEC's inquiry of 1955 are assembled from documents in: BA, B 102:7527.

32. The President of Bayer to Von Maltzan, 13 September 1949, BA, B 102:291.

33. Invloed van invoerrecht op liberalisatie, 5 April 1955, ARA, MEZ, BEB 1168.

34. N. Owen, *Economies of Scale, Competitiveness and Trade Patterns Within the European Community* (Oxford: Clarendon Press, 1983), 19-20. This work stresses the role of tariffs as impediments to the exploiting of economies of scale.

35. M. Steuer and G. Erb, "An Empirical Test of the 'GATT Hypothesis,'" *Journal of Political Economy* 74 (1966): 274-77.

36. Note of a meeting held on 23 October 1950 in Mr Nowell's room to consider whether developments in GATT or OEEC called for the early introduction of a tariff to replace the Dyestuffs Act, n.d., PRO, BT 64:4172.

37. Note of a meeting in Mr. Nowell's room on 31 October 1950 at 11:30 A.M. to consider the C.R.E problems that would arise if the introduction of a tariff for dyestuffs was delayed and we were to rely upon individual licensing as a means of protection to the home industry, n.d., PRO, BT 64:4172.

38. The Allied powers split the former chemical giant IG Farben into three large firms, Hoechst, Bayer and BASF. R. Stokes, "Recovery and Resurgence in the West German Chemical Industry: Allied Policy and the I.G. Farben Successor Companies," (Ph.D. diss., Ohio State University, 1986), 210.

39. The President of Bayer to Von Maltzan, 13 September 1949, BA, B 102:291.

40. The German tariff expert responsible for the study of unilateral tariff reductions admitted this later in 1954. Die Möglichkeit von Zollsenkungen im gewerblichen Sektor des deutschen Zolltarifs, zusammengestellt auf Grund der Beratungen des im Bundesministerium für Wirtschaft gebildeten Ausschusses zur Überprüfung des gewerblichen Sektors des deutschen Zolltarifs auf die Möglichkeit von Zollsenkungen, April 1954, BA, B 102:7314.

41. Stokes, "Recovery and Resurgence," 253-58.

42. Axenfeld (the German delegate to the OEEC) to Eichhorn, 8 July 1953, BA, B 102:56347.

43. List of commodities which Denmark requests to be examined in accordance with the Council decision of 31 January 1950, paragraphs 5 and 6, n.d., TC(50)35/04 Add.1, BA, B 102:7535.

44. Verslag van de vergadering van de ministeriële Council van de OEEC te Parijs gehouden op 26 en 27 oktober 1950, 31 October 1950, ARA, MR 590.

45. Minutes of the Economic Committee of Cabinet, 7 March 1950, ARA, MR 572.

46. R. Griffiths, "The Abortive Dutch Assault on European Tariffs," *Modern Dutch Studies: Essays in Honour of Peter King, Professor of Modern Dutch Studies at the University of Hull on the Occasion of his Retirement*, in M. Wintle, ed. (London: Athlone, 1988), 186-91.

47. Plan of Action for European Economic Integration, n.d., Kabinet, 351.66(4):33.19, Ministerie van Algemene Zaken, The Hague.

48. Minutes of the Cabinet's Economic Committee, 28 February 1950 and 7 March 1950, ARA, MR 572.

49. Plan of Action for European Economic Integration, n.d., Kabinet, 351.66(4):33.19, MAZ.

50. M. Hogan, *The Marshall Plan: America, Britain and the Reconstruction of Western Europe, 1947-1952* (New York: Cambridge University Press, 1987), 352-53; De behandeling der plannen Stikker, Petsche en Pella door Werkgroep No. 6 van het Executive Committee 28 juli–12 augustus 1950, 16 August 1950; Aanvullingen op het verslag van de Missie over de besprekingen in Werkgroep nr. 6 van het Executive Committee, 26 August 1950; Note starting 'Op 7 Juli besloot de Raad van de OEEC . . .' 7 July 1950, Ministerie van Buitenlandse Zaken, Directoraat Generaal voor Economische en Militaire Samenwerking 6117:1262.

51. Proposals and remarks submitted by Mr. Pella on behalf of the Italian government concerning methods to be adopted in the organization of the European market, 28 June 1950, MBZ, DGEM, 6218:1342.

52. Projet de création d'une banque européenne d'investissement (projet de la délégation française), 4 July 1950, ARA, MR 586.

53. Franz Blücher to Adenauer, 14 June 1950, BA, B 136:1315; Entwurf einer Stellungnahme zu den Plänen für den Herbeiführung einer wirtschaftlichen Integration in Westeuropa, n.d., B 102:11179

54. Cabinet European Economic Cooperation Committee, Record of an ad hoc meeting held in Mr. Hirschman's room, 14 June 1950, Public Record Office, Treasury Archives, 232:363.

55. Stikker Plan, 21 June 1950, PRO, T 232:363.

56. Note of a meeting between Sir James Helmore, Sir Stephen Holmes and Mr. Leckie, 23 June 1950, PRO, T 232:363; Note of a meeting of the London Committee, 30 June 1950, PRO, T 232:363; Cabinet European Economic Cooperation Committee, Integration and UNISCAN, Note by the Board of Trade, 22 November 1950, ER(L)(50)267, PRO, Board of Trade Archives 64:669.

57. Note sur les mésures à envisager en matière tarifaire (Larre), July 1950, Ministère des Affaires Étrangères, Archives Diplomatiques, Direction des Affaires Économiques et Financières, Service de Cooperation Économique 13; Propositions françaises concernant les mésures à prendre en 1951 en vue de l'intégration économique de l'Europe occidentale, 1 December 1950, MBZ, DGEM 6117:1263. The French ministry of foreign affairs had drafted this proposal in July for submission to the OEEC, but at the time it did not receive approval at cabinet level.

58. J. Wexler, *The Marshall Plan Revisited: The European Recovery Plan in Economic Perspective* (Westport, CT: Greenwood Press, 1983), 238.

59. Since the OEEC calculated countries' official liberalization percentages by looking at private trade only, member states could in fact transfer products imported under quotas from private to government accounts without officially reducing their liberalization effort as recorded by the OEEC.

60. The share of chemicals in total export of these countries were: Sweden, 1.8; Denmark 2.4; BLEU 6.7; Norway 8.1; the Netherlands 7.5; Switzerland 16.4.

61. OEEC Ministerial Council, Cabinet Mutual Aid Committee, Memorandum by Secretary-General of OEEC, "Liberalisation of Trade," 26 March 1952, MAC(52)88, PRO, CAB 134:1012.

62. The structure and procedures of the OEEC's Boards and Committees is discussed in: D. Mallet, "The History and Structure of OEEC," in *European Yearbook*, vol.1 (1955), 62-70. The Steering Board was composed of seven members who were elected annually by the Council. Its chairman was appointed annually by the OEEC's Council.

63. Maandoverzicht van de OEEC, 20 april–20 mei 1952, 21 May 1952, Algemeen Rijksarchief, Archieven van het Ministerie van Economische Zaken, Centrale raad voor het betalingsverkeer, 6570.

64. Maandoverzicht van de OEEC, 20 december–22 januari 1953, 24 January 1953, MEZ, BEB, OEEC 556.

65. Consideration of the Question of Customs Tariffs Interim Report by the Steering Board for Trade, 8 december 1952, C(52)366, BA, B 102:7538. This qualification was almost a blueprint of British delegation instructions. Burns to Button (U.K. Delegation to the OEEC), 16 December 1952, PRO,BT 11:4805.

66. Samenvatting van het besprokene tijdens de vergadering van de OEEC, 22 January 1953, MEZ, BEB, OEEC 556.

67. The background of this policy change will be discussed in chapter 6.

68. Note by the Secretary of State for Foreign Affairs and the Chancellor of the Exchequer, "A Collective Approach to Freer Trade and Currencies," 10 February 1953, C(53)56, PRO, CAB 129:59.

69. Cabinet Mutual Aid Committee, "General effects of Commonwealth Conference Proposals on European Countries," 17 February 1953, MAC(53)57 (review), PRO, CAB 134:1015.

70. Cabinet Mutual Aid Committee, Note by the Secretaries, "Brief for Visit of French Ministers: France and the Future of the EPU," 10 February 1953, MAC(53)45 (revise), PRO, CAB 134:1015.

71. Cabinet Mutual Aid Committee, "General Effects of Commonwealth Conference Proposals on European Countries," 17 February 1953, MAC(53)57 (revise), PRO, CAB 134:1015.

72. A. Milward, "Motives for Currency Convertibility: The Pound and the Deutschmark, 1950-5," in *Interaction in the World Economy: Perspectives from International Economic History: Festschrift in Honour of Wolfram Fischer,* C. Holtfrerich, ed. (New York: Harvester Wheatsheaf, 1989), 272.

73. Ibid., 269-70. For this reason, the BDI was a staunch supporter of pushing European integration and convertibility within the framework of the OEEC.

74. Gutachten über die Commonwealth Konferenz 1952 und die durch sie aufgeworfene Probleme, Im Auftrage des Bundesministeriums für den Marshallplan erstattet von Dr. V. E. Preusker, n.d., BA, B 136:2594.

75. The details of these convertibility discussions and of the British-German talks can be found in the file BA, B 102:56905.

76. Cabinet Mutual Aid Committee, "General Effects of Commonwealth Conference Proposals on European Countries," 17 February 1953, MAC(53)57 (revise), PRO, CAB 134:1015.

77. J. M. Clerx, *Nederland en de liberalisatie van het handels- en betalingsverkeer (1945-1958)* (Groningen: Wolters-Noordhoff, 1986), 125, 144-45.

78. Cabinet Mutual Aid Committee, "General Effects of Commonwealth Conference Proposals on European Countries," 17 February 1953, MAC(53)57 (revise), PRO, CAB 134:1015.

79. Note by the Dutch Minister of Foreign Affairs, 19 January 1953, no. 6921, ARA, MR 486. Marjolin's visit to the United Kingdom had failed to convince the British government of the need for prior discussions on the issue within the

OEEC. See: Note of an informal meeting between Monsieur Marjolin, Secretary-General of the OEEC, and United Kingdom officials, held in Mr. Strath's room, H.M. Treasury, 17 January 1953, PRO, T 232:343; Record of a meeting held at the Foreign Office, 16 January 1953, PRO, T 232:343.

80. Bericht über die Tagung des Handelsdirektorium in Paris in der Zeit vom 1–3. Juli 1953, 6 July 1953, BA, B 102:7538.

81. Note for Prime Minister from Chancellor of Exchequer, 6 March 1953, Public Record Office, Prime Minister's Papers 11:884; Freer Trade and Currencies: Role of the United States Policies, 1 May 1953, C(53)144, PRO, CAB 129:60.

82. Memorandum by the Foreign Secretary and the Chancellor of the Exchequer, "Collective Approach to Freer Trade and Currencies: Statement at the Council of the Organization for European Economic Cooperation," 19 March 1953, C(53)107, PRO, CAB 129:60.

83. They would also take special measures to increase imports under license of typically French and Italian products. Memorandum by the Chancellor of the Exchequer and the President of the Board of Trade, "Relaxation of Import Restrictions on Trade with Western Europe," 17 March 1953, C(53)100, PRO, CAB 129:59; Minutes of a Cabinet Meeting, 20 March 1953, CAB 128:26.

84. Note for Cherwell, 24 April 1953, PRO, PREM 11:884.

85. Bericht über die Tagung des Handelsdirektoriums der OEEC in Paris in der Zeit vom 1- 3. Juli 1953, 6 July 1953, BA, B 102:753.

86. Samenvatting van het besprokene tijdens de vergadering van de OEEC, 22 January 1953, MEZ, BEB, OEEC 556.

87. Die Möglichkeiten eines Zollabbaues im Rahmen der OEEC, 28 July 1953, BA, B 102:7538.

88. See for instance: Bericht über die Tagung des Handelsdirektoriums der OEEC in Paris in der Zeit vom 1–3. Juli 1953, 6 July 1953, BA, B 102:753; Record of the Eighth Meeting of the Anglo-Scandinavian Economic Committee (UNISCAN) held at the Foreign Office, 30 April 1953, PRO, T 236:4041.

89. A look at the liberalization percentages reached in 1954 in the different categories of products shows that the BLEU countries and Switzerland had virtually completed the removal of quota restrictions on raw materials and end products, but that they fell far behind in food and feeding stuffs (see table below). The Belgians tried to cover up their chronic problems in agriculture by insisting on a change in the reference year used for calculating the percentages. This could help them in meeting the 75 percent stage, but the remaining quotas would certainly stand out as "hard cores" of protectionism. The Dutch position was fairly comfortable in all three sectors, although a further increase in the percentage for end products would eventually mean giving up protection for a few infant industries. Norway and Denmark had much larger sectors of "weak" and infant industries for which the removal of quotas would be problematic. In Norway, the larger part of this hard core protected employment in shipbuilding, whereas in Denmark it sheltered sectors such as textiles, leatherware and

chemicals. Verslag van de vergadering van de Steering Board for Trade, 11 October 1955, MEZ, BEB, OEEC 607.

90. OECE Groupe d'étude ministeriel sur la convertibilité, Procès verbal de la 4 ième session d'experts tenue au Chateau de la Muette, Paris, 8 December 1954, BA, B 102:55346; Cabinet Mutual Ad Committee, Note of an informal meeting, 3 January 1955, PRO, CAB 134:1026.

91. Telegram, U.K. Delegation in Paris to the Foreign Office, 13 January 1955, PRO, BT 205:219; Telegram, U.K. Delegation in Paris to the Foreign Office, 17 January 1955, PRO, BT 205:219; Telegram, U.K. Delegation in Paris to the Foreign Office, 18 January 1955, PRO, BT 205:219; Council, "Decision of the Council Concerning the Extension and Stabilization of Trade," 14 January 1955, C(54) 291 final, ARA, MEZ, BEB 1131.

Chapter 4

1. These countries were: Austria, Belgium, Brazil, Burma, Canada, Ceylon, Chile, China, Cuba, Czechoslovakia, France, India, Lebanon, Luxembourg, the Netherlands, New Zealand, Norway, Pakistan, Southern Rhodesia, Syria, South Africa, the United States.

2. In trade issues, as in other fields, there are different interpretations and meanings of reciprocity. Foreign trade experts often distinguish between specific and diffuse reciprocity, where the first involves the exchange of concessions in a strictly limited and equivalent field (for example predefined tariff reductions) and the second relates to less strictly defined concessions or obligations that may also be extended to a group of countries rather than to countries individually. Here we shall use reciprocity in its specific meaning. The concept is discussed further in: R. Keohane, "Reciprocity in International Relations," *International Organization* 40 (1986): 1-27.

3. A. Shonfield, ed. *International Economic Relations of the Western World, 1959-1971*, vol. 1, *Politics and Trade* (London: University Press for the Royal Institute of International Affairs, 1976), 158. A useful account of American thinking on reciprocity and multilateralism can be found in: J. Goldstein, "Creating the GATT Rules: Politics, Institutions and American Politics," in *Multilateralism Matters: The Theory and Practice of Institutional Form*, J. Ruggie, ed. (New York: Columbia University Press, 1993), 201-32. See pages 205 to 208.

4. Shonfield, *International Economic Relations*, 156. As we shall see in chapter 5, it was only during the special review session of GATT rules in 1954 that this unwritten rule became explicitly recognized.

5. K. Kock, *International Trade Policy and the GATT, 1947-1967* (Stockholm: Almquist and Wiksell, 1969), 64.

6. This rule, laid down in article 28, was drastically changed in 1957. Instead of expiring after a maximal of three years, tariff concessions were automatically consolidated unless countries explicitly demanded modifications.

7. More data on American tariff reductions are given in R. Baldwin and A. O'Krueger, *The Structure and Evolution of Recent U.S. Trade Policy* (Chicago: Chicago University Press, 1984).

8. Other countries negotiating for accession at Torquay were Turkey, Peru and Korea.

9. "War die Konferenz von Torquay ein Erfolg?" and "Blühender Verwaltungsprotektionismus," *Frankfurter Allgemeine Zeitung,* 6 June 1951.

10. W. Diebold, Jr., *The End of the ITO* (Princeton: Princeton University Press, 1952), 6.

11. Betreft: derde verslag van de conferentie inzake de tarieven te Torquay, 27 March 1951, Ministerie van Financiën, The Hague, Netherlands, GATT 124. Parts of this story on tariff plans in GATT have been published elsewhere. See: W. Asbeek Brusse, "The Failure of European Tariff Plans in GATT," in *Die europäische Integration vom Schuman-Plan bis zu den Verträgen von Rom: Beiträge des Kolloquiums in Luxemburg, 17–19. Mai 1989,* G. Trausch, ed. (Baden-Baden: Nomos, 1993), 99-114 and Idem, "The Americans, GATT and European Integration, 1947-1957: A Decade of Dilemma," in *The United States and the Integration of Europe' Legacies of the Postwar Era,* F. Heller and J. Gillingham, eds. (New York: St. Martin's Press, 1996), 221-49.

12. Note sur les mésures à envisager en matière tarifaire (Larre), July 1950, MAE, AD, DE-CE 13; Propositions françaises concernant les mésures à prendre en 1951 en vue de l'intégration économique de l'Europe occidentale, 1 December 1950, Ministerie van Buitenlandse Zaken, Directoraat Generaal voor Economische en Militaire Samenwerking 6117:1263.

13. Summary record of the third meeting of some OEEC countries to discuss the levelling of European tariffs by multilateral negotiations, 31 January 1951, ARA, MEZ, BEB 431.

14. Bruce (Ambassador in France) to the Secretary of State, 2 September 1951, *Foreign Relations of the United States* 4 (1951), 418; "France's Trade Policy," *The Economist,* 10 February 1951.

15. The Secretary of State to the Embassy in France, 7 March 1951, *FRUS* 1 (1951), 1273.

16. Memorandum by the delegations of the Benelux countries on European Tariff Negotiations, January 1951, *FRUS* 1 (1951), 1321-23.

17. M. Hogan, *The Marshall Plan: America, Britain and the Reconstruction of Western Europe, 1947-1952* (New York: Cambridge University Press, 1987), 352-53.

18. Secretary of State to the Acting Chairman of the U.S. Delegation to the Torquay Conference, Corse, 15 January 1951, *FRUS* 1 (1951), 1323-24; Derde verslag van de conferentie inzake de tarieven in Torquay, 27 March 1951, MFin, GATT 124.

19. Notitie voor de minister via de thesaurier-generaal betreft: tariefbesprekingen te Torquay, dd.15-1-1951, MFin, GATT 124; Minutes of Cabinet's Economic Committee, 5 January 1951, ARA, MR 572.

20. Telegram, von Maltzan to the German Delegation in Torquay, 23 January 1951, BA, B 102:7348.

21. Documented in Phelps (temporary acting chairman of the United States delegation to the Torquay Conference) to the Secretary of State, 8 January 1951, *FRUS* 1 (1951), 1343-44.

22. Betr.: Zollverhandlungen in Torquay (Erhard to Adenauer), 9 March 1951, BA, B 136:1277.

23. Memorandum by the President of the Board of Trade, "Tariff Preferences and the Torquay Negotiations," 9 February 1951, EPC(51)12, PRO, CAB 134:229.

24. In Britain, the board of trade was in charge of multilateral negotiations in GATT.

25. See for a treatment of this issue: F. Romero, "Migration as an Issue in European Interdependence and Integration: The Case of Italy," in *The Frontier of National Sovereignty: History and Theory,* A. Milward, F. Lynch, F. Romero, R. Ranieri and V. Sørensen, eds. (London: Routledge, 1993), 33-58.

26. Summary record of the sixth meeting of some OEEC countries to discuss the leveling of European tariffs by multilateral negotiations, 12 February 1951, ARA, MEZ, BEB 431.

27. Phelps (temporary acting chairman of the United States delegation to the Torquay Conference) to the Secretary of State, 10 February 1951, *FRUS* 1 (1951), 1346. This Benelux proposal for automatic reductions of tariff disparities was later worked out in more detail. See: Le problème du nivellement des tarifs européens, 17 April 1951, and Memorandum soumis par les pays de l'union douanière Benelux au sujet de la resolution adoptée par les parties contractantes au G.A.T.T. à Torquay le 2 Avril 1951, 6 September 1951, ARA, MEZ, BEB 1172.

28. Betreft: gelijktrekking Europese tarieven, 16 February 1951, ARA, MEZ, BEB 1172.

29. Phelps (temporary acting chairman of the United States delegation to the Torquay Conference) to the Secretary of State, 8 January 1951, *FRUS* 1 (1951), 1343-44; Telegram, von Scherpenberg to Beye, 3 February 1951, BA, B 102:7348.

30. De Montremy worked at the customs tariffs service of the ministry of economic affairs.

31. Avant des 'Dix' pour la solution du problème de l'alignement des tarifs européens, 2 May 1951; Betreft: rechttrekking der Europese tarieven (verder overleg met de Fransen, 8 May 1951, ARA, MEZ, BEB 1172.

32. Déclaration de M. Pierre Pflimlin, président de la délégation française, 19 September 1951; Telegram, Pflimlin to the French Delegation in Torquay, 19 September 1951, MAE, AD, DE-CE 13.

33. W. Vermeulen, *Europees landbouwbeleid in de maak: Mansholts eerste plannen, 1945-1953,* vol. xx, *Historia Agriculturae* (Groningen: Nederlands Agronomisch-Historisch Instituut, 1989), 193.

34. Telegram, Wormser to the Economic Cooperation Service of the General Directorate of Economic Affairs and Finance at the Ministry of Foreign Affairs, 4 July 1951, MAE, AD, DE-CE 13.

35. Note au sujet des propositions soumises à la 6ème session des parties contractantes à l'Accord Général en vue de l'abaissement des tarifs douaniers, 8 November 1951, MAE, AD, DE-CE 13. Bernard Clappier was 'Directeur de Cabinet' under Schuman. Despite their 'assistence' in redrafting the text, neither Montremy nor Clappier agreed with Pflimlin's new approach. See for example: Objet: nivellement des tarifs européen (Clappier), n.d., MAE, AD, DE-CE 13.

36. Note pour monsieur le secretaire général, 15 September 1951, MAE, AD, DE-CE 13; Note au sujet des propositions soumises à la 6ème session des parties contractantes à l'Accord Général en vue de l'abaissement des tarifs douaniers, 8 November 1951, MAE, AD, DE-CE 13.

37. Memorandum, Perkins (assistant secretary of state for foreign affairs) to Cabot, Director of International Security Affairs, 24 July 1951, *FRUS* 4 (1951), 409-12.

38. "Problematischer Preispolitik in Frankreich," *Neue Zürcher Zeitung,* 25 September 1951.

39. At a meeting with representatives of the state department in July, the Americans had again insisted on a nonpreferential approach to the disparity issue but the French had remained adamant that the results would be disappointing. Sixième session des Parties Contractantes, "Conversations Franco-Américains des 30 et 31 juillet 1951," 1 August 1951, MAE, AD, DE-CE 13.

40. Lecuyer to the French Embassy in The Hague, 4 October 1951, MAE, AD, DE-CE 13. The note reports on the meeting between Pflimlin and, among others, van Blankenstein and Spierenburg in the Hague.

41. Note pour l'ambassadeur, secretaire général, 2 October 1951, MAE, AD, DE-CE 13.

42. Note pour monsieur Wormser a.s. le Conseil de l'Europe et le "Low Tariff Club," 27 December 1951, MAE, AD, DE-CE 13.

43. This 'final version,' although by no means recognized as such by all the governments involved in the talks, was published as an official GATT document: General Agreement on Tariffs and Trade (GATT), *A New Proposal for the Reduction of Customs Tariffs* (Geneva, 1954).

44. French proposal for a general lowering of customs tariffs, note of problems arising out of the plan contained in GATT/IW2/5, 8 November 1951, PRO, BT 205:12.

45. The term "demarcation line" is used to make a distinction between the weighted average tariffs of all countries together and the weighted average of the tariff items of each individual country.

46. The formula for calculating this proportional reduction (X) was the following:

$$X = 30\% \times \frac{N-P}{D-P}$$

with X representing the reduction required, N the average incidence, D the demarcation line and P the floor level (defined as D–30%).

If we take the example of the Benelux tariff in sector IX, the following reduction of this tariff would be required:

$$30\% \times \frac{10-7}{11-7} = 23\% \text{ over 3 years, or } 7.6\% \text{ per annum}$$

47. Council of Europe, *Low Tariff Club: A Council of Europe Contribution to the Study of the Problem of Lowering Customs Barriers as between Member-Countries* (Strasbourg, 1952).

48. Council of Europe, *The Strasbourg Plan: Proposals for Improving the Economic Relations Between Member States of the Council of Europe and Their Overseas Countries With Which They Have Constitutional Links* (Strasbourg, 1952).

49. Verslag van het tweede deel der derde zitting van de raadgevende vergadering van de Raad van Europa, 24 December 1951, MAZ, 351.88(4)1.075.

50. Trade Negotiations Committee, Subcommittee on Tariffs, GATT, "Report of the United Kingdom Delegation to the Meeting of Sub-group of Intercessional Working Party on the Reduction of Tariff Levels," 15–26 July, 1952, PRO, BT 205:13; Conseil de l'Europe. Comité des Ministres. 12ème session. Neuvième réunion des délégués des ministres, 10 February 1953, CM(53)8, MAE, AD, DE-CE 15.

51. Letter, Minister of Industry to the Minister of Foreign Affairs, 8 April 1952, MAE, AD, DE-CE 14.

52. Letter, Minister of Industry to the Minister of Foreign Affairs, 8 April 1952; Commission interministerielle au sujet des travaux du sous-groupe d'Intersession du GATT sur l'abaissement des tarifs douaniers, 20 May 1952, MAE, AD, DE-CE 14.

53. Minister of Industry to the Minister of Commerce, "Proposition française d'abaissement général des tarifs douaniers," 12 December 1951, MAE, AD, DE-CE 14.

54. Extracts from Minutes of the First Meeting of the U.K. Delegation to the Seventh Session of the Contracting Parties to the GATT, 2 October 1952, PRO, BT 205:13; De 7e bijeenkomst van de Verdragsluitende Partijen van de Algemene Overeenkomst inzake Tarieven en Handel (GATT), 18 September 1952, ARA, MR 598.

55. Memorandum by the delegations of the Benelux countries on European tariff negotiations, January 1951, *FRUS* 1 (1951), 1321-23.

56. Vermerk über eine inoffizielle Besprechung im franz. Wirtschaftsministerium über die technische durchfürbahrkeit des Pflimlin-Planes, 24 February 1953, BA, B 102:7350.

57. Extract from Minutes of the Ninth Meeting of the U.K. Delegation to the Seventh Session of the Contracting Parties to the GATT, 11 October 1952, PRO, BT 205:13.

58. Annex V to: Note by the Chancellor of the Exchequer, "Freer Trade and Currencies: The Role of the United States Policies," 1 May 1953, PRO, CAB 129:60.

59. Note by the Chancellor of the Exchequer, "Freer Trade and Currencies: The Role of the United States Policies," 1 May 1953, PRO, CAB 129:60; Extract from Minutes of First Meeting of the U.K. Delegation to the Seventh Session of the Contracting Parties to the GATT, 2 October 1952, PRO, BT 205:13.

60. See for instance: Minutes, Sanders to Sinclair, 4 December 1953; Minutes, Nowell to Hewitt, 8 December 1954, PRO, BT 11:5100.

61. Extract from a letter from G. Parker of the British Embassy in Washington, 14 April 1954, PRO, BT 11:5100.

62. J. Kaufmann, "Trends in United States Tariff Policies," *Kyklos* 6 (1953), 72. This body was appointed in 1953 to investigate all security aspects of American trade policy.

63. Economic Commission for Europe, *Economic Bulletin of Europe* 7 (1955), 11.

64. One very clear indicator of the tension between European countries and the United States over import policies was the increasing amount of trade conflicts in GATT, which in some cases lead to retaliatory measures imposed with GATT's permission. See: Paper Prepared in the Bureau of Economic Affairs, 17 May 1954, *FRUS* 1 (1952-1954), 71.

65. P. Bidwell, *What the Tariff Means to American Industries* (New York: s.n., 1956), 286.

66. H. Piquet, *Aid, Trade and the Tariff* (New York: Cromwell, 1953). His calculations were incorporated in the Randall Committee's Report on Trade and Tariffs.

67. Obviously it would be wrong to define high American tariffs according to an average that included the Benelux countries, Denmark, Sweden and Norway. After all, it was a direct consequence of the existing European tariff disparity that these rates pulled down the European average, thus covering up what were considered "average" tariff levels in France, Britain, West Germany and Italy.

68. Piquet, *Aid, Trade and the Tariff,* 48-59; W. Salant and B. Vaccara, *Import Liberalisation and Employment: The Effect of Unilateral Tariff Reductions in United States Import Barriers* (Washington: The Brookings Institute, 1961); See also: Bidwell, *What the Tariff Means.*

69. Canada's market shares were particularly large for synthetic rubber, primary aluminum, motors and generators, communication equipment, primary

batteries, heavy trucks and buses, aircraft and parts, and motor vehicles and parts.

70. See M. Wasserman, C. Hultman, and R. Moore, *The Common Market and American Business* (New York: Simmons-Boardman Publishing Company, 1964), 286-89. These pages refer to Appendices A and B, summing up leading commodities in the United States import and export trade with the EEC for 1956-1960.

71. This was published under the title: Staff Papers Presented to the Commission of Foreign Economic Policy, Washington, 1954; See: R. Pastor, *Congress and the Politics of U.S. Foreign Economic Policy, 1929-1976* (Berkeley: University of California Press, 1980), 102.

72. The 5 percent reductions were to apply to rates existing in the first year of the reduction. Thus, a tariff of 40 percent would be reduced by an annual maximum of 2 percent.

73. Clair Wilcox, head of the American delegation to GATT, described the working of the peril point procedure as follows: "It is not the President . . . who does the negotiating. That is done by the boys down in the shop. And the members of Congress whose constituents are then hurt by the tariff concessions will not call the President in and say to him: Why did you do this? They will use a different technique. They will find out who negotiated this agreement and put him on the griddle. And there are not many people who are willing to face the kind of attack they will meet. The purpose of the peril point provision is to intimidate the negotiators. That is what it has always been for, and it is a very effective measure." K. Knorr and G. Patterson, eds. *A Critique of the Randall Commission Report on United States Foreign Economic Policy* (Princeton, NJ: Princeton University Press, 1954), 20.

74. Royer to Eichhorn, 11 February 1954, BA, B 102:3751; G. Parker (British embassy in Washington, D.C.) to Sinclair, 1 February 1954, PRO, BT 11:5100.

75. Both quotes are from: Memorandum by Kalijarvi (deputy assistant secretary of state for economic affairs) to the Secretary of State, 27 May 1954, *FRUS* 1 (1952-1954), 199-200.

76. Telegram, British Embassy in Washington to the Foreign Office, 19 May 1954, PRO, BT 205:14.

77. L. Krause, "The U.S. Trade Position and the Common Market," in *The Common Market: Progress and Controversy*, L. Krause, ed. (Englewood Cliffs, NJ: Prentice Hall, 1964), 151.

Chapter 5

1. G. van Roon, *Kleine landen in crisistijd: Van Oslostaten tot Benelux, 1930-1940* (Amsterdam, Elsevier, 1985), 96-97. For these interwar initiatives see also: P. Blaisse, *De Nederlandse handelspolitiek: De Nederlandse volkshuishouding tussen*

twee wereldoorlogen (Utrecht: Het Spektrum, 1952); E. Bloemen, "Tussen vrijhandel en protectie: Colijn en de internationale economische congressen, 1927-1933," in *Colijn: Bouwstenen voor een biografie*, J. de Bruijn and H. Langeveld, eds. (Kampen: Kok, 1994), 235-58; H. Klemann, *Tussen Reich and Empire: De economische betrekkingen van Nederland met zijn belangrijkste handelspartners: Duitsland, Groot-Brittannië en België en de Nederlandse handelspolitiek, 1929-1936* (Amsterdam: Nederlands Economisch Historisch Archief, 1990); A. Kersten, "Oorsprong en inzet van de Nederlandse Europese integratiepolitiek," in *Het Benelux-effect: België, Nederland en Luxemburg en de Europese integratie, 1945-1957*, E. Bloemen, ed. (Amsterdam: Nederlands Economisch Historisch Archief, 1992), 1-12; and J. Brouwer, "In het kielzog van Frankrijk? Enkele opmerkingen over het buitenlands beleid van het groothertogdom Luxemburg, 1945-1950," in *Het Benelux-effect: België, Nederland en Luxemburg en de Europese integratie, 1945-1957*, E. Bloemen, ed. (Amsterdam: Nederlands Economisch Historisch Archief, 1992), 33-53.

2. J. Wemelsfelder, *Het herstel van de Duits-Nederlandse economische betrekkingen na de Tweede Wereldoorlog* (Leiden: Stenfert Kroese, 1954), 18.

3. Betreft: Handels- en betalingsverkeer met West-Duitsland, 7 September 1949, MAZ 351.88(43)33; Betreft nadere besprekingen in Frankfurt inzake de uitvoering van het nieuwe handelsaccoord met West Duitsland van 22 t/m 24 Sept.'49, 26 September 1949, MAZ 351.88(43)33.

4. Wemelsfelder, *Het herstel van de Duits-Nederlandse economische betrekkingen*, 49.

5. Minutes of the Cabinet Economic Committee, 8 February 1950, ARA, MR 572.

6. R. Griffiths, "The Stranglehold of Bilateralism," in *The Netherlands and the Integration of Europe, 1945-57*, R. Griffiths, ed. (Amsterdam: Nederlands Economisch Historisch Archief, 1990), 20.

7. Wemelsfelder, *Het herstel van de Duits-Nederlandse economische betrekkingen*, 54. Some calculations even suggested the figure would drop to 21 percent. See for the talks on this issue: Samenvatting van het besprokene tijdens de vergadering van de Raad op ministerieel niveau van 6 en 7 October 1950, 10 October 1950, ARA, MEZ, BEB 403; Minutes of the Cabinet Economic Committee, 3 October 1950, ARA, MR572; Minutes of the Cabinet Economic Committee, 18 October 1950, ARA, MR 572.

8. W. Asbeek Brusse, "The Stikker Plan," in *The Netherlands and the Integration of Europe, 1945-1957*, R. Griffiths, ed. (Amsterdam: Nederlands Economisch Historisch Archief, 1990), 82.

9. As a result of a political compromise between the coalition partners in the new cabinet, the Dutch had two ministers of foreign affairs in this period. Beyen was in charge of all European matters excluding Benelux issues.

10. The EPC and Beyen initiatives are described in: P. Gerbet, *La construction de l'Europe*, rev. ed. (Paris: Imprimerie Nationale Éditions, 1994), 137-54; R.

Griffiths, "The Beyen Plan," in *The Netherlands and the Integration of Europe, 1945-1957*, R. Griffiths, ed. (Amsterdam: Nederlands Economisch Historisch Archief, 1990), 165-82; R. Griffiths and A. Milward, "The Beyen Plan and the European Political Community," in *Noi si mura: Selected working papers of the European University Institute*, W. Maihofer, ed. (Florence: European University Institute, 1986), 596-621; G. Trausch, ed., *Die europäische Integration vom Schuman-Plan bis zu den Verträgen von Rom: Beiträge des Kolloquiums in Luxemburg, 17 -19. Mai 1989* (Baden-Baden: Nomos, 1993).

11. The classic on the EDC is E. Fursdon, *The European Defence Community: A History* (London: Macmillan, 1980). See also H.-E. Volkmann and E. Schwengler, eds., *Die Europäische Verteidigungsgemeinschaft: Stand und Probleme der Forschung* (Boppard am Rhein: Boldt, 1985).

12. Ontwerp van een memorandum bestemd voor de regeringen, 28 January 1953, ARA, MR 486; Europese Politieke Gemeenschap, 9 February 1953, ARA, MR 486; Minutes of Cabinet, 9 February 1953, ARA, MR 398.

13. F. Romero, "Migration as an Issue in European Integration: The Case of Italy," in *The Frontier of National Sovereignty*, A. Milward, F. Lynch, F. Romero, R. Ranieri, and V. Sorensen, eds. (London: Routledge, 1993), 43-44.

14. Griffiths, "The Beyen Plan," 170.

15. J. Eck, *Histoire de l'économie française depuis 1945* (Paris: Armand Colin, 1988), 22-23.

16. An extensive overview of these economic measures is provided by J. Benard, "Economic Policy in France, 1949 to 1961," in *Economic Policy in Our Time*, vol. 3, *Country Studies*, E. Kirschen, ed. (Amsterdam: North Holland, 1964), 325-28.

17. United Nations Economic Commission for Europe, *Economic Survey of Europe in 1954* (Geneva, 1955), 189-90; L. Vincent and G. Matthys, "La situation économique," *Revue Economique* 5 (1952), 714; L. Vincent and G. Matthys, "La situation économique," 6 (1953), 922; L. A. Vincent, "La situation économique," 7 (1954), 616.

The differences in price levels between France and other European countries are given in the table below:

Price indices of GNP
(CONVERTED INTO CURRENT DOLLARS), 1950 = 100

	France	West Germany	U.K.	Italy	Netherlands
1952	138	113	117	113	115
1956	152	120	135	121	126

Source: J. Carré, P. Dubois and E. Malinvaud, eds., *La croissance française: Un essai d'analyse économique causale de l'après-guerre*, rev. and enl. (Paris: Seuil, 1972), 467.

18. The deficit on current account was reduced from 1,063 million U.S. dollars in 1951 to 220 million in 1953, but this reduction resulted largely from an increase in American offshore purchases in France.

19. Liberalisation: OEEC Examination of Remaining Quantitative Restrictions on Imports, 19 March 1954, PRO, T 232:434.

20. Again, it must be remembered that these percentages were calculated by taking 1948 as a base year, and that they excluded state trade. With 22 percent in 1953, France still had the highest percentage of state trade among the OEEC countries. If taken as a share in actual trade, this amounted to 35 percent.

21. Minister of Foreign Affairs to the Secretary of State for Economic Affairs, "Réponse à addresser à l'OECE concernant les tarifs douaniers européens," 26 July 1954, MAE, AD, DE-CE 16.

22. C. Bourdache, *Les années cinquante: La vie politique en France, l'économie, les relations internationales, l'Union française* (Paris: Fayard, 1980), 437.

23. Note by the Secretaries, Cabinet Mutual Aid Committee, Ministerial Council of OEEC, Liberalisation Position of OEEC, 29 April 1954, MAC(54)90, PRO, CAB 134:1022; Liberalisation: OEEC Examination of the Remaining Quantitative Restrictions on Imports, 19 March 1954, PRO, T 232:434.

24. Présidence du Conseil, Commissariat général au plan de modernisation et d'équipement, Commission des industries de transformation, Rapport du groupe de travail des industries d'équipement à caractère industriel, April 1954, Archives Nationales 80 AJ/46.

25. Note by the Secretaries, Cabinet Mutual Aid Committee, Ministerial Council of the OEEC, Liberalisation Position of OEEC. 29 April 1954, PRO, CAB 134:1022.

26. Vermerk betr.: Niederländisches Memorandum vom 5.5.1953—hier: Vereinbarkeit der Niederländischen Vorschläge mit der Satzung der OEEC und dem Liberalisierungs-Kodex, n.d., BA, B 146:1844.

27. Germany's position during the EPC negotiations is discussed by P. Fischer, "Die Bundesrepublik und das Projekt einer Europäischen Politischen Gemeinschaft" in *Vom Marshall Plan zur EWG: Die Eingliederung der Bundesrepublik in der westliche Welt*, L. Herbst, W. Bührer, and H. Sowade, eds. (München: Oldenbourg, 1990), 279-99.

28. These calculations were based on a simple statical analysis of real imports in 1952 and the average tariff incidence (weighted by import values) for three categories of products: raw materials, agricultural products and manufactures. The impact on the Dutch import bill of removing internal barriers was expressed in terms of the trade coverage of imports from West Germany, Italy and France. Ontwerpverdrag, houdende het Statuut ener Europese gemeenschap. Bijlage I. Enkele zeer voorlopige calculaties omtrent de gevolgen van de tariefgemeenschap voor Nederland, n.d. MAZ, Kabinet 351.88(4)075:32.

29. Notitie Wemelsfelder betreffende de verhoudingen op het gebied der invoer-rechten tussen het niet-deelnemende en het wel aan de tariefgemeenschap deelnemende gebied, 18 April 1953, ARA, MEZ, BEB 1024.

30. P. Verdoorn, "Welke zijn de achtergronden en vooruitzichten van de economische integratie in Europa, en welke gevolgen zal deze integratie hebben, met name voor de welvaart in Nederland," in *Welke zijn de achtergronden en vooruitzichten van de economische integratie in Europa, en welke gevolgen zou deze integratie hebben, met name voor de welvaart in Nederland? Prae-adviezen van Prof. Dr. P. Kuin, Prof. Dr. P. J. Verdoorn,* Vereeniging voor Staatshuishoud-kunde (The Hague: Vereeniging voor Staatshuishoudkunde, 1952), 112-17.

31. Verdoorn, "Welke zijn de achtergronden," 113-15.

32. Minutes of the Cabinet, 29 April 1953, ARA, MR 398.

33. Harmonization should be avoided, though, because, unlike coordination, this would mean having to surrender national policies and powers of implementation.

34. Compte-rendu de la 4ième séance du Groupe de Travail du Marché Commun (CPE), 17 July 1953, MAE (Bel) 17.771:1.

35. Rapport aux ministres des affaires étrangères, 9 October 1953, Ministerie van Buitenlandse Zaken, The Hague, 913.100:19.

36. Ibid.

37. Ibid.

38. Nederlandse vertegenwoordigers in de Economische Commissie ter Parijse Studieconferentie, 10 February 1954, MAZ, Kabinet 351.88(4)875:32.

39. Nota betreft: vergadering Economische Commissie EPG op 3 en 4 Juni 1954, 8 June 1954, MBZ 913.100.4207.

40. Nederlandse vertegenwoordigers in de Economische Commissie van de Parijse Studieconferentie Europese Politieke Gemeenschap, 21 May 1954, MAZ, Kabinet 351.88(4)075:32.

41. Bijlage 2 bij E.C. 20. De vrijmaking van het goederenverkeer na de integratie-besprekingen te Parijs, n.d., MAZ, Kabinet 351.88(4)875:32.

42. Ibid.

43. Verslag van de heer Van Alphen over besprekingen betreffende tariefplannen met de Duitsers Dr. Eichhorn en Dr. Herwig en de Belgien Dubois en Arends, 20 February 1954, MAZ, Kabinet 351.88(4)075:32.

44. Matters were further complicated because some Belgian and German exports questioned the need for adopting a CET. They hinted that a free trade area would require certificates of origins to avoid trade deflection but that it allowed states to keep their own schedules, which better suited national interests.

45. Minutes of the Cabinet, 13 April 1954, ARA, MR 399.

46. Kort verslag van de economische werkgroep, 30 September 1953, MBZ 913.100.100.4197.

47. Notes sur les travaux de la Commission économique de la conférence de Rome, October 1953, MAE (Bel) 17.771.

48. P. Gerbet, *La construction de l'Europe*, 142-51.

49. P. Gerbet, "La Relance européenne jusqu'à la Conférence de Messine," in *Il rilancio dell'Europa e i Trattati di Roma (The Relaunching of Europe and the Treaties of Rome)*, E. Serra, ed. (Milan: Giuffrè, 1989), 68.

50. Nota inzake de Europese integratie, 24 March 1955, ARA, MR 509.

51. Gerbet, *La construction de l'Europe*, 68.

52. A. Harryvan and A. Kersten, "The Netherlands, Benelux and the Relance Européenne," in *Il rilancio dell'Europa e i Trattati di Roma (The Relaunching of Europe and the Treaties of Rome)*, E. Serra, ed. (Milan: Giuffrè, 1989), 134.

53. Griffiths, "The Beyen Plan," 178; H.-J. Küsters, *Fondements de la Communauté Economique Européenne* (Brussels: Editions Labor, 1990), 30.

54. Gerbet, "La Relance européenne jusqu'à la Conférence de Messine," 73.

55. In March 1955 the German cabinet eventually approved an agreement with France whereby it would import a half million tons of French wheat each year during a period of three years. This was decided despite strong opposition from the German ministries of agriculture and finance. Extracts of Minutes of the Cabinet Session on 23 March 1955, BA B 136:1259.

56. J. van Tichelen, "Herinneringen van de Onderhandelingen van het Verdrag van Rome" in *De rol der Belgen en van België bij de Europese opbouw*, Interuniversitaire Studiecommissie van het Koninklijk Instituut voor Internationale Betrekkingen, ed. (Brussels: Koninklijk Instituut voor de Internationale Betrekkingen, 1981), 347-48.

57. Between 1954 and 1955, though, Belgian export growth recovered. It rose by 47.5 percent, whereas French exports increased by 43 percent. However, there is little doubt that at the time the Belgian government worked with the export figures of 1953 and the beginning of 1954.

58. Griffiths, "The Beyen Plan," 178.

59. Harryvan and Kersten, "The Netherlands, Benelux and the Relance Européenne," 137.

60. Compte rendu de la deuxième séance de la Commission interministerielle chargée de l'étude des problèmes relatifs à la Communauté politique européenne, 5 June 1953, MAE (Bel) 17.771:1.

61. Harryvan and Kersten, "The Netherlands, Benelux and the Relance Européenne," 151.

62. Küsters, *Fondements de la Communauté Economique Européenne*, 116.

63. H.-J. Küsters, "The Federal Republic of Germany and the EEC-Treaty," in *Il rilancio dell'Europa e i Trattati di Roma (The Relaunching of Europe and the Treaties of Rome)*, E. Serra, ed. (Milan: Giuffrè, 1989), 497.

64. Extracts of Cabinet Minutes of a Meeting, 6 July 1955; Niederschrift über die Besprechung am Donnerstag, dem 7. Juli 1955 unter Vorsitz des Vizekanzlers Dr. Blücher im Hause Carstanjen betr. Weisung an den deutschen Vertreter bei der Vorbereitung der Brüsseler Vorkonferenz, 10 July 1955, BA, B 136:1310.

65. Gerbet, "La Relance européenne jusqu'à la Conférence de Messine," 75.

66. Benard, "Economic policy in France, 1949 to 1961," 382.

67. E. Bjøl, *La France devant l'Europe: La politique française européenne de la IVe République* (Copenhagen: Munksgaard, 1966), 193-94; Gerbet, *La construction de l'Europe,* 185.

68. A full account of the Green Pool negotiations can be found in: G. Noël, *Du pool vert à la Politique Agricole Commun: Les tentatives de Communauté agricole européenne entre 1945 et 1955* (Paris: Economica, 1988).

69. F. Lynch, "Restoring France: The Road to Integration," in A. Milward, F. Lynch, F. Romero, R. Ranieri, and V. Sørensen, *The Frontier of National Sovereignty: History and Theory* (London: Routledge, 1993), 77-82.

70. See: Comité intergouvernemental créé par la conférence de Messine, *Rapport des chefs de délégation aux ministres des affaires étrangères* (Brussels, 1956).

71. The Benelux schedule counted as one.

72. Note by the Joint Secretaries, Cabinet Official Committee on the Review of GATT, Tariffs, 29 December 1954, RG(0)(54)79, PRO,CAB 134:1155.

73. Vermerk über die Sitzung der Arbeitsgruppe II am 15.12.1954, 20 December 1954, BA, B 102:7351. The GATT now stated: "Binding against increase of low duties or of duty-free treatment shall, in principle, be recognized as a concession equivalent in value to the reduction of high duties," (article 28). Quoted in: *International Economic Relations of the Western World, 1959-1971,* vol. 1, *Politics and Trade,* A. Shonfield, ed. (London: University Press for the Royal Institute of International Affairs, 1976), 156. It also gave countries the right to complain if a new and higher tariff, clearly imposed to compensate for the removal of an import quota, was shown to be hampering trade considerably. Tariffs which frustrate the effect of removing tariffs, n.d., PRO, BT 205:84; Note by the President of the Board of Trade, Review of the General Agreement on Tariffs and Trade, 5 February 1954, EA(55)22, PRO, CAB 134:855.

74. These initiatives were launched in view of the American president's newly obtained powers for tariff reductions under the Trade Agreements Extension Act which was due to expire in July 1956.

75. Stand van het vraagstuk der tariefverlagingsplannen, 13 July 1955, ARA, MEZ, BEB, GATT 2294; White (U.K. delegation to the GATT) to Sanders, 30 June 1955, PRO, BT 11:5338.

76. Telegram, Ellis-Rees (U.K. Delegation in Paris) to the Foreign Office, 4 July 1955, PRO, BT 205:220; Minute Frost, 5 July 1955, PRO, BT 205:3; Thorneycroft to Butler, 6 July 1955, PRO, BT 11:5338.

77. Revenue duties, tariffs on seasonal and perishable products would also be excluded. Betreft: stand van het vraagstuk der tariefverlagingen, 13 July 1955, MEZ, BEB, GATT 2294.

78. Organization for European Economic Cooperation, Negotiating Procedures for the Proposed Round of GATT Tariff Negotiations to be Held Early in 1956, 18 July 1955, PRO, BT 11:5338; GATT Tariff Reductions Proposals, 8 July

1955, PRO, BT 11:5338; Telegram, U.K. Delegation in Paris to the Foreign Office, 3 August 1955, PRO, BT 11:5338.

79. Richards, (U.K. Delegation to the OEEC) to Dennehy, 5 August 1955, PRO, BT 205:3.

80. Bretherton, Future Work in the OEEC, 11 November 1955, PRO, BT 11:5454.

81. R. Bullen, "Britain and Europe, 1950-1957," in *Il rilancio dell'Europa e i Trattati di Roma (The Relaunching of Europe and the Treaties of Rome)*, E. Serra, ed. (Milan: Giuffrè, 1989), 334.

82. Note by the Secretaries, Cabinet Mutual Aid Committee, The United Kingdom and a European Common Market, 24 October 1955, MAC(55)199, PRO, CAB 134:1030.

83. See for a detailed account of the political considerations: S. Burgess and G. Edwards, "The Six Plus One: British Policy-Making and the Question of European Economic Integration, 1955," *International Affairs* 64 (1988), 393-413; J. Young, "The Parting of Ways? Britain, the Messina Conference and the Spaak Committee, June–December 1955," in *British Foreign Policy, 1945-56*, M. Dockrill and J. Young, eds. (Basingstoke: Macmillan, 1989), 197-224.

84. Note by the Secretaries, Cabinet Mutual Aid Committee, The United Kingdom and a European Common Market, 24 October 1955, MAC(55)199, PRO, CAB 134:1030.

85. Ibid.

86. Ibid.

87. Record of Conversation, European Integration, 3 September 1955, T232:431.

88. The American role in the Common Market negotiations is discussed by P. Winand, *Eisenhower, Kennedy and the United States of Europe* (New York: St. Martin's Press, 1993); C. Boccia, "L'amministrazione Eisenhower e l'integrazione economica dell'Europa occidentale, 1953-1961," (Ph.D. diss., University of Genoa, 1993). The American view is also documented in *FRUS*, 1955-1957, 261-569.

89. European Integration, 16 January 1956, MAC(56)6 (Clarke), PRO, T 234:182.

90. Thorneycroft to Eden, 20 January 1956, PRO, FO 371:122022.

91. Minutes of the Meeting of the Mutual Aid Committee, 27 October 1955, PRO, CAB 134:1026.

92. Minute, Figgures to Clarke, 30 January 1956, PRO, T 232:183.

93. Clarke to Caccia, 1 March 1956, PRO, FO 371:122024.

94. Working Group on a United Kingdom Initiative in Europe, Final Report, 20 April 1956, (RWBC 1.15/15 FIN), PRO, T 234:190.

95. Memorandum by the President of the Board of Trade, Initiative in Europe, 22 May 1956, PRO, T 232:190.

96. Future Tariff Policy, 14 May 1956, PRO, BT 11:5454.

97. Bretherton to Cohen, Tariff Action in Europe, 11 May 1956, PRO,BT 11/5454.

98. General Agreement on Tariffs and Trade, Trade Negotiations Committee, Low Tariff Group's Proposal for Reducing Tariffs in OEEC, Potential Benefits to United Kingdom Exports, 7 August 1956, TN(56)11, PRO,BT 11:5454.

99. Tariff Discussions in OEEC, 16 May 1956, PRO, BT 11:5454.

100. Memorandum by the Chancellor of the Exchequer and the President of the Board of Trade, Organization for European Economic Cooperation and Tariffs, 9 July 1956, CP(56)172, PRO, CAB 129:82.

101. Minutes of the Cabinet Meeting, 12 July 1956, PRO, CAB 128:30.

102. De gemeenschappelijke lijst bij de OEEC, 4 August 1956, ARA, MEZ BEB 1700.

103. Gerbet, La construction de l'Europe, 180-81.

104. P. Guillen, "La France et les negociations des Traités de Rome; l'Euratom," in Il rilancio dell'Europa e i Trattati di Roma (The Relaunching of Europe and the Treaties of Rome), E. Serra, ed. (Milan: Giuffrè, 1989), 519. There is some discussion on the exact date at which the French government decided to press for a Common Market. Gerbet, Griffiths and Milward suggest the decision fell in January–February 1956, when the Mollet government came to power. Lynch and Guillen place it in July. Lynch sees it as a reaction to the threat posed by the British proposal for a wider free trade area within the OEEC, whereas Guillen associates it with the National Assembly's support for Euratom. Others place the final decision later still, and see it as a response to the diplomatic isolation following the Suez debacle.

105. Weekbericht no. 7, 10–13 September 1956, MAZ, Kabinet, 351.88(4)075:32.

106. Küsters, Fondements de la Communauté Economique Européenne, 218.

107. R. Girault, "La France entre l'Europe et l'Afrique," in Il rilancio dell'Europa e i Trattati di Roma (The Relaunching of Europe and the Treaties of Rome), E. Serra, ed. (Milan: Giuffrè, 1989), 362.

108. Note sur le Comité d'Etudes de Coordination Economique de l'Ensemble Français, 19 June 1954, AN, 80 AJ/72.

109. Le Marché commun européen et l'Union douanière de la Zone Franc, 20 April 1956, MAE, AD, DE-CE 21.

110. See article 113 of the EEC Treaty, European Communities, Treaties Establishing the European Communities: Amending Treaties: Other Basic Instruments (Luxembourg, 1983).

111. Groupe du Marché Commun, Note concernant les dispositions relatives à l'élimination des droits de douane et à la supression des restrictions quantitatives à l'interieur de la Communauté, que le président du groupe du Marché Commun propose comme base de discussion lors de la deuxième lecture, 6 November 1956, MAE 510/56, ARA, MEZ, BEB 1403.

112. The total customs receipts were specified as the basic rates multiplied by the value of imports from other member states in 1956. The minimum reductions required were 5 percent of the basic rate.

113. Again, the minimum reduction required for each tariff line in each of these steps was 5 percent. These stages in the elimination of internal customs duties are described in the articles 12-17 of the EEC Treaty.

114. Küsters, *Fondements de la Communauté Economique Européenne*, 234.

115. Griffiths, "The Common Market," in *The Netherlands and the Integration of Europe, 1945-1957*, R. Griffiths, ed. (Amsterdam: Nederlands Economisch Historisch Archief, 1990), 197.

116. Copie. M. Jean François-Poncet, secretaire général de la délégation française à M. Calmes, "Propositions d'amendements au classement des produits en matière premières, demi-produits et produits finis, tel qu'il est etabli sur Annexes I et II du Rapport des Experts douanières du 22 mars 1956," 29 August 1956, MAE/78/65, ARA, MEZ, BEB 1400.

117. Proposition allemande concernant le mandat du sous-groupe "Questions douanière" a créer auprès de la Conference de Bruxelles pour l'integration économique, 12 July 1956, MAE 164/56, ARA, MEZ, BEB 1400; Kabinettsvorlage Betr.: Brüsseler Regierungskonferenz für den Gemeinsamen Markt und Euratom, hier: Gemeinsamer Markt, 2 October 1956, BA, B 146:1845.

118. Bijlage III. Commentaar op het Brusselse rapport over de gemeenschappelijke markt, 15 May 1956, ARA, MR 523; Europese integratie, commissie Beyen 158 betreft: Buitentarief Europese Gemeenschap, n.d., MBZ, 913.100.

119. Weekbericht No. 16, 6 June 1956, MAZ, Kabinet 351.88(4)075:32; Fernschreiben aus Brüssel an AA, Bonn, 4 September 1956, BA, B 126/3017.

120. Samenvatting van de op 26,27 en 28 januari te Brussel gehouden besprekingen van de ministers van buitenlandse zaken van de Zes EGKS-landen inzake de nog hangende problemen met betrekking tot de instelling van een Europese gemeenschappelijke markt en Euratom, n.d. MAZ, Kabinet 351.88(4)075:32.

121. Weekbericht No. 19, 10–14 December 1956, MAZ, Kabinet 351.88(4)075:32.

122. Groupe du marché commun. Note sur le tarif extérieur commun de la communauté presenté par la délégation française, 28 November 1956, MAE 656/56, ARA, MEZ, BEB 1404.

123. Weekbericht 20, 17–20 December 1956, MAZ, Kabinet 351.88(4)075:32.

124. Comité des chefs de delegation. Proposition de compromis relatif à l'établissement du tarif extérieur, 27 January 1957, MAE 308/57, ARA, MEZ, BEB 1406.

125. Redaction approuvée par les ministres des affaires étrangères au cours de leur réunion du 4 février 1957 concernant les articles 20 et 39, quiquies du traité relative au tarif extérieur commun, 6 February 1957, MAE 409/57, ARA, MEZ, BEB 1406.

126. Projet de procès-verbal de la conference des ministres des affaires ètrangères des etats membres de la CECA (Bruxelles, 26,27,28 janvier et 4 fevrier 1957), 12 February 1957, MAE 498/57, ARA, MEZ, BEB 1407.
127. The minimum reduction required for each tariff line in each of these steps was 5 percent.
128. Quoted in: R. Griffiths, "The Common Market," 202.
129. Letter Löbke to Adenauer, 16 March 1957, BA, B 136:1313.

Chapter 6

1. Many international political economy studies of protectionism now try to move beyond the realist approach whereby commercial policy and levels of protection are seen as the outcome of objective, rational decisions of states acting in the national interest. They answer the appeals for an approach that combines the state-oriented perspective with that focusing on nonstate actors in their own right. See for instance: C. Hill and M. Light, "Foreign Policy Analysis," in *International Relations: A Handbook of Current Theory*, M. Light and A. Groom, eds. (London: Pinter, 1985).
2. The following general approaches to protectionism have been helpful in the analysis of these domestic forces: Organization for Economic Cooperation and Development, *Costs and Benefits of Protection* (Paris, 1985); R. Baldwin, "The Political Economy of Protectionism" in *Import Competition and Response*, J. Bhagwati, ed. (Chicago: Chicago University Press, 1982), 263-86; W. Brock and S. Magee, "Tariff Formulation in a Democracy," in *Current Issues in Commercial Policy and Diplomacy*, J. Black and B. Hindley, eds. (New York: St. Martin's Press, 1980), 1-9; J. Ruggie, "International Regimes, Transactions and Change: Embedded Liberalism in the Post-War International Economic Order," *International Organization* 36 (1982): 379-416.
3. By 1954, several products of these industries were still protected by quantitative restrictions. The OEEC produced a long list of German quotas on products for which liberalization was said to depend solely on "relevant action of the authorities." Examination of negative lists, products of category A, 24 June 1954, TFD/td/620, ARA, MEZ, BEB 1900; Het Duitse justificatiememorandum, 25 March 1954, ARA, MEZ, BEB 1134.
4. F. Jerchow, "Außenhandel im Wiederstreit: Die Bundesrepublik Deutschland auf dem Wege in das GATT 1949-1951," in *Politische Weichenstellungen im Nachkriegsdeutschland, 1945-1953*, A. Winkler, ed. (Göttingen: Vandenhoeck und Ruprecht, 1979), 283.
5. Aufzeichnung betr.: vorläufige Nichtanwendung von Torquay-Zollermässigungen, 25 September 1951, BA, B 136:1277; P. Schade, "Die Entwicklung des Zolltarifes der Bundesrepublik Deutschland bis zum EWG-Außentarif" (Ph.D. diss., Eberhard Karls University, Tübingen, 1963), 94. These rates covered several food products such as beef, pork fats and bacon, meat extracts

and some types of fish, fruits and vegetables. For instance, the tariff of 25 percent on bacon imports, levied on top of already high world market prices, imposed a heavy burden on consumer budgets and had to be temporarily reduced to 10 percent. In another case, a new tariff on willow twigs endangered the jobs of some 15,000 home workers in the basket making industry. It, too, had to be suspended. Bundestag, *Drucksachen,* nr. 2544: Entwurf einer Verordnung über Zolländerungen, 12 August 1951 (German Parliamentary Paper).

6. Meeting of the West German Cabinet, 11 March 1952, in *Die Kabinettsprotokolle der Bundesregierung,* K. von Jena, ed., vol. 5, *1952,* (Boppard am Rhein: Harald Boldt, 1989), 206.

7. Among these were aluminum, wood, base metals and base metal manufactures. Schade, *Entwicklung des Zolltarifes der Bundesrepublik Deutschland,* 82; Bundestag, *Drucksachen,* nr. 2460: Entwurf einer Verordnung über Zolländerungen, 9 July 1951. Some metal processing industries, for instance, had already in 1950 warned that replacing the old, specific tariffs with the new ones of 1951 would lead to unacceptable increases in the costs of metal semimanufactures and end products. At their insistence, some specific metal tariffs were eventually reduced or suspended. Betr.: Angleichung der Zollsätze des gegenwärtige Tarifs an die des Entwurf eines deutschen Zolltarifs, 23 August 1950, BA, B 102:57880.

8. Because Switzerland was not a contracting party to GATT, the German government was forced to conclude a separate agreement to safeguard its very large export interests in this market. The Swiss government, for its part, also insisted on immediate tariff negotiations, because its exporters felt seriously hampered by the sharp tariff increases that occurred after the introduction of the new German tariff schedule. When the delegations met, the Swiss insisted on tariff cuts for no less than 505 items in exchange for consolidations of all their own tariffs. Niederschrift über die Sitzung des Handelspolitischen Auschusses, 30 October 1951, BA, B 146:787; Bundestag, *Drucksachen,* Nr. 3108, Entwurf eines gesetzes über den Zollvertrag zwischen der Bundesrepublik Deutschland und der Schweizerischen Eidgenossenschaft, 20 December 1951.

9. Von Mangold to the Ministry of Marshall Plan, 9 November 1951, BA, B 102:56727. The ECA and the OEEC's special restricted committee charged with investigating the German balance of payments position urged for a 60 percent liberalization in all sectors, while the Managing Board of the EPU pressed for 75 percent. On 18 October, the Council of the OEEC officially insisted on a minimum of 40 and, possibly, of 60 percent. Niederschrift über die Sitzung des Handelspolitischen Ausschusses, 18 September 1951, BA, B 146:787. West Germany's first steps within the OEEC are described in: W. Bührer, "Erzwungene oder freiwillige Liberalisierung: Die USA, die OEEC und die westdeutsche Außenhandelspolitik 1949-1952," in *Vom Marshall Plan zur EWG: Die Eingliederung der Bundesrepublik in der westliche Welt,* L. Herbst, W. Bührer and H. Sowade, eds. (München: Oldenbourg, 1990), 139-63.

10. Von Mangold to Erhard, 9 November 1951, BA, B 102:56727.

11. Betr.: 75-ige Liberalisierung und Verhandlungen zur Liste Commune (Werkmeister to the ministry of Marshall Plan), 15 December 1951, BA, B 146:326.

12. Niederschrift über die Sitzung des Handelspolitischen Ausschusses, 17 March 1953, BA, B 146:789.

13. Niederschrift über die am 19. Mai 1953 im BMWI stattgefundene Ressortbesprechung über die stellungnahme der Bundesrepublik zum revidierten Pflimlin-Plan, betreffende Senkung des Niveaus der Zolltarife, 19 May 1953, BA, B 102:7350; ERP Unterlage 1/53. Betrifft: Integrationsstudien im Rahmen der OEEC. Stand 15. Januar 1953. Anlage 2. Pressenotiz 'Die Integrationsaufgabe der OEEC'. Entschliessung der BDI, 28 March 1953, BA, B 102:11180; Vermerk über die Dienstreise nach Köln am 25.2.1953, 2 March 1953, B102:7351; Betr.: GATT Plan zur internationale Senkung der Zölle (Letter of the BDI to the ministry of economic affairs), 12 June 1953, B 102:7351.

14. The German government announced it would consider these reductions at the GATT session in October 1953. Declaration made by the German delegation leader to the tariff session of GATT in Geneva, 14 October 1953, BA, B 102:7350.

15. Extracts of the Minutes of the Cabinet Session on 21-12-1953: "Punkt 2. Aussprache über die Besprechung im BMWI am 4. November 1953 über schwebende zollpolitische Fragen," 7 November 1953, BA, B 136:2595.

16. Revenue duties were excluded from the operation. Niederschrift über die Besprechung im BMWI über schwebende zollpolitische Fragen, 9 January 1954, BA, B 102:7308; Niederschrift über die Besprechung im BMWI am 4. November 1953 über schwebende zollpolitische Fragen, 7 November 1953, BA, B 102:7308.

17. Niederschrift über die Besprechung im BMW am 10 Februar 1954 über schwebende zollpolitische Fragen, 15 February 1953, BA, B 102:7308. At this meeting, representatives of industry talked to the secretaries of state of the ministries of economic affairs and agriculture.

18. German producers could not reduce their prices because the government subsidized wheat.

19. Niederschrift über die Besprechung im BMW am 21. Mai über Grundsatzfragen des Systems der Gleitzölle, Anlage 2. Grundsätzliches zur Frage der Gleitzölle, 28 May 1954, BA,B 102/56253.

20. Niederschrift über die Sitzung des Handelspolitischen Ausschusses, 16 March 1954, BA, B 146:790; Niederschrift über die Besprechung im BMW am 21. Mai über grundsätzliche Fragen des Systems der Gleitzölle, 28 May 1954, B 102:56253.

21. Niederschrift über die Sitzung des Handelspolitischen Ausschusses, 23 November 1953, BA, B 146:789. In 1955 and 1956, Denmark issued complaints in GATT against Germany's use of sliding-scale tariffs.

22. Auszug aus dem Schreiben der Bundesminister für Ernährung, Landwirtschaft und Forsten vom 26.1.1954—VIIA 1–7055 an den Bundesminister für

Wirtschaft, Betr.: Liberalisierung, 4 March 1954, BA, B 102:7308. The assessments were that the new measures for removing quotas, covering about 20-30 agricultural and 200 industrial products, would be very limited. Their practical impact would be in the order of a rise in the liberalization percentage of 0.5–0.8 percent. However, the Germans expected that the "psychological impact" on OEEC members would be very favorable indeed. Extracts of the minutes of the cabinet session of 21 December 1953, "Punkt 2. Aussprache über die deutschen Zahlungsüberschüsse," BA, B 136:2595.

23. Die Möglichkeit von Zollsenkungen im Gewerblichen Sektor des deutschen Zolltarifs, zusammengestellt auf Grund der Beratungen des im Bundesministeriums für Wirtschaft gebildeten Ausschusses zur Überprüfung des gewerblichen Sektors des deutschen Zolltarifes auf die Möglichkeit von Zollsenkungen, April 1954, BA, B 102:7314.

24. K. Knauß, President of Wolldeckfabrik Zoeppritz Aktiengesellschaft, to Erhard, 7 September 1954, BA, B 102:7312; Erhard to K. Knauß, 12 October 1954, BA, B 102:7312; Betr.: Erhöhung des Zollsatzes für fertiggestellte Decken (Secretary Michel to Max Spörl), n.d., BA, B 102:7312.

25. One important modification in the original proposals imposed at the insistence of the parliamentary committee on foreign trade was to exempt optical instruments.

26. Betr.: Ermächtigung zur Zollsatzänderungen (Erhard and Schäffer to the Secretary of State of the Bundeskanzleramt), February 1955, BA, B 136:378.

27. One major complaint was that such measures also hampered growth in sectors that were clearly not "overheated."

28. Extracts of the Minutes of the Cabinet Session, 3 March 1955, "Zu Punkt 1. der T.O.—Preissituation in der Bundesrepublik, insbesondere Ermächtigung zur Zollsatzänderungen," BA, B 136:378.

29. A. Milward, "Tariffs as Constitutions," in *The International Politics of Surplus Capacity: Competition for Market Shares in the World Recession*, S. Strange and R. Tooze, eds. (London: Allen and Unwin, 1981), 57-67. This article highlights the traditional role of tariffs as institutionalized mirror images of power divisions within societies. See also: Fischer, "Swings Between Protection and Free Trade in History," in *Free Trade in the World Economy: Towards an Opening of Markets*, H. Giersch, ed. (Tübingen: Mohr, 1987), 20-32.

30. The complexity of the British schedule was not merely the result of the numerous separate finance acts and other acts covering tariff provisions, but also of the fact that goods chargeable under one act were sometimes also chargeable under another. Composite goods, for instance, could be chargeable under more than one part of the schedule, so that some duties were superimposed on others.

31. It is impossible to provide more details of the complicated British tariff system. The literature on the topic is extensive. See for instance: H. Hutchinson, *Tariff Making and Industrial Reconstruction: An Account of the Import Duties Advisory*

Committee, 1932-1939 (London: Harrap, 1965); E. McGuire, *The British Tariff System* (London: Methuen, 1951); F. Capie, *Depression and Protectionism: Britain Between the Wars* (London: Allen and Unwin, 1983), 31.

32. Since laws in existence before the signing of GATT could be maintained during the first years of GATT's existence, it was no violation of GATT rules. In practice, however, this caused friction with other contracting parties and hampered tariff negotiations.

33. OEEC, Exercise on tariff disparities, 5 August 1955, PRO, BT 205:222.

34. For the full text of the Agreement see: Cabinet Economic Steering Committee, Sub-Committee on the Removal of Quantitative Restrictions and Tariff Policy, Report on the Duty-free Entry for Commonwealth Goods, 5 May 1956, ES(QT)(56)11, PRO, CAB 134:1244.

35. Among these goods were iron and steel bolts, screws and wire, veneers, domestic pottery, plate and sheet glass, illuminating glass, clocks and watches, electric cables, radio valves, electric lamps, electric lighting appliances, X-ray apparatus, agricultural machinery, food preparation and sterilizing machinery, jute piece goods and fur and fur manufactures. Tariff policy, Brief prepared by IMG for the president, n.d., EPC(49)62, PRO, BT 64:2420.

36. Memorandum by the President of the Board of Trade, Tariff Policy, Cabinet Economic Policy Committee, 4 March 1949, EPC(49)16, PRO, CAB 134:221.

37. Tom Williams to Stafford Cripps, 21 February 1949; Stafford Cripps to Wilson, 25 February 1949, PRO, BT 64:2420.

38. Minutes of the Economic Policy Committee, 11 March 1949, PRO, CAB 134:220.

39. A. Cairncross, *Years of Recovery: British Economic Policy, 1945-51* (London: Methuen, 1987), 280-87.

40. Memorandum by the Chancellor of the Exchequer and the President of the Board of Trade, Import Policy, Cabinet Economic Policy Committee, 29 March 1949, EPC(49)30, PRO, CAB 134:221.

41. Ibid.

42. It concentrated on the effects of a quota relaxation on British industrial competitiveness at home and abroad, while leaving aside the monetary aspects.

43. Usually, these domestic restrictions had been imposed to give dollar exports priority over domestic consumption or to restrict the use of scarce raw materials. See: Cairncross, *Years of Recovery,* 286.

44. The committee admitted that the British clock and watch industry, which also received a key industry tariff of 33.3 percent, could not be protected "by any tariff rates [it] could reasonably impose." Import Licensing Committee, Working Party on Import Licensing Relaxations, Notes of an ad-hoc meeting at the Board of Trade, 5 January, 1950, PRO, BT 64:4644.

45. Minutes of the Meeting Held at the Board of Trade, Import Licensing Committee, Working Party on Import Licensing Relaxations, 21 December, 1949, PRO, BT 64:4644.

46. Minutes of a Meeting Held at the Board of Trade, Import Licensing Committee, Working Party on Import Licensing Relaxations, Sub-committee on Engineering Consumer Goods and Goods for Industry, 8 March, 1949, PRO, BT 64:4642.

47. Memorandum by the President of the Board of Trade, Tariff Policy, 10 June 1949, EPC(49)62, PRO, CAB 134:222; Minutes of the Economic Policy Committee, 26 July 1949, PRO, CAB 134:220.

48. Memorandum by the Chancellor of the Exchequer and the President of the Board of Trade, Relaxation of Import Controls, 20 September 1949, EPC(49)97, PRO, CAB 134:222; Minutes of the Economic Policy Committee, 22 September 1949, PRO, CAB 134:220.

49. Cairncross, *Years of Recovery,* 286. Cairncross himself, on behalf of the treasury, had been involved in the inquiry into import quotas.

50. Among them were Robert Boothby, Lord Layton and Leo C. Amery. See also: N. Hariss, *Competition and the Corporate Society: British Conservatives, the State and Industry, 1945-1964* (London: Methuen, 1972), 230.

51. J. Barnes and D. Nicholson, *The Empire at Bay: The Leo Amery Diaries, 1929-1945* (London: Hutchinson, 1988), 1051-55. Between 1948 and 1950, leaders of the Conservative Party were urged by their party members to denounce the no-new-preference rule of GATT. In 1950 and 1951, this policy appeared in the party's election statements. A. Seldon, *Churchill's Indian Summer: The Conservative Government, 1951-55* (London: Hodder and Sloughton, 1981), 180.

52. Memorandum by the Secretary of State for Foreign Affairs, Council of Europe, Assembly Resolution No. 21: Proposal for a Europe-Commonwealth Conference, 13 May 1952, PRO, CAB 129:52. Neither the foreign office nor the treasury and board of trade had been prepared to take it seriously. Boothby, in his memoirs, argued: "It was a good plan—certainly better that what we have seen since. It was pole-axed overnight by the British treasury." R. Boothby, *Recollections of a Rebel* (London: Hutchinson, 1987), 315.

53. Note by the Secretaries, Cabinet Working Party on External Economic Policy, The Problems of External Economic Policy, 22 July 1952, GEN (General Cabinet Committee) 412/7, PRO, CAB 130:78.

54. Of the major dominions, Canada had already in 1947 insisted on the reciprocal canceling of contractual rights to preferential treatment. It wanted to obtain complete freedom to negotiate reductions in the margins of preferences. Over the years, it had been only too willing to bargain away the British preferences in its domestic market in exchange for freer access to the American market. South Africa had never granted many preferences to the British. Australia and New Zealand did attach large value to their preferential access to the British market, but they themselves did not want to facilitate access of British industrial producers to their domestic markets. Finally, India, Pakistan and Ceylon were said to be rather hostile to the system of Imperial Preference, which they

associated with colonialism and exploitation by British industrial interests. In the colonies, the situation was slightly different. Most of them did not want to lose revenue by reducing their preferential rates. Moreover, a number of them (such as Nigeria, Kenya and Northern Rhodesia) no longer had a system of preferential tariffs because of obligations outside GATT. Others (such as Hong Kong, Malaysia and Singapore) imported most of their goods duty free from all sources. Cabinet Working Party on External Economic Policy. External Policy and the Commonwealth, 16 July 1952, GEN (General Cabinet Committee) 412/3(final), PRO, CAB 130:78.

55. Note by the Joint Secretaries, Cabinet Working Party on External Economic Policy, The Problems of External Economic Policy, 22 July 1952, GEN 412/7, 22 PRO, CAB 130:78.

56. Note by the Joint Secretaries, Cabinet Working Party on External Economic Policy, Imperial Preference, 5 September 1952, GEN 412/26, PRO, CAB 130:78.

57. Cabinet Working Party on External Economic Policy, Record of a Meeting, 15 August, 1952, PRO, CAB 130:78.

58. Minutes of the Meeting of Cabinet, 3 November 1952, PRO, CAB 128:25.

59. Cherwell to Churchill, 13 September 1952, PRO, PREM 11:22.

60. See for instance in: Note by the Secretaries, Review of GATT, Use of Quantitative Restrictions for Protective Purposes, 31 December 1954, EA(54)149, PRO, CAB 134:853; Cabinet Economic Policy, Report of a Working Party of Officials on the Effects of Removing Quantitative Import Restrictions, with special reference to Dollar Imports, 29 August 1955, EP(55)37, CAB 134:1227.

61. Cabinet Economic Policy Committee, Report of a Working Party of Officials on the Effects of Removing Quantitative Import Restrictions, with special reference to Dollar Imports, 29 August 1955, EP(55)37, CAB 134:1227.

62. F. T. Blackaby, "Economic Policy in the United Kingdom, 1949 to 1961" in *Economic Policy in Our Time,* vol. 2, *Country Studies,* E. Kirschen, ed. (Amsterdam: North Holland Publishing Company, 1964), 96.

63. The Tariff, 9 November 1954, PRO, T 236:4033.

64. Ibid.

65. J. de Vries, *The Netherlands Economy in the Twentieth Century: An Examination of the Most Characteristic Features in the Period, 1900-1970* (Assen: Van Gorcum, 1978), 101. See for other examples: J. van Zanden and R. Griffiths, *Economische geschiedenis van Nederland in de 20e eeuw* (Utrecht: Het Spectrum, 1989), 184 and H. de Liagre Böhl, J. Nekkers and L. Hot, eds., *Nederland industrialiseert!* (Nijmegen: Socialististiese Uitgeverij Nijmegen, 1981), 131.

66. In 1928, more than 28 percent of total industrial production depended directly on imported raw materials. For agriculture, this percentage was 37. Blaisse, *De Nederlandse handelspolitiek: De Nederlandse volkshuishouding tussen twee wereldoorlogen* (Utrecht: Het Spectrum, 1952), 17-18.

67. For more details: W. Asbeek Brusse, "The Stikker Plan," *The Netherlands and the Integration of Europe, 1945-1957*, R. Griffiths, ed. (Amsterdam: Nederlands Economisch Historisch Archief, 1990), 83-85.

68. De achtergrond van het werk van de Afdeling Technisch Economische Vraagstukken op het gebied der industrialisatie in de periode 1 September 1945–1 Augustus 1947 door Drs. A. Kohnstamm, 25 August 1947, MEZ, hoofdarchief 738:1; Kort verslag van de discussie betreffende het voorlopig industrialisatieprogramma, in de vergadering van 16 augustus ten departmenete van economische zaken, kamer 338, 16 August 1946, MEZ, DG Industrialisatie 94/2.

69. Industrialisatienota, n.d., Ministerie van Economische Zaken, Directoraat Generaal voor Handel en Nijverheid 216:1. Such "cooperation agreements" often included cartel practices.

70. Telex, Blaisse to van Tuyll, 27 October 1950, MBZ, DGEM 6117:1263.

71. BEB to Teppema, Letter no. 4892, 20 November 1952, ARA, MEZ, BEB 1131

72. Onderzoek naar de mogelijkheid van de toepassing van globale contingenten, 14 January 1956, ARA, MEZ, BEB 1168. This gives an overview of remaining hard core quotas.

73. Telegram no. 221, Ellis Rees to the Foreign Office, 30 March 1954, PRO, BT 64:4558.

74. Minutes of the Cabinet's Economic Committee, 18 November 1953, ARA, MR 573.

75. Minutes of the Cabinet's Economic Committee, 11 March 1953 and 24 February, 1954, ARA, MR 573.

76. GATT Contracting Parties, Fourth Session, Summary record of the twelfth meeting, 9 March 1950, ARA, MR 584.

77. Conseil des accords commerciaux. Procès verbal de la réunion tenue à Bruxelles les 1er et 2 mars 1950, n.d., ARA, MEZ, BEB 738; Minutes of Cabinet's Economic Committee, 28 February 1950 and 7 March 1950, ARA, MR 527.

78. Betreft: eventuele terugtrekking van tariefconcessies te Genève en Annecy verleend, 12 August 1950, ARA, MEZ, BEB 1924.

79. Korte notitie naar aanleiding van de vergadering van de raad voor de handelsaccoorden gehouden the Brussel op 28 augustus 1950, 30 August 1950, ARA, MEZ, BEB 738.

80. It mainly concerned tariffs on meat products which, following a special ministerial decision, could not be bound in any tariff negotiations. Door Nederland in the nemen standpunt in de bijeenkomst van de sub-groep van het GATT (15 juli a.s. the Genève), 4 July 1952, ARA, MR 598.

81. Betr.: besprekingen met de Belgen en Fransen over Franse plan tot verlaging der tarieven, 11 July 1952, MEZ, BEB, GATT 2294.

82. Betreft: de verschillende plannen tot verlaging der tarieven, 20 March 1953, MEZ, BEB 2756.

83. Vraagstuk inzake de tarieven in het kader van de Benelux, 2 December 1952, ARA, MEZ, BEB 1172.
84. This is discussed in contributions by Bloemen, Boekestijn, Harryvan and Van Zanden in the volume: E. Bloemen (ed.), *Het Benelux-effect: België, Nederland en Luxemburg en de Europese integratie, 1945-1957* (Amsterdam: Nederlands Economisch Historisch Archief, 1992). See for older contributions in English (which are less critical on Benelux): J. Meade, *Negotiations for Benelux: An Annotated Chronicle, 1943-1956* (Princeton, NJ: Princeton University Press, 1957) and J. Meade, H. Liesner and S. Wells, *Case Studies in European Economic Union: The Mechanics of Integration* (Oxford: Oxford University Press, 1962).
85. Memorandum DEU/Be aan S. via Chef DEU betreft Benelux handelspolitiek, 8 September 1955, MBZ, Benelux, Permanente Commissie voor de handelspolitiek, commentaar vergaderingen deel I, 1955.

Conclusion

1. Quoted in: J. Finlayson and M. Zacher, "The GATT and the Regulation of Trade Barriers: Regime Dynamics and Functions," *International Organization* 34 (1981): 575.
2. For a Keynesian model, see: Pelkmans, *The Process of Economic Integration* (Tilburg, Netherlands: Tilburg University Press, 1975).

Appendix

1. The problems involved in standardizing national tariff schedules on an international trade nomenclature such as the Standard International Trade Classification or the Brussels Tariff Nomenclature are dealt with in J. Tumlir and L. Till, "Tariff Averaging in International Comparisons," in *Effective Tariff Protection: Proceedings of a Conference Sponsored by the General Agreement on Tariffs and Trade and the Graduate Institute of International Studies,* H. Grubel and H. Johnson, eds. (Geneva: GATT, 1971), 147-60.
2. Bertrand, "Comparaison du niveau des tarifs douaniers des pays du Marché Commun." *Cahiers de l'Institut de Science Economique Appliqué,* série R, Etudes et Materiaux pour le Marché Commun (1958): no. 2.
3. Generally, therefore, weighted tariff comparisons tend to give lower protection rates than unweighted tariffs.
4. Furthermore, since not all commodities enter international trade, these indices also distort the picture.
5. See for a critique of effective protection theory: W.P. Travis, "A Critical Rehabilitation of Effective Protection Theory" in *Effective Tariff Protection: Proceedings of a Conference Sponsored by the General Agreement on Tariffs and Trade and the Graduate Institute of International Studies,* H. Grubel and H. Johnson, eds. (Geneva: GATT, 1971), 217-45.

6. Many calculations, such as the pioneering ones of Balassa, have been based on the input-output coefficients of the Benelux countries. This method has proven to be unreliable as a proxy for the free trade situation because for many industries Benelux countries had substantial rates of effective protection. G. Sampson and A. Yeats, "On the Use of Belgium-Netherlands Coefficients for Effective Protection Analysis," *Oxford Economic Papers* 3 (1979), 496-507.

7. F. Capie, *Depression and Protectionism: Britain Between the Wars* (London: Allen and Unwin, 1983), 116-17. The latter method of assuming unchanged technology has been adopted by Capie in his assessments of the protective impact of the Import Duties Act of 1932. He argues that "The clear conclusion here is that, since the two biggest sectors (construction and iron and steel) generally accredited with the principal contribution to economic recovery had very low effective rates of protection, the tariff played an insignificant part in the upturn out of depression. Indeed, the role in stimulating the manufacturing sector must have been small." The problem with this conclusion is that it relies heavily on the findings for these two industries. The iron and steel industry, which—in Capie's analysis—covers everything from pig iron to finished steels and special steels, is too broad a category to produce meaningful assessments on levels of effective tariff protection. It is also a highly cyclical industry, and therefore more likely to have been protected by quantitative restrictions and cartel arrangements. The building industry, for which negative rates of effective tariff protection were calculated, is equally unreliable as an indicator for the impact of tariff protection because this is a sector par excellence where nontradable commodities dominate. In addition, it is also a sector that experienced technological improvements in the 1930s, so that a neglect of technological factors in the calculations is likely to distort the assessments. See for a more extensive treatment of Capie's methods: M. Kitson and S. Solomou, *Protectionism and Economic Revival: The British Interwar Economy* (Cambridge: Cambridge University Press, 1990), 36-41. For the interwar period, the issue of measuring effective protection is further discussed by V. Hentschler, "Zur Politik internationaler Wettbewerbsbeschränkungen in der Zwischenkriegszeit—Maßnahmen und Wirkungen. USA, Grossbrittanien, Deutschland und Frankreich," in *Wettbewerbsbeschränkungen auf internationalen Märkten: Referate und Diskussionsbeiträge des 10. Wissenschaftlichen Symposiums der gesellschaft für Unternehmersgeschichte am 25-27. September 1985 in Lüneburg*, H. Pohl, ed. (Stuttgart: Steiner Verlag, 1988), 114-121.

8. The source for this comparison is: GATT, Subgroup of the Working Party on Reduction of Tariff Levels, data furnished by members of the subgroup pursuant to Annex F of IW.2/15, June 1952, PRO, BT 11:4901.

Bibliography

This bibliography is limited to published sources cited in the notes. A list of archival references is presented on page ix.

Published documents, statistics and organizational publications

Comité intergouvernemental créé par la conférence de Messine. *Rapport des Chefs de Délégation aux Ministres des Affaires Étrangères*. Brussels, 1956.

Council of Europe. *European Yearbook*. The Hague. Various volumes.

Council of Europe. *Low Tariff Club: A Council of Europe Contribution to the Study of the Problem of Lowering Customs Barriers as Between Member-Countries*. Strasbourg, 1952.

Council of Europe. *The Strasbourg Plan: Proposals for Improving the Economic Relations Between Member States of the Council of Europe and Their Overseas Countries With Which They Have Constitutional Links*. Strasbourg, 1952.

European Communities. *Treaties Establishing the European Communities: Amending Treaties: Other Basic Instruments*. Luxembourg, 1983.

France. Ministère des Finances. "La politique commerciale et douanière de la France et d'Allemagne occidentale." *Statistiques et Etudes Financières*. 1958. Supplement 113.

General Agreement on Tariffs and Trade (GATT). *A New Proposal for the Reduction of Customs Tariffs*. Geneva, 1954.

General Agreement on Tariffs and Trade (GATT). *Basic Instruments and Selected Documents, Second Supplement*. Geneva, 1954.

German Federal Republic. Bundestag. "Entwurf einer Verordnung über Zolländerungen." *Drucksachen*. 9 July 1951. Nr. 2460 (Parliamentary Paper).

German Federal Republic. Bundestag. "Entwurf einer Verordnung über Zolländerungen." *Drucksachen.* 12 August 1951. Nr. 2544 (Parliamentary Paper).

German Federal Republic. Bundestag. "Entwurf eines gesetzes über den Zollvertrag zwischen der Bundesrepublik Deutschland und der Schweizerischen Eidgenossenschaft." *Drucksachen.* 20 December 1951. Nr. 3108 (Parliamentary Paper).

Jena, K. von, ed. *Kabinettsprotokolle der Bundesregierung.* Vol. 5, *1952.* Boppard am Rhein: Harald Boldt, 1989.

League of Nations. *Commercial Policy in the Inter-war Period.* Geneva, 1942.

League of Nations. *Quantitative Trade Controls: Their Causes and Nature.* Geneva, 1943.

League of Nations. *International Currency Experience: Lessons of the Interwar Period.* Geneva, 1944.

League of Nations. Economic Intelligence Service. *World Production and Prices.* Geneva, various years.

Organization for European Economic Cooperation. *Twelfth Annual Economic Review.* Paris, 1961.

Organization for Economic Cooperation and Development. *Costs and Benefits of Protection.* Paris, 1985.

Political and Economic Planning. *Atlantic Tariffs and Trade.* London, 1962.

United Nations. *Economic Bulletin for Europe: The Journal of the United Nations Economic Commission for Europe.* 1950. 2; 1955. 3; 1955. 7.

United Nations Economic Commission for Europe. *Economic Survey of Europe in 1951.* Geneva, 1952.

United Nations Economic Commission for Europe. *Economic Survey of Europe Since the War.* Geneva, 1953.

United Nations Economic Commission for Europe. *Economic Survey of Europe in 1954.* Geneva, 1955.

United Nations Economic Commission for Europe. *Economic Survey of Europe in 1956.* Geneva, 1957.

United Nations Statistical Office. Department of Economic Affairs. *Yearbook of International Trade Statistics.* Vol. 1, *Trade by Country.* New York, 1951.

United Nations Statistical Office. Department of Economic Affairs. *Yearbook of International Trade Statistics.* Vol. 2, *Trade by Commodity.* New York, 1951.

U.S. Department of State. *Foreign Relations of the United States,* vol. 1 and 4: (1951); Vol. 1 (1952-1954); Washington DC: U.S. Government Printing Office.

Books and articles

Abelshauser, W. "Der Kleine Marshallplan: Handelsintegration durch innereuropäische Wirtschaftshilfe, 1948-1950." In *Wirtschaftliche und Politische Integration In Europa im 19. und 20. Jahrhundert,* edited by H. Berding, 212-24. Göttingen: Vandenhoeck & Ruprecht, 1984.

Adams W., R. Amacher, S. Arndt, et. al. *Tariffs, Quotas and Trade: The Politics of Protectionism.* San Francisco: Institute for Contemporary Studies, 1979.

Aldcroft, D. *From Versailles to Wall Street, 1919-1929.* London: Allen Lane, 1977.

Arndt, H. *The Economic Lessons of the Nineteen-Thirties: A Report.* London: Oxford University Press, 1944.

Asbeek Brusse, W. "The Stikker Plan." In *The Netherlands and the Integration of Europe, 1945-1957,* edited by R. Griffiths, 69-92. Amsterdam: Nederlands Economisch Historisch Archief, 1990.

Asbeek Brusse, W. "The Failure of European Tariff Plans in GATT." In *Die europäische Integration vom Schuman-Plan bis zu den Verträgen von Rom: Beiträge des Kolloquiums in Luxemburg, 17–19. Mai 1989,* edited by G. Trausch, 99-114. Baden-Baden: Nomos, 1993.

Asbeek Brusse, W., "The Americans, GATT and European Integration, 1947-1957: A Decade of Dilemma." In *The United States and the Integration of Europe: Legacies of the Postwar Era,* edited by F. Heller and J. Gillingham, 221-49. New York: St. Martin's Press, 1996.

Ashwort, W. *A Short History of the International Economy Since 1850.* 3rd ed. London: Longman, 1975.

Bairoch, P. *Economics and World History: Myths and Paradoxes.* New York: Harvester Wheatsheaf, 1993.

Balassa, B. "Tariff Protection in Industrial Countries: An Evaluation." *Journal of Political Economy* 73 (1965): 573-94.

Balassa, B. "Trade Creation and Trade Diversion in the European Common Market." *The Economic Journal: The Journal of the Royal Economic Society* 77 (1967): 1-17.

Balassa, B. *Trade Liberalization Among Industrial Countries: Objectives and Alternatives.* New York: McGraw-Hill, 1967.

Baldwin, R. "The Political Economy of Protectionism." In *Import Competition and Response,* edited by J. Bhagwati, 263-86. Chicago: Chicago University Press, 1982.

Baldwin, R., and A. O'Krueger, *The Structure and Evolution of Recent U.S. Trade Policy.* Chicago: Chicago University Press, 1984.

Barnes, J., and D. Nicholson, *The Leo Amery Diaries, 1929-1945.* Vol. 2, *The Empire at Bay.* London: Hutchinson, 1988.

Benard, J. "Economic Policy in France, 1949 to 1961." In *Economic Policy in Our Time,* edited by E. Kirschen, 286-388. Vol. 3, *Country Studies.* Amsterdam: North Holland, 1964.

Bertrand, R. "Analyse du tarif douanier français par industries." *Cahiers de l'Institut de Science Economique Appliquée,* série R, Etudes et Materiaux pour Le Marché Commun, no. 2 (1958).

Bertrand, R. "Comparaison du niveau des tarifs douanier des pays du Marché Commun." *Cahiers de l'Institut de Science Economique Appliqué,* série R, Etudes et Materiaux pour le Marché Commun, no. 2 (1958).

Bhagwati, J. *Protectionism.* Cambridge, MA: MIT University Press, 1988.

Bidwell, P. *What the Tariff Means to American Industries.* Westport, CT: Greenwood, 1956.

Bjøl, E. *La France devant l'Europe: La politique française européenne de la IVe République.* Copenhagen: Munksgaard, 1966.

Black, J. "Arguments for Tariffs." *Oxford Economic Papers* 2 (1950).

Blackaby, F. "Economic Policy in the United Kingdom, 1949 to 1961." In *Economic Policy in Our Time.* Vol. 2, *Country Studies,* edited by E. Kirschen, 89-154. Amsterdam: North Holland Publishing Company, 1964.

Blacksell, M. *Post-War Europe: A Political Geography.* 2nd ed. London: Hutchinson, 1981.

Blaisse, P. *De Nederlandse handelspolitiek: De Nederlandse volkshuishouding tussen twee wereldoorlogen.* Utrecht: Het Spectrum, 1952.

Bloemen, E., ed. *Het Benelux-effect: België, Nederland en Luxemburg en de Europese integratie, 1945-1957.* Amsterdam: Nederlands Economisch Historisch Archief, 1992.

Bloemen, E. "Tussen vrijhandel en protectie: Colijn en de internationale economische congressen, 1927-1933." In *Colijn: Bouwstenen voor een biografie,* edited by J. de Bruijn and H. Langeveld, 235-58. Kampen: Kok, 1994.

"Blühender Verwaltungsprotektionismus." *Frankfurter Allgemeine Zeitung* (German Federal Republic). 6 June 1951.

Boccia, C. "L'amministrazione Eisenhower e l'integrazione economica dell'Europa occidentale, 1953-1961." Ph.D. diss., University of Genoa, 1993.

Boekestijn, A. "Een nagel aan Adam Smiths doodkist: De Benelux-onderhandelingen in de jaren veertig en vijftig." In *Het Benelux-effect: België, Nederland en Luxemburg en de Europese integratie, 1945-1957,* edited by E. Bloemen, 143-68. Amsterdam: Nederlands Economisch Historisch Archief, 1990.

Boekestijn, A. "The Formulation of Dutch Benelux Policy." In *The Netherlands and the Integration of Europe, 1945-1957,* edited by R. T. Griffiths, 27-48. Amsterdam: Nederlands Economisch Historisch Archief, 1990.

Boothby, R. *Boothby: Recollections of a Rebel.* London: Hutchinson, 1987.

Bossuat, G. "La politique française de libération des échanges en Europe et le plan Schuman (1950-1951)." In *Die Anfänge des Schuman-Plan: Beiträge des Kolloquiums in Aachen, 28–30. Mai 1986,* edited by K. Schwabe, 319-32. Baden-Baden: Nomos, 1988.

Bossuat, G. "Pierre Mendes France, une volonté pour l'Europe, 1944-1974." In *Pierre Mendes France et l'économie: Penseé et action,* edited by M. Margairaz, 167-99. Paris: Edition du Seuil, 1989.

Bossuat, G. *La France, l'aide américain et la construction européenne, 1944-1954.* Paris: Imprimerie nationale, 1992.

Bourdache, C. *Les années cinquante: La vie politique en France, l'économie, les rélations internationales, l'Union française.* Paris: Fayard, 1980.

Boyer, F., and J. Sallé. "The liberalisation of intra-European trade in the framework of OEEC." *International Monetary Fund Staff Papers* 4 (1955): 179-216.

Brock, W., and S. Magee. "Tariff Formulation in a Democracy." In *Current Issues in Commercial Policy and Diplomacy,* edited by J. Black and B. Hindley, 1-9. New York: St. Martin's Press, 1980.

Brouwer, J. "In het kielzog van Frankrijk? Enkele opmerkingen over het buitenlands beleid van het groothertogdom Luxemburg, 1945-1950." In *Het Benelux-effect: België, Nederland en Luxemburg en de Europese integratie, 1945-1957,* edited by E. Bloemen, 33-53. Amsterdam: Nederlands Economisch Historisch Archief, 1992.

Brown, W. *The United States and the Restoration of World Trade: An Analysis of the ITO Charter and the General Agreement on Tariffs and Trade.* Washington, DC: The Brookings Institute, 1950.

Bruijn, J. de, and H. J. Langeveld, eds. *Colijn: Bouwstenen voor een biografie.* Kampen: Kok, 1994.

Buchheim, C. "Einige wirtschaftspolitische Maßnahmen Westdeutschlands von 1945 bis zur Gegenwart." In *Wettbewerbsbeschränkungen auf internationalen Märkten: Referate und Diskussionsbeiträge des 10: Wissenschaftlichen Symposiums der gesellschaft für Unternehmersgeschichte am 25–27. September 1985 in Lüneburg,* edited by H. Pohl, 213-26. Stuttgart: Steiner Verlag, 1988.

Bührer, W. *Ruhrstahl und Europa: Die Wirtschaftsvereinigung Eisen- und Stahlindustrie und die Anfänge der europäischen Integration, 1945-1952.* München: Oldenbourg, 1986.

Bührer, W. "Erzwungene oder freiwillige Liberalisierung: Die USA, die OEEC und die westdeutsche Außenhandelspolitik, 1949-1952." In *Vom Marshall Plan zur EWG: Die Eingliederung der Bundesrepublik in der westliche Welt,* edited by L. Herbst, W. Bührer and H. Sowade, 139-63. München: Oldenbourg, 1990.

Bullen, R. "The British Government and the Schuman Plan, May 1950–March 1951." In *Die Anfänge des Schuman-Plans 1950/51: Beiträge des Kolloquiums in Aachen, 28–30. Mai 1986,* edited by K. Schwabe, 199-210. Baden-Baden: Nomos, 1988.

Bullen, R. "Britain and Europe, 1950-1957." In *Il rilancio dell'Europa e i Trattati di Roma (The Relaunching of Europe and the Treaties of Rome),* edited by E. Serra, 315-38. Milan: Giuffrè, 1989.

Burgess, S., and G. Edwards. "The Six Plus One: British Policy-Making and the Question of European Economic Integration, 1955." *International Affairs* 64 (1988): 393-413.

Cairncross, A. *Years of Recovery: British Economic Policy, 1945-51.* London: Methuen, 1987.

Calleo D., and B. Rowland. "Free Trade and the Atlantic Community." In *International Political Economy: Perspectives on Global Power and Wealth,* edited by J. Frieden and D. Lake. New York: St. Martin's Press, 1987.

Camps, M. "Comment." In *From Marshall Plan to Global Interdependence: New Challenges for the Industrialized Nations,* 30-47. Paris: Organization for Economic Cooperation and Development, 1978.

Capie, F. *Depression and Protectionism: Britain Between the Wars.* London: Allen and Unwin, 1983.

Capie, F. *Tariffs and Growth: Some Illustration from the World Economy, 1850-1940.* Manchester: Manchester University Press, 1994.

Carré J., P. Dubois, and E. Malinvaud, eds. *La croissance française: Un essai d'analyse économique causale de l'après-guerre.* Rev. and enl. Paris: Seuil, 1972.

Cavalcanti, M. *La politica commerciale italiana, 1945-1952: Uomini e fatti.* Naples: Edizione Scientifiche Italiane, 1984.

Clerx, J. M. *Nederland en de liberalisatie van het handels- en betalingsverkeer (1945-1958).* Groningen: Wolters-Noordhoff, 1986.

Cohen, B. "The Political Economy of International Trade." *International Organization* 44 (1990): 261-81.

Cooper, R. "Tariff Dispersion and Trade Negotiations." *Journal of Political Economy* 72 (1964): 597-603.

Cuddington, J., and R. McKinnon. "Free Trade versus Protectionism: A Perspective." In *Tariffs, Quotas and Trade: The Politics of Protectionism,* edited by W. Adams, R. Amacher, S. Arndt, et al. San Francisco: Institute for Contemporary Studies, 1979.

Curzon, G. *Multilateral Commercial Diplomacy: An Examination of the Impact of the General Agreement on Tariffs and Trade on National Commercial Policies and Techniques.* London: Joseph, 1965.

Dam, K. *The GATT: Law and International Economic Organization.* Chicago: University of Chicago Press, 1970.

Dell, S. *Trade Blocs and Common Markets.* London: Constable, 1963.

Dell, S. "Economic Integration and the Example of the United States." In *The Common Market: Progress and Controversy,* edited by L. Krause, 76-81. Englewood Cliffs: Prentice Hall, 1964.

Diebold, Jr., W. *The End of the ITO.* Princeton, NJ: Princeton University Press, 1952.

Diebold, Jr., W. *Trade and Payments in Western Europe: A Study in Economic Cooperation, 1947-1951.* New York: Harper and Brothers, 1952.

Diebold Jr., W. *The Schuman Plan: A Study in Economic Cooperation, 1950-1959.* New York: Praeger, 1959.

Dockrill, M., and J. Young, eds. *British Foreign Policy, 1945-56.* Basingstoke: Macmillan, 1989.

Dumke, R. "The Political Economy of German Economic Unification: Tariffs, Trade and the Policies of the Zollverein Era." Ph.D. diss., University of Wisconsin, Madison, 1977.

Eatwell, J., M. Milgate, and P. Newman, eds. *The New Palgrave: A Dictionary of Economics.* London: Macmillan, 1987.

Eck, J. *Histoire de l'économie française depuis 1945.* Paris: Armand Colin, 1988.

Finger, J. "Trade Liberalisation: A Public Choice Perspective." In *Challenge to a Liberal International Trade Order,* edited by R. Amacher, G. Habeler, and Th. Willet. Washington, DC: American Enterprise Institute for Public Policy Research, 1979.

Fischer, P. "Die Bundesrepublik und das Projekt einer Europäischen Politischen Gemeinschaft." In *Vom Marshall Plan zur EWG: Die Eingliederung der Bundesrepublik in der westliche Welt,* edited by L. Herbst, W. Bührer, and H. Sowade, 279-99. München: Oldenbourg, 1990.

Fischer, W. "Swings Between Protection and Free Trade in History." In *Free Trade in the World Economy: Towards an Opening of Markets,* edited by H. Giersch, 20-32. Tübingen: Mohr, 1987.

Fleury, A. "La situation particulière de la Suisse au sein de l'Organisation européenne de cooperation économique (OECE)." In *Histoire des débuts de la construction européenne, mars 1948–mai 1950 (Origins of the European Integration, March 1948–1950),* edited by R. Poidevin, 95-117. Paris: Libraire général de droits et de jurisprudence, 1989.

Foreman-Peck, J. *A History of the World Economy: International Economic Relations Since 1850.* 2d ed., rev. New York: Harvester Wheatsheaf, 1995.

"France's Trade Policy." *Economist* (London), 10 February 1951.

Fremdling, R. "Die Zoll- und Handelspolitik Großbritanniens, Frankreichs und Deutschlands vom späten 18. Jahrhundert bis zum ersten Weltkrieg." In *Wettbewerbsbeschränkungen auf internationalen Märkten: Referate und Diskussionsbeiträge des 10: Wissenschaftlichen Symposiums der gesellschaft für Unternehmersgeschichte am 25–27. September 1985 in Lüneburg,* edited by H. Pohl. Stuttgart: Steiner Verlag, 1988.

Frey, B. *International Political Economics.* Oxford: Basil Blackwell, 1984.

Frieden, J., and D. Lake, eds. *International Political Economy: Perspectives on Global Power and Wealth.* New York: St. Martin's Press, 1987.

Fursdon, E. *The European Defence Community: A History.* New York: St. Martin's Press, 1980.

Gardner R. *Sterling-Dollar Diplomacy: The Origins and the Prospects of Our International Economic Order.* Rev. and enl. New York: McGraw-Hill, 1969.

Gerbet, P. *La construction de l'Europe.* Rev. ed. Paris: Imprimerie Nationale Éditions, 1994.

Giersch, H., ed. *Free Trade in the World Economy: Towards an Opening of Markets.* Tübingen: Mohr, 1987.

Gerbet, P. "La relance européenne jusqu'à la Conference de Messine." In *Il rilancio dell'Europa e i Trattati di Roma (The Relaunching of Europe and the Treaties of Rome),* edited by E. Serra, 61-91. Milan: Giuffrè, 1989.

Gillingham, J. *Coal, Steel and the Rebirth of Europe, 1945-1955: The Germans and French from Ruhr Conflict to Economic Community.* Cambridge: Cambridge University Press, 1991.

Girault, R. "La France entre l'Europe et l'Afrique," In *Il rilancio dell'Europa e i Trattati di Roma (The Relaunching of Europe and the Treaties of Rome),* edited by E. Serra, 351-78. Milan: Giuffrè, 1989.

Goldstein, J. "Creating the GATT Rules: Politics, Institutions and American Politics." In *Multilateralism Matters: The Theory and Practice of Institutional Form,* edited by J. Ruggie, 201-32. New York: Columbia University Press, 1993.

Grieco, J. *Cooperation Among Nations: Europe, America, and Non-Tariff Barriers to Trade.* Ithaca NY: Cornell University Press, 1990.

Griffiths, R. "The Abortive Dutch Assault on European Tariffs." In *Modern Dutch Studies: Essays in Honour of Peter King, Professor of Modern Dutch Studies at the University of Hull on the Occasion of his Retirement,* edited by M. Wintle, 186-91. London: Athlone, 1988.

Griffiths, R. "The Schuman Plan Negotiations: The Economic Clauses," In *Die Anfänge des Schuman-Plans 1950/51: Beiträge des Kolloquiums in Aachen, 28–30. Mai 1986,* edited by K. Schwabe, 35-71. Baden-Baden: Nomos, 1988.

Griffiths, R. "The Beyen Plan." In *The Netherlands and the Integration of Europe, 1945-1957,* edited by R. Griffiths, 165-82. Amsterdam: Nederlands Economisch Historisch Archief, 1990.

Griffiths, R. "The Common Market." In *The Netherlands and the Integration of Europe, 1945-1957,* edited by R. Griffiths, 183-208. Amsterdam: Nederlands Economisch Historisch Archief, 1990.

Griffiths, R. "The Schuman Plan." In *The Netherlands and the Integration of Europe, 1945-1957,* edited by R. Griffiths, 113-35. Amsterdam: Nederlands Economisch Historisch Archief, 1990.

Griffiths, R. "Creating a High Cost Club: The Green Pool Negotiations: 1953-1955." In *The Green Pool and the Origins of the Common Agricultural Policy,* edited by R. Griffiths, and B. Girvin, 21-50. Bloomsbury: Lothian Press, 1995.

Griffiths, R., and W. Asbeek Brusse. "The Dutch Cabinet and the Treaties of Rome." In *Il rilancio dell'Europa e i Trattati di Roma (The Relaunching of Europe and the Treaties of Rome),* edited by E. Serra, 461-93. Milan: Giuffrè, 1989.

Griffiths, R., and D. Barbezat. "The European Integration Experience." In *Promoting Regional Cooperation and Integration in Sub-Saharan Africa,* 83-101. Brussels: Global Coalition for Africa, 1992.

Griffiths, R., and F. Lynch. "L'Échec de la `Petite Europe': les négociations Fritalux/Finebel, 1949-1950." *Revue Historique* 274 (1985): 159-93.

Griffiths, R., and F. Lynch. "L'Échec de la 'Petite Europe': Le Conseil Tripartite 1944-1948." *Guerres Mondials et Conflits Contemporains* 252 (1988): 39-62.

Griffiths, R., and A. Milward. "The Beyen Plan and the European Political Community." In *Noi si mura: Selected Working Papers of the European University Institute,* edited by W. Maihofer, 595-621. Florence: European University Institute, 1986.

Grossman, G., and J. Richardson. *Strategic Trade Policy: A Survey of Issues and Early Analysis.* Special Papers in International Economics. No. 15. Princeton NJ: Princeton University Press, 1985.

Grubel, H. "Effective Tariff Protection: A Non-Specialist Guide to the Theory, Policy Implications and Controversies." In *Effective Tariff Protection: Proceedings of a Conference Sponsored by the General Agreement on Tariffs and Trade and the Graduate Institute of International Studies,* edited by H. Grubel, and H. Johnson, 1-15. Geneva: GATT, 1971.

Grubel, H., and H. Johnson. "Nominal Rates, Indirect Taxes and Effective Rates of Protection: The Common Market Countries, 1959." *The Economic Journal* (1967): 761-76.

Guillen, P. "La France et les negociations des Traités de Rome: l'Euratom." In *Il rilancio dell'Europa e i Trattati di Roma (The Relaunching of Europe and the Treaties of Rome),* edited by E. Serra, 461-93. Milan: Giuffrè, 1989.

Guillen, P. "Le projet d'union économique entre la France, l'Italie et le Benelux" In *Histoire des débuts de la construction européenne, mars 1948–mai 1950 (Origins of the European Integration, March 1948–May 1950)*, edited by R. Poidevin, 143-64. Paris: Libraire général de droits et de jurisprudence, 1989.

Guisinger, S., and D. Schydlowsky. "The Empirical Relationship Between Nominal and Effective Rates of Protection." In *Effective Tariff Protection: Proceedings of a Conference Sponsored by the General Agreement on Tariffs and Trade and the Graduate Institute of International Studies*, edited by H. Grubel and H. Johnson, 269-86. Geneva: 1971.

Hagelstam, J. "Mercantilism Still Influences Practical Trade Policy at the End of the Twentieth Century." *Journal of World Trade* 25 (1991): 95-105.

Hardach, G. *The First World War, 1914-1918.* London: Allen Lane, 1977.

Harris, N. *Competition and the Corporate Society: British Conservatives, the State and Industry, 1945-1964.* London: Methuen, 1972.

Harryvan, A., and A. Kersten. "The Netherlands, Benelux and the Relance européenne, 1954-1955." In *Il rilancio dell'Europa e i Trattati di Roma (The Relaunching of Europe and the Treaties of Rome)*, edited by E. Serra, 125-49. Milan: Giuffrè, 1989.

Hentschel, V. "Zur Politik internationaler Wettbewerbsbeschränkungen in der Zwischenkriegszeit—Maßnahmen und Wirkungen: USA, Grossbrittanien, Deutschland und Frankreich." In *Wettbewerbsbeschränkungen auf internationalen Märkten: Referate und Diskussionsbeiträge des 10. Wissenschaftlichen Symposiums der gesellschaft für Unternehmersgeschichte am 25–27. September 1985 in Lüneburg*, edited by H. Pohl, 114-21. Stuttgart: Steiner Verlag, 1988.

Herbst, L. "Die Zeitgenössische Integrationstheorie und die Anfänge der europäischen Einigung, 1947-1950." *Vierteljahrshefte für Zeitgeschichte* 34 (1986): 161-205.

Hieronymi, O. *Economic Discrimination against the United States in Western Europe (1945-1958): Dollar Shortage and the Rise of Regionalism.* Geneva: Droz, 1973.

Hogan, M. *The Marshall Plan: America, Britain and the Reconstruction of Western Europe, 1947-1952.* New York: Cambridge University Press, 1987.

Hogg, R. L. "Belgium, France and Switzerland and the End of the Gold Standard." In *The Netherlands and the Gold Standard, 1931-1936:*

A Study in Policy Formation and Policy, edited by R. Griffiths, 193-210. Amsterdam: Nederlands Economisch Historisch Archief, 1987.

Hutchinson, H. *Tariff Making and Industrial Reconstruction: An Account of the Import Duties Advisory Committee, 1932-1939.* London: Harrap, 1965.

Isaacs, W. *International Trade, Tariffs and Commercial Policies.* Chicago: Irwin, 1948.

Jerchow, F. "Außenhandel im Wiederstreit: Die Bundesrepublik auf dem Weg in das GATT, 1949-1951." In *Politische Weichenstellungen im Nachkriegsdeutschland, 1945-1953*, edited by A. Winkler, 254-89. Göttingen: Vandenhoeck und Ruprecht, 1979.

Kaufman, B. *Trade & Aid: Eisenhower's Foreign Economic Policy, 1953-1961.* Baltimore: Johns Hopkins University Press, 1982.

Kaufmann, J. "Trends in United States Tariff Policies." *Kyklos* 6 (1953): 55-74.

Kenen, P. *The International Economy.* 3rd ed. Cambridge: Cambridge University Press, 1994.

Kenwood, A., and A. Lougheed. *The Growth of the International Economy, 1820-1980: An Introductory Text*, London: Allen and Unwin, 1987.

Keohane, R. "Reciprocity in International Relations." *International Organization* 40 (1986): 1-27.

Kersten, A. "Oorsprong en inzet van de Nederlandse Europese integratiepolitiek." In *Het Benelux-effect: België, Nederland en Luxemburg en de Europese integratie, 1945-1957*, edited by E. Bloemen, 1-12. Amsterdam: Nederlands Economisch Historisch Archief, 1992.

Kindleberger, C. *The World in Depression, 1929-1939.* Berkeley: University of California Press, 1973.

Kindleberger, C. "The Rise of Free Trade in Western Europe." *Journal of Economic History* 35 (1975): 20-55.

King, P., ed. *International Economics and International Economic Policy: A Reader.* New York: McGraw-Hill, 1990.

Kitson M., and S. Solomou. *Protectionsm and Economic Revival: The British Interwar Economy.* Cambridge: Cambridge University Press, 1990.

Klemann, H. *Tussen Reich and Empire: De economische betrekkingen van Nederland met zijn belangrijkste handelspartners: Duitsland, Groot-Brittannië en België en de Nederlandse handelspolitiek, 1929-1936.* Amsterdam: Nederlands Economisch Historisch Archief, 1990.

Knipping, F. "Que faire de l'Allemagne? French Policy toward Germany, 1945-1950." In *France and Germany in an Age of Crisis, 1900-1960: Studies in Memory of Charles Bloch*, edited by H. Shamir, Leiden: Brill, 1990.

Knorr, K., and G. Patterson, eds. *A Critique of the Randall Commission Report on United States Foreign Economic Policy*. Princeton, NJ: Princeton University Press, 1954.

Kock, K. *International Trade Policy and the GATT, 1947-1967*. Stockholm: Almquist and Wiksell, 1969.

Krasner, S. "State Power and the Structure of International Trade." *World Politics* 28 (1976): 317-47.

Krause, L. "European Economic Integration and the United States." *American Economic Review*, Papers and Proceedings (1963): 185-96.

Krause, L. "The U.S. Trade Position and the Common Market." In *The Common Market: Progress and Controversy*, edited by L. Krause. Englewood Cliffs: Prentice Hall, 1964.

Kreinin, E. "On the 'Trade-Diversion' Effect of Trade Preference Areas." *Journal of Political Economy* 67 (1959): 398-401.

Krier, E. "L'industrie lourde luxembourgeoise et le Plan Schuman." In *Die Anfänge des Schuman-Plans 1950/51: Beiträge des Kolloquiums in Aachen, 28–30. Mai 1986*, edited by K. Schwabe, 357-66. Baden-Baden: Nomos, 1988.

Krugman, P. "Is Free Trade Passé?" In *International Economics and International Economic Policy: A Reader*, edited by P. King, 91-107. New York: McGraw-Hill, 1990.

Kurgan-van Hentenryk, G. "La Belgique et le relèvement économique de l'Allemagne 1945-1948." *Relations Internationales* 51 (1987): 343-63.

Küsters, H.-J. *Die Gründung der europäischen Wirtschaftsgemeinschaft*. Baden-Baden: Nomos, 1983.

Küsters, H.-J. "Zollunion oder Freihandelszone? Zur Kontroverse über die Handelspolitik Westeuropas in den fünfziger Jahren." In *Wirtschaftliche und politische Integration in Europa im 19. und 20. Jahrhundert*, edited by H. Berding, 296-308. Göttingen: Vandenhoeck and Ruprecht, 1984.

Küsters, H.-J., "The Federal Republic of Germany and the EEC-Treaty." In *Il rilancio dell'Europa e i Trattati di Roma (The Relaunching of Europe and the Treaties of Rome)*, edited by E. Serra, 495-506. Milan: Giuffrè, 1989.

Küsters, H.-J. *Fondements de la Communauté Economique Européenne.* Brussels: Editions Labor, 1990.

Lake, D., ed. *The International Political Economy of Trade.* Vols. 1 and 2. Aldershot: Edward Elgar, 1993.

Lake, D. "Leadership, Hegemony, and the International Economy: Naked Emperor or Tattered Monarch with Potential?" *International Studies Quarterly* 37 (1993): 459-89.

Laurent, P.-H. "America's Ally, Britain's Opponent: Belgium and the OEEC/EPU Debates, 1947-50." *Millennium: Journal of International Studies* 16 (1987): 453-66.

Lerdau, E. "On the measurement of tariffs: the U.S. over 40 years." *Economia Internazionale* 10 (1957): 232-47.

Liagre Böhl, H. de, J. Nekkers, and L. Hot, eds. *Nederland industrialiseert!* Nijmegen: Socialistiese Uitgeverij Nijmegen, 1981.

Light, M., and A. Groom, eds. *International Relations: A Handbook of Current Theory.* London: Pinter, 1985.

Lipgens, W. *A History of European Integration.* Vol. 1, *1945-1947: The Formation of the European Unity Movement.* Oxford: Clarendon Press, 1982.

Lipsey, R. *An Introduction to Positive Economics.* 4th ed. London: Weidenfeld and Nicholson, 1975.

Lynch, F. "The Role of Jean Monnet in Setting up the European Coal and Steel Community." In *Die Anfänge des Schuman-Plans 1950/51: Beiträge des Kolloquiums in Aachen, 28–30. Mai 1986,* edited by K. Schwabe, 117-29. Baden-Baden: Nomos, 1988.

Lynch, F. "Restoring France: The Road to Integration." In A. Milward, F. Lynch, F. Romero, R. Ranieri, and V. Sørensen, *The Frontier of National Sovereignty: History and Theory.* London: Routledge, 1993.

Machlup, F. *A History of Thought on Economic Integration.* London: Macmillan, 1977.

Maddison, A. *Dynamic Forces in Capitalist Development: A Long Run Comparative View.* Oxford: Oxford University Press, 1991.

Magnusson, L. *Mercantilism: The Shaping of an Economic Language.* London: Routledge, 1994.

Mallet, D. "The History and Structure of OEEC." *European Yearbook* 1 (1955): 62-70.

Marcy, G. "Libération progressive des échanges et aide à l'exportation en France depuis 1949." *Cahiers de l'Institut de Science Economique Appliqué,* série P (1959): no. 2.

Mayall, J. "The Institutional Basis of Post-War Economic Cooperation." In *International Institutions at Work,* edited by P. Taylor and A. Groom, 53-74. London: Pinter, 1988.

Mayrzedt, H. *Multilaterale Wirtschaftsdiplomatie zwischen westlichen Industriestaaten. Instrumente zur Stärkung der multilateralen und liberalen Handelspolitik.* Bern: Lang, 1979.

McGuire, E. *The British Tariff System.* London: Methuen, 1951.

McKeown, T. "Hegemonic Stability Theory and 19th Century Tariff Levels in Europe." *International Organization* 37 (1983): 73-91.

McKeown, T. "A Liberal Trade Order? The Long Run Pattern of Imports to the Advanced Capitalist States." *International Studies Quarterly* 35 (1991): 151-72.

Meade, J. "Negotiations for Benelux: An Annotated Chronicle, 1943-1956." Princeton Studies in International Finance. No. 6. Princeton University, 1957.

Meade, J., H. Liesner, and S. Wells. *Case Studies in European Economic Union: The Mechanics of Integration.* London: Oxford University Press, 1962.

Milner, H., and D. Yoffe. "Between Free Trade and Protectionism: Strategic Trade Policy and a Theory of Corporate Trade Demands." *International Organization* 43 (1989): 239-72.

Milward, A. *War, Economy and Society, 1939-1945.* London: Allen Lane, 1977.

Milward, A. "Tariffs as Constitutions." In *The International Politics of Surplus Capacity: Competition for Market Shares in the World Recession,* edited by S. Strange and R. Tooze, 57-67. London: Allen and Unwin, 1981.

Milward, A. *The Reconstruction of Western Europe, 1945–51.* Cambridge: Methuen, 1987.

Milward, A. "The Belgian Coal and Steel Industries and the Schuman Plan." In *Die Anfänge des Schuman-Plans 1950/51: Beiträge des Kolloquiums in Aachen, 28.–30. Mai 1986,* edited by K. Schwabe, 437-53. Baden-Baden: Nomos, 1988.

Milward, A. "Motives for Currency Convertibility: The Pound and the Deutschmark, 1950-5." In *Interaction in the World Economy: Perspectives from International Economic History. Festschrift in Honour of Wolfram Fischer,* edited by C. Holtfrerich, 260-84. New York: Harvester Wheatsheaf, 1989.

Milward, A. *The European Rescue of the Nation-State.* London: Routledge, 1992.

Milward, A., F. Lynch, F. Romero, R. Ranieri, and V. Sørensen, *The Frontier of National Sovereignty: History and Theory.* London: Routledge, 1993.

Möller, H. "The Reconstruction of the International Economic Order after the Second World War and the Integration of the Federal Republic of Germany into the World Economy." *Zeitschrift für die gesammte Staatswissenschaft* 137 (1981): 344-66.

Mommens, T. "Agricultural Integration in Benelux." In *The Netherlands and the Integration of Europe, 1945-1957,* edited by R. Griffiths, 49-69. Amsterdam: Nederlands Economisch Historisch Archief, 1990.

Noël, G. *Du pool vert à la Politique Agricole Commun: les tentatives de Communauté agricole européenne entre 1945 et 1955.* Paris: Economica, 1988.

O'Krueger, A. "Theory and Practice of Commercial Policy: 1945-1990." Working Paper No. 3596, National Bureau of Economic Research, Cambridge, MA, 1990.

Organization for European Cooperation and Development. *From Marshall Plan to Global Interdependence: New Challenges for the Industrialized Nations.* Paris: OECD, 1978.

Owen, N. *Economies of Scale, Competitiveness and Trade Patterns within the European Community.* Oxford: Clarendon Press, 1983.

Pastor, R. *Congress and the Politics of U.S. Foreign Economic Policy, 1929-1976.* Berkeley: University of California Press, 1980.

Patterson, G. *Discrimination in International Trade: The Policy Issues, 1945-1965.* Princeton NJ: Princeton University Press, 1966.

Pelkmans, J. *The Process of Economic Integration.* Tilburg: Tilburg University Press, 1975.

Pelkmans, J. "Effects of the Community's Customs Union: Revision and Extension of Conventional Theory." In *Integrationskonzepte auf dem Prüfstand,* edited by R. Bieber et al, 49-67. Baden-Baden: Nomos, 1983.

Pelkmans, J. *Vrijhandel of protectionisme: Een Europa dat openstaat voor de wereld.* The Hague: Stichting Maatschappij en Onderneming, 1985.

Peters-Godts, S. "La Politique européenne du gouvernment belge, septembre 1944–mai 1950." Ph.D. diss., European University Institute, Florence, 1987.

Piquet, H. *Aid, Trade and the Tariff.* New York: Cromwell, 1953.

Pohl, H., ed. *Die Auswirkungen von Zöllen und andere Handelshemnissen auf Wirtschaft und Gesellschaft vom Mittelalter bis zur Gegenwart.* Stuttgart: Steiner Verlag, 1987.

Poidevin, R. "Le facteur Europe dans la politique allemande de Robert Schuman." In *Histoire des débuts de la construction européenne (mars 1948–mai 1950): Actes du colloque de Strasbourg, 28–30 novembre 1984,* edited by R. Poidevin, 311-26. Paris: Libraire général de droits et de jurisprudence, 1988.

Pollard, S. *European Economic Integration, 1815-1970.* London: Thames and Hudson, 1974.

Pomfret, R. *International Trade Policy with Imperfect Competition.* Special Papers in International Economics. No. 17. Princeton, NJ: Princeton University, 1992.

Preeg, E. *Traders and Diplomats: An Analysis of the Kennedy Round of Negotiations under the General Agreement on Tariffs and Trade.* Washington, DC: The Brookings Institute, 1970.

"Problematischer Preispolitik in Frankreich." *Neue Zürcher Zeitung* (Switzerland). 25 September 1951.

Ranieri, R. "L'espansione alla prova del negoziato—l'industria italiana e la comunita' del carbone e dell' acciaio, 1945-1955." Ph.D. diss., European University Institute, Florence, 1988.

Ranieri, R. "The Italian Steel Industry and the Schuman Plan Negotiations." In *Die Anfänge des Schuman-Plans 1950/51: Beiträge des Kolloquiums in Aachen, 28.–30. Mai 1986,* edited by K. Schwabe, 345-56. Baden-Baden: Nomos, 1988.

Romero, F. "Migration as an Issue in European Interdependence and Integration: The Case of Italy." In *The Frontier of National Sovereignty: History and Theory,* edited by A. Milward, F. Lynch, F. Romero, R. Ranieri, and V. Sørensen, 33-58. London: Routledge, 1993.

Roon, G. van. *Kleine landen in crisistijd: Van Oslostaten tot Benelux, 1930-1940.* Amsterdam, Brussels: Elsevier, 1985.

Rothbarth, E. "Causes of the Superior Efficiency of U.S.A. Industry as Compared with British Industry." *The Economic Journal: The Journal of the Royal Economic Society* 56 (1946) 383-90.

Ruggie, J. "International Regimes, Transactions, and Change: Embedded Liberalism in the Postwar International Economic Order." *International Organization* 36 (1982): 379-415.

Salant, W., and B. Vaccara. *Import Liberalisation and Employment: The Effect of Unilateral Tariff Reductions in United States Import Barriers.* Washington, DC: The Brookings Institute, 1961.

Sampson, G., and A. Yeats. "On the Use of Belgium-Netherlands Coefficients for Effective Protection Analysis." *Oxford Economic Papers* (1979): 496-507.

Saul, S. *Studies in British Overseas Trade, 1870-1914.* Liverpool: Liverpool University Press, 1960.

Schade, P. "Die Entwicklung des Zolltarifes der Bundesrepublik Deutschland bis zum EWG Außentarif." Ph.D. diss., Eberhardt Karls University, Tübingen, 1963.

Schmieding, "How to Fill a 'Dollar Gap'?: Observations on the Liberalisation of West Germany's External Trade and Payments, 1947-1958." Working Paper no. 291, Institut für Weltwirtschaft, Kiel, 1987.

Schwartz, H. *States versus Markets: History, Geography and the Development of the International Political Economy.* New York: St. Martin's Press, 1994.

Seldon, A. *Churchill's Indian Summer: The Conservative Government, 1951-55.* London: Hodder and Sloughton, 1981.

Sellekaerts, W. "How Meaningful Are Empirical Studies on Trade Creation and Trade Diversion?" *Weltwirtschaftliches Archiv* 109 (1973): 519-53.

Shonfield, A., ed. *International Economic Relations of the Western World, 1959-1971.* Vol. 1, *Politics and Trade.* London: University Press for the Royal Institute of International Affairs, 1976.

Shutt, H. *The Myth of Free Trade: Patterns of Protectionism Since 1945.* Oxford: Basil Blackwell, 1985.

Simmons, B. *Who Adjusts? Domestic Sources of Foreign Economic Policy During the Interwar Years.* Princeton, NJ: Princeton University Press, 1994.

Solomon, R. *The International Monetary System, 1945-1981.* New York: Harper and Row, 1982.

Steuer M., and G. Erb. "An Empirical Test of the 'GATT Hypothesis'." *Journal of Political Economy* 74 (1966): 274-77.

Stokes, R. "Recovery and Resurgence in the West German Chemical Industry: Allied Policy and the I.G. Farben Successor Companies." Ph.D. diss., Ohio State University, 1986.

Strange, S., and R. Tooze, eds. *The International Politics of Surplus Capacity: Competition for Market Shares in the World Recession.* London: Allen and Unwin, 1981.

Svennilson, I. *Growth and Stagnation in the European Economy.* The Hague: Martinus Nijhoff, 1954.

Taylor, P., and A. Groom, eds. *International Institutions at Work.* London: Pinter, 1988.

Thompson, W., and L. Vescera. "Growth Waves, Systemic Openness, and Protectionism," *International Organization* 46 (1992): 493-532.

Tichelen, J. van. "Herinneringen van de onderhandelingen van het Verdrag van Rome." In *De rol der Belgen en van België bij de Europese opbouw,* edited by Interuniversitaire Studiecommissie van het Koninklijk Instituut voor Internationale Betrekkingen, 343-60. Brussels: Koninklijk Instituut voor de Internationale Betrekkingen, 1981.

Thorbecke, E. *The Tendency Towards Regionalization in International Trade.* The Hague: Martinus Nijhoff, 1960.

Thorbecke, E. "European Economic Integration and the Pattern of World Trade." *American Economic Review* 53 (1963) 147-74.

Tilly, C. *Coercion, Capital, and European States.* Cambridge, MA: Basil Blackwell, 1990.

Trausch, G., ed. *Die europäische Integration vom Schuman-Plan bis zu den Verträgen von Rom: Beiträge des Kolloquiums in Luxemburg 17–19. Mai 1989,* Baden-Baden: Nomos, 1993.

Travis, W. "A Critical Rehabilitation of Effective Protection Theory." In *Effective Tariff Protection: Proceedings of a Conference Sponsored by the General Agreement on Tariffs and Trade and the Graduate Institute of International Studies,* edited by H. Grubel and H. Johnson, 217-45. Geneva, 1971.

Tumlir, J., and L. Till. "Tariff Averaging in International Comparisons." In *Effective Tariff Protection: Proceedings of a Conference Sponsored by the General Agreement on Tariffs and Trade and the Graduate Institute of International Studies,* edited by H. Grubel and H. Johnson, 147-60. Geneva: 1971.

Verdier, D. *Democracy and International Trade: Britain, France and the United States, 1860-1990.* Princeton, NJ: Princeton University Press, 1994.

Verdoorn, P. "Welke zijn de achtergronden en vooruitzichten van de economische integratie in Europa, en welke gevolgen zal deze integratie hebben, met name voor de welvaart in Nederland." In *Welke zijn de achtergronden en vooruitzichten van de economische integratie in Europa, en welke gevolgen zou deze integratie hebben, met name voor de welvaart in Nederland? Prae-adviezen van Prof. Dr. P. Kuin, Prof. Dr. P.J. Verdoorn,* edited by Vereeniging voor Staatshuishoudkunde, 112-17. The Hague, 1952.

Vermeulen, W. *Europees landbouwbeleid in de maak: Mansholts eerste plannen, 1945-1953.* Vol XX, *Historia Agriculturae XX.* Groningen: Nederlands Agronomisch-Historisch Instituut, 1989.

Vincent, L. "La situation économique." *Revue Economique* 7 (1954).

Vincent, L., and G. Matthys. "La situation économique." *Revue Economique* 5 (1952).

Vincent, L., and G. Matthys. "La situation économique." *Revue Economique* 6 (1953).

Viner, J. *The Customs Union Issue.* New York: Carnegie Endowment for International Peace, 1950.

Volkmann, H., and E. Schwengler, eds. *Die Europäische Verteidigungsgemeinschaft: Stand und Probleme der Forschung.* Boppard am Rhein: Boldt, 1985.

Vries, J. de. *The Netherlands Economy in the Twentieth Century: An Examination of the Most Characteristic Features in the Period, 1900-1970.* Assen: Van Gorcum, 1978.

Wallace, W. *The Dynamics of European Integration.* London: Pinter, 1992.

"War die Konferenz von Torquay ein Erfolg?" *Frankfurter Allgemeine Zeitung* (German Federal Republic). 6 June 1951.

Wasserman, M., C. Hultman, and R. Moore. *The Common Market and American Business.* New York: Simmons-Boardman Publishing Company, 1964.

Webb, M., and S. Krasner. "Hegemonic Stability Theory: An Empirical Assessment." *Review of International Studies* 15 (1989): 183-98.

Wemelsfelder, J. *Het herstel van de Duits-Nederlandse economische betrekkingen na de Tweede Wereldoorlog.* Leiden: Stenfert Kroese, 1954.

Wexler, I. *The Marshall Plan Revisited: The European Recovery Plan in Economic Perspective.* Westport, CT: Greenwood Press, 1983.

Wilcox, C. *A Charter for World Trade.* New York: MacMillan, 1949.

Winand, P. *Eisenhower, Kennedy and the United States of Europe.* New York: St. Martin's Press, 1993.

Woytinsky, W., and E. Woytinsky. *World Commerce and Governments: Trends and Outlook.* New York: Twentieth Century Fund, 1955.

Young, J. "The Parting of Ways? Britain, the Messina Conference and the Spaak Committee, June–December 1955." In *British Foreign Policy, 1945-56*, edited by M. Dockrill and J. Young, 197-224. Basingstoke: Macmillan, 1989.

Zanden J. van, and R. Griffiths. *Economische geschiedenis van Nederland in de 20e eeuw*. Utrecht: Het Spectrum, 1989.

Index